UNCERTAIN BUSINESS:
RISK, INSURANCE, AND THE LIMITS OF KNOWLEDGE

Uncertain Business explores insurance industry practices and what they tell us about risks and uncertainties in contemporary society. The core of the book is a set of unique ethnographic studies of the insurance industry. Addressing four fields of insurance – life, disability, earthquake, and terrorism – these studies reveal that a high degree of uncertainty pervades the insurance business, the very industry that is charged with transforming uncertainty into manageable risk. The authors show how scientific data on risk are often absent, inadequate, controversial, contradictory, or ignored, and how insurers often impose meaning on uncertainty through non-scientific forms of knowledge that are intuitive, emotional, aesthetic, moral, and speculative. Furthermore, the nature of uncertainty and the response to it varies substantially across the areas studied, showing how contemporary society is characterized by competing interests and forms of logic in regard to risk.

Insurers' perceptions and business decisions – with potential for huge profits as well as catastrophic losses – create crises in insurance availability and generate new forms of inequality and exclusion. *Uncertain Business* demonstrates that, while insurers act as a bulwark against uncertainty, they also play a key role in fostering it.

RICHARD V. ERICSON is the director of the Centre for Criminological Research at the University of Oxford and is a fellow of All Souls College.

AARON DOYLE is an assistant professor in the Department of Sociology and Anthropology at Carleton University.

UNCERTAIN BUSINESS

Risk, Insurance, and the
Limits of Knowledge

Richard V. Ericson and
Aaron Doyle

UNIVERSITY OF TORONTO PRESS
Toronto Buffalo London

© University of Toronto Press Incorporated 2004
Toronto Buffalo London
Printed in Canada

ISBN 0-8020-8759-0 (cloth)
ISBN 0-8020-8562-8 (paper)

Printed on acid-free paper

National Library of Canada Cataloguing in Publication

Ericson, Richard V., 1948–
Uncertain business : risk, insurance, and the limits of
knowledge / Richard V. Ericson and Aaron Doyle.

Includes bibliographical references and index.
ISBN 0-8020-8759-0 (bound)   ISBN 0-8020-8562-8 (pbk.)

1. Risk (Insurance)   I. Doyle, Aaron   II. Title.

HG8054.5.D69 2004   368   C2003-906779-3

University of Toronto Press acknowledges the financial assistance to its
publishing program of the Canada Council for the Arts and the Ontario
Arts Council.

University of Toronto Press acknowledges the financial support for its
publishing activities of the Government of Canada through the Book
Publishing Industry Development Program (BPIDP).

Contents

Acknowledgments

In this book we advance the view that society is formed by institutions that coalesce around specific interests, objectives, and procedures. The insurance industry is especially important because it intersects with all other major institutions in society to provide systems of governance, risk management, risk taking, and security.

This book is itself a product of collaboration across many institutions. First and foremost we thank the members of the insurance industry who gave us access to their organizations. They deepened and broadened our understanding of what they do and how their actions contribute to the constitution of society.

A number of institutions provided financial, organizational, and intellectual support for our research. A project grant awarded by the Social Sciences and Humanities Research Council of Canada was essential for the extensive field research that forms the core of this book. Richard Ericson enjoyed the enormous leave privileges of a Killam Research Fellowship sponsored by the Killam Programs, Canada Council for the Arts. He also received generous support as a Visiting Fellow of All Souls College, Oxford, during the 1998–9 academic year. In particular, he thanks Andrew Ashworth, Roger Hood, and Lucia Zedner for their friendship and encouragement. Substantial support has been provided by the University of British Columbia, and in particular, Green College. We are especially grateful to Dean Barry, Diana Ericson, Dene Matilda, Rosanne Rumley, and Lillian Yee for their research assistance.

Among the scholars who have most influenced this work are Tom Baker, Aditi Gowri, Ian Hacking, Kevin Haggerty, Carol Heimer, Pat O'Malley, Michael Power, Nikolas Rose, Violaine Roussel, and

Jonathan Simon. We are especially grateful to Tom Baker for his detailed comments on the full manuscript, and for his enthusiastic support of our research program on insurance. Early formulation of ideas and research results was helped by critical response to talks given by Richard Ericson at All Souls College, Oxford, the University of Edinburgh, the London School of Economics and Political Science, the City University of New York, the University of Connecticut, the University of Toronto, and the University of British Columbia.

Last, and by no means least, we thank the University of Toronto Press. Along with the other organizations mentioned above, University of Toronto Press is an important cultural institution that shares the value of independent scholarly inquiry. We are especially grateful to Virgil Duff for his wise advice and unfailing encouragement. We also thank Allyson May for her copy-editing skills, which have made this book much better.

RICHARD V. ERICSON
AARON DOYLE

UNCERTAIN BUSINESS:
RISK, INSURANCE, AND THE LIMITS OF KNOWLEDGE

1 Risk, Insurance, and the Limits of Knowledge

The knowledge of the world is only acquired in the world, and not in a closet.
Lord Chesterfield, Letter to his son (1774)

In civil business; what first? boldness; what second and third? boldness: and yet boldness is a child of ignorance and baseness.
Frances Bacon, Essays 'of Boldness' (1625)

Thus, while the aggregate of human suffering and calamity remains undiminished, thus, while the uncertainty of their visitation remains unremoved, human ingenuity and cooperation equalize the distribution of the fearful aggregate, and alleviate the terrors of uncertainty ... a great fund ... to which none could be said to contribute gratuitously, from which none but the needy should be aided: a great reserve fund, held in readiness for the uncertain case of want.
D.R. Jacques, 'Society on the Basis of Mutual Life Insurance,'
Hunt's Merchants (1849)

Introduction

In our previous book, *Insurance as Governance* (Ericson, Doyle, and Barry 2003), we demonstrated how the private insurance industry works with the state to spread the costs of risk and provide security. While the state has enormous legal power to spread risk and responsibility among different sectors of society, the insurance industry also has regulatory power. For example, through industry associations, it regulates insurance company practices; through the insurance contract, it regulates the insured. While the state has formidable military and police power, the insurance industry mobilizes private security systems. It forces policyholders to implement security measures intended to provide an efficient level of prevention and thereby minimize actual harm and the future cost of harm. The state has the deepest pockets, by virtue of its powers of taxation, minting money, and financing indemnity over time. But the insurance industry also has deep pockets, tailored by premium income and investment returns that form enormous capital assets. These assets are used to compensate losses for which the state might otherwise be compelled to pay. They also give insurance companies creditworthiness – not equivalent to the state's creditworthiness, but substantial nonetheless – with which they can take risks in underwriting and investment. While the state has the greatest array of information resources, the insurance industry is also information rich. Databases on policyholders and their assets are used for a wide range of surveillance and control functions. They are also investment commodities that are sold to various private corporate and state institutions. While the state is the ultimate risk manager (Moss 2002), in an insurance-based society such as ours the state cannot manage without the insurance industry. In all of the ways specified above, the industry is crucial for governing the everyday world of safety and security.

In *Insurance as Governance*, we underscored the importance of research on the insurance industry for addressing contemporary debates about the risk society. Research on how the insurance industry uses diverse means to treat different risks offers a more nuanced understanding of how risk society is constituted.

In the present book we pursue our research interest in how the private insurance industry helps shape the contours of risk society as well as the problems faced by that society. While we continue our interest in analysing the governance practices of the insurance industry, our particular focus in this regard is the problems of knowledge which insurers are forced to confront in risk society. What are the limits to the scientific understanding and technical control of risks, and how does the insurance industry operate in the context of such limits? In pursuing these questions, we intend to make a significant contribution to the sociology of knowledge, and in particular, to the sociology of science and technology. We also enhance sociological understanding of organizations, institutions, professions, governance, and political economy.

As a probability statement, risk is the frequency with which an unwanted outcome is likely to occur and the severity of losses suffered when it does occur. Risk is surrounded by uncertainty. Uncertainty is the lack of secure knowledge about an unwanted outcome. Insecure knowledge may result because of unavailable or unreliable data about frequency and severity. With regard to severity, the loss may be irreplaceable and the risk therefore non-distributable, as in the loss of a treasured heirloom, or of the life of a loved one. In such cases the risk assessment is overlain with non-probabilistic reasoning that is aesthetic, emotional, and experiential.

Our thesis is that a high degree of scientific and technical uncertainty permeates the insurance industry, the very business that is charged with transforming uncertainty into risk. Insurers do not necessarily back off from a high degree of uncertainty. Rather, they respond with a range of creative and sometimes ingenious solutions. However, they also regularly confront the limitations of their own science, technology, and institution for addressing risk. Scrutiny of how insurers face their own incapacities reveals that theirs is an uncertain business, and that we live not so much in a risk society as in an uncertain society.

Insurance is a key institution in which to understand knowledge of risk and uncertainty. It is one of the great modern institutions of science and technology, indeed, insurance was central to the development of the sciences of risk and probabilistic thinking (Hacking 1975, 1990, 2003).

Insurance is *the* institution of applied knowledge and social necessity. Insurers have an enormous social responsibility to assess and act upon risk. Their decisions in this regard have society-wide implications for the operation of capital, loss prevention measures, systems of compensation for loss, social planning, and the freedom to take risks (Ericson, Doyle, and Barry 2003). Ideally, insurers call upon the latest science regarding each risk they are addressing in order to specify the insurance contract conditions and premium rates, assess the validity of claimed losses, and organize loss prevention measures. Ideally, their own science of actuarialism converts myriad risks in the world into insurance technologies that spread and compensate losses with fairness and efficiency.

In practice, insurers run up against the limits of scientific knowledge and its technical applications. These limits are by no means peculiar to how the insurance industry operates, but rest more broadly in the capacities of science and technology and their role in society. A brief excursion into the sociology of science and technology makes evident some of the fundamental problems of knowledge faced by insurers, and why we live in an uncertain society.

Scientific Knowledge of Risk and Uncertainty

Sociologists of science have shown that the limitations of scientific knowledge and technology are revealed in everyday efforts to ascertain and manage risk. Uncertainty is confronted as 'the basic condition of human knowledge' (Douglas 1985: 42). Realities that are apprehended through probabilistic reasoning about risk are experienced as erratic, equivocal, changeable, unreliable, unconvincing, and doubtful. Science itself articulates 'the uncertainty principle' (Hawking 1988). In some quarters uncertainty even trumps risk. While the language of risk 'used to be sufficient to describe all types of insecurity, the new paradigm sees uncertainty reappear in the light of even newer science. It bears witness to a deeply disturbed relationship with a science that is consulted less for the knowledge it offers than for the doubt it insinuates' (Ewald 2002: 274).

Why has scientific and technological progress in the 'taming of chance' (Hacking 1990) led to so much uncertainty, and as a corollary, the view that we may be taking too many chances?

Because risk is a probability statement, it is always surrounded by uncertainty. 'Risk is a close relation to uncertainty. Where we cannot be certain about the relation between cause and effect we clutch at the straw of probability ... Estimates of the probability of particular harms are quantified expressions of ignorance' (Adams 2003: 90). At best, risk is a 'known chance' or measured uncertainty (Knight [1921] 1964: 231). It reaches more 'objective' weight in highly controlled contexts, such as the dice gaming table, where it is possible to measure behaviour within 'an invariant, existing and delimited system' (Pixley 2002: 43). In less controlled contexts, risk frays into uncertainty, fear, speculation, and unanticipated consequences.

A known risk may be difficult to assess and therefore to ameliorate through management strategies. Indeed, this quality of apprehension without obvious capacity for assessment and action is a definition of uncertainty. Many of the new 'global risks' have this character. Are weather patterns a sign of irreversible interruption through 'global warming' or only deviation from historical trends (Von Storch and Stehr 2000)? Is Islamic terrorism a danger emanating from specifiable 'cells' or a sign of a new kind of war that is sustained and systematic (Esposito 2002)? Is the 'virtual risk' (Adams 2003) of BSE so contaminating that the only viable policy is slaughter of animals without evidence of the risk (Roussel 2003)? Such decisions are beyond a risk calculus of probability and severity. They achieve certainty through a different logic, that of precaution, vigilance, and pre-emption.

Scientific knowledge of risk also produces uncertainty because of its 'reflexive' character (Giddens 1990, 1991; Beck, Giddens, and Lash 1994). On a given topic of risk, there is a stream of incoming knowledge from various experts who offer counter-factual assessments and conflicting advice on what action to take. Furthermore, when action is taken, it changes how the risk is perceived and subsequently assessed. There is perpetual reflexive monitoring of the risk, knowledge is never settled, and uncertainty is normalized. The prevailing sensibility is 'radical doubt' (ibid.).

Related to the last point, aggregate scientific data on risk are not directly applicable to decision making in the particular case under consideration. For example, when a medical practitioner deals with a given patient, 'obtaining more data about different individuals is irrelevant to the particular case of the patient [he or she wishes] to treat' (Hacking 1990: 86). Adams (2003: 91) offers the example of trying to estimate the probability of someone dying as a result of a road accident. The data available are from previous years. There is enormous, multifactoral variation by driver characteristics, road conditions, vehicle conditions, and so on. Risk analysis fragments into uncertainty analysis, to the point where 'The veneer of scientific authority imparted by scientific probability often can withstand little scratching' (ibid.).

Science and technology are often producers of new risks with potentially disastrous consequences. This is the main thrust of Beck's (1992a) work, and of many others who have analysed the impact of scientific knowledge on social relations (Stehr and Ericson 1992). Drugs used to manage the risks of one disease can cause other diseases (Malleson 2002). Technological innovations to control dangerous processes – for example, nuclear energy production – can increase the complexity of the technological system and the possibility of disaster (Perrow 1984). The accumulating consequence of risks produced by science and technology is uncertainty compounded by fear. 'We are, in fact, seeing the proof that our societies and their members are threatened by risks that can be disastrous but are introduced by the very acts that sought to reduce those risks' (Ewald 2002: 293–4).

The unintended negative consequences of risks produced through science and technology are typically responded to with more science and technology. While political authorities and social movements have a voice, scientific experts are charged with the solution because the risk exists in their knowledge of it. This is nicely captured in Beck's (1992b: 212) observation about environmental risks that 'no amount of collective coughing, scratching, or sighing helps. Only science does.' There is a belief that more science and technology will work where less has not, creating an endless cycle of scientific research and technological development on the modern view that rational knowledge of risk is the key to progress and well-being. Radical doubt, indeed distrust, in science and technology cannot be taken too far because science and technology must still be looked to for solutions. 'This is no doubt explained by the fact that one wants to maintain a principle of economic and social development, which prohibits inaction in the face of uncertainty, at the same time as one seeks to limit as far as possible its harmful consequences. Hence, the idea of "sustainable development"' (Ewald 2002: 287).

Institutions and professions are producers of new risks with potentially disastrous consequences. Institutions and professions have a propensity to be iatrogenic. This term commonly refers to a disease or other harm caused by medical examination or treatment (from *iatros*, Greek for physician, and -genic, produced by). It is well established that the health care institutions and professions cause a great deal of harm as well as good, not least because they continually invent new health risks and new technologies that go in search of dubious uses to control these risks (Illich et al. 1977; Malleson 2002). Baker (2002a: 352) argues the need to broaden the concept of iatrogenesis to encompass any 'situation in which efforts to prevent one kind of harm creates another.' Institutions and their professional experts regularly take harm reduction measures in the context of available knowledge and capacity to act, but in retrospect their knowledge and actions appear wrong and generate uncertainty.

The story of asbestos exemplifies Baker's point. Asbestos was introduced in building construction as a fire-resistant technology that would greatly reduce risks to property and persons. It was celebrated by the scientists who created it, innovative building engineers, and grateful customers. It was also promoted by insurance risk experts, who are always eager to introduce new technologies of loss reduction. But then asbestosis was discovered, a health risk that trumped fire risk. At last count, in the United States alone, the insurance industry was $65 billion out-of-pocket in asbestos-related claims. Dozens of commercial enterprises went out of business because they could not bear their share of liabilities.

Hacking (2003: 30) makes the important observation that the institutionalization and professionalization of the field of risk analysis contributed to the culture of uncertainty and fear. He distinguishes risk analysis, which is concerned with fear, and risk management, which is concerned with balancing hope and fear (especially the hope of bottom-line profit against the fear of financial loss). 'Why did risk analysis emerge in 1969? Was it because we had entered a new and scary epoch in the history of industrial civilisation? No we had not, but that is what it felt like. Collective non-distributable risks were experienced as never before. That in turn was part of the larger picture of politics and activism that characterised the late 1960s. This was a "cultural" phenomenon' (ibid.: 32).

Non-Scientific Knowledge of Risk and Uncertainty

As Hacking indicates, the uncertainties swirling around risk are not confined by scientific knowledge, whether statistical calculations of probabilities or otherwise. When science and technology fail to bolster confidence about how risks are being addressed, or worse still, when they evidently produce more dangers, other knowledge of risk becomes ascendant. As Adams (2003: 92) remarks, 'We do not respond blankly to uncertainty. We impose meaning(s) upon it.'

Risk analysis has taught us that risk perception is based on criteria other than the rational knowledge of probabilities. Huber and colleagues (1997) show that people have great difficulty interpreting probabilities in the course of decision making, and often do not even want probabilistic data when it is available. Moreover, when asked to search for information that would help them make managerial decisions, they rarely seek data on probabilities. Kunreuther (2001: 11) observes that homeowners in California tend to purchase earthquake insurance only after they have experienced an earthquake. 'When asked whether the probability of a future event was more likely, the same, or less likely than before the disaster, most people responded by saying "less likely"' (ibid.).

'[T]he very notion of "risk" entails making calculable the uncalculable or the monitoring of contingency' (Lash 1993: 6). As such, risk is a quest for certainty. Certainty remains elusive, more within us as a yearning than outside us as a fact. There may be no clear guidelines for monitoring, and efforts to produce them can create even more ambivalence and uncertainty. In such circumstances, there may be no obvious course of action to take. The same decision makers will change their approach in different contexts. At times they will expend further resources in an effort to understand and control the risk. At other times they will take a fatalistic view and forge ahead in a state of uncertainty.

People do not reflect at all on some types of risk. They do not consciously mull over possible harms that might result from each choice available, but simply act on the basis of conventional and habitual routines (Taylor 1992). In their 'habitus' (Bourdieu 1984, 1990; Bourdieu and Wacquant 1992) of daily routines, people simply avoid risks or take risks without a thought. Driving is one such context. People routinely secure their seatbelts, and change lanes in heavy traffic or at high speed, in an habitual manner. Indeed, too much reflection upon every driving move can itself pose a major risk on the road.

When people are reflexive about risk, they use knowledge beyond rational cognition of probabilities and/or normative categories. They engage in self-interpretation as well as self-monitoring. That is, they actively examine their self and identity in risky social processes in order to assign significance to their actions and to the institutions in which they participate. This 'aesthetic' (Lash 1993, 1994) dimension of risk addresses aspects such as the pleasures of risk taking, taste, lifestyle, and a sense of belonging to a community. It can be highly conscious, as in the pursuit of extreme sports (Simon 2002, 2003). On the other hand, as part of a habitus, it can be embedded in 'background assumptions and unarticulated practices and in intuition, feeling, emotion and the spiritual ... It is a product of an individual's embodied "being-in-the-world," in which knowledge about the world is developed through – and not just in relation to – the body (Merleau-Ponty 1962). Aesthetic reflexivity relies upon an individual's membership of a community, the moral and culturally learned and shared assumptions, preferences, and categories to which Douglas refers in her work on risk' (Lupton 1999: 118). For example, people take risks in sexual activity not simply on the basis of knowledge about sexually transmitted diseases provided by experts, but also in relation to their emotions and acculturation about who and what represents purity and danger (Maticka-Tyndale 1992).

The emotional dimension of addressing risk and uncertainty is especially salient. Knowledge of risk and uncertainty are sources of great fear, and this emotion can fundamentally affect how people approach security. Most risk analysts view fear and its effects on security-related behaviour as irrational when measured against data on 'actual' risks.

This view is typical among the many analysts who have studied fear of crime. A characteristic line of argument is that the mass media over-represent violent crime and dramatize urban legends about dangerous criminals to the point where people grossly overestimate their likeli-hood of victimization and buy expensive security devices that restrict them more than those they imagine to be preying upon them (e.g., Doob and Macdonald 1979; Best and Horiuchi 1985; Gunter 1987; Sparks 1992; Altheide 2002).

The same logic is applied to other areas of risk. For example, in *The Culture of Fear: Why Americans Are Afraid of the Wrong Things*, Barry Glassner (1999) uses aggregate data on risk and commentary about media coverage to argue that Americans are not only irrational about crime, but also about the risk of unemployment, poor health, and so on. As Haggerty (2003: 197) observes about Glassner's work, 'The implicit assumption of his and comparable studies is that to be afraid of the "right" things would involve some kind of actuarial calculus whereby what we fear and take action to allay closely correspond with what is likely to harm us. Individuals are consequently held to a stan-dard of calculative rationality where they are expected to attend to and mitigate the real risks they face as demonstrated by the statistical likeli-hood that something will cause them harm. When they take actions to mitigate a risk that is probabilistically low, they face the prospect of being accused of acting irrationally or having been swept away by a moral panic.'

Risk analysts are in the business of making peoples' fears appear irrational against the template of probabilistic data on risk. While such knowledge may help people to allay their fears and make more 'ratio-nal' decisions, it is only partially successful in doing so. Fears persist, and form a basis for action beyond probabilistic thinking. Terrorists rely on this: they are explicitly in the business of creating uncertainty and inducing fear. Governments that respond to terrorism also know this: they are in the business of enhancing security by inducing fear. In such contexts, fear is intended to serve as 'an effective pre-rational warning system' (De Becker 1997) connected to other emotional and cognitive elements such as suspicion, precaution, and vigilance.

Emotions enter into the most rational contexts of decision making about risk. Pixley (2002) shows that financial institutions, such as banks, insurance companies, and investment dealers, generate finan-cial risk expectations and make decisions through socially based emo-tions. Following Barbalet (1996, 1998), she argues that emotions have their own rationality in decision processes. 'The future orientations of trust, confidence, fear, and less conspicuous "emotional energy" (Collins's term [1993]) are routinely drawn on as decisions *ex ante* cannot be made without them. They necessarily play some part in actually fostering "rational" decision-making in finance organizations and in defining the alleged "fundamentals"' (Pixley 2002: 42).

In *The Crisis of Global Capitalism*, George Soros (1998: 24) recounts his experience at Quantum Hedge Fund: 'As a fund manager, I depended a great deal on my emotions ... The predominant feelings I operated with were doubt, uncertainty, and fear. I had moments of hope or even euphoria, but they made me feel insecure. By contrast worrying made me feel safe ... By and large, I found managing the hedge fund extremely painful. I could never acknowledge my success, because that might stop me from worrying, but I had no trouble recognizing my mistakes ... [W]hen I looked around, I found that most people go to great lengths to deny or cover up their mistakes.'

From Keynes (1937) onward, many economists have made the same point about the emotional basis of financial decisions on the interpersonal, micro level. While they are generally in accord with other types of risk analysts in seeing these emotions as irrational against a template of quantitative data (e.g., Shiller 2000), economists nevertheless recognize that emotions shape the capacity to act. Pixley observes that emotions also play a significant role at the meso or organizational level. There is a need to establish trust among organizations as a basis for rendering uncertainty bearable and creating the capacity for routine transactions. In 'the primary "futures institutions" where agents are entrusted to act for principals (banks, investment and insurance firms),' many standard terms have emotional meanings: '"securities," "insurance," which means to guarantee, credit (to believe), "trust," "fidelity," "guardian," "assurance," "beneficial," and "equitable" (Shapiro 1987: 628)' (Pixley 2002: 53). In Canada, one of the traditional pillars of the financial institution system is the 'trust company.' The largest banks have taken over some of these companies, but still retain the trusty name, for example, Toronto-Dominion Canada Trust and Royal Trust (a branch of Royal Bank of Canada). 'Clearly the future-oriented emotions in the finance sector are overtly managed, manipulated, and also commodified. The trust-inducing names of the firms are part of the commodification of trust and reputation, the appearance that all is in order (Lewis and Weigart 1985: 974)' (Pixley 2002: 55).

Decisions about risk and uncertainty are also moral decisions (Ericson and Doyle 2003). Risks are inevitably moralized in assessments of the severity of the dangers involved (Douglas 1990, 1992). They are also moralized in the process of classifying indicators of risk and making probability statements about these indicators (Hacking 1990). As a result, efforts to manage risk in practical decisions are infused with moral criteria, or what we have termed 'moral risk' (Ericson, Doyle, and Barry 2003: chap. 3). Thus, Adams (2003: 87) observes, 'Risk management decisions are moral decisions made in the face of uncertainty.' He develops a typology of how decision makers approach risk with 'ethical filters.' '[B]ound up with every rationality, solidarity or perceptual framework, one finds sets of moral principles and ethical codes that inform risk taking behavior' (ibid.: 94). Faced with uncertainty, especially about 'virtual risks' that scientific experts contend are there but no one can see, decision makers fall back on myths of nature. Adams describes hierarchist, fatalist, individualist, and egalitarian perceptions of nature and how each entails different views on moral behaviour about risks in both physical and social environments.

The cacophony of different moral views on risk has led to the rise of ethics and its institutionalization in organizational life (Rose 1999; Power 2003). For example, institutes of applied ethics have sprung up in universities to scrutinize environmental ethics, business ethics, scientific research ethics, and so on. University ethics committees audit research projects for their procedural propriety and have become increasingly stringent about the research process and even what is researchable (Van den Hoonaard 2002). The result of all such efforts to institutionalize ethical reflexivity is further doubt and uncertainty. 'Science now seeks its own legislation. It never ceases doubting the effects of its own development' (Ewald 2002: 294).

Surrounded by uncertainty, people use moral criteria as a necessary basis for deciding what risks are a special threat and therefore a priority for preventive action (Douglas and Wildavsky 1982; Douglas 1990, 1992; Hacking 2003). Again, this process operates not only at the level of individuals, but also among organizations and at the societal (nation-state) level. For example, faced with perceptions of non-distributable risks of high severity, a collective will include in its 'risk portfolio' those threats that articulate with its moral codes. In Douglas's terms, the risk is treated as a 'pollution' that threatens the 'purity' of the collective and is subject to strong reaction. There are efforts to pre-empt the risk through heavy preventive security and extreme vigilance. The reaction in North America to the remote (low probability) but non-distributable (high severity) risk of child abduction is a case in point, as is the response to terrorism after 11 September 2001 and to Severe Acute Respiratory Syndrome (SARS) in 2003.

Different collectivities react differently to potentially disastrous non-distributable risks. For example, in the face of nuclear fear, Germany is phasing out nuclear energy production while neighbouring France continues to embrace it as less polluting than the alternative of coal-fired energy plants. As Hacking (2003: 41) remarks, 'The relevant question is not whether it "really" is pollution, but whether in the rhetoric of debates something is presented either as pollution, or as an assault from across the border on purity ... I may wish to make distinctions between real, figurative, metaphorical, and symbolic pollution, but in real social life these run together.'

In summary, while contemporary Western society is commonly depicted as 'risk society' (Beck 1992a, 1992b, 1999) and 'knowledge society' (Stehr and Böhme 1986; Stehr and Ericson 1992; Stehr 1992, 1994, 2002), it can just as reasonably be viewed as the 'uncertain society.' Indeed, it is peculiar that Beck himself did not title his work 'The Uncertain Society,' because his primary contention is that science and technology are out of control to the point of producing non-distributable risks that are disastrous and irreversible. Risk society must assume that scientific knowledge of probabilities will continue to order the world, but Beck's view is one of a post-risk-calculation, post-insurance capacity, *uncertain* society. In the uncertain society, the focus is on the limits of scientific knowledge of risk and imagining unintended consequences of that knowledge. The prevailing sensibility is radical doubt, and this leads to a new responsibility for precaution. 'Precaution starts when decisions must be made by reason of and in the context of uncertainty' (Ewald 2002: 294): 'This implies that from now on, along with what one can learn from science, in a context that is always relative, it will also be necessary to take into account what one can only imagine, suspect, presume or fear ... an active use of doubt, in the sense Descartes ([1641] 1992) made canonical in his *Meditations on First Philosophy.* Before any action, I must not only ask myself what I need to know, what I dread or suspect. I must, out of precaution, imagine the worst possible, the consequence that an indefinitely deceptive malicious demon could have slipped into the folds of an apparently innocent enterprise' (ibid.: 286).

Insurers' Knowledge of Risk and Uncertainty

Of course, it is not news to insurers that they operate in societal conditions of uncertainty. They make decisions on uncertainty as a daily routine.

There is often no scientific data available on the risks to be insured. When such data are available, they are often subject to scientific controversy. There is uncertainty among scientific experts, let alone among those who hope to apply their knowledge. Scientific knowledge is subject to constant development and fluctuation. As a result, insurers experience liability for things they did not know existed at the time of underwriting (e.g., asbestosis), or did not visualize with respect to severity of catastrophic loss (e.g., the terrorist activity of 11 September 2001). Actuarialism is more art than science (Porter 1995; Glenn 2000; Ericson, Doyle, and Barry 2003). Risk pooling and spreading efforts can appear flawed in retrospect, as insurers discover unforeseen problems of moral risk, adverse selection, concentration risk, and aggregation risk (Baker 1996, 2003a; Baker and Simon 2002; Ericson, Doyle, and Barry 2003).

Consider how uncertainties are an inevitable fact of life in complex technological systems. A series of unintended technical failures can interact to yield catastrophic accidents (Perrow 1984). In assessing how both to prevent and insure against such catastrophic loss, there can only be a trade-off among the different risks involved, and uncertainty always looms.

The case of asbestosis is again illustrative. Asbestos was introduced to prevent harm from fire, and it continues to serve this function. Asbestosis was discovered as a new harm to personal health. There was a trade-off to consider: what is the greater harm to prevent, and what liabilities should insurers be responsible for in each case? This trade-off cannot be addressed on a once-and-for-all, either/or basis, but shifts according to each context in which asbestos prevents one harm and causes another. For example, Lahnstein (2002: 6) observes that in the World Trade Center catastrophe of 11 September 2001, 'responsibilities in connection with the initially suspected massive use of sprayed asbestos were discussed. After it became clear that the use of sprayed asbestos to protect steel girders had stopped from the 40th floor onwards of the first tower as early as 1971, the discussion shifted more onto the question of whether sprayed asbestos would have protected the steel structures for longer than the replacement product then used, and thus allowed more extensive evacuation.' Insurance is an uncertain business, and enormous liabilities may be assumed no matter what risk trade-off is made. As Ewald (2002: 291) asks about such 'development risks,' 'Is it not unjust to judge an act from the perspective of another state of awareness than that under which it was carried out? Is it fair, even for purposes of compensation, to appraise an act in accordance with suspicions and doubts that one is only capable of having after the event?'

Lahnstein (2002) also makes the important point that the meaning of risk and uncertainty is negotiated in insurance claims settlement processes. In the case of long-tailed liability claims such as asbestosis or other areas of products liability, this negotiation occurs over many years (ibid.: 16). The meaning of the risks involved and losses incurred changes significantly over time, as legal, media, and political forces negotiate liability scenarios that serve different interests. The meaning of risk and loss also changes significantly across different jurisdictions, because each jurisdiction has its own distinct legal liability system as well as media and political culture. The negotiated meaning of risk and insured loss is illustrated by a catastrophic explosion in Toulouse, France, just ten days after the 11 September 2001 attacks in the United States.

> A topical example of explosion damage in production and storage facilities was the explosion of ammonium nitrate on 21st September 2001 at a plant in Toulouse belonging to the TotalFinaELF Group: over 80,000 claims, 27,000 damaged dwellings, 10,000 claims for bodily injury, including 4,800 industrial accidents and 30 deaths. The total loss, largely insured, has been put at over 2 billion. The suspicion of terrorism was neither proved nor disproved; debate about it has ended – a case of successful government risk management? A second terrorist attack ten days after 11th September would in fact have created greater uncertainty in the global economy and motivated copycats. The problem of excluding terrorism from liability or insurance cover is becoming clear. (Lahnstein 2002: 4)

There are also many uncertainties embedded in the complex systems of insurance technology itself (Ericson, Doyle, and Barry 2003). For example, in pricing life insurance policies, there are speculative assumptions about interest rates, investment markets, policy lapse rates, and so on. Many of these assumptions prove wrong in retrospect, sometimes with windfall profits for insurers, at other times with huge losses and even insolvency. More generally, market-based insurance is highly competitive, and therefore subject to the same market pressures as any other commodity. Insurers develop specialized market segments and sell unique products to each segment in the hope of turning a profit. They often do so with a focus on the competition and the need to generate premium revenue more than on the knowledge of sound underwriting practice or strict loss prevention requirements.

Reinsurance is another complexity in the insurance system (Ericson, Doyle, and Barry 2003: 114–25). The originating or primary insurer takes out its own insurance protection with reinsurers in order to spread its risk exposure. When a major risk with catastrophic loss potential is involved, there can be dozens of partners in the reinsurance agreement. The system is so complex that a given party may not be aware of all of the partners, or of the details of their actual risk exposure. When a major catastrophe does occur, there is often shock at the level of overexposure and resultant heavy losses. Lloyd's of London syndicates are an infamous example of this process (Luessenhop and Mayer 1995; Swiss Re *Sigma* No.3/2002), but the uncertainty is embedded in the reinsurance system more generally. The complexities of reinsurance can yield the insurance technology equivalent of 'normal accidents' (Perrow 1984).

One option for insurers faced with uncertainty is to simply refuse to participate in underwriting a particular risk. This option is frequently exercised after a major catastrophic loss – Hurricane Andrew, the Northridge earthquake, and the terrorist activity of 11 September 2001 are prime examples – or in face of the 'development risk' entailed in product liabilities. Refusal to participate in particular risks also occurs in the process of excluding certain populations from a given insurance pool because they threaten the integrity and profitability of that pool. 'Redlining' in property insurance is a prime example (Squires 1997).

There are also many types of risk that the insurance industry regards as uninsurable (Moss 2002). For example, it is not possible to purchase insurance against the risk that the home one purchases will decrease in value over a specified period of time. Some risks uninsurable in the private market – for example, the risk of unemployment, or of flooding in specific regions – are addressed by government insurance schemes. Other such risks are not insured at all.

It is possible to make almost anything insurable. All that it takes is two parties agreeing to a contract. The history of the origins of insurance is rife with stories of such contractual arrangements in conditions of uncertainty (O'Malley 2003). For example, life insurance appeared long before actuarial tables. In effect, it was transacted at gaming tables where the parties were literally 'betting on lives' (Clark 1999). Marine insurance contracts had the same character, with one party betting the ship sailing in uncharted waters would return safely and the other betting it would not (Heimer 1985). Stories about the speculative gambling of the Lloyd's of London syndicates are legendary, although that system is now experiencing its own demise (Swiss Re *Sigma* No. 3/ 2002). The sensibility in the insurance world was, if at first you don't succeed, try Lloyd's. The London market remains *the* locus for insuring risks that have proven too difficult to insure elsewhere (ibid.; see also Froot 1999).

Perhaps the most remarkable thing is that insurers decide to insure as much as they do, regardless of whether or not they have detailed knowledge of the risk. On the one hand, insurance is a tireless effort to produce knowledge, to make the seemingly incalculable subject to calculation. In this effort it literally produces risks and finds ways to insure what had previously been regarded as uninsurable. On the other hand, even when this process fails – there is an inability to provide meaningful calculations, there are no probability statistics – they may still insure and assume liabilities for the unknown.

Why is this so? A simple answer is profits. Insurers are happy to gamble intelligently knowing that they can play on the uncertainty and associated emotions of the insured.

A complex answer is found in how insurers manage to achieve profits. Profits are pursued through the capital logic of insurance. There is a conversion of the event, process, or state of affairs represented by the risk, known scientifically or otherwise, into the insurance logic of capital risk and its distribution. Insurers reconfigure the uncertainties of others – of scientists' knowledge of risk and uncertainty, and of the insured in search of more security – into capital against whose loss they offer a guarantee. What is insured is not the actually lived or suffered loss: the effects of the loss of a loved one, or of property with sentimental value, are indeed incalculable. But insurance can at least provide some certainty that capital will be there to repair whatever damage can be expressed in monetary terms. In short, the insurance industry addresses uncertainty by protecting capital from risk. Ironically, it does so by putting capital at risk, especially but not exclusively its own. Insurers are risk takers in conditions of uncertainty.

Profits are also pursued through the governance mechanisms of the insurance industry (Ericson, Doyle, and Barry 2003). These mechanisms are organized around the concept of loss ratio: premium revenue minus administrative expenses minus loss prevention expenses minus reinsurance premiums minus insured losses plus reinsurance claims plus investment returns. While the actual implementation of this formula in insurance operations is highly complex (ibid.), some basic elements follow.

Premium revenue depends on market-based underwriting, offering products that are at once competitive and based on pools with good insurable risk characteristics. Administrative expenses are managed more efficiently through limiting the workforce, making the sales force dependent on commissions, introducing new information technologies, and outsourcing various services. Loss prevention needs are managed through insurance contract stipulations that make the insured responsible for loss reduction measures. Insured losses are managed through the selection of who is accepted into the insurance risk pool to begin with, loss prevention stipulations in the insurance contract, and control of the claims process by adjusters and investigators. Reinsurance taken out by the insurance company also limits and distributes insured loss claims. If all of the above governance mechanisms prove effective, the insurer has substantial sums available to invest in capital markets. Good investment returns will augment the insurer's capital base to further address expenses and insured loss claims, and to enhance profits. Obviously the myriad forms of insurance as governance are entwined with the capital risk logic of the industry.

How insurers address the limits of knowledge, capital risks, and loss ratios varies substantially across different lines of insurance. Each line poses unique problems of uncertainty regarding the scientific knowledge available, underwriting decisions, administration, loss prevention, claims management, reinsurance, and investment. As a result, each line entails different approaches to risk, attributions of responsibility for risk, and abilities to respond to uncertainty ('response ability').

Recognizing variation across lines of insurance is important for understanding conceptions of risk and risk society. Academic literature on risk often conflates different types of risk as well as frameworks for analysing it (Garland 2003). Social scientists are entangled in the particular model they wish to advance. In an effort to capture essential trends in society at the moment, they overlook counter-evidence and complexity.

The risk society thesis of Ulrich Beck (1992a, 1992b, 1999) is a case in point. As mentioned previously, Beck's focus is on catastrophes brought on by science and technology, for example, industrial accidents (Bhopal) and nuclear accidents (Chernobyl). This focus highlights risk as danger and is used to advance the view that modern society is undergoing transformation because it must increasingly respond to catastrophic threats that it itself has manufactured and is responsible for. To the extent that Beck addresses risk as probability estimates, he wishes to show that many actual and potential catastrophes are beyond such calculus. In the post-risk-calculation society, there is an inability to deal with the question of frequency of events because of the unpredictability of complex technological systems and the new environment of normal accidents. There is an inability to deal with the question of severity because events such as Bhopal and Chernobyl yield unimaginable consequences for the immediate victims, subsequent generations, and their environments. Beck is actually concerned with the uncertain society. He offers the sociological counterpart to Hawking's (1988: chap. 11) view that, 'In effect, we have redefined the task of science to be the discovery of laws that will enable us to predict events up to the limits set by the uncertainty principle.'

Beck uses his particular focus on science and technology to make inferential leaps about society as a whole. One such leap is the view that technological disasters have become 'uninsurable.' Technological disasters no doubt place a strain on the insurance system. However, disasters of this type and many others – for example, hurricanes, earthquakes, terrorism, and corporate fraud liabilities – are regularly addressed by the capital risk and loss ratio governance mechanisms of the insurance industry.

Mary Douglas (1990, 1992; Douglas and Wildavsky 1982) prefers a cultural framework. She is concerned to show the necessary conditions through which major risks, especially ones that appear relatively non-distributable, become part of the 'risk portfolio' of a given political culture. She emphasizes the moral dimension, which arises in particular from the fact that 'risk is not only the probability of an event but also the probable magnitude of its outcome, and everything depends on the value that is set on the outcome. The evaluation is a political, aesthetic and moral matter' (Douglas 1990: 10). The selection of a risk into the portfolio is an articulation of values, and in turn a means to mobilize moral communities for dealing with dangers in particular ways, and to force accountability. The word 'danger' was sufficient in the past, but in highly individualistic liberal societies trying to respond to globalized culture, the scientism of risk analysis has greater rhetorical effect. The word 'sin' also sufficed in the past to translate dangers into moral and political issues, but sin like danger is becoming obsolete as a mobilizer of moral community compared to 'the modern, sanitized discourse of risk ... A neutral vocabulary of risk is all we have for making a bridge between the known facts of existence and the construction of a moral community ... Risk, danger, and sin are used around the world to legitimize policy or discredit it, to protect individuals from predatory institutions or to protect institutions from predatory individuals' (ibid.: 4–5).

Douglas and her followers (e.g., Hacking 2003) ignore the way in which the risks at the centre of a culture's risk portfolio *are* distributable through the capital logic and loss ratio mechanisms of insurance. A given political culture's most dreaded risks – for example, nuclear energy production, child safety, terrorism, global warming – may be non-distributable when viewed through the cultural lens of severity and the limits of scientific knowledge. Such risks will inevitably be subject to extreme forms of precaution, vigilance, and suppression. However, this cultural reaction does not make them non-distributable from an insurance viewpoint. For example, Hacking (2003: 43) observes that after the terrorist activity of 11 September 2001, insurers recoiled and immediately stopped underwriting terrorism coverage. Many insurers did act in this manner, temporarily. However, the insurance system not only paid an estimated $55 billion to cover this loss, it also immediately set about the task of reconfiguring this risk so as to continue insurance coverage and profit from it.

Another framework is provided by Baker and Simon (2002), who argue that we are now living in an era of 'embracing risk.' Their focus is on the relative shift from welfarism to neo-liberalism, which places more onus on the individual to be self-sufficient in the life course. Crackdowns in disability insurance programs such as workers' compensation (McClusky 2002), and the rise of welfare-to-work programs (Gilliom 2001), exemplify this shift. The new emphasis is on managing one's own political economy to foster wealth and health. This new personal risk portfolio includes, for example, education and training that will make one a desirable 'human resource'; conscientiousness about health risks (e.g., eating habits, fitness programs, pharmaceutical consumption); investment in capital markets; and ample provision of life, health, property, and casualty insurance.

Many of the trends pointed to by Baker and Simon (2002) are now well established in all Western societies (see also Ericson, Doyle, and Barry 2003). However, 'embracing risk' is only one aspect of the present conjuncture and the role of insurance in it. Embracing risk was indeed the sensibility of the 1990s, as welfare programs were slashed, capital markets ballooned, and those able to afford it bought into regimes of being a valuable human resource, through fitness, personal investment, insurance, and so on. On the other hand, state health, welfare, and social security programs persist (Atkinson 1999, 2000), albeit with a new mix of public and private insurance. Moreover, in some areas, such as catastrophic loss through natural (e.g., storms, earthquakes) and human-made (e.g., nuclear energy, terrorism) forces, the strong state is advancing as the ultimate insurer (Moss 2002).

Uncertain Business

In the substantive chapters that follow, we compare and contrast uncertainty in four fields of insurance: life, disability, earthquake, and terrorism. These fields were chosen to document how insurers face real empirical variation in types of risk and uncertainty that is not simply reducible to their own insurance logics and processes (Hacking 1999). Each field involves unique problems of knowledge, approaches to risk, conceptions of responsibility, and response ability. In developing distinctive approaches to risk and uncertainty in each field, the insurance industry plays quite different roles as a central institution in risk society. Our empirical investigations of how these different roles are played show why risk society theorists must take into account real empirical variation in types of risk and uncertainty, and how such variation is addressed through different logics and processes.

A typology that highlights the distinctive features in each field is presented in figure 1.1. Detailed case studies of each field are then presented in chapters 2 to 5. In this section, we provide a brief summary of each chapter.

Life

The uncertainties of life have been addressed by insurance since the early modern period (Zelizer 1979; Clark 1999). Life insurance has evolved into an institution for the prolongation of prosperous lives and the management of civilized death. Prosperity and civilized death are to be achieved through life insurance and personal investment strategies

Figure 1.1
Uncertainty, Risk, Responsibility, and Response Ability

Uncertainty	Risk	Responsibility	Response Ability
Life	Embracing	Prudence	Investment
Disability	Spreading	Solidarity	Welfare
Earthquake	Absorbing	Mitigation	Infrastructure
Terrorism	Pre-empting	Precaution	Vigilance

that yield self-sufficiency into old age, a decent funeral, and the continued well-being of dependants after death. As such, life insurance offers economic rationalization of human capital: it is a method of finance involving speculation on the medically supervised prolongation of life (Defert 1991: 212). It injects utilitarian morality into the management of life and death, which is otherwise emotionally laden and thus a possible locus of nonutilitarian behaviour and mismanagement.

Life insurance appears as a quintessential institution of actuarial science, and of modern science more generally. Morbidity and mortality rates are relatively straightforward, and provide a reasonable means to establish underwriting criteria and premium levels. As such, life insurance seems to be a certain business, and indeed a highly lucrative one. But as we show in chapter 2, life insurance is not straightforward and is full of uncertainties.

Life insurance operated long before life expectancy tables were introduced in 1868. Even after the introduction of these tables, life insurance was typically underwritten with crude data that created an artificial order (Porter 1995). In some contemporary forms of life insurance, for example, group life plans, the subtleties of ratings continue to be eschewed in favour of absorbing differences into the law of large numbers.

Aggregate actuarial knowledge across populations is invariably compromised in the context of a given insurance company's local market position. Life tables and rate structures do not provide objective measurements for local practices and are often unsophisticated for practical purposes. Moreover, the calculus is further complicated by a loss ratio formula that takes into account such things as administrative expenses, policy lapse rates, reinsurance, and investment returns. Pricing decisions are partly based on guesswork in support of gambling, with both unexpected windfalls and catastrophic losses.

In recent years, increasingly specialized medical underwriting has been introduced to refine risk pools and segment markets for life insurance. This medical underwriting intensifies as the value of the life policy increases, and it yields more certainty in some respects. On the other hand, it also produces new uncertainties, as increasingly specialized market segments, risk pools, and product features are created. Actuaries often have no prior history data on which to price these products, and must use their best guesses about the future rather than wisdom about the past in order to design and price them.

Parallel specialization has occurred in the financial product features of life insurance. Life insurance has been repositioned as part of the competitive retailing of life course management and retirement provision. The welfarist notion that retirement provision is a 'merit good' based on a lifetime of hard work that needs to be protected by employers and the state has been turned on its head. Retirement income is now to be based on the individual's merit in being self-reliant, including her acquisition of life insurance investment products that hopefully will pay off. The customer is brought to the gaming table and presented with a bewildering array of speculative options: investment certificates, bond index funds, daily interest savings, equity market index funds, and so on. Annuity market, capital market, and inflation risks are all meritoriously transferred to the individual as part of her liberal powers of 'freedom' to embrace risk.

Insurers also embrace risk with these new products, which are typically created with limited knowledge or experience on how to rate and price them. Assumptions are made which often enough prove lucrative, but are also sometimes disastrous. When wrong assumptions lead to potential catastrophic loss for the insurer, efforts are made to change the assumptions in existing policies, or to convert policyholders to new contracts with assumptions more favourable to the insurer. This activity borders on, and frequently traverses, market misconduct and fraud (Ericson, Doyle, and Barry 2003: chap. 6).

Uncertainty is no deterrent to underwriting. Rather, life insurers turn to knowledge of local markets to lay their bets. They do everything possible to find applicants acceptable for some type of life insurance. For example, in Canada the industry typically rejects only about 3 per cent of all applicants, but policies vary enormously according to market segmentation criteria. As mentioned above, in the contemporary market-based underwriting of life insurance, the products blend into wealth management and become more life protection than death protection. Only a small fraction (15 to 20 per cent) of a large Canadian multinational life insurer's business is in life insurance policies per se, with the remainder in wealth management through myriad financial instruments. Financial market risks are increasingly embraced along with health and lifestyle risks.

These new dimensions of life insurance exemplify the shift to 'embracing risk' characterized by Baker and Simon (2002). The individual is made more responsible for her prudent choices about how to build, protect, and use financial assets over the life course on the principle that 'one person cannot transfer to another the burden of what happens to him' (Ewald 2002: 274). Risk taking in conditions of uncertainty is valourized in life insurance markets, as it is in the wider culture. '[P]rivate pensions, annuities, and life insurance are engaged in an historic shift of investment risk from broad pools (the classic structure of risk spreading through insurance) to individual (middle-class) consumers and employees in return for the possibility of a greater return' (Baker and Simon 2002: 4). Again, this embracement entails not only greater risk taking on the part of the insured, but also by insurers. Insurers fiercely compete in financial product markets and are always watching rating agency assessments and shareholder value.

The way in which both the life insured and their insurers embrace risk indicates that insurance involves much more than spreading risks and losses (ibid.: 2). It further suggests that risk is not only a danger or harm, but also something that has positive value for those willing to play with it. Furthermore, it indicates that risk is not limited to the technical calculation of probabilities. While probabilistic thinking and risk spreading are part of both the enterprising self and life insurance company operation, they are only one component. In this field, probability and harm take on new meaning. Moreover, they are sometimes absent as insurers design new products and the insured embrace them with a great deal of uncertainty.

The uncertainties of embracing risk are addressed by a responsibility for prudence. The insured is responsible for being circumspect about life course management. Through careful purchase and ongoing monitoring of life insurance investment products, she is to ensure not only death and survivor benefits, but also life, health, and well-being benefits to herself in her senior years. For its part, the insurer is to be a prudent manager of loss ratios and investment portfolios. This responsibility is signified by the 'prudent person' rule of insurance regulators: company officers are to treat the company's investment portfolio as if it were their own personal one (Ericson, Doyle, and Barry 2003: 107). It is also symbolized in the marketing of life insurance products, most famously that of The Prudential, which claims to be a safe and solid locus of investment, 'like a rock.'

Hacking (2003: 25) observes that prudence and risk have been in close association for five centuries. From its inception in the sixteenth century, a key use of the word risk was 'a new sense of life and morality.' Prudence shifted from denoting 'cowardice, the lowliness of the frugal, devoid of honor, selfish' to signifying 'the wise who accepted the moral duty of attending to the future, of saving for a rainy day, the virtue of foresight ... The new prudence and the idea of risk leads to insurance' (ibid.: 25–6).

Responsibility for prudence leaves those who make the wrong choices with no excuse. If something untoward occurs and the individual has not provided for its eventuality, it is her fault and she must bear the burden. It is her responsibility to prepare in advance by being aware of the risks she faces and taking prudent measures in relation to them. 'This is how insurance came to be promoted throughout the nineteenth century – as the institution of rational providence. In the world of providence, one has no other resources than calculation and virtue. Faced with the accidents that one can hardly anticipate, the only possible tactic is to learn how to offset them. And insurance, which makes this possible, cannot be made compulsory, since the obligation would rule out the exercise of the virtue of providence' (Ewald 2002: 277).

The response ability is investment for the future. The responsible individual buys life insurance products and services that ostensibly yield wealth, health, and well-being. Combined with other 'lifestyle management' practices, this is a lifelong process that requires continuous adjustment and learning from past mistakes. '[F]ailures and sufferings are able to become the indeterminate principle of their own remedy. The principle of responsibility, based on fault, thus serves as a universal converter of bad into good' (ibid.: 275).

In the new marketing of life insurance, response ability includes perpetual investment in the health of one's body. Aided by new risk analysis fields such as 'health promotion,' the individual is urged to invest in physical fitness regimes and to avoid risk habits such as excessive tobacco, alcohol, drug, and cholesterol consumption. Health promotion remains largely a state function, but there is increasing emphasis on governing healthy bodies in private corporate work settings, backed up by insurance requirements. There is also a burgeoning self-help industry of fitness counsellors, books, websites, and so on. Private insurers contribute to this self-help discourse on healthy lifestyles through educational materials tied to their marketing. Their message is that people living longer through better health promotion regimes will also need more prudence in investment to finance their longevity. They capitalize on the opportunity to be the life-course merchants to all prudent clients who want to construct their personal political economy with them. Recognizing the structural relationship between wealth and health, they are especially keen to pursue wealthy clients as a valuable commodity.

Disability

Disability insurance operates within a markedly different framework of uncertainty, risk, responsibility, and response ability. Disability insurance arose as an important institution for addressing the uncertainties of engagement with science and technology. In particular, temporary or permanent injuries suffered as a result of work and traffic accidents are met by insurance schemes that spread risks across broad pools as an expression of solidarity and exemplar of welfare. Disability insurance recognizes that modern science and technology have disastrous consequences on a *routine* basis. The best way to manage this state of affairs is to make insurance compulsory, and either fully managed by the state (e.g., workers' compensation in all Canadian provinces, and vehicle insurance in British Columbia, Saskatchewan, Manitoba, and Quebec), or, if not, then heavily regulated by the state (e.g., vehicle insurance in the remaining Canadian provinces).

While disabilities result from the modern advance of science and technology, they are also responded to through science and technology, especially that of the health sciences and medicine. New disabilities are constantly being discovered by the health sciences, and through the use of medical technologies. Associated treatments are then claimed to be a 'medical necessity.' Insurers must address how they will rate the new risk and compensate treatment programs. This is a very uncertain business because there is often little or no observable evidence of the disability nor of what constitutes successful treatment (Malleson 2002).

The disability insurance system responds by negotiating the meaning of disability in medical-legal contexts and in the everyday world of claims management. Disability is first and foremost an insurance term for inability to work and a construct for deciding how much productive ability a person has left. For example, various medical definitions of 'functional impairments,' related to restrictions on the use of the body for productive purposes, are established according to the insurance terms and conditions, including compensation levels available. One scientific task force of health professionals, grappling with how to establish recovery from whiplash associated disorder, declared that recovery occurs when insurance compensation is terminated (Spitzer et al. 1995)! The meaning of disability is constantly negotiated in the pragmatic contexts of insurance claims settlement. Surveillance systems and procedural regularity replace accurate scientific knowledge as the basis for assessment in many fields of disability insurance.

Disability insurance systems are also prone to problems of moral risk (Ericson, Doyle, and Barry 2003; Ericson and Doyle 2003b). This proneness results from the highly reactive nature of disability risk. Determinations of the meaning of disability and of losses worthy of compensation are made in routine transactions among claimants, medical professionals, legal professionals, and insurance claims officials. The subjective nature of injuries means that what is regarded as a legitimate disability, and as a reasonable level of compensation for loss, varies enormously across insurance claims cultures. It also means that there is plenty of room for exaggeration and fraud on the part of all parties to the insurance relationship. This highly reactive aspect of the disability insurance system is its distinctive feature relative to the life, earthquake, and terrorism insurance systems that we analyse.

The proliferation of disabilities, problems in establishing acceptable knowledge about them, and reactive moral risk problems all mean that disability is a risky area for insurers. Nevertheless, they underwrite a wide range of disabilities. Moreover, even when there might be some knowledge available that would assist in underwriting, it is often deemed too expensive to acquire and use. Disability risks are often underwritten on speculation, and investigation only occurs when claims are made and there is a need to minimize or deny them to control costs. Lack of investment in underwriting investigations leads to adverse selection problems, whereby those with a propensity to the disability being insured are more likely to want and acquire insurance. It also leads to moral risks at the level of the insured, who may benefit as much or more from disability claims than from working. These circumstances have led to cases where there have been massive underwriting shortfalls and consequent financial crises for insurers. Unable to control claims and therefore to protect loss ratios, many private disability insurers have left the field and there has been a general consolidation in this part of the insurance industry.

These problems of uncertainty in underwriting explain why many disability insurance programs are organized by the state. State involvement allows the compulsory spreading of risk across broad pools. The law of large numbers combined with the deep pockets of the state helps to address the problems posed by the limitations of medical knowledge, adverse selection, and moral risk. Ideally, the individual receives necessary health care and is at least financially protected from a lifetime of uncertainty. Organizations and institutions are also protected. In the case of workers' compensation, employers are protected from the uncertainties of long-term and expensive litigation as each serious work injury arises. In the case of vehicle insurance, vehicle manufacturers, road designers, and traffic engineers are also protected from the uncertainties of accident-by-accident litigation.

As mentioned previously, these society-wide mechanisms of risk spreading were recognized as essential in dealing with the untoward consequences of scientific and technological progress. '[A]ccidents are the by-product, necessary though always more marginalized, of scientific and technological progress. These are special or abnormal risks, the responsibility for which should be spread over the community' (Ewald 2002: 282). If the person's misfortune is truly an accident, and if work, transportation, and other technologically associated risks are routine and 'normal,' then individual fault and responsibility cannot be assigned. The community must take responsibility on the principle of solidarity.

In principle, solidarity is the opposite of embracing risk. Responsibility resides with the community, which in practice means its organizational and institutional entities. The employer in a workers' compensation scheme is held responsible by conceptions of social rights and fairness embedded in that scheme. In most instances in Canada, the employer is responsible for paying workers' compensation insurance premiums and for effecting work safety measures stipulated in insurance contracts. While the worker is also responsible for work safety, it is more as 'a link in a technical system in which faults are considered less as individual than as organizational' (Ewald 2002: 281).

Personal injury insurance systems, especially those governed by the state, have a strong accident prevention and safety mandate. This mandate is one aspect of how responsibility for solidarity depends on the response ability of welfarism. Welfarism entails a capacity to spread risks not only through the capital risk and loss ratio logics of insurance, but also through knowledge of how to prevent and treat every mishap in life. In this respect, welfarism represents another 'scientific and technical utopia, in which society may have the possibility of controlling itself, where knowledge may have an indefinite priority over power. At its philosophical foundations, it is inseparable from the imperative of prevention: prevention of illnesses ... crimes ... accidents ... poverty and social insecurity' (ibid: 273).

The response ability of welfarism has been under strain since the inception of the welfare state, and increasingly so in the last decade. The unravelling of welfare and its ethic of solidarity has been widely analysed and debated in both public policy and academic contexts (e.g., O'Conner 1973; Giddens 1998, 1999; Atkinson 1999, 2000; Broadbent 2001). We do not intend to retrace this development, but we will mention three features that are relevant to our analysis.

First, on the ideological level, there has been a substantial and relatively successful attack on welfarism by neo-liberalism, which advocates a minimal state, market fundamentalism, risk taking, individual responsibility, the inevitability of social inequality and vigilant critique of the state (Ericson, Barry, and Doyle 2000; Ericson, Doyle, and Barry 2003). Second, on the practical level of prevention and treatment of problems, there has been a realization of the limits of knowledge, including the iatrogenic tendencies of professions and institutions to compound rather than correct problems (Malleson 2002). Third, on the practical level of political economy, there has been a realization of the limits on both private and government insurers to keep raising premiums to the extent necessary to address insured claims and other expenses, and the limits on government as the ultimate insurer to increase taxes when its pockets need deepening. As Foucault observed, 'A machinery set up to give people a certain security in the area of health has, then, reached a point in its development at which we will have to decide what illness, what type of pain, will no longer receive coverage – a point at which, in certain cases, life itself will be at risk. This poses a political and moral problem not unrelated, all things considered, to the question of the right enjoyed by a state to ask an individual to go get himself killed in war ... The question that now arises is how people are going to accept being exposed to certain risks without being protected by the all-providing state' (Foucault 1988: 171–2; see also Sullivan and Baranek 2003).

These ideological and practical dimensions are transforming the response ability of welfare systems and their responsibility for solidarity. Disability insurance systems are a prime example. Underpinned by neo-liberalism, the limits of knowledge, and the limits of revenue, there has been a shift in the direction of embracing risk. Individuals are expected to take more responsibility for accident prevention by seeking education about risks and constantly being reflexive about them. They are also to assume more responsibility for the consequences of accidents. If they should have known about the risks in advance and taken preventive action, and an accident still occurs, then they can be faulted for the consequences. Indeed, in some fields of personal injury, such as vehicle accidents, the word 'accident,' which implies no fault, is replaced by 'crash,' which describes the event in more neutral terms so that fault can be attributed (Green 1997; Ericson, Doyle, and Barry 2003). The faulty individual who failed to prevent the crash can also be compensated less.

There is an attendant crackdown on insurance terms and conditions. For example, there have been increased restrictions on eligibility for insurance, and on benefits, in both vehicle insurance (Ericson, Doyle, and Barry 2003) and workers' compensation insurance (McClusky 2002). When costs are rising exponentially, and experts do not have accepted knowledge to diagnose and treat problems, the insurance system increasingly dictates the limits to both knowledge and compensation capacity. One dimension of this is intensified surveillance and policing of claims, including a crackdown on insurance fraud (Ericson, Doyle, and Barry 2003: chap. 9; Ericson and Doyle 2003b, 2004). Another dimension is work-hardening regimes (McClusky 2002, Butler 2002). In a retreat from solidarity, the responsibility of both injured persons and of the helping professions who treat them shifts from addressing the injury alone to also getting the disability claimant back to work as efficiently as possible to save the system, and especially insurers, money. Work-hardening regimes are grounded in the view that too much insurance protection can be harmful, forcing the injured claimant into a state of dependency and compounding the iatrogenic tendencies of the helping professions.

Chapter 3 captures the tensions faced by disability insurers in trying to spread risk while also forcing the insured individual to embrace more risk. Insurance contract–based sanctions and incentives are used at the point of underwriting. One mechanism is to substantially under-insure the policyholder in order to control malingering, for example, by keeping income replacement levels for the prospective disability claimant to about one-half of the person's normal income on the experience that a higher level can severely affect loss ratios. Various return-to-work incentives are also built into contracts, and underwriting increasingly anticipates the claims negotiation process.

Disability insurers step up safety education campaigns designed to reduce personal injury accidents and therefore claims costs (Ericson, Doyle, and Barry 2003: chap. 8). For example, in relation to work contexts and the driving of vehicles, there are advertising campaigns, education programs, environmental engineering programs, on-site inspections, and law enforcement crackdowns that are collectively aimed at persuading people to act more safely. These programs focus on the individual responsibility of risk takers to ensure safety of self and others. Each act of individual responsibility contributes an increment to the social responsibility of causing less accident-induced disabilities. Health, education, media, and legal experts are mobilized to make everyone obsessed with safety and smarter about the risks they take.

Physicians and other health care professionals are mobilized in the crackdown on disability claimants, while at the same time being sub-ject to more control over the services they provide. It is difficult to untangle the locus of inflated disability claims because claimants' views of their disabilities are constituted by the practices of health pro-fessionals and of the insurance system itself. Instead of placing the onus on the insurance and health care systems to produce better knowledge for diagnosis and treatment of such things as soft tissue injuries and back pain, ignorance is confessed. This confession enables a shift to the production and distribution of knowledge useful in getting the claimant back to work quickly and off disability benefits. Surveillance-based knowledge places responsibility on health pro-fessionals to police malingering and fraud, and on the claimant to do her part in learning to risk manage her pain at work as a kind of non-monetary 'deductible' or co-insurance payment.

As part of 'work-hardening' disability claimants, health profession-als are encouraged to abandon notions of cure in favour of teaching claimants to self-manage their disabilities at work. They are required to serve as ongoing claims investigators, for example, obtaining details on the accident that led to the claim to ascertain if those details corroborate other reports on the accident or suggest fraud. Clinical diagnosis and treatment sessions are also used for surveillance purposes, for example, checking whether the patient is making bodily movements that might belie her claims of functional impairment and pain.

Just as disability insurers promote preventive medicine among their insured populations, so they try to prevent medicine among health care providers for fear that too much surplus value will pass into their hands. They assign disability case coordinators to monitor the fine-grained detail of diagnosis and treatment regimes. In many contexts, they require that all cases be handled through designated assessment centres where they can control more fully who provides the assessment and treatment of claimants. Physicians and other service providers are taught to be more reflexive about the iatrogenic effects of their practices in order to make them more self-governing about what they are prescribing to patients for profit. Indeed, it is difficult to adhere to the Hippocratic oath, the essence of which is harm minimization, when both the physician and patient must prove that the patient is ill for the purpose of collecting insurance.

Health professionals are governed through the very technologies they use to assess and treat their disabled patients. New computer-based technologies for assessing functional impairment and pain check not only on the reliability of the claimant's story, but also on the health professional's rendition of that story. Health professionals are further subject to 'epidemiological surveillance' as they are required to report on standardized forms. The controlling formats of these forms yield some consistency in classifications of disabilities, and therefore procedural regularity in place of scientific objectivity. Procedural regularity is underpinned by professional liability insurance requirements which govern the health care working environment.

All of these trends in disability insurance underwriting and claims processing are aimed at making both the insured and health professionals more responsible for embracing risk. In the new disability insurance culture of surveillance and suspicion, solidarity loosens and welfare mixes uneasily with age-old principles. For example, there is a re-emergence of the view that good people are those who work hard to consume more, and those who are responsible for their own (mis)fortunes. Nevertheless, solidarity and welfare remain as essential components of disability insurance. Through their technologies for spreading risk, insurers continue to offer benefits for many disabilities that are easy to imagine but impossible to prove.

Earthquake

Knowledge of risk and uncertainty has a fundamentally different character in the case of earthquakes. Unlike other risks we have discussed to this point, earthquakes result from natural processes. They are not a consequence of advances in science and technology, nor is it possible to intervene proactively in what causes them in order to alter the course of events.

Earthquake science is very shaky. The timing, location, and effects of earthquakes are unpredictable. For example, recent catastrophic earthquakes in Northridge, California, and Kobe, Japan, were not predicted. The risk of a substantial earthquake in a Canadian urban environment is very low in probability, but very high in severity. Severity is extremely difficult to assess because there are so many variables in what buildings and infrastructures would be destroyed, what businesses would be interrupted, and what lines of insurance would be concentrated in the losses. Sophisticated models for estimating probable maximum loss are in use, but data collection and analysis involve dubious assumptions and subjective criteria related to what might happen over the next several hundred years. One statistical approach to 'quantify uncertainty' of earthquakes is called the 'bootstrap method' (Low 1997: 144)! Following the unpredicted earthquake at Northridge, reliance on the historical record for estimating probable maximum loss was rendered obsolete (Wallace and White 1997: 5).

Insurers still underwrite earthquake coverage in these conditions of uncertainty. We refer to this underwriting as 'absorbing risk.' The insured cannot be expected to embrace the risk of earthquake because they have no proactive capacity to intervene and help prevent an earthquake from occurring. While prevention is possible with most other types of risk – even the 'natural' hazard of hailstorms can be offset by using a fleet of aircraft to seed storm clouds with chemicals – earthquakes are a force of nature. Their catastrophic consequences must be absorbed by the entire society, and in particular the insurance industry in collaboration with government as the ultimate insurer and deep pocket for disaster relief.

In earthquake coverage, the capital logic of the insurance system is especially salient. The insured seeks protection of major capital assets from a remote but catastrophic loss. The insurer seeks to build capital capacity and risk spreading over the long term through some combination of premium revenue, investment returns, capital reserves, reinsurance, and government participation (for example, as a reinsurer at higher levels of loss; offering insurers tax benefits to allow them to build their reserves).

Beyond these means of capital protection and capacity building, insurers sell earthquake coverage on the basis of local market conditions. More conservative insurers conduct multiple probable maximum loss tests using the latest science and take out extra reinsurance beyond what these tests recommend. They do so in the knowledge of uncertainty, not really knowing whether they could keep their promise to pay in the event of a catastrophe. Less conservative companies try to get by with the minimum test and reinsurance levels required by regulators. In soft (highly competitive) markets, they sell earthquake insurance at low rates or even give it away as a 'loss leader' to attract other property and casualty insurance business.

Of course, it is difficult to identify low or high insurance premium rates without a more solid understanding of the risk. Insurance consumers are necessarily in the dark, and therefore respond to this market-based underwriting largely on the basis of local cultural perceptions. The cultural economy of earthquake underwriting is revealed in comparing British Columbia with Quebec. While Vancouver and Montreal have similar risks of catastrophic earthquake, only 5 per cent of homeowners in Montreal purchase earthquake insurance, compared to 60 per cent of homeowners in Vancouver. Among commercial insurance policyholders, 30 per cent of those in Quebec have earthquake coverage compared to 80 per cent in British Columbia (Wallace and White 1997: 13).

Earthquake risk can also be absorbed through design and construction of the built environment. As Lahnstein (2002: 2) observes, 'The causes of an earthquake cannot be attributed to anyone, but foreseeable or avoidable consequences of construction defects or poor disaster management can.' The responsibility is mitigation, taking steps that might make the effects of an earthquake less severe. The response ability lies in infrastructure: buildings, communication networks, bridges, roads, sewers, fuel lines, and so on can be built to absorb the shock. Some response ability is also available through disaster preparedness. Individuals can be educated about survival kits, emergency communication channels, and shelter options in the event of an earthquake.

In practice, responsibility for mitigation and response ability via infrastructure are difficult to mobilize through the insurance system. Earthquake risk is seen as remote and many choose not to insure at all.

Many who do insure take the view that they will not invest heavily in infrastructure protection: if a catastrophic earthquake occurs, they will simply walk away with whatever monetary compensation the insurer and government provide.

The usual mechanism for loss prevention incentives is the insurance contract. However, in the case of earthquake, any effort to enforce costly contract sanctions can lead the policyholder to simply switch to a more high-rolling insurer. Most earthquake loss prevention efforts are therefore left to the state, while insurers sporadically encourage their policyholders to improve the shake-resistant features of their properties.

Absorbing earthquake risk falls back on the capital risk logic of insurance and is a highly uncertain business. Insurers underwrite earthquake coverage in the knowledge they may become insolvent and unable to meet their obligations to policyholders, not only regarding earthquake coverage, but also regarding other property and casualty coverage as well. An insurance industry catastrophe may follow an earthquake catastrophe. For example, in 1997 it was estimated that a large magnitude earthquake in Vancouver might cost $30 billion, but less than half of that amount could be covered by the insurance industry's capacity, creating an economic shock ten times greater than the most recent recession (Wallace and White 1997: 8).

An additional exposure in Canada is the property and casualty insurance industry's policyholder compensation scheme. This scheme was established primarily as a means of protecting policyholders from isolated insolvencies that arise occasionally from insurance operations. Its arrangements are manageable in the event of single company failures that arise from time to time. However, there are potentially catastrophic consequences if several companies collapse at once: the claims against remaining companies will be so large that some of them may also fail, in a house-of-cards effect. Insurers who underwrite earthquake coverage in a highly speculative manner in effect transfer the risk to more responsible companies who would have to pay through the compensation scheme in the event of a major earthquake, and might themselves collapse as a result.

There is potential for a similar problem with reinsurance arrangements. Most earthquake risk is laid off with reinsurance partners, some of which may also take on too much exposure and not be able to meet obligations in the event of a catastrophe.

The state is drawn into this capital risk alchemy because of its obligations to citizens following a major catastrophe. Not wishing to appear as the ultimate deep pocket, the state declares that catastrophe insurance is to be provided by private industry and 'disaster relief' is at the discretion of the state after-the-fact. It is political death to say no to disaster relief when the causes of catastrophe cannot be attributed to anyone. But it is also political death to tell citizens they do not need private insurance because the state has deep enough pockets to take care of everything. The state's compromise is to help manage the capital risk distribution, for example, by giving the industry tax concessions on an investment reserve fund dedicated to earthquake catastrophe claims.

Terrorism

Terrorism can have catastrophic consequences of the same magnitude as earthquakes. In contrast to earthquakes and other natural hazards, terrorism is intentional catastrophe. It not only results in severe destruction of property and tragic loss of life, but also in the disestablishment of broader social, cultural, political, and economic infrastructures. It is literally an attack on the fabric of society.

Terrorists are in the business of uncertainty. They use random attacks to intimidate and to generate extreme fear. They play on the culture of fear that is already dominant in risk societies (Glassner 1999; Altheide 2002). They also play on the intensification of security in risk societies. Governments, in collaboration with institutions of civil society, including the insurance industry, are in the business of providing security as guarantees against loss. Terrorists randomly breach security to further dramatize uncertainty.

The insurance industry is a key player in defining and responding to terrorism. One Canadian property and casualty insurance company, adopting a standard definition developed by the Insurance Bureau of Canada, defined terrorism as 'an ideologically motivated unlawful act or acts, including but not limited to the use of violence or force or the threat of violence or force, committed by or on behalf of any group(s), organizations(s), or government(s) for the purpose of influencing any government and/or instilling fear in the public or a section of the public.' As documented in chapter 5, following the terrorist activity of 11 September 2001, insurers paid much closer attention to the definition of terrorism in order to limit their terrorism coverage or exclude it altogether. Their definitions varied substantially depending on the type of coverage they offered, and the various reinsurance and other partners involved in underwriting this risk. As such, the meaning of terrorism was under continuous negotiation, and changed from contract to contract.

Prior to 11 September 2001, terrorism in North America was viewed as a low frequency and moderate severity event. The previous worst insured loss resulting from terrorist activity in North America was the World Trade Center event of 1993. The loss from that event was $725 million, compared to $20 billion for Hurricane Andrew and $15 billion for the Northridge earthquake. Insurers' worst case scenario for the World Trade Center was a small aircraft striking one of the towers and destroying two stories. This estimate of probable maximum loss, combined with a very competitive insurance market in the 1990s, meant that insurers did not generally underwrite terrorism as a special coverage with a separate premium. Instead, they simply included terrorism as part of 'all perils' coverage in various lines of insurance. So exposed, they experienced an estimated $55 billion in insured losses from the events of 11 September 2001.

These considerations suggest that prior to 11 September 2001, terrorism was regarded as a relatively remote risk in North America that, if it occurred, would result in an easily manageable loss. However, terrorism in some jurisdictions outside North America has occurred regularly as a known risk. Palestinian suicide bombers in Israel, Irish Republican Army bombers in the United Kingdom, and ETA bombers in Spain testify to this fact. Moreover, there was good evidence that Islamic terrorists planned a renewed attack with catastrophic consequences on the World Trade Center (Lesser et al. 1999; Public Broadcasting System *Frontline* 2002). If anything was ripe for risk analysis as an effort to address the fear of collective, non-distributable risks, it was terrorism, and there was a burgeoning terrorism risk research industry long before 11 September 2001.

As we document in chapter 5, a deep sense of uncertainty set in after 11 September 2001. Insurers fretted about the seeming impossibility of making terrorism risk calculable with respect to frequency and location of events. They also began to imagine cataclysmic scenarios, such as nuclear, biological, and chemical attacks on major urban centres, the severity of which would be impossible to calculate.

The World Trade Center collapse also gave insurers a new appreciation of uncertainties in the insurance system itself. Some insurers and reinsurers experienced unprecedented 'correlation risk': they unwittingly discovered that they had underwritten World Trade Center coverages across lines of insurance that interacted to compound their losses. They also experienced unprecedented 'concentration risk' or 'aggregation risk,' having multiple insurance contracts with different insurance and reinsurance company partners that compounded their insured losses in previously unknown ways.

The uncertainties of future terrorist activity, as well as of their own technologies and systems, drove insurers into a mode of 'pre-empting risk.' Pre-emption took two forms. First, there was an effort to pass exposure to other parties by refusing to underwrite terrorism risk, or underwriting it under very costly and stringent terms. Reinsurers shifted exposure to primary insurers, who in turn tried to pass it on to the insured. Insurers struggled to involve the U.S. federal government as the ultimate insurer. There were various proposals for a government 'backstop' or reinsurance participation scheme. Second, there was an effort to pre-empt terrorist activity. Unlike earthquakes, in relation to which only risk absorption is viable, terrorist activity can be subject to active disruption and elimination. Such pre-emption entails a responsibility for extreme precaution, and the response ability of vigilance through surveillance. Here government took the lead, with heavy military and police involvement, but there was also an intensification of private security compelled by the insurance industry.

The model of pre-empting risk, precaution, and vigilance is fostered in conditions of deep uncertainty. The hope is that governments, in partnership with the institutions of civil society, including the insurance industry, are up to the task of security provision. But the very effort to implement the model fosters greater uncertainty. Perpetual news discourse about terrorism and vigilant security screening in public places are daily reminders of profound insecurity. Terrorists sporadically manipulate security systems to augment the terror. Ironically, the more the model of pre-emption, precaution, and vigilance is implemented, the more the terror is heightened.

While the uncertainties of life, disability, and earthquake all provide challenges to insurance technologies and systems, terrorism upsets the very 'postulates of an insurance-based society, which is to attribute to a threat an objective value and price' (Ewald 2002: 285). If frequency and severity cannot be reasonably calculated and assessed, the viability of insurance appears doubtful, and the primary task is to do whatever seems necessary to prevent the catastrophe from occurring. Pre-emption trumps compensation as the primary goal, and precaution and vigilance dominate. As Ewald (2002: 299) remarks about the precautionary principle in general, 'Solidarity had almost made us riskophiles; now we are almost riskophobes, individually and collectively, and will remain so for some time.' Cost-benefit analysis, so salient in embracing the risks of life and spreading the risks of disability, seems less applicable in the case of terrorism. Cost-benefit analysis assumes acceptance of residual risk, but when the focus is on pre-empting risk, there is no acceptable residual. There is 'zero tolerance' in the hope of achieving 'zero risk,' that is, a risk that has no price (Ewald 2002: 285).

The use of the precautionary principle and vigilance through surveillance did not originate with the terrorist activity of 11 September 2001. While precaution and vigilance have reached extremes in relation to the threat of terrorism, they have been dominant in other contexts of failure to protect citizens from risk (Jonas 1984; Ewald 2002; Baker 2002a; Haggerty 2003). Baker (2002a) observes that there has been a general retreat from the belief that harm can be predicted and controlled in advance. This retreat is evident in the law of products liability, which imposes strict liability on manufacturers. Even where there is no reasonable scientific evidence that the product actually caused the harm alleged – for example, that silicon breast implants cause chronic fatigue syndrome and other illnesses – the courts have sometimes imposed massive liabilities on manufacturers. The objective is to force a precautionary approach in product design and development through the threat of major financial sanctions if things eventually go wrong. The increasing criminalization of environmental law in the United States (ibid.), and of responsibility for various risks to health and safety in France (Mangon 1995; Roussel 2000, 2002, 2003), provide further evidence that limits to knowledge of risk will be dealt with by a political and legal emphasis on pre-emption at all costs. Baker (2002a: 356) outlines the implications for the insurance system.

If the risk is not foreseeable to the manufacturer, then it is not foreseeable to insurers, either. This means that liability insurance pricing is at best an estimate, coupled to the fervent hope that the good bets cancel out the bad and the future will not be too different than the past. Because of this [product] development risk, insurers design their insurance contracts so that they can run away from the loss at the earliest possible moment. As a result, limited liability and bankruptcy come to play too large a role in the management of development risk, so that victims do not in fact have the protection against loss that law claims to provide for them (Lo Puki 1996).

The inevitable consequences are uncompensated victims, a clamour for criminalization, and a call for extreme efforts to prevent loss in the future.

There is some parallel to the field of personal injury accidents and disability insurance. Harms that are difficult to predict and assess, especially those that are entangled in iatrogenic processes, do not square with the loss ratio logic of the insurance system. The emphasis shifts to prevention, surveillance, and enforcement in ways that not only disadvantage the insured but also encourage a precautionary approach and vigilant practices among those who diagnose and treat disabilities.

The precautionary approach entails a 'decline of innocence' (Priest 1990; Lowi 1990; Ericson 1994a; Ewald 2002). Under other approaches to responsibility – for example, the traditional model of *actus reus* and *mens rea* in criminal law – uncertainty spells innocence. Under the precautionary principle, uncertainty is no excuse, but rather a mobilizer of vigilance through intensified surveillance. Boundless liability 'leaves no room for innocence' (Ewald 2002: 296). Everyone is held responsible for doing their part in the preventive safety effort and assessed against the standard of the worst case scenario, not the probabilities of risk. When this negative logic is translated into decision making, it appears as a 'least worst' approach directed at preservation, impediment, and restriction. The precautionary principle addresses 'the irreparable, the irremediable, the incompensible, the unpardonable, the nonprescriptive ... Precautionary logic is, above all, a logic of decision applicable to situations of uncertainty, including that of remedying injuries ... Precautionary logic does not cover risk ... it applies to what is uncertain – that is, to what one can apprehend without being able to assess' (Ewald 2002: 284–6).

In short, the responsibility for precaution and response ability of vigilance with respect to terrorism arose in political cultures that were already attuned to pre-empting risk in myriad contexts of uncertainty. In the case of terrorist activity, governments stepped in quickly to mobilize the pre-emption of risk. There has been an enormous enhancement of surveillance and coercive security, involving personnel (military, police, private security), technologies (weapons, surveillance), and law (enabling legislation to ensure security system rights over individual due process, as well as private duties of protection). The cost of this enterprise, even in the short term, has been multiples of the $55 billion compensation paid by insurers to victims of the terrorist activity on 11 September 2001.

Ironically, but predictably, the uncertain society fell back into the familiar trap of believing that more science and technology would work where less had not. Research and development of new weapons and electronic surveillance technologies, and massive spending on whatever technologies were available, went in search of certainty. New risks and uncertainties were created in the process. Pre-empting risk, precaution, and vigilance against terrorism produce new forms of discrimination, restrict liberty, invade privacy, reduce public account-ability, result in inequality in security protection, consume massive resources, and yield more terror.

While governments take the lead in precaution and vigilance against terrorism, the insurance industry plays a significant role. In spite of all the uncertainties of terrorism, it has reconfigured its systems to pro-vide terrorism insurance coverage in various forms and contexts. The capital logic of insurance is especially salient. The potential for sub-stantial profits from terrorism insurance was a major catalyst for the mobilization of new capital brought into the insurance industry after 11 September 2001, and for the invention of new terrorism coverages underwritten as special risks. Bets were laid that there would not be another terrorist event of such catastrophic proportions. These bets were laid off with reinsurers. Efforts were made to involve govern-ments as the insurers of last resort above a certain loss limit. Insurers also played a supporting role in precaution and vigilance by forcing the insured to implement security arrangements as a condition of ter-rorism insurance coverage. Even in exorbitant conditions of uncer-tainty, insurance is a crucial technology in search of more security.

Research Approach

The following case studies of life (chapter 2), disability (chapter 3), and earthquake (chapter 4) insurance are based on extensive field research conducted in 1997, 1998, and 1999. This is the same field research that formed the basis of our earlier book, *Insurance as Governance* (Ericson, Doyle, and Barry 2003). A fuller description of the field research is available in that volume (ibid.: 91–8).

The field research involved 276 researcher days. It was mostly con-ducted in Canada, but we also collected data in the United States. A tri-angulation research approach (Miles and Huberman 1994) was adopted to develop multiple perspectives on knowledge of risk and uncertainty and how they are dealt with in each field of insurance. There was trian-gulation of data sources (e.g., persons, times, places), methods (e.g., interviews, observations, document analyses), researchers (e.g., a team field research approach), and data types (e.g., qualitative texts, tape-recorded interviews, observations, quantitative data).

We conducted 224 open-focused interviews with participants in the insurance industry. All but a few of these interviews were tape-recorded and transcribed. Interviewees included fifty-nine employees of private insurance companies, thirty professionals (e.g., actuaries, data analysts, lawyers, doctors) in expert systems that serve the insur-ance industry, ten representatives of insurance brokerages, forty-eight employees of state-run insurance operations, twenty-one state repre-sentatives who were involved in the regulation of private insurance, and fifty-six insurance consumers.

Observations of insurance practices transpired in various contexts. We attended industry conferences that addressed the future of the industry, corporate management, reinsurance, marketing, and insur-ance fraud. Selected conference sessions were tape-recorded and tran-scribed, and we also talked informally with conference participants. We observed insurance sales practices, including regional sales meet-ings between managers and agents, call centre operations, and agent-client meetings. We observed claims-processing operations regarding vehicle, health, and workers' compensation insurance.

During our interviews and observations we were given several hun-dred documents that proved useful for our analysis. From insurance companies we obtained training and operations manuals for sales agents, claims adjusters, loss prevention inspectors, and fraud investi-gators; underwriters' rating manuals; marketing research and strategy documents; and sales promotional material. We obtained documents from expert service providers to the insurance industry, for example, regarding expert systems used in marketing, underwriting, claims pro-cessing, and fraud investigation. Insurance brokers provided us with sales material as well as policy documents regarding the rapidly changing sales distribution system. State regulators of insurance prac-tices provided us with documents pertaining to policy, standards of insurance practice, the training and licensing of sales agents, and con-sumer complaint systems. Corporate risk managers gave us docu-ments on policy and procedures. Consumer association representatives provided material on particular cases of complaint or actions against insurance industry practices. A few individual consumers gave us material pertaining to their specific complaints or actions against the insurance industry.

Field research for the case study on terrorism insurance (chapter 5) was conducted in 2002 in both Canada and the United States. It included attendance at an industry conference on insurance markets following the terrorist activity of 11 September 2001. The entire conference proceedings were tape-recorded and selectively transcribed. There were sixteen presenters at the conference, including insurance and reinsurance company executives, insurance industry regulators, experts in legal liability, and experts in insurance risk and decision processes. In separate field trips, we also conducted open-focused interviews with thirteen senior executives in insurance companies, reinsurance companies, and regulatory agencies. We obtained various documents from conference participants and interviewees, as well as from the websites of insurance companies, insurance industry information service companies, and insurance regulatory bodies.

The format of chapter 5 differs somewhat from that of the case studies in earlier chapters. Chapter 5 addresses the dynamics of the insurance industry and government reactions to a specific catastrophic event.

The terrorist activity of 11 September 2001 continued to reverberate on insurance markets and government policy well beyond our data collection period. Therefore, the reader must appreciate that chapter 5 only tries to capture how the uncertainties of terrorism were addressed in the first year after the catastrophe. Moreover, the data are limited to what we could glean from the sources outlined above. Nevertheless, we are confident that chapter 5 includes rich and unique data relevant to our concerns about how the insurance industry operates in conditions of uncertainty. The uncertainties of terrorism pose unique problems for insurance logic and industry operations, and chapter 5 therefore provides an important comparative analysis in the context of the other three case studies.

We must also point out the limitation of our comparative studies of insurance as an uncertain business. We ourselves are producers of limited knowledge. In particular, we are constrained by the limits of our research approaches and ways of knowing. Moreover, we have only compared four fields of insurance, selected in order to sharply contrast types of uncertainty, risk, responsibility, and response ability faced by the insurance industry and societies in general. If other fields of insurance were subject to similar analysis, further conundrums of knowledge and complexities of the insurance industry would be revealed, and our claims would no doubt require modification.

We are now in a position to enter the field. We begin with a case study of the uncertainties of life, and how these are managed through an insurance system that fosters the embracing of risk, the responsibility of prudence, and the response ability of investment.

2 Uncertainties of Life: Embracing Risk, Prudence, and Investment

One must take all one's life to learn how to live, and, what will perhaps make you wonder more, one must take all one's life to learn how to die.

Seneca, *On the Shortness of Life* (1st c.)

Our fear of death ought to be proportional not only to the magnitude of the harm, but also to the probability of the event. Just as there is hardly any kind of death more rare than being struck by lightning, there is hardly any that ought to cause less fear.

Arnaud and Nicole, *Logic, or the Act of Thinking, Containing, besides Common Rules, Several New Observations Appropriate for Forming Judgment* (1662)

[Life insurance is] semi-religious and semi-business ... an unprecedented combination of the moral and the material, of conviction and reason, of preaching and mathematics, of the zeal of the fanatic and the dispassion of the business contract.

Kingsley, *Militant Life Insurance* (1911)

Uncertainties of Life

Life insurance appears as a paradigmatic institution of modernity. Relying upon actuarial science and probabilistic reasoning, it enables rational choice about provision for the future. Among various lines of insurance, it is viewed as exemplifying actuarialism at its finest, generating data about life expectancy (mortality) and health conditions (morbidity) of the population that facilitate accurate pricing of insurance policies and determination of required benefits. Against this backdrop, life insurance is marketed as offering greater certainty in face of the contingencies of life and unpredictability of death.

Beneath the veneer of certainty, life insurance is a very uncertain business. As we document in this chapter, uncertainty is pervasive for a number of interconnected reasons. Actuarial data on mortality and morbidity are often crude and of limited applicability in local underwriting contexts. Aggregate actuarial knowledge is always compromised in the practical decision making of each insurance company competing in local markets. In the past two decades, highly specialized medical underwriting has been introduced to refine risk pools and segment markets for life insurance. New sources of uncertainty have been introduced, as increasingly specialized market segments, risk pools, and product features are created for which actuaries have no prior history. Over the same period, specialization has also occurred in the financial product features of life insurance. Life insurance is increasingly repositioned as part of retirement provision. The policyholder is presented with a bewildering array of investment options tied to the policy that promise to assist in the accumulation of retirement assets. The compounding effects of medical and financial product market segmentation force policyholders to embrace the uncertainties of their health conditions and financial risk taking.

Life insurers also embrace the uncertainties of these new products, which are typically created with little knowledge or experience on how to rate and price them. Insurers fiercely compete in broader financial product markets and are driven by rating agency assessments and shareholder value. Seeking windfall profits but also exposed to catastrophic losses, they exemplify neo-liberal risk taking in conditions of uncertainty.

In efforts to control their uncertain environment, life insurers invest heavily in governance of the insured. Although they themselves are often imprudent in their underwriting and investment decisions, they foster a strong sense of responsibility for prudence among the insured. The insured is to be prudent about her own life course management through wise investment in life insurance products, as well as participation in various self-disciplinary programs of health promotion, lifestyle, and well-being. If she makes wise choices she will benefit in the long term; if she makes the wrong choices it is her fault and she must bear the burden.

While Baker and Simon (2002) capture some aspects of these processes as 'embracing risk,' we show in this chapter that it is more a matter of embracing uncertainty. Life insurance has always entailed a considerable degree of uncertainty. However, the recent proliferation of fine-grained medical underwriting, financial product features, and market fragmentation have greatly accelerated uncertainty. Life insurance entrepreneurs push beyond the capacity of life insurance technology in order to be competitive, and the life insured often suffer negative consequences of this entrepreneurialism.

Uncertainty surrounds the ways in which the life insurance industry manufactures the product. Key ingredients in the manufacturing process include mortality rates, persistency or lapse rates, administrative expenses, investment strategies, medical ratings, and market segmentation practices. Each of these ingredients is a source of uncertainty, involving speculation and risk taking beyond rational knowledge of risk as probability calculations. Moreover, uncertainties are compounded by the interaction of all of these elements in the manufacture of a given life insurance product.

The life insurance industry has a long history of insuring lives based on limited knowledge of mortality. In the United States, the first life expectancy table for pricing life insurance did not appear until 1868, but life insurance operated as a profitable business long before that date (Zelizer 1979: 14). In England, life insurance began in the eighteenth century as a purely speculative 'betting on lives' (Clark 1999, 2002). In contrast to its present-day image of restraint and security, life insurance was a form of gaming in which the time of death of an identified other – including a person in whom one did not have an insurable interest – was the subject of wager. Although actuarial science developed in the nineteenth century and eventually became institutionalized in life insurance underwriting, it bore no direct relation to decision making.

Even if there were general 'laws of mortality,' a matter of controversy among the actuaries, they provided no adequate basis for the institution of life insurance. Nineteenth-century actuaries recognized that their work required creating a domain of artificial order. This they aimed to accomplish mainly through the skillful selection of lives ... The selection of lives presented a difficult problem of trust and surveillance. A sound company would take care that medical as well as financial expertise was represented on its board. The customary practice among life insurance companies in the early decades of the industry was to require a personal appearance of every applicant before the assembled directors. There, an inspection would take place and a decision would be reached about whether this was indeed a 'select' life. But sometimes an inspection was grossly inconvenient, especially if the applicant lived far from London. Charles Babbage reported in his study of insurance institutions in 1826 that most companies were willing to dispense with this visit for a certain percent. How much this ought to be, he added disapprovingly, had never been calculated. (Porter 1995: 39–40)

A number of these observations about nineteenth-century life insurance underwriting continue to be relevant. A personal inspection of the prospect is useful to assess not only financial and medical details, but also to combine this technical knowledge with an assessment of moral character. However, if such assessments seem too expensive or inconvenient, they can be waived as long as the premium price can be adjusted upward to compensate for the imagined additional risks entailed.

Aggregate actuarial knowledge across populations is invariably compromised in the local context of the company's market position. Life tables and rate structures do not provide objective measurements for local practices. 'Because of the essential heterogeneity of company practices and the populations insured, no mere process of collecting and tabulating results from the population at large could yield numbers that would be valid for any particular company' (Porter 1995: 102–3).

We attended a brokers' conference where reinsurance specialists lectured on industry trends. One specialist observed that into the 1970s life insurers worked with large general risk pools and therefore with little detailed knowledge of their clients' financial and medical risks. They were not 'as concerned about seeking out where they got a competitive advantage, whether they did bring something genuine to the consumer or to the distributor, and where they should focus on.' A colleague said that during this period, actuarial tables were very unsophisticated and of little use to a company underwriting with sensitivity to local market conditions: 'In terms of mortality experience, what companies used in 1975, they used a table that is called C50–58, which is the commissioner's standard ordinary table, and that was an aggregate table based on older data and it wasn't that relevant to what the marketplace was in the 1970s. Companies were trying to get into mortality improvement in their tables, and trying to figure out what is a real mortality table. As I said, smaller companies had a hard time doing that.'

This life-underwriting expert used the example of how smoker and non-smoker rates were introduced on a very crude aggregate basis. The original rate structure was especially disadvantageous to non-smokers and lucrative for insurers. When more refined preferred rating became available, insurers were reluctant to adopt it. A more fine-grained preferred rating system would not only reduce the excessive premium revenue they were generating from the existing system, it would also create problems of adverse selection. Initially there was

flat adjustment of 60 per cent of an aggregate table [for non-smokers] and 120 per cent for smokers – that was very arbitrary, based on Stats Canada statistics or other types of the general population not directly related to insurance. So a lot of those prices were a bit offline [i.e., too expensive] and companies tended to be a bit conservative ... [Over time] non-smokers that were healthy were moving from their aggregate rates to [preferred] non-smoker rates. So basically, all the companies had left in their in-force block of business were either smokers or not as healthy non-smokers. So there was a bit of deterioration there, and that's probably one of the key reasons why preferred took so long to get into Canada. Companies with big blocks of in-force business were reluctant to come out with us just because if you come out with preferred products you may eat up your in-force, and have all these with healthy lives going to this preferred basis. And all your in-force bought would be worse mortality.

A colleague of this expert said that the term insurance rate for a healthy male non-smoker dropped by 80 per cent between 1975 and 1997. He attributed this sharp decline in premium to a combination of aggressive competitive pricing with preferred products, better data on the effects of smoking, improved mortality experience for non-smokers, and new reinsurance arrangements that offer participation in larger pools for more specialized products.

A second source of uncertainty is persistency or lapse rates: how long consumers hold onto their life insurance policies. Historically, life insurance companies have profited enormously from high lapse rates. In late nineteenth-century America, only 10 per cent of life insurance policies were actually terminated by death (Gowri 1997: 20). It is still the case that only a minority of policies mature or result in death payments, these being financed by the majority that lapse (Clarke 1999: 87). Term life insurance policies are especially lucrative when they eventually lapse, because they carry no cash surrender value (Zelizer

1979: 128). On the one hand, term policyholders have an incentive to keep paying premiums even if they find them costly so as not to lose their 'investment.' On the other hand, they may allow the policy to lapse, either because they have accumulated other assets to meet their needs or because they find the premiums too expensive, especially on policies where the premiums increase with age.

The actual lapse calculus is tied in with mortality, administrative expenses, and investment return and, as such, varies with each type of product. For example, if the life policy has investment value there may be a surrender charge (e.g., a mutual fund with a back-end load). This product is predicted to have a low lapse rate until the surrender charge falls off, at which time lapses will increase, then drop down again as the committed policyholders persist. If a level premium is charged year after year ('guaranteed premium' product), the insurer over-charges in the early years to compensate for the fact that the client is effectively paying less over time and the lapse rate will be very low. Where a product has cash value, the cash value itself becomes an inducement for people to lapse when they grow older. A marketing actuary for a life insurance company explained in interview, 'It's assumed that if somebody is age eighty, the kids are no longer an issue for them and they want to take a world cruise ... there's that incentive to surrender ... Because the product is "lapse-supported," you can tend to charge less for it ... because the people that do surrender early in those cases often experience a bit of a loss, but that loss is spread to the policyholders who persist.'

Clearly there is a lot of guesswork regarding lapse rates and the gamble does not always pay off. A solvency regulator we interviewed said that he had to step up regulation and demand greater capital ade-quacy because too many companies were making wrong bets on lapse supported products. 'If they all drop the policies too soon they back your initial cost, but if ... everybody keeps them going to the end in fact it's not adequately priced. Some companies got themselves in a bit of a box by assuming more lapses would occur. If this is a hot seller, very competitive product, if you could convince yourself that enough would lapse you would have the best price in town, you'd do a lot of business. So a couple of companies have got really heavily into this ... In one instance the scenario involved declining interest rates and low-lapse rates, [it] did not paint a very pretty picture for this company.'

There are cases of lapse rate miscalculations even on apparently straightforward products. One case in Canada involved a level-premium product known as T100. This is a term insurance product that the policyholder is entitled to keep to age one hundred at a fixed premium rate. The development of this product was described in an industry newsletter published in 1997:

> An intensely competitive marketplace and the high interest rates during the 80s also spawned low-cost, lapse-supported T100 (term-to-100) life insurance policies. The T100 policy design is a permanent policy with guaranteed level premiums for life (to age 100) and a guaranteed death benefit but no cash surrender value. Consequently, the reserves which the insurance company establishes with the premium revenues are forfeited by the policyholder if the policy is surrendered or lapses before death. In pricing T100 policies, the insurance company projects a potential windfall gain from these forfeitures and reduces premiums accordingly. Because of the guaranteed nature of the T100 policy, long-term assumptions of mortality, lapse rate and investment yield are critical in designing a profitable product for the insurance company.

By the late 1990s, insurers realized that the 'potential windfall' gain was turning into an actual windfall loss. Policyholders held onto these policies to the point that, in 1998, the lapse rate was 'close to zero' (*Globe and Mail*, 6 July 1998). Declining interest rates and less-than-expected investment returns over the same period accentuated the problem, and regulators demanded higher capital reserves to cover the anticipated payouts. A former life insurance sales agent we interviewed said that from the agents' perspective, the T100 product was a problem at the outset but companies failed to heed their warnings. 'They were lapse-supporting the price ... They had these wild assumptions that didn't hold true ... Agents, the grassroots people, knew that this wasn't holding true. And the companies were getting information from their agents, but they weren't acting on the information ... to raise ... the premium.'

Administrative expenses pose a third source of uncertainty in life insurance underwriting. Assumptions about long-term inflation rates are embedded in insurance policies regarding all aspects of company operations (e.g., employee compensation, office rental, supplies, services, and so on). The insured is subject to a host of policy charges, with inflation assumptions built in, to cover myriad administrative expenses. These expenses include, but are not limited to, sales agents' commissions, which are front-loaded and very high; ongoing operational expenses; reinsurance premiums; insurance on the insurance policy, in the form of compulsory premiums paid to the industry compensation scheme to protect policyholders whose insurer becomes insolvent; and directors' and officers' employment liability and errors and omissions insurance to cover problems of company fraud (Ericson, Doyle, and Barry 2003: chaps. 5, 6).

A fourth element of uncertainty is the fact that life insurance is based on the performance of financial markets. Life insurance companies invest available capital in diversified portfolios of equities, commercial bonds, government bonds, real estate, and so on. In doing so, they make assumptions about what fields of investment will yield the best returns over time to offer value to policyholders and profit to shareholders. Placing too great a stake in the wrong investment field at the wrong time can yield very negative returns and threaten solvency. The Confederation Life Insurance Company of Canada became insolvent in the early 1990s through gross over-exposure to property markets that collapsed, combined with highly speculative means of financing these investments (McQueen 1996; Ericson, Doyle, and Barry 2003: chap. 4). This was the largest single insurance company failure in North American history at the time, but it was not a unique occurrence. Both Sovereign Life and Les Coopérants Mutual Life Assurance Society preceded Confederation Life into insolvency, and for many of the same reasons.

The combined multibillion-dollar losses in these cases meant that they were catastrophes within an insurance definition of that term. They were catastrophes because they triggered enormous losses with disastrous ramifications for policyholders, debtors, creditors, and the companies' own employees and pensioners. In this respect, life insurance is similar to other lines of insurance that are more usually thought of as addressing catastrophes, such as earthquake or terrorism coverage. All of these lines expose the uncertainties of the insurance business and the potential for disastrous consequences.

As seen in the previous example of the T100 product, interest rate assumptions are also crucial and a source of great uncertainty because of the long-tailed nature of life insurance products. Another catastrophe for multinational life insurers developed in the context of retirement annuity markets in the United Kingdom. Life insurers sold retirement annuity contracts at high guaranteed rates of return between the 1950s and 1980s. The high interest rate and mortality assumptions on which these contracts were based proved erroneous in retrospect, leading to a situation in 1999 where life insurers faced

£11 billion liabilities in paying out these contracts. Many companies were threatened with insolvency as a result, and turned to the government for catastrophe relief.

> The Government is coming under pressure from the City [of London financial institutions] to use its borrowing powers to bail out insurers threatened by the £11 billion cost of paying guaranteed annuity rates to policyholders ... Buoyed by inaccurate assumptions about long-term trends in interest and mortality rates, few thought they would ever have to honour the guarantees, which in some cases promised to pay people an 11 percent annual income when they retired. However, in recent years increased life expectancy and declining gilt yields have pushed annuity rates to a post-war low of 5 percent, making the guarantee extremely valuable to policyholders. With annuity rates predicted to fall still further, insurers are just beginning to count the cost of their mistakes. Scottish Amicable has already earmarked £300 million, Scottish Mutual £200 million and Sun Life of Canada £114 million to meet their liabilities. Such figures are bound to rise and could prompt more consolidation in the industry ... The Treasury has already caused controversy over its handling of the crisis over guaranteed annuities. Last week Martin Roberts, director of the Insurance Directorate, wrote to the heads of insurance companies outlining how they should treat policyholders with guaranteed annuity options. Insurers, he said, were entitled to make policyholders pay for the guarantee provided it did not clash with their 'reasonable expectations.' He said insurers could, in some cases, reduce the terminal bonuses that investors receive at retirement. Charles Levett-Scrivener, director of product services at Towry Law, said that Mr. Robert's decision allowed companies to impose charges retrospectively to correct their earlier mismanagement. 'It is like a car company offering free airbags for drivers and passengers and then at a later date, when a crash occurs and the airbags inflate, to suddenly levy an additional charge.' (*The Times*, 2 January 1999, 22)

As these cases illustrate, uncertainties of life insurance company investment assumptions and practices create uncertainties for policyholders. Large catastrophes can lead to a substantial reduction in the investment returns originally promised to the policyholder or, in the case of insolvencies, to joining the queue of supplicants for whatever value is left. In such cases consumers are starkly aware that life insurance is an uncertain business. Furthermore, as we have documented elsewhere (Ericson, Barry, and Doyle 2003: chap. 6), policyholders can be affected by the uncertainties of life insurance investment practices without even knowing it. With the introduction of more complex investment policies in the last two decades, such as Universal Life II, the uncertainties are shifted even more to the policyholder, while the insurance company covers its own risks through several related pricing strategies and investment mechanisms. For example, policyholders are offered 'investment bonuses' as they persist in paying into their policies over time, but what remains hidden is the fact that these bonuses are funded by extremely low interest rates. If the insurer's mortality experience is worse than projected, it can reduce the interest rate credited to the accumulated fund to cover the difference. While there may be a guaranteed level cost of insurance, this means little because the insurance company simply funds the policy through decreasing investment returns as necessary. Policy lapse rates, which are more volatile, are dealt with in the same way. In some cases companies require that a large balance be kept in a low interest account, with only funds in excess of a specified amount being transferable to higher-yielding investments. There are also cases in which a portion of funds invested is withdrawn by the company to cover administrative charges, including some products where the level of withdrawal increases with investment returns.

A fifth source of uncertainty is advances in medical science and technology. These advances contribute to the fact that people are living longer, but therefore face greater uncertainties about health problems and how they are going to pay for them over time. These advances also promote more fine-grained medical rating of life insurance applicants and policyholders. The refinement of medical ratings creates new uncertainties about medical knowledge and how it can be used by insurers to exclude or to include with differential premiums and contract conditions.

These advances in medical science and technology combine with new demographics and changing forms of governance beyond the state to alter the life insurance institution fundamentally (Ericson, Doyle, and Barry 2003). While life insurance still provides 'death protection' for beneficiaries of those who die too soon, it is increasingly tied to 'life protection' for those who live longer. It blends into wealth management strategies for persons hoping to live well in their senior years and therefore adds even more financial market risk to health and lifestyle risk as integral components of underwriting.

The life insurance product is now supposed to provide 'living bene-fits' for illness and long-term care eventualities and for retirement income needs. Such uses of life insurance instruments are actively encouraged by the state. In relation to critical illness and long-term care in senior years, the state sees private insurance as a crucial vehicle for managing the increasing financial burden of an aging population. A senior civil servant responsible for health insurance in Ontario said in interview, 'We have 7,000 new people turn 65 every month ... You always lose people off [by death], we have a net of 4,000 every month ... people that are using the health services obviously. We still spend most of our money in the last year of life. Are we going to say no to those people in the last year of life? ... That's where you come down to your clinical parameters ... and that's where getting private insurance is going to have to start ... You can cost shift to them.'

A government commission in Ontario recommended the legaliza-tion of a viatical industry as one way to address the problem of costly old people. The viatical industry allows the terminally ill to collect their life insurance payouts in advance, but at a substantial discount. At the time of our research, it was legal in some jurisdictions – for example, Quebec, Nova Scotia, New York, Michigan, and California – but not in others, including Ontario, where section 115 of the Insurance Act 'prohibits trafficking in or offering to purchase life insurance poli-cies.' The prohibition is related to the moral risks involved in having people take out life insurance policies with an eye on this market, and in having the terminally ill pressured to sell an asset at a discount because of their condition. However, the commission considered these moral risks minor compared to the cost-saving benefit the viatical industry would bring to the state. 'There could be substantial savings to the province in avoiding public assistance for patients unable to work. Savings could arise from enabling patients to afford sufficient in-home care to defer or avoid institutionalization. Section 115 is prevent-ing this industry and its associated jobs from being established ... [T]he demographic reality of an aging population, along with recent social trends such as a higher rate of divorce and a considerable increase in the number of single-person households, will likely contribute to growing consumer demand for viatical settlements.'

The Canadian federal state promotes individual responsibility for retirement income through a Registered Retirement Savings Plan (RRSP). An individual is allowed to avoid current taxation of a portion of her annual income by investing in an RRSP. If held to senior years, the accumulated wealth in the RRSP can be converted into annuities or other retirement investment products and taxed only then. Life insurers are major players in selling both RRSP investment products and retirement instruments such as annuities.

In Canada and the United States, the life insurance industry has experienced a steady decline of individual policy sales and a rise in investment product and annuity sales. The vice-president of a large life insurance company's Canadian division told a brokers' conference we attended that only 15 per cent of his company's business was in life insurance per se, while the other 85 per cent was 'wealth business' such as 'large mutual fund investments.' In Canada in 1997, 78 per cent of life insurance agents were also licensed to sell mutual funds, up from 59 per cent in 1993 (Life Insurance Marketing Research Association [LIMRA] 1997: 13).

The shift into the wealth business has brought life insurers into direct competition with other financial institutions. Most large mutual insurance companies owned by policyholders have demutualized and become stock companies owned by shareholders. Life insurance companies have bought into banking and other retail financial operations. In turn, other financial institutions, especially banks, have established insurance operations. Specific to our current concern, insurance companies only held their position among financial institutions in the sale of RRSPs between 1985 and 1995, while gains were made by banks and especially mutual fund companies.

In this transformed life insurance environment, medical, and broader 'well being' ratings are entwined with financial and wealth ratings. This entanglement is summarized in the term 'lifestyle,' which means the standard of living the insured hopes to sustain into retirement. Retirement is conceptualized as a risk to personal resources management with uncertainty to time of death. 'Longevity risk' is not only a matter of having *sufficient* resources, but the *correct* resources for the individual's desired consumption. As the asset value of the life insurance policy increases, so does the intrusion into the individual's life and body. When the policy value stakes are high, every conceivable inquiry may be made into the individual's medical history and condition, work history, leisure, drug consumption, spending habits, and so on (Ericson, Doyle, and Barry 2003: chap. 6).

These considerations point to a sixth source of uncertainty in life insurance underwriting, namely, market segmentation. Different products and prices are offered to those with varying health and lifestyle attributes or deficiencies. For example, while there was no separate underwriting for smokers compared to non-smokers until the 1960s, smokers, as greater health risks, were eventually treated separately with higher premiums and more stringent contract conditions. More recently, there is a finer gradation among smokers themselves: there are preferred rates for those who use certain smoking products with certain frequency (e.g., occasional cigar smokers) compared to others (e.g., regular cigarette smokers, occasional cannabis smokers), and for those on a program to reduce and eventually quit smoking. This gradation of health and lifestyle rating is paralleled in other areas of life insurance underwriting, all with the intention of selling policies to as many customers as possible provided the premium levels are appropriate to the minutiae of their every condition and habit. Only about 3 per cent of life insurance applicants are refused (Canadian Life and Health Insurance Association [CLHIA] 1996: 9), but the policies vary enormously according to market segmentation criteria.

Health and lifestyle market segmentation combines with financial risk segmentation to accelerate fragmentation in life insurance products and services. Broadly, the market is segmented into the following: those who can only afford a term insurance policy that offers death benefits to cover final expenses; those whose term policy also includes a lump-sum payment that will provide for dependants; those who purchase policies that have cash value, increasingly tied to investment portfolios; and those who additionally use life insurance as part of wealth management with tax considerations. The lower-end customers are given less advice and service and are encouraged to buy directly from the insurers themselves. The higher-end customers are given special advice and service in which agents are repositioned as expert advisers to individuals planning their retirement years.

The accelerating segmentation of life insurance products in recent years has not enhanced certainty in underwriting. Ironically, features based upon more knowledge about medical conditions, and upon investment options, have resulted in so many gradations of products and prices that uncertainty is accentuated. Speaking to a life insurance brokers' conference, a reinsurance specialist warned that, with so many specialist products and the anti-selection problems they create, 'some of the prices out there are simply insufficient for some of the risk involved: not only how do you price them, but how do you manage your risk? How do you spread your risk around? There is no way the reinsurer will keep going naked on them, just hoping the risk charge is going to be enough. It is a question of how you are going to manage your exposure after the risk and how you are going to hedge yourself.'

This interviewee is referring to the way in which the 'feature creep' of ever-finer life insurance products and market segments leads competing companies into actuarial speculation rather than precision. As new product features creep into new market segments, a given company cannot afford to stay out of the game. There is not only fear of failing to attract new business, but also fear of losing existing policyholders who are good risks. However, simply borrowing new product features from competitors often means that actuaries and other company officials have little knowledge about how to price them. The temptation is to offer low prices in order to attract new business competitively.

As we have shown elsewhere (Ericson, Doyle, and Barry 2003: chap. 5; see also Zelizer 1979; Porter 1995; Clark 1999; Glenn 2000), the actuarialism of life insurance faces many of the same limits to knowledge as actuarialism in other insurance lines. Life actuaries must engage the major uncertainties analysed above – mortality, persistency, administrative expenses, investment returns, medical ratings, and market segmentation – to price their products in advance of actual costs being known. In putting a present value on future contingent events, they do not offer predictions as much as make estimations based on assumptions. Moreover, their assumptions and interpretive judgments are shaped by the corporate culture of their company and the local political economy of competitive markets. Many things cannot be taken into quantitative account because science, technology, law, company practices, political environments, and market conditions are in perpetual flux. As such, actuaries are more corporate managers than calculators. They experiment with different assumptions and methodologies. They respond variously to data, audits, and advice to make 'guesstimates' and place their bets.

Embracing Risk

The uncertainties of life insurance underwriting make evident a commitment to embracing risk. The goal of not only protecting but expanding assets for all parties to the life insurance relationship – policyholders, shareholders, service providers, employees, officers, and directors – can be accomplished only through substantial risk taking by each of these parties. With respect to policyholders, new investment-related life insurance products shift mortality, persistency, administrative expense, investment return, medical rating, and market segmentation uncertainties to them, whether they are aware of it or not (Ericson, Doyle, and Barry 2003: chap. 6).

Accelerating participation in investment markets is one manifestation of how individuals are embracing more risk. This participation may be voluntary, for example, through the purchase of investment-related life insurance policies, stocks, and bonds. It may also be compulsory, for example, through employer group pension schemes. Many employer group pension plans have shifted from a 'defined benefit' collective pool approach to a 'defined contribution' approach in which the individual must choose investment options and face the consequences of her choices, including the fact that her retirement years may be less comfortable than imagined. As Baker and Simon (2002: 4) observe, 'private pensions, annuities and life insurance are engaged in an historic shift of investment risk from broad pools (the classic structure of risk spreading through insurance) to individual (middle-class) consumers and employees in return for the possibility of greater return.'

This shift is rooted in neo-liberal politics and economic globalization (Rose 1999; Ericson and Stehr 2000; Ericson, Doyle, and Barry 2003: chap. 1). The new political economy of neo-liberalism and globalization is to be reflected in the personal political economy of the individual as risk taker. Too much protection organized by paternalistic institutions is no longer seen as a public good but a corrosive bad. Individuals must assume responsibility for their well-being by embracing risks. 'The idea that some amount of risk is good for people and that too much protection is harmful has important consequences for the development of insurance technologies, institutions, and forms, as well as the development of personal identity and social institutions other than insurance' (Baker and Simon 2002: 10).

This view of social change and embracing risk is not simply a matter of academic abstraction and debate. It is embedded in how the life insurance industry understands contemporary society and organizes in relation to it. According to a life insurance industry document that addresses social change and individual responsibility, we have returned to an era of 'rugged individualism' and speculative risk taking. This document includes a graph, reproduced in figure 2.1, that depicts twentieth-century trends in retirement funding. A shift occurred from individual responsibility backed by informal commu-

Figure 2.1
Return to 'Rugged Individualism'

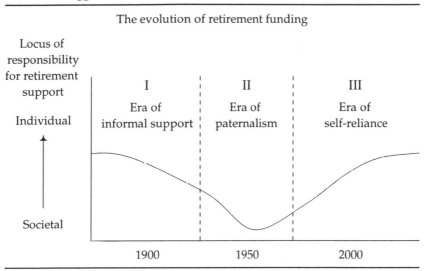

The evolution of retirement funding

Locus of responsibility for retirement support

Individual

Societal

	I	II	III
	Era of informal support	Era of paternalism	Era of self-reliance

1900   1950   2000

nity support to state paternalism backed by state social program support, and then to 'rugged individualism' backed by nothing except 'self-reliance.'

The document continues by noting, 'Chief characteristic of future-state retirement marketplace the repositioning of individual at centre of decision-making process.' This is accompanied by a second figure (2.2) that shows the individual at the centre of three institutions: government, employer, and financial services. The individual is depicted in interaction with these institutions making choices among what each has to offer. Government is shown as backing off, being a 'provider of last resort.' Its role is also to help regulate the market and enforce a retirement savings regime through employers and financial service providers. Employers also back off, being 'procurement providers' from financial service institutions rather than providing more directly for the retirement of their employees. Their role is to use their group capacity to obtain good rates and deals, but the menu of benefits is up to the individual employee to select. Financial service retailers move to the forefront, providing investment choices along with insurance arrangements and other retirement-related packages. At the hub, next

Figure 2.2
Future-State Retirement Services Marketplace

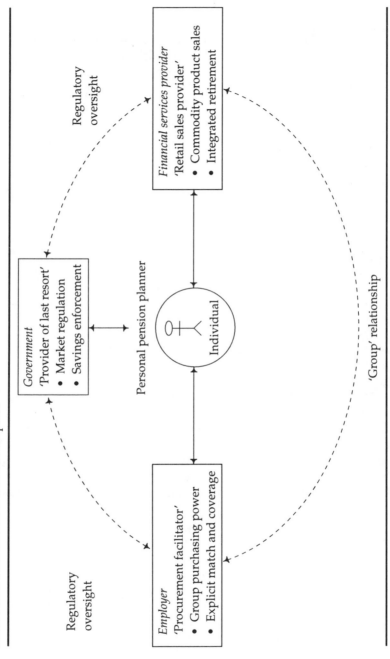

Government
'Provider of last resort'
• Market regulation
• Savings enforcement

Financial services provider
'Retail sales provider'
• Commodity product sales
• Integrated retirement

Employer
'Procurement facilitator'
• Group purchasing power
• Explicit match and coverage

Individual

Regulatory oversight

Regulatory oversight

Personal pension planner

'Group' relationship

to the individual risk taker, is the life agent as 'personal pension planner.' Her task is to broker the individual's relationship with the institutions, procuring what appear to be the best bets for the future.

With the rugged individual so positioned in the financial marketplace, the need for state involvement in retirement provision is deemed less necessary. First, made reflexively aware of the risks of living too long or dying too soon and of investment options available, people will no longer be myopic about their retirement needs. Second, while consumer society continues to encourage people to spend beyond their means, insurance and retirement investment products are marketed as simply another consumer desirable. They are portrayed as a durable good, allowing one to continue consumption at a desirable level well into the future. Third, the old notion that retirement provision is a 'merit good' based on a lifetime of hard work that needs to be protected by employers and the state is turned on its head. Retirement income is now to be based solely on the individual's merit in being self-reliant, including her gambles on life investment products. Annuity market, capital market, and inflation risks are all meritoriously transferred to the individual as part of portraying her powers of freedom in embracing risks.

Prudence

In casting human beings as 'rugged individualists' in the 'era of self-reliance,' institutions make individuals responsible for choices about the future. In some respects little is new in this regard. The word risk originated in European languages of the sixteenth century to articulate the need for individual prudence, being circumspect about actions today in ways that contribute to well-being in the future (Hacking 2003).

The promotion of prudence about life and death has always been morally charged from religious and other cultural standpoints (Zelizer 1979, 1997; O'Malley 2002). With origins in gambling on life and death (Clark 1999, 2002), the life insurance policy itself was once a symbol of immorality, turning what should be sacred into one of the most profane human activities of all. But the moral meanings of life insurance gradually transformed. Life insurance can cement the sacred by making funds available for lavish funerals and gifts which sanctify death. Provision for life insurance – like other forms of financial prudence such as personal savings and investments – can be a socially worthy activity of discipline and responsibility. It protects one's self from the disgrace of poverty in old age and a pauper's funeral. It spares one's dependants from sharing financial and other burdens of long-term care and funeral expenses. It saves the state from the expensive consequences of privileging social responsibility over individual responsibility. It can reduce other risks and social responsibilities, for example, crime risks that might be posed by impoverished dependants. It facilitates risks taken during the life course, such as marriage and childrearing. These positive features combine to offer moral gratification in exchange for hefty premiums and risky economic pay-offs in the future. Those without it are made to feel morally inferior.

The meaning of prudence has shifted again in the contemporary context of embracing risk. The individual is expected to commodify herself as a 'human resource,' valuable to herself and others as a machine-like producer of assets that will grow and prosper continuously. The spirit of this 'new prudentialism' (O'Malley 2002) is evident in contemporary instructional material for life insurance sales agents. For example, a booklet for sales agents depicts human beings as simply earning machines that require maintenance programs and plans for obsolescence.

> The service you sell insures a value just as tangible as any other form of property ... Make your prospects aware of the fact that the most valuable pieces of property they own are themselves ... Every gainfully employed person is an earning machine ... Living expenses ... might as well be called 'upkeep' or 'maintenance' since your prospect must have food, clothing and shelter to continue to function successfully as a money machine. Second, you must recognize that the human earning machine is subject to the two hazards that overshadow all functioning income-producing machines: sudden destruction and gradual obsolescence ... When death calls a person whose earning power is not yet worn out, the resulting economic loss is as genuine as if a piece of productive machinery were destroyed by accident, or a piece of income-producing real estate were destroyed by fire ... Our schools teach the value of property, but seldom teach the value of human life. Most people take a person's earning power for granted, and seldom stop to think of the value of a machine that would produce the same amount of income.

The booklet goes on to offer the agent a number of gambits to use in convincing the sales prospect of his or her worth as a money machine. For example, family values are to be reinforced by saying to the prospect, 'If you had a machine that turned out money, you'd insure it, wouldn't you? Well, as far as your family is concerned, you are such a machine.' If a more pithy remark is required, the agent can use, 'Death is quicker than inflation' or other phrases which remind the client that the hearse will be backed up to the door sooner or later.

Instructional materials given to clients elaborate on the ways in which they can maintain themselves prudently. These materials emphasize how demographics and medical advances indicate that people are living longer and must therefore be prepared for health and wealth management for an extended retirement period. They also underscore the fact that the state has shifted more of the responsibility for self-sufficiency to the individual. Life, health, and long-term care insurance, as well as retirement savings plans and annuities, are marketed as desirable commodities in this demographic and political context.

A typical promotion was contained in a financial institution's newsletter to customers called 'Possibilities.' Distributed with customers' monthly financial statements, the newsletter cover featured a caricature of a fit man with a long beard and '100' (years) inscribed on his athletic vest. At the top of this caricature was the title of the newsletter's theme, 'Live Longer and Better: Eight Ways to Stay Healthier Longer.' This cover sets the stage for the eight tips on health and well-being, and for the subsequent promotion of the financial institution's products, by noting that Canadian males now live on average to age seventy-five and females to eighty-one. 'And that average is steadily rising thanks to a downward trend in smoking and drinking, an upward trend in fitness, and our ever-increasing awareness of nutritional health and preventative medicine. "The number of people living into their late seventies, eighties, and beyond is definitely increasing," says Louis Plouffe, Manager of the Section of Knowledge Development at Health Canada's Division of Aging and Seniors. "It's not inconceivable that the baby boomers will have an even greater chance of living past 90 than their predecessors."'

The checklist on being healthy and happy in later life is presented like a car maintenance schedule. It declares that the secret to health and happiness is 'consistent maintenance' as follows:

• Think Prevention: 'If you're smart you'll rely on vigilance. It's a mind set. You do it every day and over the years it pays off.' (Advice is offered on healthy breakfasts, exercise, and nutritional supplements, and on avoiding excess fatty foods, alcohol, and stress.)

- Eat Healthfully – Habitually.
- Consider Supplements: 'The key is daily routine. People who swear by supplements usually place them somewhere they can't be missed – beside the coffee maker or on the bedside table. Consistency is everything.' (Cites a self-help book, *Prescription for Nutritional Healing* by James and Phyllis Balih.)
- Make Exercise Easier: e.g., 'a cross-country ski machine for 20 minutes while listening to high-energy music on the headphones.' (Also advocates weight training for seniors into their seventies and eighties.)
- Reduce Stress.
- Value Sleep: 'A good night's rest is an effective healing technique that will abort many incipient illnesses ... [use] a common folk remedy such as spreading a few drops of lavender oil on your palms and inhaling deeply several times. The effect is wonderfully relaxing.' (Cites a self-help book, *Spontaneous Healing*, by Andrew Weil.)
- Know Your Options. (Advises to seek out popular books and magazines about self-care.)
- Indulge – with moderation: 'longevity is abetted by a positive attitude.'

This section of the newsletter ends with a call for testimonials on the secret to longevity, with a fifty dollar award to each person whose testimonial is selected for publication in the next issue. It then moves into the sales pitch, which follows from adherence to the eight-point 'consistent maintenance' schedule. Entitled 'Planning for 90,' the sales pitch opens with the statement, 'Living a longer and healthier life is in all ways desirable – unless you are unprepared financially.' The reader is thereby transfigured from prudence regarding health risks to prudence about financial risks. 'Too many people reach the age of 65 without adequate funds. Struggling through such penury is uncomfortable enough for 10 to 15 years. It's worse for 30.' The solution is disciplined savings and financial management throughout the adult life course. 'All things being equal, a 21-year-old contributing $200 per month will have more money at 55 than someone starting at 35 and contributing $1000 per month. Those early contributions, however modest, will make a big difference in your seventies, eighties or nineties.' The reader is then reminded what this financial discipline is for: being an active older person who can travel, golf, and 'experience things.' An inactive older person requires extended care 'that can really eat up your savings.'

The newsletter concludes with words of wisdom from both ordinary folks and great statesmen and philosophers. The ordinary folks are represented by contributors who responded to calls for submissions in the previous newsletter, entitled 'Lifelong Learner.' Awarded fifty dollars for their expertise – enough to buy one share in the financial institution on the equity markets – they gave their own tips on health, wealth, and happiness. Among the contributors is a seventy-eight-year-old who said he took up juggling at age seventy-one: 'my doctor says I'll live to be 90.' A university teacher instructs students to forget about marks and be passionate about learning, to seek advice from elders, and to adopt the saying that the person who hesitates is lost: learn from your decisions and 'if you approach a fork in the road, take it.' This wisdom about embracing risk from a professor sets up the higher learning of famous statesmen and intellectuals who offer moral lessons in prudence under the title, 'The Meaning of Money: Financial Wit and Wisdom.' Their sayings are printed above caricatures of two men, one with an overflowing moneybag, the other with a bag that sags half empty.

He that waits upon prosperity is never sure of a dinner.

Benjamin Franklin

Fortunes made in no time are like shirts made in no time; it's ten to one if they hang long together.

Douglas Jerrold

Fortune knocks at every man's door once in a life, but in a good many cases the man is in a neighbouring saloon and does not hear her.

Mark Twain

The gratification of wealth is not found in mere possession or in lavish expenditure, but in its wise application.

Miguel De Cervantes

Prosperity makes friends; adversity ties them.

Publilius Syrus

When prosperity comes, do not use all of it.

Confucius

The individual is exhorted by these timeless voices of authority to create her own political economy in the pursuit of health, wealth, and happiness. This pursuit requires rigid discipline regarding health risks. 'You do it everyday and over the years it pays off ... consistency is everything' – whether 'it' is keeping supplements beside the coffee maker, driving harder on the cross-country ski machine, or inhaling lavender oil. This pursuit also requires rigid discipline regarding financial risks. To avoid being 'unprepared financially' and 'struggling through penury' the individual must buy into the financial services marketplace at the onset of adulthood and sustain regular purchases forever. Here too the moral lesson is that if you do it every day, over the years it pays off because consistency is everything. While all this conjuring of health and wealth may only allow one to be a happy juggler at the age of seventy-one, at least one has the prospect of continuing in this role to age ninety.

Here we learn of the unique ways in which financial service institutions express the need for prudence. They do not want to lose the opportunity to be the life course merchant to all such morally fit clients who want to construct their individual political economy with them. Recognizing only too well the structural relationship between health and wealth, they pursue the more morally fit clients as a valuable commodity.

Investment

These lessons in responsibility for prudence make investment obvious. Investment is the response ability each individual has to meet his or her responsibility for prudence. Investment refers to both financial matters, applying money in the hope of future wealth, and health matters, applying self-discipline for future fitness. Ideally, the proper blending of wealth and fitness will provide the desired prosperous lifestyle in the long term.

The ability to respond through investment plays back upon the responsibility for prudence. Another meaning of 'invest' is to endue a person with special qualities and powers. The prudent investor is someone who will rise in social rank and be 'invested' as having achieved a successful 'lifestyle.' Lifestyle is the new cultural code for standard of living. According to neo-liberal state policy and financial institution marketing, it is the responsibility of each member of society to invest prudently in search of the desired lifestyle.

The focus on individual investment for wealth, health, and happiness leads life insurers into new and more intensive *investigations*. These investigations are directed at the aforementioned effort to create market segments based on a blend of financial and health criteria. The new social hierarchy of lifestyles is crafted by the life insurance industry in its investigative efforts to create specialized risk pools that prove profitable.

A life insurance underwriting specialist for a multinational insurer told a brokers' conference we attended that all aspects of 'health and lifestyle are essentially built into pricing ... We're almost moving to individual pricing as you look at the refinement, we're more and more moving to, "How old are you? How much do you weigh? How much ...?" And you put that on a spreadsheet, in the end you come up with a different rate for different people.' This approach to fine-grained fragmentation of populations was common across life insurance companies we studied. A marketing actuary for a life insurance company said in interview that his job is perpetually 'figuring out more ways to cut and dice ... end result being that you want to offer the best rate out there, even though less than 1/10 of 1 per cent of the people could actually qualify.'

An industry document on marketing trends instructs on the need to engage in 'value-based segmentation' related to customer profitability. The need is established by documenting that under traditional life insurance marketing – with one set of intermediary agents involved in distribution – the top customers who are highly profitable end up subsidizing the services provided to the less profitable. The document presents data (table 2.1) showing that for whole life (cash value) policies, the 'top two customer deciles create nearly 220 percent of portfolio value, cross-subsidizing remaining 80 percent of marginally profitable or profit-destroying customers.' With captions such as 'Best Clients Footing the Bill for Value-Destroying "Free Riders,"' the document says that high-end customers are being 'underserviced' and bottom-end customers 'overserviced.' The particular danger is that special niche market companies, termed 'category killers,' will cream off customers. Top-decile customers will be creamed by niche companies who can offer better products at lower 'unbundled' prices. Bottom-decile customers will be creamed by direct sellers who offer cheaper products because they have minimal service and administrative frills. The company that does not move into value-based segmentation is left with serious adverse selection problems.

Table 2.1
Whole Life Insurance Profit Contribution Deciles

Deciles	Profit Contribution (%)
1	171.85
2	45.81
3	14.39
4	1.63
5	(4.12)
6	(7.01)
7	(7.92)
8	(10.23)
9	(22.68)
10	(81.72)

The solution is to change distribution strategies according to the value of the customer: high-end customers should receive full-service financial planning, marginally profitable customers should be given a convenient retail outlet and no-pressure sales, and low-end customers should be given call-centre access. The solution is represented schematically in figures 2.3 and 2.4. An additional recommendation is to make the segmentation visible by offering a status incentive program similar to those available with credit card or frequent-flier programs (silver, gold, platinum, sapphire). The high-flying life insured receives all the benefits of wealth inequality, while the person barely above water is kept at a distance. The model involves a 'four-tiered classification system based upon customers' total assets invested with institution; each tier receives servicing levels, retention focus commensurate with profit contribution ... Institution notifies top customer tiers of 'upgrade' in servicing, provides customers with new toll-free number connecting each tier to specialized servicing staff; highest tier customers connected to personal servicing representative; next tier level connected to a member of elite pool of top servicing staff, lower tiers offered "virtual" relationship services.'

This market segmentation is not only reflected in the type of distribution facilities and services offered, it is also a basis for adjusting actuarial standards and rates. A senior executive of an institute of actuaries explained in interview that all companies adjust standard mortality table rates in relation to their 'market base. Are they high end? white collar? blue collar? ... Are you closer to people who are buying annuities? ... top category of people who say, "I'm going to live for-

Figure 2.3
Service Delivery Management Matrix

	High cost	Delivery mechanism	Low cost
	Personal intermediation	Virtual relationship	Electronic access
High profit	A Value/service equilibrium	Retention risk from underservicing	Retention risk from underservicing
Market segment	B Expense risk from overservicing	Value/service equilibrium	Retention risk from underservicing
Low profit	C Expense risk from overservicing	Expense risk from overservicing	Value/service equilibrium

Source: Life Insurance Marketing Trends Document, 1995

ever," whereas your general population mortality table, a lot of people who aren't employable.'

This tendency towards fragmentation of life insured populations, and to zero in on the profitable top segment, was epitomized by an agent who said that in the previous three months he had worked on the completion of only two sales. Both prospects were considering whole life policies with tax advantages. One client's policy would yield a commission of $30,000, which the agent said was 'almost one-third of my income for one year.' He said that in his segment of the business, the initial meeting with a prospect was not to do everything possible to close even a modest sale, but rather to deselect the less prosperous.

With the initial meeting all I'm trying to do ... is meet somebody, see if I want them as a client: [I avoid those I know will be] a pain in the neck ... They've always got a better idea, or they've got their second cousin, twice removed, who is a lawyer, an accountant, saying, 'That doesn't work. It's useless.' ... You leave them alone and get out of there and ... go out and look for people who fit your profile, the kind of person you want to go and sell to ... Excuse me, more money [laughs] ... did a little analysis on the people that I'd already sold the biggest premiums that got paid to me ... [younger people] between thirty-two and forty-two, their offices were downtown ... professionals ... brokerage business or they owned

Figure 2.4
Custom–Tailored Distribution Strategy

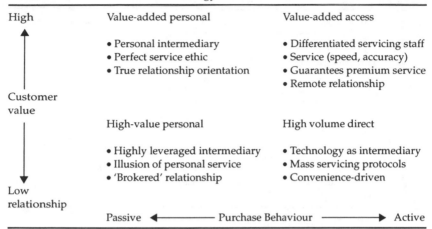

their own business. And when I asked for referrals, I always put that profile in front of somebody ... You're selling to people that you like, that's
what it is. I mean, the great thing about this business is, if you don't like
somebody, you don't have to deal with them ... [I like them] because they
do more or less the same thing as I do. They're responsible for their own
bottom line. And it is a horrible thing, but they eat what they kill.

Another agent described the case of a client who was taking out a
policy on his seventy-seven-year-old mother as an investment and tax
vehicle. The policy would have $5 million cash demand value and
carry an annual premium of $255,000.

Quite frankly there are people that I don't want to do business with, people that are a pain in the ass ... This client that's paying $255,000 if his pre-
mium was $20,000 a year I would have blown him off a long time ago.
Because I put so much work into this, and I've been working on this for
six years, I'm not going to blow him off ... I've got clients in the U.S., one
of whom phoned me up right out of the blue looking for something, and
she threw a dinner party for me and one of the people at the dinner party
was the president of a large retail company.

The bottom end of the scale is served by companies that use television ads and brochure prospectuses directed at a market segment that can only afford 'final expenses' coverage. Typical is an appeal to those between fifty and seventy-five for coverage to a maximum of $25,000. One brochure and prospectus directed to this market pictured an elderly couple eating together, then the grandfather fishing with his grandson, then the grandmother hugging her grandson. Here the intergenerational legacy is not an inheritance, but a decent funeral and not leaving heirs with debt. The premiums were steep: for example, at fifty the annual premium for $25,000 coverage was $250 (1 per cent of coverage). In comparison, a university faculty group term policy for a fifty-year-old provided $250,000 coverage for an annual premium of $600 (.24 per cent of coverage).

Between the $25,000 term policy with $250 premium and the $5 million cash value, tax advantaged policy with $255,000 premium lie many more market segments based on wealth positions in the life course. A life insurer's manual for agents included a section on 'target markets,' headed by an illustration of a dart in the bull's eye of a dartboard. The agent was directed to fourteen possibilities beyond the traditional market of nuclear family protection.

1) Juvenile – life insurance as a funding mechanism for future education, business, wedding;
2) Young, unmarried – life insurance as a 'changing lifestyles' funding mechanism: sell flexible premiums and death benefits or 'higher premiums than in the later years when he/she gets married and starts a family';
3) Seasonal worker/employer – load premium payments into working months 'and take a premium vacation if needed during the off-season';
4) Affluent market – sell tax deferral of cash value: 'pre-pay future premiums with tax-advantaged dollars ... interest earnings can pay the cost of his/her insurance';
5) Estate protection;
6) Registered retirement savings plan and registered retirement investment fund protection;
7) Pension maximization;
8) Mortgage protection;
9) Charitable giving;
10) Estate equalization;
11) Leveraging life insurance – 'the growing cash value inside the policy

can be used as bridge financing for retirement, share redemption for a
retiring shareholder etc.';

12) Buy term insurance and invest the rest in segregated funds (insurance
company mutual funds);
13) Education savings for children;
14) Business market – life insurance on key persons, creditor insurance,
buy/sell.

We interviewed various market segmentation specialists who said
that their job is to find segments within segments. For example, an
interviewee who described himself as a 'business gerontologist' said
he specialized in the risk profiling and segmentation of populations
over fifty years of age. As an adviser to insurance marketing operations he helps them to

understand the dynamics of aging plus the different segments of the
seniors as a mature market. So we just don't say '50+', there are very different segments above that. And even as the boomers age, we will notice
that they segment more and more – if nothing else, based on lifestyle,
income, health profiles, and so on ... [I train young insurance sales agents
on] what the older person is about. How they think, how they buy, what
their behaviours are, and even to some degree what the human factors are
like as age changes ... sight, hearing ... what they need to accommodate
when they are dealing with older customers ... playing into this increasing
need for security ... As we get older, issues around security become more
important, and that's why the insurance companies are capitalizing.

These fragmented populations of older people are encouraged to
remain prudent through continuous investment in their 'chosen' lifestyles. Referred to within the industry as 'the competitive retailing of
retirement,' the goal is to capitalize on every detail of the individual's
wealth and lifestyle desires. The competitive retailing of retirement
turns the life insurance agent into a retirement counsellor who will
help the individual manage his or her lifestyle. Thus a document prepared by a life insurance industry expert service recommends 'full
scope retirement planning' for a client, including financial services,
long-term care, and assisted-living services. There should be 'heavy
emphasis on educating individuals on how to manage retirement ...
seminars supplemented by one-on-one "counselling" sessions ... insuring against longevity, finding more active lifestyle.' Suggested services

beyond life insurance include health insurance, financing, wealth transfer, travel, other leisure activity, volunteer work, relocation, twenty-four-hour medical information line, medical bill payment and claims filing service, discount pharmacy cards, a 'senior net,' a beneficiary book, a twenty-four-hour retirement life answer line 'staffed by experts on retirement lifestyle, eldercare issues,' and a 'financial gerontology group.'

Such an approach is supposed to address 'the "vacuum" left by exit of government [and] employers from retirement provision system.' It *capitalizes* on current supply-side fragmentation within "retirement" industry by positioning provider as client's "retirement manager": provider relieves pressure on consumer to ensure personally that all components of retirement planning process are adequately integrated.' If insurance agents get in early on this approach it will help them to 'realize premium pricing ... by embedding commodity product within array of value-added services, practice represents most advanced strategy yet identified for escaping the "commodity trap".' Finally, it is a 'counterattack against nonfinancial providers' forays into the financial services marketplace; given excellent "fit" of nonfinancial offerings in context of lifetime customer stewardship, forgone conclusion that increasing number of providers will adopt such strategies.'

This retailing of retirement approach positions the individual consumer as the decision maker who draws upon expert services in lifestyle management as needed. A similar positioning of the individual as choice maker with powers of freedom is evident throughout contemporary life insurance marketing and sales approaches. For example, in Canada the London Life Insurance Company had a long-standing 'Freedom 55' marketing campaign. Now run by Freedom 55 Financial, this campaign promises retirement at fifty-five with a prosperous lifestyle for those who are prudent enough to invest with the company at an early stage of the life course.

A manual for agents selling universal (investment-based) life insurance policies emphasizes repeatedly that agents must make the consumer feel empowered as a participant in the investment process. In approaching the prospect by telephone or letter, the agent is instructed to declare at the outset that the relationship will be a partnership with the client as choice maker. Thus a suggested gambit for approaching the prospect is, 'Our first meeting will allow you and I to mutually discover if there is anything we can do to provide help to you with regard to your insurance and retirement needs.'

In introducing the prospect to universal life insurance, the agent is directed to list ten features, all of which indicate the prospect's choice and flexibility in embracing risk. First, the policy is based on 'custom design ... incredible *flexibility* and *choice* ... [we] can design a policy to fit the needs of any market.' Second, various options allow the policy value to grow on a tax-deferred basis. Third, there are flexible payment options, including an increase or decrease in premium payments according to one's financial situation, as well as 'premium vacations.' Fourth, a wide choice of death benefit options is provided. Fifth, death benefits can be changed according to the performance of the policy. Sixth, there are various options pertaining to cost of insurance (front- and back-end loads, surrender charges, premiums related to lapse prevention, etc.). Seventh, many investment options are available to the policyholder regarding how premiums will be allocated. Eighth, future premium payment options are available using the accumulated cash value of the policy. Ninth, special options are available to increase insurance coverage over time. Tenth, the policy value can be used as a source of emergency funds, with withdrawals permitted under certain conditions, as well as loan provisions.

In order to work her way through all of this choice, the prospect completes a questionnaire, 'Determining Your Investment Risk Profile.' The cover of the questionnaire booklet pictures the pieces of a jigsaw puzzle along with the company's logo and universal life product logo. The individual is situated as the one who solves the jigsaw puzzle, starting with a self-rating as 'conservative,' 'moderate,' or 'aggressive' on eight items designed to constitute 'your personal risk profile.' Thus even the degree to which one embraces risk is subject to risk profiling. This profiling forms in effect the individual's prudence risk. Nevertheless, the company's agents are there to provide tips on the better bets. Thus the booklet declares:

> The world of investing can be puzzling. Some investments can fluctuate from time-to-time. Their values can move up or down, sometimes rapidly. This is known as 'investment risk.' One very important piece of the puzzle is understanding the concept of 'risk and reward,' particularly when investing for the long term. Although the Universal Life II plan is primarily a life insurance policy intended to provide insurance protection, a very important component of the performance of the plan is your choice of investment options. A Universal Life II policy from [company name] provides a wide choice of investment options to suit your own individual risk profile. We'll help you fit the pieces of the puzzle together.

This document is designed to give the prospect the sense that she is deciding her own financial future. The next step involves a computer-based system called 'The Profiler.' The Profiler constantly changes the products and features to be presented and the questions to ask the prospect as she provides data about herself. As such, it is a 'format of control' (Altheide 1995: chap. 2) that governs the agent's work at the same time that it channels the prospect into choices framed by the insurance company. The Profiler agents' manual says the technology has the ability to make decisions *like an expert* ... The visual presentation motivates your clients to act while accurate analysis is done behind the scenes.' The prospect's needs can be evoked by the emotional as well as cognitive power of the technology. 'The presentation turns all the analytical facts into a detailed sales presentation that appeals to both the emotional and the logical thought processes.'

The technology is designed to have the client imagine the future and its (in)securities. For example, under 'retirement' there is a prompt to '"Put more Aside." This is an excellent *what if* screen. It enables you to show your client what impact retirement savings and savings amounts will have in the shortfall in the savings plan.' The prospect is then reminded that financial security is not only a matter of savings amounts but also how that money is put to work. She must embrace the risk of financial markets in order to appreciate fully the prospect of prosperity. To this end the Profiler includes a presentation called the 'coin game.' 'The coin game is configured to help clients choose among the types of products available based on the characteristics they are looking for in the portfolio ... This is one of the key features, and is crucial for helping your client decide what types of investment are appropriate for their Risk Profiles.'

The individual is asked to take her hard-earned money, put it into play, and hope that it will in turn work for her. There is a clear gaming aspect: the prospect is brought to the gaming table and presented with myriad speculative options. Should the premiums be allocated to investment certificates, a bond index fund, a daily interest savings account, a Standard and Poor's 500 index fund, a Toronto Stock Ex-change 35 fund, or something else? Moreover the individual is not making a one-shot decision but engaging in a perpetual process of embracing risk and second-guessing.

A client determines their premium allocation for ULII policies by considering their investment risk profile ... The circumstances of each client will determine what may be a suitable premium allocation for them ... A premium allocation is not static, and will likely change over time ... A premium allocation mix that is appropriate today will need to be reviewed over time. While your clients should not panic at every market turn (getting out in a downturn will only lock in losses), they must recognize that in an 'unbundled' product like Universal Life II, the responsibility and the risk on the investment side is transferred from the Insurance Company to the individual policyholder.

Also, as his or her circumstances change, a policyholder's ability and willingness to accept risk will change, and the premium allocation will need to be reviewed and potentially changed. Factors influencing this are:

- Clients may become more averse to the risk through increased sophistication and exposure
- The difference between [guaranteed investment certificate and equity market] rates may make one more or less attractive than the other
- The client's ability to withstand potential market-related losses will change with their own financial circumstances.

Clearly both client and agent must become sophisticated financial market analysts. One potential risk for the agent and the company is that the client will actually become sophisticated enough to be averse to the risks posed by this type of insurance policy! One potential risk for the client is that the agent is not a professional investment specialist. Thus another manual for agents from the same company includes a bold 'WARNING: Agents are not investment professionals and therefore should refrain from offering specific investment advice. Ultimately the client must make specific investment decisions.' Another potential risk for the client is that expertise is embedded in the Profiler, constraining both the agent and the client to work within the parameters of the insurance company.

Perplexities do not end with the determination of investment options. Beneath all of the visualizations of financial futures on the Profiler screen are additional costs. Each choice made has tax implications for the client, for example, regarding investments, withdrawals, surrenders, loans, policy changes (e.g., duration, insurance amount, age, sex, smoking status), and change of ownership. There are also many company charges for administering the policy. These charges are higher than for other life insurance policies because of the increased number of options that have to be administered. Front-end load charges, administrative fees, compensation scheme contributions to cover the policyholder in the event the company cannot meet its obligations, surrender charges, lapse prevention premium pricing weighted higher over the first years of the policy, and bonuses for policyholder asset accumulation over time are all part of the calculus. All of these features signify that this form of life insurance may not be much of an investment after all. As a company manual for agents emphasizes, 'It is important to keep in mind that ULII is life insurance. Cash values are available in the policy as an extra benefit and to allow pre-funding of future costs as much as to provide cash to the policyholder.'

Wealth profiling is not sufficient for either the individual or the insurance company. Health profiling is also necessary for the contentment of the individual and the insurer's bottom line. Therefore, medical investigations are undertaken to market segment healthy bodies as they articulate with the wealth management strategies of both the individual and the insurer.

A life insurance marketing specialist said in interview that the companies no longer have a choice on whether or not to market segment. Companies that refine segmentation cream off the wealthier and healthier risks and leave the risks of adverse selection to those companies that have not been quick enough off the mark. 'We all have to do it ... [otherwise] you're going to be left with all the unhealthy risks. So if you want your fair share of the healthy risks and healthiest risks, then you better have qualifications that are similar to competitors.'

The result is that even term insurance products splinter into super-preferred, preferred, and standard rates. For example, a company had six categories of preferred rates for term insurance, with 80 per cent of its policyholders spread over these categories and only 20 per cent left in the standard category. An underwriting specialist described this process of making the standard rate no longer standard as having 'segmented everybody so it is like auto insurance rates for driving records.' He continued with the observation that in term insurance sales 'you *have to* differentiate yourself ... I'm not sure though it is still going to be the easiest insurance sale because of the rotation you have to have with your client in terms of getting a feel for really how healthy they are and where can I expect them to fit in terms of my preferred class.' He added that the differentiation of companies means that they also become segmented: they seek specialization in particular market niches they think they know best. It also means that reinsurers are increasingly brought into the picture to handle the rippling effects of term insurance pools hit with adverse selection problems. 'Because your rates are so much higher [than companies with finer gradations of preferred rates], there's a big tendency for a healthy person to rese-lect and go buy a new policy that is much less expensive for him. So what the companies are left with at that point are not a good risk. A lot of them ... they're just moving that to the reinsurers that have more experience over a longer period of time.'

Market segmentation makes each preferred risk category a desirable commodity. Indeed, stepping up to the next rung in the preferred risk hierarchy is marketed to prospects and policyholders as an achieved status available to prudent individuals who manage to become wealth-ier and healthier. This new preferred market-based underwriting turns both underwriters and brokers into managers of client expectations.

A company published a booklet for brokers entitled 'We Can Help You Settle Substandard Cases.' This booklet instructs brokers on how to cool out applicants when they learn of their substandard rating, and thereby ease them into the extra charges and surveillance mechanisms entailed. Brokers are to use the booklet to become 'more comfortable and, hopefully, more successful in what is already a highly lucrative market.' It reminds them that 'substandard business ... comes naturally with the older age market we target.' Since the target is both natural and lucrative, the question is 'How do you get your client to buy into the decision and pay the higher premium?' Among the many tips offered is the suggestion of using the client's personal physician as an ally: 'have the evidence sent to your client's doctor. Our underwriters ... will include an explanation for the assessment. They will speak to the doctor if that will help her understand our decision. If the doctor is unwilling to speak with the underwriter, our Medical Director is also available.' Another gambit is to tell the client that she has received a valuable service in being told about the undesirable condition(s) that make her life substandard for insurance purposes. 'Consider it a service that you are providing to your client when an abnormality is uncovered for the first time during the underwriting process. Had these results not been uncovered – for example, high blood pressure, elevated blood sugar or an abnormal EEG – your client would not even be aware that a problem existed. Who knows how much this could have advanced by the time they did seek medical assistance! You could be playing a sig-nificant role in the well being of the individual! In addition, some rat-ings of this nature can be reviewed soon after treatment has been instituted. Many can be reduced and others removed entirely.'

The booklet also suggests various strategic moves the broker can make in the event that the prospect's medical rating is inferior. Again the underlying rationale for these moves is that somehow the lives in question can be underwritten. 'Who knows better than you how difficult it is to get someone to agree that they need to purchase life insurance? So when there is agreement to make the purchase, completion of the application should not be risked. This may be the most important part of the sales process.' If additional medical tests are an option to disprove or modify the inferior rating, the broker is advised nevertheless to 'place the coverage first. Failure to do so may result in loss of that offer should the additional test results be unfavourable!' Another option is 'to shop the application to other insurers for their opinion. Shop to one company at a time to avoid confusion and delays due to flooding of the reinsurance market.' If the premium remains excessive because of the substandard life classification, as a last resort the broker should 'consider term insurance rather than permanent, a mixture of term and permanent, or a reduction in the face amount. Considering the changing demographics in our society, with an aging population, the future will bring a larger percentage of impaired risks into the insurance-buying population. There will be a real opportunity to successfully sell insurance to these risks if you learn how to manage impaired risks in a proactive manner today.'

Life insurance agents and brokers are constituted as agents of surveillance regarding 'impaired risks.' They are instructed that failure to be vigilant will be costly in the long run. We attended a brokers' conference at which an underwriting specialist warned brokers to think beyond 'that $4,000 commission I'm going to get is going to be wonderful when I go to Hawaii next week.' The first thought must be about the health-risk selection criteria for preferred rates and deselection criteria for substandard rates or exclusion.

The agent as medical interrogator is to treat the insurance prospect as suspect. The above-mentioned underwriter instructed his audience of brokers about their role as interrogators. He introduced his address by saying that he was there to teach them about preferred market segmentation, 'to get a better feel for where do people fall – which category do they fall into? And also to help you train, and coach you as to how to do it.' The central lesson was the need for good data on risk rather than acting on stereotypes or appearances. 'How many of you here think [names an athletic movie star] is a super-preferred risk and up? You must read the tabloids then ... he had aortic valve replacement surgery a while back ... You see people, they look great to you, just as a friend of mine in Toronto did about two weeks ago when I went out to visit him – two days prior to his five-vessel bypass surgery.'

The need for thorough investigation was underscored with reference to smoking tobacco and illegal drugs. Brokers were told to probe for 'marijuana, nicotine gum, the patch,' and to be aware of 'smoker's amnesia' which afflicts '3 to 7 per cent of the population ... They seem to think they have never smoked in the last twelve months and then, bingo, for whatever reason, the cotinine reading or the major metabolite of nicotine shows up at a whopping 8.3 on the scale 0 to 9.9.' Knowledge of science and ethnic culture is also helpful. If the client is from an East Indian or other Asian background, high cotinine readings may result from consumption of betel nuts. 'So if you have someone of the Asian descent or Indian descent or whatever, and they say they're eating a lot of betel nuts, put it down in the application ... because [otherwise] it can blow your preferred rates.' To emphasize that everyone should be suspected, he told the story of a Supreme Court judge in a Canadian province whose urine sample revealed traces of cocaine. 'You've got to be pretty clean ... Otherwise it throws the actuary right out of whack, and if we're going to fit everybody in who's a standard into a super preferred it isn't going to work.'

Brokers were also instructed on how to prepare clients for their medical tests in ways that would allow them to be administered efficiently and therefore save money for the insurer. Saliva tests are often administered by agents themselves and come with detailed instructions for procedural propriety. Blood tests require a 'fasting state, no booze, no cigarettes if you can for at least two hours ... Pee first ... because a full bladder can actually cause minor abnormalities.' Brokers were told about subtle interactions between health and lifestyle. For example, 'Protein in your urine may be indicative of kidney problems, or it could mean that you are a long distance runner ... If you have a long distance runner, don't let him run a marathon the day before he goes to have a test.'

Inspection service companies are contracted to ask questions of applicants and conduct investigations of them that are too awkward for the broker to pursue. Such inspection services are also a means of investigating the brokers themselves, who have the most immediate incentive for misrepresentation because high front-end load commissions are at stake. A senior executive of an inspection service company said in interview, 'Usually applicants are applying for life insurance ... [because] they've got a need for it, or disability insurance, and they're not there to con. If anything the agent is probably the worst one because ... he wants to get his sale, so he may not take all the information down ... What that becomes is a negative [inaccurate] database.'

Agents are also held financially responsible if inspections and investigations undertaken are subsequently deemed unnecessary given the amount of insurance or other factors. One life company's underwriting booklet for brokers declared, 'Any excess fees or unnecessary evidence will be charged to the agent.'

We interviewed the head investigator for a company that provides investigative services to the life insurance industry. He said that the degree of investigation depends on the level of policy coverage and who has a financial stake in it. Even if the coverage is high, the primary insurer may not pursue detailed investigations if most of the policy is reinsured. On the other hand, if reinsurers have a very high stake they may compel the primary insurer to undertake more detailed investigations as a condition of their participation in the contract.

This interviewee observed that life insurers are now relying more on medical examinations and less on other detailed investigations about the applicant's risk-taking lifestyle. A primary reason for this shift is that informal investigations of lifestyle, for example, talking to the applicant's neighbours, have become impractical because of the changing character of community life. Neighbours do not know each other well enough to be good informants. At the same time institutions know their populations much better. It is easier to obtain institutionally certified knowledge about a person's health, wealth, and habits. In particular, medical surveillance has become much more refined to include details on a person's broader lifestyle and well-being attributes.

Medical investigations usually intensify as age and the policy coverage increase. Table 2.2 is one life insurer's grid for the escalation of medical screening required by age and amount of insurance. At one extreme there is no medical investigation for children insured up to $200,000, those aged sixteen to fifty insured up to $100,000, and those fifty-one to fifty-five insured up to $50,000. At the other extreme are five different major investigations for those seeking high amounts of insurance, especially as they age: a medical history report from the applicant's physician, independent blood profile including HIV test, microscopic urinalysis, treadmill exercise electrocardiogram, and X-ray.

Table 2.2
Medical Investigation Requirements by Age and Amount of Insurance

Age	Amount of Insurance ($)	Medical Investigation Requirement
0–15	to 199,999	Non-med
	200,000 – 300,000	Aps
	300,001+	Individual consideration
16–35	to 99,999	Non-med
	100,000 – 500,000	Non-med, O
	500,001 – 1,000,000	Para, Ibp, Mu
	1,000,001+	Med, Ibp, Mu
36–40	to 99,999	Non-med
	100,000 – 250,000	Non-med, O
	250,001 – 500,000	Para, O
	500,001 – 1,000,000	Para, Ibp, Mu
	1,000,001 – 4,999,999	Med, Ibp, Mu, Ecg
	5,000,000+	Med, 1bp, Mu, Tmt, X-ray
41–45	to 99,999	Non-med
	100, 000 – 500,000	Para, O
	500,001 – 1,000,000	Para, Ibp, Mu
	1,000,001 – 2,999,999	Para, Ibp, Mu, Ecg
	3,000,000+	Med, 1bp, Mu, Tmt, X-ray
46–50	to 99,999	Non-med
	100,000 – 500,000	Para, O
	500,001 – 1,000,000	Para, Ibp, Mu,Ecg
	1,000,001 – 2,999,999	Med Ibp, Mu, Ecg, X-ray
	3,000,000+	Med, 1bp, Mu, Tmt, X-ray
51–55	to 50,000	Non-med
	500,000 – 99,999	Para, Mu
	100,000 – 500,000	Para, Ibp, Mu
	500,001 – 1,000,000	Med, Ibp, Mu, Ecg
	1,000,001+	Med, 1bp, Mu, Tmt, X-ray
56–60	to 99,999	Para, Mu
	100,000 – 250,000	Para, Ibp, Mu
	250,001 – 1,000,000	Med, Ibp, Mu, Ecg
	1,000,001+	Med, 1bp, Mu, Tmt, X-ray
61–65	to 99,999	Para, Mu
	100,000 – 1,000,000	Med, Ibp, Mu, Ecg
	1,000,001+	Med, 1bp, Mu, Tmt, X-ray

Table 2.2 (*Concluded*)

Medical Investigation Requirements key:

APS	attending physician statement
Ecg	electrocardiogram, standard 12 lead
Ibp	independent blood profile including HIV test, using approved blood kit
Med	medical history report from physician
Mu	microscopic urinalysis using a urine specimen container from approved paramedical facilities
Non-med	none
O	orasure saliva test for HIV, cocaine, nicotine
Para	paramedical examination form completed by licensed physician or para-medical service
Tmt	treadmill exercise electrocardiogram
X-ray	chest x-ray

Source: Life insurance company studied

The company that used these medical investigation criteria also required broader lifestyle investigations of applicants seeking more than $500,000 coverage. The primary source of investigation was consumer reports, which were used to both verify information on the application and to provide additional data on consumption habits related to income. An investigator who contracted with the insurance industry said that lifestyle investigations beyond consumer reports are based on particular judgments of what appears morally suspect to the insurer, for example, 'Is your partner male? ... the medical shows you have a drinking or drug habit ... it could be the environment you're in, for example a stripper they will usually ask for an inspection report.'

Policies with a low amount of coverage usually do not require any financial, medical, or lifestyle investigation at the point of underwriting. This fact is frequently used in promoting these policies. Thorough investigation at the point of underwriting is simply too expensive for such policies. Rather, potential problems of financial, medical, and moral risk are addressed by having the applicant self-report every imaginable detail about their wealth and health. Investigation is only initiated in the event of a claim. Typical is a company that sold a policy with maximum $25,000 death benefit coverage to the fifty to seventy-five age group. It required not only self-reported detail, but the following signed authorization by the applicant to allow access to information from every conceivable institution that might have wealth and health information about her:

> We hereby authorize any health care professionals as well as any other public or private health or social service establishment, any insurance company, the Medical Information Bureau, financial institutions, personal information agents or detective agencies, and any public body holding information concerning ourselves or our family, particularly medical information, to supply this information to [name of company] and its reinsurers for the risk assessment or investigation necessary for the study of any claim. We also authorize our insurer, or its reinsurers, to exchange the personal information contained in this application with other insurers, or financial institutions, and to inquire of them for the appraisal of the risk or in the event of a claim. In case of death or disability, the beneficiary, the heir or the liquidator of my estate, is expressly authorized to supply [name of company], when required by the latter, with all the information and authorizations necessary to study the death benefit and obtain the required justifications.

When the policy stakes are high enough to warrant investigation at the point of underwriting, the investigation is aimed at fine-grained market segmentation on medical criteria. One company we studied produced various guides for brokers about their preferred underwriting program. One guide said the program is 'designed to identify "healthier" lives or better mortality, and reward those clients by charging them lower insurance premiums.' Rating points were assigned on the following criteria:

- Build – height and weight.
- Blood pressure – maximum acceptable increases slightly with age – exclude 'currently or previously treated hypertensive clients.'
- Total cholesterol – varies by underwriting programs; limit increasing with age.
- Total cholesterol/HDL ratio – total cholesterol to high density lipoproteins.
- Family medical history regarding specified diseases – requires detailed history of father, mother, and siblings, whether adopted.
- Personal history regarding specified disease – 'typically any ratable history will exclude a client from the preferred classes.'
- Driving record – 'of particular importance in the younger age mar-

ket, especially if your client is male. Underwriters will probably want a motor vehicle report for any applicant under age 35. Several moving violations or an impaired charge will exclude a client from most preferred programs.'

- Hazardous sport participation.
- Drug/alcohol use – if past abuse will consider 'how long the client has been sober, how their life has changed and whether or not they are still participating in a support group.'

This company also provided brokers with an 'impairment guide' which listed from A to Z the health and lifestyle criteria that could be used to select applicants into preferred ratings; to deselect them into substandard pools and much higher premiums; or to exclude them altogether. This guide addressed each specific medical condition and lifestyle habit regarding the nature of the problem and its rating. Selected examples illustrate the intensity of surveillance.

Starting with specific medical conditions, a person with angina and myocardial infarction is given the life insurance equivalent of a criminal probation order. The applicant so diagnosed is assigned 'a temporal rating, in place for the first five years following the episode, which covers the high additional mortality present during this period of time,' as well as a permanent rating 'which relates to the permanent additional mortality.' The rating is to vary by the prognosis, for example,

- Unstable angina, increasing episodes, difficult for doctor to manage: decline.
- Stable angina, few episodes, no other risk factors, over age 50: +50 – +100
- Anteroseptal myocardial infarction, age 48, one year ago: +150 – +200 and $7.50/1000 insured for four years.
- Inferior myocardial infarction, age 55, no other factors. Two years ago: +100 and $5.00/1000 for three years.

The calibration of breast cancer was also subject to both temporal and permanent ratings which make the applicant pay for the ongoing risks of her illness. Breast cancer is 'not insurable for three years following diagnosis and completion of treatment (surgery, radiation, or chemotherapy) although carcinoma-in-situ may be insurable sooner. Thereafter, there will be a permanent rating of +50 and a temporary rating in the range of $7–$12 per thousand for another six years. The permanent rating results from the long-term risk of a recurrence which can occur as late as fifteen to twenty years after the original illness.' In the case of eating disorders, a history of 'repeated relapse' results in coverage being denied. Those deemed fully recovered are rated substandard for a minimum of one year, then graduated towards standard rates in three to five years. Organ transplant history is also differentially rated. Heart and lung transplant cases are uninsurable, but kidney transplant cases are insurable after two years of stability: 'Ratings begin at +100 and $10.00 per thousand (permanently) if donor is a living relative and +150 and $13.50 per thousand if donor a cadaver, in best cases.'

Turning to lifestyle criteria, occupations were rated according to named dangerous locations and hazardous materials handling, with flat fee extras starting at $2.50 per $1,000 coverage. The extra premium could be negotiated depending on the applicant's experience and training in safety. Medical history could also be considered in relation to the occupation. 'Rarely, medical history in combination with occupational duties may preclude insurance (e.g., epilepsy with marine diving).' In some cases special occupational risk policies were underwritten with respect to critical illness and care to death. For example, the company offered occupational HIV infection insurance for health care workers. The terms and conditions of this coverage were especially stringent regarding claims investigations, reporting requirements, and moral risk exclusions. For example:

- The insured must report anything giving rise to potential claims within fourteen days – the incident must be investigated by appropriate authorities as usual.
- A blood test within this period must show HIV negative.
- Three to six months after, blood tests must confirm HIV positive.
- 'The company must be given access to independently test all the blood samples used and to take such additional samples as deemed necessary.'
- 'HIV infection resulting or transmitted by any other means, including sexual activity or recreation drug use' is excluded.
- 'This benefit will not apply if the person insured has elected not to take any vaccine affecting protection against the HIV which becomes available prior to the accident or where a cure against the HIV has become available prior to the accident.'

Pilots pose another occupational lifestyle risk. If the applicant is involved in aviation, a detailed questionnaire must be completed out-lining experience, type of aircraft flown, nature of occupation, and so on. 'Aviation risks are assessed on the number of hours flown (more is generally better), where generally, if a pilot has many hours of experi-ence, flies fixed wing aircrafts on scheduled routes and not into remote areas, and does not participate in risky activities such as crop dusting or others mentioned above, he or she will likely be standard to $2.50 [excess] per thousand [insured].'

Foreign travel may also be rated. Foreign countries are risk assessed on the basis of 'political or military instability or poor socio-economic and medical service.' A traveller to a substandard country may be given a substandard rating. Another Canadian company we studied declared in its manual for underwriters, 'Clients travelling to, visiting or planning on residing in all countries *except*: Western Europe, USA, Hong Kong, Singapore, Japan, Taiwan, Australia, New Zealand must be submitted on a Trial basis (no premium is collected and the Condi-tional Insurance Agreement may not be issued.). Note: Clients visiting, residing or travelling to Middle East countries, Africa or any country experiencing political instability are not acceptable.'

Persons with deviant lifestyles involving drugs are also subject to excess premium ratings or exclusion for their excesses. A person who consumes alcohol with too much regularity must complete a special questionnaire which affects the rating. A confirmed alcoholic who sub-sequently becomes abstinent is placed on probation with variable rat-ing depending on evidence of longer-term abstinence. "A minimum abstinence of one year from alcohol would probably be rated +200 with yearly rating reconsiderations being available if no relapses or criticisms or health history may be considered for standard rates." In the case of illegal drug users, another questionnaire is required. Mari-juana use is equated to preferred tobacco use (e.g., occasional pipes, cigars). 'Marijuana use in isolation, of four to six times a month, would generally be considered at standard smoker rates. More frequent use would be rated +50 to decline.' However, users of other illegal drugs are treated like confirmed alcoholics. 'Current use of other illegal drugs is a decline. Coverage may be considered two to three years after the last use and ratings would be +200. Reconsideration yearly with continued abstinence would be available.'

Legal drug use is also subject to rating considerations. If the person is required to take prescription drugs as part of addressing a medical condition, then prescribed use of that drug may also be an insurance condition. For example, insulin rated diabetics, already charged higher premiums for their condition, find that 'with poor control or compliance, ratings increase or the risk becomes uninsurable.' Similarly, the person diagnosed with high blood pressure (hypertension), is subject to the following edict: 'Blood pressure that is not well controlled, for an applicant who does not follow his doctor's orders or does not see his doctor for regular follow-ups, will result in rated coverage and possibly even a decline.'

For people whose pursuit of happiness includes Prozac, the habit is to be read as a symptom of disorders it is designed to overcome, for example, obsessive-compulsive disorders, eating disorders, and depression. As such it is rated +50 or higher. 'The exceptional case can be standard if the history is minor and well followed by a doctor. Prozac is a relatively new drug and treatment has been controversial.' Nervous disorders such as depression may be tolerable if they do not interfere with work and therefore income stability. Long-term depression with work stability is to be rated standard, but 'Coverage will likely be declined or postponed if symptoms are increasing in severity, difficult to control or the applicant is unable to work.'

Many explicit exclusions are stated as contract conditions. For example, the accidental death benefit provision of a company we studied explicitly excluded deaths from suicide or drugs; deaths occurring in the course of the commission of a criminal offence; and deaths occurring as a result of driving under the influence of alcohol. There was also room for exclusion of this benefit from a life policy that was otherwise accepted if the applicant showed signs of being accident-prone. For example, 'Accidental death benefit will not be offered to certain borderline risks which may be granted universal life insurance coverage, such as proposed insureds with poor driving records.'

Other exclusions are not written into insurance contracts but are made evident to applicants who apply. Life insurance is for those who exhibit stability in their domicile, work, and sources of income. It is for good citizens or those who give every indication that they are on the road to being good citizens. A company we studied excluded temporary residents of Canada, for example, domestics with temporary work permits, students with student visas, visitors, and diplomats. Landed immigrants in Canada during their first year were not considered without evidence of employment or 'demonstrable wealth.' Refugees were considered to be a particular moral risk and therefore a longer period of residency was required before considering coverage, along with other indicators of domestic, financial, and health stability. Refugees from all geographical locations had to meet the following criteria to be considered:

- Provide proof of residency in Canada for a minimum of 24 months.
- If married, spouse and dependent children must reside in Canada.
- Must be gainfully employed and provide a copy of his/her most recent income tax return as proof of employment. A client investing in Canada (home, business ownership) would be considered more favourably than one with no investment.
- Insurance amount must be consistent with the client's income and assets in Canada.

Note: Landed Immigrants and/or Refugees from any country living in Canada less than 1 year require a Medical Exam and Independent Blood Profile in addition to any other automatic or discretionary evidence required to assess the risk.

A client who is given an unfavourable medical rating on any criterion may be granted the capacity to have the rating reviewed by another medical examiner. However, the review is typically on the condition that she must pay any expenses involved. If the initial rating is overturned, reimbursement of expenses may be made.

The applicant's health status at the point of underwriting is also a focus of investigation when she dies and a claim is made. In assessing a claim a company investigates possible misrepresentation at the point of underwriting. A claims specialist for a life company we studied said that if the person dies two years or more after the initial application, it is necessary to 'prove fraud ... and proving the intent when the person's dead is pretty hard. In the United States you can't even go the fraud route after two years, but in Canada you can.' He gave as an example of a clear-cut fraud case a person who had not disclosed a major surgery for cancer and the claim was denied outright.

We interviewed a private investigator who contracted with life insurance companies to investigate claims. He said his work mainly entailed searches for evidence showing the person had violated the exclusion clauses of the insurance contract. For example, in the case of a person who died of a drug overdose, did that person falsely report not using those drugs prior to the application? Many such cases pertain to the accidental death provisions of the contract, and hinge upon the determination of what caused the accident and whether the cause relates to an exclusion clause. For example, did the accident result from alcohol or other drug impairment? Did the person have a heart attack causing death prior to the vehicle crash? Did the person commit suicide by purposely driving into an oncoming vehicle?

Investigations are further complicated if the death occurs in a foreign country. Several interviewees said that this is an increasing problem for two reasons. First, there are fraud rings that manufacture false documents with respect to the reported death of someone who departed Canada permanently. Second, many people who emigrate to Canada return to their home country as they age and their health deteriorates. Either way, it is necessary to document the death. One interviewee said that, in the past, local Canadian consulates in the country concerned would do the necessary verification. However, they no longer do so and it is therefore necessary to contract with private security firms to 'go to the hospital, go to the graveyard ... interview people around.'

The investigative process is facilitated by access to information authorization signed by the insured at the point of application (see above), and by having next-of-kin, usually the beneficiary, sign a similar authorization at the point of claim. An investigator told us that if the next-of-kin refuses to sign the authorization he is simply told that the company is unable to process the application. He added that in his long experience he had never had such a case.

A routine aspect of the investigation is to match the claim with other insurers to ascertain whether the person took out multiple small policies to avoid more stringent investigations at the point of underwriting. For example, the person might have ten policies with $25,000 coverage on each rather than having a single $250,000 policy that would have precipitated medical and other investigations upon application. During the claims investigation this possibility is explored by matching the claim with claims received by other companies, a self-report requirement by the beneficiary on the claims form, and direct questions to the beneficiary or next-of-kin.

Clearly, investment in life insurance products entails rigorous investigation by life insurance companies. This investigation reflects prudence on the part of insurers, trying to protect the integrity of each fragmented risk pool for the benefit of other insured within it and the insurer's bottom line. But as shown at the beginning of the chapter, this fine-grained underwriting does not inevitably create more certainty for any party to the insurance relationship. The key elements of life insurance loss ratios – mortality rates, persistency rates, administrative expenses, investment strategies, medical ratings, and market segmentation practices – each involve speculation and embracing risk beyond rational knowledge of risks as probability calculations. The interaction of all of these elements in the manufacture of a given life insurance product often compounds uncertainties for the insured and the insurer. Beyond the powers of actuarialism and trust in numbers, life insurance is an uncertain business.

3 Uncertainties of Disability: Spreading Risk, Solidarity, and Welfare

I reckon being ill is one of the great pleasures of life, provided one is not too ill and is not obliged to work till one is better.

Samuel Butler, *The Way of the Flesh* (1903)

Preserving the health by too severe a rule is a wearisome malady.

La Roche-Foucauld, *Maxims* (1665)

Uncertainties of Disability

In this chapter we examine disabilities that arise from work and vehicle accidents and how they are dealt with by the insurance system. Our particular focus is the subjective nature of personal injury accident assessment and not simply the compensation of physical disabilities such as smashed limbs following an accident. As we shall see, personal injuries are often entirely subjective. Even when there is objective physical impairment, a strong subjective component shapes the ways in which insurance claims are managed and compensated.

We demonstrate that moral risk problems are especially acute in this field because of the subjective nature of personal injuries and the reactive way in which disability risk is defined and responded to (Ericson, Doyle, and Barry 2003; Ericson and Doyle 2003b). Injuries such as whiplash following vehicle accidents and lower back pain suffered in work environments are notoriously difficult to diagnose and treat (Malleson 2002). This situation leaves considerable scope for the institutions and professions involved – medical, legal, and insurance – to shape the meaning of disability and how it will be compensated in a local jurisdiction.

Each of these institutions and professions pose moral risks as they use the system to serve their respective interests. Medical professionals have plenty of scope to invent new illnesses and treatments that will fuel demand for their services. Lawyers for plaintiffs can work with the medical profession to build insurance claims and their own fees. Insurers can counter with their own medical and legal expertise, as well as stringent claims procedures, to deny what are viewed as legitimate claims by disabled claimants and their caregivers. There are also moral risks at the level of the insured. They too have considerable room to negotiate the meaning of disability and what it is worth. Whether they accept the illness categories and treatment regimes urged by their doctors and lawyers for the purpose of making an insurance claim, decide to exaggerate in the interest of inflating a claim, or fraudulently report that they are suffering in ways they are not, claimants too can take advantage of uncertainties in the disability insurance environment.

Disability is a key word in contemporary risk society. It addresses the obsession with health and well-being on both the individual level and in political culture. Disability generally refers to a physical incapacity – caused by congenital defects, injury, or disease – or to a lack of some other attribute that limits one's ability to do something. Because the term is applied to a full range of physical and mental impairments, few people escape personal experience of disability. Indeed, according to the U.S. National Council on Disabilities, at a given time, forty-nine million Americans are suffering from a disability (O'Brien 2001: 1). In this view, disability can be seen as a 'normal' part of the life course, something that needs to be addressed in the prudent management of one's life, as discussed in chapter 2.

The fact that physical and mental impairments abound poses uncertainties for the insurance industry. Focusing on disabilities arising from vehicle accidents and work-related injuries, we discover that the insurance institution is enmeshed with the medical and legal institutions in the perpetual politics of classifying, commodifying, and indemnifying human productive capacities. Disability becomes a construct of these institutions for deciding how much productive ability a person has left following an injury.

The medical institution defines disability first and foremost in relation to work and the income derived therefrom. For example, the diagnostic manual of the American Medical Association [AMA] (1993: 2) declares, 'A disability arises out of the interaction between impairment and external requirements, especially of a person's occupation. Disability may be thought of as the gap between what a person *can* do and what the person *needs* or *wants* to do.'

Disability insurers work within the framework that disability is based not only on medical assessment, but also on the prognostic criteria of insurance logic. For example, a workers' compensation board's manual on permanent functional impairment states that while physicians determine the level of functional impairment, disability 'is not a purely medical condition ... [It is] an administrative and not solely a medical responsibility or function. It is an appraisal of the worker's present and future ability to engage in gainful activity as it is affected by such diverse factors as age, sex, education, economic and social environment, in addition to the definitive medical factor of permanent injury.'

The courts also take 'a broad and free-wheeling functional definition of disability' (O'Brien 2001: 15). Consistent with the insurance framework, the courts consider what the worker can and cannot do in the context of myriad personal and societal factors. In this consideration, the courts not only seek to restore the person to her station in life, but also to ensure that she actively embraces whatever personal, expert, or technological devices will help to mitigate her condition (ibid.: 16).

Insurance is crucial in this interinstitutional nexus. As observed by a work and health specialist we interviewed, 'Whether somebody is disabled in a short term, medium term or long term, is a matter of how they get insured, not a matter of, really, a significant difference in health.' Research confirms that insurance arrangements have a determining influence on medical diagnoses and treatment regimes for disabilities arising from vehicle and work-related accidents (Butler et al. 1997; Malleson 2002).

The influence of insurance logic on medical assessments can be further demonstrated by considering the process through which the degree of physical impairment is ascertained. Figure 3.1 illustrates the commodification of various body parts by medical practitioners on behalf of insurers. In this depiction of the insurance value of body parts, we find that the left arm is rated at 12 per cent, amputation at 45 per cent, spine at 13 per cent, and so on. It is this quantification of the impairment of bodily functions for insurance purposes that the medical specialist is asked to perform.

Figure 3.1
The Commodification of Body Parts

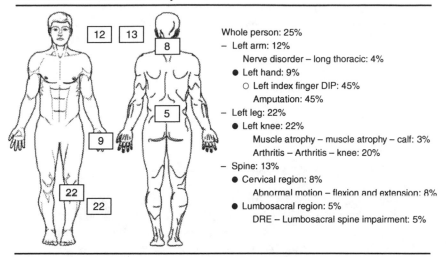

Whole person: 25%
– Left arm: 12%
    Nerve disorder – long thoracic: 4%
  ● Left hand: 9%
    ○ Left index finger DIP: 45%
      Amputation: 45%
– Left leg: 22%
  ● Left knee: 22%
    Muscle atrophy – muscle atrophy – calf: 3%
    Arthritis – Arthritis – knee: 20%
– Spine: 13%
  ● Cervical region: 8%
    Abnormal motion – flexion and extension: 8%
  ● Lumbosacral region: 5%
    DRE – Lumbosacral spine impairment: 5%

Source: Insurance Bodily Injury Claims Assessment Manual

We interviewed the director of corporate planning for a workers' compensation insurer in Canada. He explained how insurance underwriting logic is embedded in the percentage figures that medical experts arrive at when determining functional impairment. For example, AMA (1993) standards on functional impairment are set in relation to the weeks of compensation a claimant is entitled to by insurers. The interviewee began by referring to a published article in which the editor of the AMA manual described the standard-setting process:

Well, we sat around a table like this and said 'What do you think an arm is worth? Yeah, OK, 25 per cent for the arm at the elbow, 50 per cent for the arm and shoulder, that's what we'll decide it is.' Now the people who were sitting around the table brought with them their experiences from their own milieu, which was primarily U.S. insurance workers' compensation, disability, social security. And the milieu there was that these disability ratings ... [are] paid on the basis of the number of weeks you're entitled to ... [T]he most common rate is five hundred weeks. So when these people are sitting around a table, they're thinking what this is going to work out to in real terms with this individual, the average individual, let's say thirty-four years of age at the top. So that's what they did, they looked at the average wages, what the average person would get, and they come up with a percentage that they thought was reasonable. And they made a lot of caveats about not wanting really to do the disability side, but they're really talking about impairment. They're talking about what the physical limits are, not what the impact of earnings will be. But you can't really separate the two, they're so much interrelated that you really have to look at what the effect would be ... [Everything] is engineered in meetings ... At least there's agreement interjurisdictionally in about seventeen states now that actually say they're going to use AMA guides. The problem is ... there's not a lot of comparability between editions. That also raises other problems about what you do ... retroactively with cases. Maybe we've disadvantaged, or over-compensated ... It's a big worry.

This interviewee also said that his workers' compensation board did not adopt the AMA guides because American jurisdictions have substantially lower levels of insurance compensation than is available in his Canadian jurisdiction. The AMA panel of experts sets the functional impairment percentages high in order to obtain somewhat reasonable levels of compensation. However, if these inflated percentages are imported into the higher compensation environment in Canada, they would yield too high levels of compensation. Accordingly, his board adopted its own definitions and calculus of functional impairment for disability assessment. '[The AMA guides] were developed in a milieu where people didn't get a lot of money for workers' compensation cases, so the percentages are higher than the percentages we give. What's really important is not to compare the percentages but to compare the net present values with dollars that are going into the person's hands. And in every measure, with the exception of backs, we are way over what everybody else pays. Backs, we're a tiny bit out.'

These considerations make it clear that disability is indeed a social, political, economic, and cultural construct beyond whatever capacity a medical examiner might have to ascertain the degree of functional impairment. At least functional impairment is in some respects measurable. As we shall see, many of the claims of disability that arise from vehicle and work-related accidents are not reasonably measurable. They are based on subjective complaints such as whiplash-associated disorders and low back pain that require medical practitioners to be specialists of the invisible. Disability becomes a 'moral battle' (Sontag 1979, 1989) fought via classification schemes, metaphorical language, and figurative reasoning. Physicians struggle with the believability of patients' claims; lawyers with efforts at claims suppression by insurers; insurers with how to manage their loss ratios in the face of iatrogenic health services and nomogenic legal services; and claimants with insurance, medical, and legal obstructions that seem to impair them more than their disabilities.

The conundrum facing disability insurers is captured in the term 'somatoform': complaints by patients for which there is no apparent physical illness. When patients nevertheless insist they have a physical illness, health professionals may view it as 'psychosomatic': a psychological problem being expressed as a physical illness. However, the tendency in medical science has been to accept somatoform symptoms as indicative of physical disease and to pursue the physical causes and most helpful treatments (Shorter 1992, 1994). What appears in the somatoform 'symptom pool' (ibid.) as indicative of physical disease varies enormously in time and place. The symptom pool that is brought to the centre of the risk portfolio of a local patient-doctor-lawyer-insurer culture varies enormously with social, political, economic, and technological change. Somatoform illnesses are invented, proliferate, and disappear according to the culture of legitimate claims that prevails in a local context.

As the history of medicine shows, the invention of new technologies is accompanied by the invention of new illnesses. For example, the invention of the railway in 1830 was followed by frequent accidents and horrific injuries. While many of the injuries were physically evident – loss of sight, limb, or appendage – others could only be imagined. A new illness of 'railway spine' (Trimble 1981) was invented to capture all of the imagined possibilities associated with concussion of the spinal cord. The injured were seen as suffering from ailments that ranged from 'shock' to spinal anemia and meningitis.

New technologies introduced into work contexts have also been accompanied by the invention of new illnesses. When quill pens were replaced with steel nibs in the British Civil Service circa 1850, many civil servants claimed disability (Tyrer 1994). At the turn of the twentieth century, 'telegraphists' cramp' was invented along with the telegraph keypad and eventually reached epidemic proportions (ibid.). A national committee in Britain established 'that a nervous instability in the operator combined with the rapidity of the keypad movements overwhelmed the nervous system, causing a "nervous breakdown"' (Malleson 2002: 53). Telegraphists' cramp eventually disappeared, but nervous breakdown persisted in covering all manner of mental illness claims. And, with the invention of the computer, 'repetitive strain injury' (RSI) has arisen as the new keyboard malady. In the early 1990s, RSI was estimated to cost $7 billion annually in the United States, and thousands of multimillion dollar lawsuits were pursued throughout the decade (ibid.: 70).

Health service professionals have a propensity to underwrite culturally legitimate somatic claims for a number of reasons. First, they are socialized to be sympathetic to patients. Second, they have ongoing relationships of trust with patients that lead them to dispense helpful diagnoses and treatments routinely. For example, in Winnipeg recently, 'As a form of protest, 107 police officers called in sick on the same day. Faced with the threat of losing a day's pay, 91 officers produced a doctor's note certifying that they were sick' (ibid.: 63). Third, health service professionals are well aware of the limits of medical science. In the absence of objective evidence, they go with the flow of medical consensus as shaped by insurance and legal systems. Fourth, they are backed by enormous resources, largely from public and private insurance schemes, that facilitate invention of diagnoses and treatments that seem legitimate at the time. Treatments proliferate to the point where they make the diagnoses to which they refer seem obvious in retrospect. With respect to somataform illnesses in particular, treatment often underscores the imagined physical basis of the illness for both patient and doctor (Shorter 1992, 1994). 'In our society, nothing defines the diagnosis more than the treatment: "No treatment, no illness!" ... In treatment, the power of mystery often wins out over the transparency of science' (Malleson 2002: 65, 367). Fifth, following upon the heavily resourced infrastructure, the health professions are iatrogenic, generating business in order to expand their enterprises as well as, hopefully, the well-being of their patients. In this respect, 'human bodies and car bodies are similar. All the pre-accident damaged and malfunctioning parts get lumped in with damage caused by the accident. Again like body shop owners, health care practitioners are on the lookout for work – and often again like body shop owners, almost double their charges when an insurance company pays' (ibid.: 197). Sixth, medical practitioners are always half-watching in terms of another show, namely, the involvement of lawyers and the law. On the one hand, they fear malpractice suits. On the other hand, they appreciate that lawyers also participate in the invention and perpetuation of disabilities, contributing to nomogenesis in tandem with iatrogenesis.

In this chapter, we focus on the most common personal injury insurance claims that arise from accidents. Neck injury, or whiplash, is the most frequent personal injury claim following vehicle accidents (Livingston 1998; Swerdlow 1998; Malleson 2002). About 75 per cent of vehicle injury claims are for whiplash, and 10 per cent of claimants are deemed permanently disabled. While estimates vary widely, millions of North Americans sustain a whiplash injury each year. In the United States, the high-end estimate is that five million sustain a whiplash injury every year, and three million do not fully recover in the short term. In 1994, 2.6 million Americans reported chronic pain following whiplash injury, and for 650,000 the pain was ongoing (Malleson 2002: 4, 10).

Back injury is the most frequent personal injury claim following work-related accidents (Waddell 1998). Once absorbed as an unfortunate accompaniment of daily life, back pain became increasingly diagnosed as an injury in need of sustained medical attention. Malleson (2002: 8) records that in 'the United Kingdom, days lost through low back disability increased more than tenfold in the period from 1955 to 1999 ... In 1970 one per cent of the working Swedish population was off work with back pain for an average of twenty days; by 1987, 8 per cent were off work for an average of thirty-four days. During this period there was a 6000 per cent increase in the number of Swedes receiving permanent disability pensions for low back pain.' Similar to whiplash, about 10 per cent of low back pain cases are deemed permanently disabled.

Since whiplash and low back pain both involve attributions of spinal injury, the two conditions have a great deal in common and often fold into each other (ibid.: 77). Singly or together, they represent the most common reasons for visiting a health care specialist whether one has been involved in an accident or not. The majority of adults experience some low back pain each year, and this experience is severe enough to make it the second most common reason for visiting a family physician and the most common reason for visiting specialists such as chiropractors, osteopaths, neurosurgeons, and orthopaedic surgeons. Neck pain is so common that someone not involved in a vehicle accident is as likely to experience it as someone who was involved in a vehicle accident four weeks previously. The problem with all of this visitation is that, while whiplash and back pain are attributed to structural damage spinal injury, it is extremely difficult to provide physical evidence of such injury. 'Despite years of intensive search ... no convincing physical cause has been found to explain the ongoing pain of whiplash or occupational low back pain in about 97 per cent of cases. Low back pain plagues the work force of the industrialized world, and neck pain plagues the auto insurance industry' (ibid.: 79).

Medical classifications abound. In the case of non-specific low back pain classifications include: 'lumbar sprain, lumbar strain, lumbago, sciatica, discal hernia, discopathy, facet syndrome, lumbar myositis, ligamentitis, minor invertebral displacement, dysfunction of the intervertebral joint, fibromyositis, fibrositis, facutis, myofasciitis, articular hypomobility and hypermobility, discarthrosis, metameric celluloteno-periostomyalgic syndrome, posterior branch syndrome, rhizopathy. The length of the list reflects the brevity of what is known about the causes of low back pain' (Malleson 2002: 83, referring to Spitzer et al. 1987).

In the case of whiplash, the rage to invent diagnoses and treatments has spiralled. The one-third of accident victims in North America who claim whiplash are treated to a rich menu of medical possibilities.

> Ophthalmologists report whiplash damage to the eyes. ENT surgeons report whiplash damage of the inner ear that causes distressing and disabling dizziness, buzzing in the ears, and sometimes deafness. Dentists report mandibular whiplash leading to chronic and incapacitating temporo-mandibular joint disorder. Orthopaedic surgeons report whiplash to be a potent cause of persistent backache and other musculoskeletal pains, and rheumatologists that whiplash victims frequently develop fibromyalgia [also known as fibrositis: severe muscle aches and pains, unrefreshing sleep, constant exhaustion].
>
> Minds can be damaged in accidents as well as bodies. Psychologists and psychiatrists emphasize that the deleterious effects of the frightening experience of the collision cause victims to develop a post-traumatic stress disorder. Recent studies into the psychological effects of motor vehicle accident victims (mostly whiplash victims) seeking treatment for ongoing physical symptoms have signs of post traumatic stress disorder. (Malleson 2002: 12–13)

Many of these whiplash-associated disorder diagnoses are somatoform and lack objective evidence. Post-traumatic stress disorder is a clear case in point. Easy to imagine but difficult to prove, post-traumatic stress disorder went from being non-existent to being part of almost half of all vehicle accident claims in fourteen years (ibid.: 212).

Table 3.1
Workers' Compensation Board of British Columbia Claims Costs 1996

Type of claim	N	Cost
Health care	71,438	$ 22,663,943
Short-term disability	69,021	337,821,750
Long-term disability	4,667	334,398,947
Fatal	152	38,863,587
	145,278	733,748,227

Source: Workers' Compensation Board of British Columbia 1996: 7

Fibromyalgia has also had a meteoric rise. Because it addresses diffuse aches and pains, insomnia, and exhaustion, fibromyalgia has enormous potential for magnification by health care professionals (Hadler 1997). Moreover, these symptoms provide scope for alternative health practitioners, and for the burgeoning self-help industry on the Internet and in popular books. Indeed, physicians receive less than half of the insurance dollars following bodily injury claims. Referring to data reported by the Insurance Research Council (1994), Malleson (2002: 258–9) documents the average number of visits to various health care practitioners in connection with bodily injury claims: chiropractors (25), physical therapists (19), psychotherapists (11), unspecified health care practitioners (9), MD/osteopath other than the initial emergency room visit (8), dentists (7), unspecified medical professionals (6), MD/ osteopath emergency room visit (1).

The cost of disabilities arising from work-related and vehicle accidents forms a significant part of all Western political economies. For example, in the case of disabilities resulting from work-related accidents, the Province of British Columbia, with a 1996 population of about four million and a GDP of about $100 billion, had a workers' compensation scheme that paid out $734 million in claims (table 3.1). About 25 per cent of the short-term disability claims paid by the Workers' Compensation Board of British Columbia [WCBBC] each year are for back strains (WCBBC 1996: 10, 12). Extrapolating from the data in table 3.1, this means that in 1996, 17,255 claimants received compensation for back strains at a cost of $84.5 million.

Figures from workers' compensation insurers alone do not tell the whole story. Additional costs are covered through claims to provincial health care insurance programs and to private disability insurers. An estimate of total cost must also include employer loss of productivity and other uninsured expenses. A workers' compensation official we interviewed said it is reasonable to assume these expenses double what is covered by insurance. Operating with this assumption, 'in Canada we spend about $6.7 billion in benefits, and that means the cost to firms in this country is about $13.7 billion per year ... That's 10 per cent more than the annual contribution of all Canadian employers and workers in the Canada Pension Plan, about 1.6 per cent of estimated GDP, and it's more than the federal income tax paid by corporations.'

Disabilities arising from traffic accidents are also staggering in terms of economic costs. In 1995 the British Columbia vehicle insurance corporation, Insurance Corporation of British Columbia (ICBC), paid out personal injury claims of $1.185 billion or roughly 1 per cent of the provincial GDP. Again this figure does not include additional payments by other insurers, such as the provincial health care insurance system, and workers' compensation for drivers whose traffic accident occurred on the job. Moreover, it does not include all costs associated with lost time at work for those disabled by traffic accidents. A researcher for ICBC said in interview that a study they conducted found the economic impact of lost work time as a result of vehicle accidents was five times greater than the economic impact of all crime victimization that occurred in the province.

ICBC pays enormous compensation for whiplash-associated disorders (WAD). According to their sources, almost three-quarters of the bodily injury claims received at their claims centres are for whiplash injuries. More precisely, as illustrated in figure 3.2, 92 per cent of all bodily injury claims paid are for temporary disabilities, and 80 per cent of these are soft tissue (WAD) 'subjective' injuries. A research organization partly funded by ICBC reports that on average a whiplash patient sees a family physician five times, a physiotherapist thirty-eight times, and a chiropractor forty-two times (Physical Medicine Research Foundation n.d.). A leading actuarial expert with knowledge of ICBC operations said that for 1997, bodily injury claims were about $1.3 billion, of which about $.5 billion went to pay the 'subjective' injuries. She said an average automobile insurance policy in the province carried a $600 annual premium for bodily injury risks, and 'about $250 of that is for stiff necks and sore shoulders.'

Whiplash claims costs are also substantial in other jurisdictions. In the United States, the annual national claims costs for whiplash are

Figure 3.2
Insurance Corporation of British Columbia Bodily Injury Claims

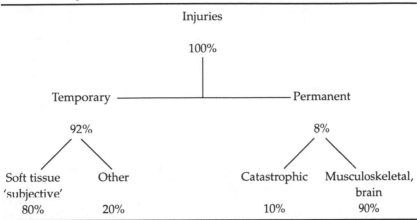

Source: ICBC 1997: 36

estimated to range from US$13 billion to US$18 billion annually, while in Britain a recent estimate is £3.1 billion (Malleson 2002: 10, 28). In the United States in the late 1980s and early 1990s, bodily injury claims costs increased at an annual growth rate of 7.4 per cent (ibid.: 256). 'Between 1980 and 1993, the number of BI claims per 100 insured vehicles rose 33 per cent, from 17.9 to 29.3, and the likelihood of a BI claim being filed in an accident that involved a property damage claim rose 64 per cent in the same time period' (ibid.: 254).

Growth was also experienced in Canadian jurisdictions. For example, a consultant's report to ICBC uses the concept 'social inflation' to address 'the tendency within society to demand greater entitlements for injury or inconvenience and to a growing element of litigious behaviour' (Insurance Corporation of British Columbia 1996: 27). Social inflation results in 'the claims process being viewed as an avenue to achieve financial gain as opposed to a mechanism for ensuring the recovery of good health and replacing real economic loss' (ibid: 22–3). The escalation of claims payments is attributed in particular to 'a greater propensity for maximizing claims for non-economic losses (i.e. "pain and suffering") ... increasing expectations for payment after collisions, regardless of actual nature of injury ... [and] increased levels of advertising by lawyers and a greater likelihood of claimants seeking legal representation' (Insurance Corporation of British Columbia 1997a: 4; see also Insurance Corporation of British Columbia 1996: 20-1). Social inflation and legal inflation are entwined: 'the dynamics of the liability system have made it possible to get relatively large awards for pain and suffering ... and led to a growing expectation of such compensation when minor accidents occur' (Insurance Corporation of British Columbia 1996: 21). The cumulative result of 'social inflation' is that '"pain and suffering" awards have increased dramatically resulting in auto premium increases of 138 per cent during the past decade. The percentage is nearly twice the Consumer Price Index increase (66 per cent) during the same period. For 1996, "pain and suffering" awards for temporary injuries are expected to total $400 million or 18 per cent of the $2.238 billion in crash and auto crime claims' (Insurance Corporation of British Columbia 1997a: 4).

It has been well documented that whiplash claims rates vary enormously across jurisdictions. For example, the British Columbia Whiplash Initiative (1997: 8) published data on whiplash claims rates per 100,000 across various jurisdictions. These data are limited by the fact that they pertain to different years and involve different definitions and systems for dealing with claims. Nevertheless, the differences are marked. The year and rates per 100,000 for each jurisdiction follow: New Zealand (1987) 13; Australia (1987) 39; Quebec (1987) 70; Sweden (1990) 200; Britain (1995) 450; Saskatchewan (1987) 700; British Columbia (1992) 850.

A comparison of relatively similar jurisdictions also reveals substantial variation in whiplash claims rates. For example, in the mid-1980s, Victoria, Australia, and New Zealand were similar in size and standard of living. They also had similar rates of rear-end collisions, but the rate of whiplash claims in Victoria was 800 per cent greater than in New Zealand, and the amount paid for whiplash injury was 300 per cent greater (Malleson 2002: 32, citing Awerbuch 1992; Mills and Horne 1986). In Canada, even provinces with state vehicle insurance systems vary enormously in whiplash claims rates. For example, in 1997 the rate per 100,000 in Quebec was 70, Manitoba 700, Saskatchewan 800, and British Columbia 1,600 (Malleson 2002: 297). In the United States, bodily injury claims, three-quarters of which involve whiplash, also vary substantially across jurisdictions. For example, 'In 1993 Metropolitan Los Angeles had 98.8 BI claims per 100 property damage claims, while Franklin County, Florida, had only 8.8 such claims. The wide variability in the rates of BI claims compared to auto damage claims extends throughout the States and appears independent of the insurance system in use and of the probable *elasticity* of vehicles involved. In 1993, North Dakota had 5.6 BI claims per 100 property damage claims, while Massachusetts had 34.8; both are *no-fault* states. Wyoming had 17.6 such claims compared to California's 60.7; both are *tort* states' (ibid.: 256).

We interviewed an expert on vehicle insurance claims patterns who served as a consultant to insurance companies. He offered additional observations about variation in whiplash claims across jurisdictions.

> You go to North Dakota, no one believes it. They have 6 per cent, the whiplash rate, and people just think, 'Oh, your car got bumped. You lived. You're happy.' You go to Lithuania, they have zero, they don't believe in it. No one knows. You interview people, there are *no* victims of whiplash. *There are none* [see Schrader et al. 1996; Merskey 1997] [In British Columbia] the average number of treatments is twice as much as in pure tort systems ... The probability of disability is 50 per cent higher than the North American norm and the period of disability is 300 per cent higher because they pay for it ... Norway allows permanent lifetime disability from whiplash, except in Norway it's paid. So in a country of 4.2 million, 70,000 are permanently disabled from whiplash. It's a national disaster. You get to retire if you get rear-ended! It's a joy! ... And what's more, if you went and talked to the people, I am sure, overwhelmingly they're very sincere and think that the accident ruined their life ... In Canadian dollars, in British Columbia you pay $209 in whiplash claims, in California $56, as part of annual premium.

This remarkable variation in claim rates can be understood through examination of the three major institutional players in the system: insurance, medicine, and law. The epidemiology and political economy of disability claims depends on the local structure and culture of insurance arrangements, health services, and legal services.

From an insurance perspective, the most fundamental consideration is whether the prevailing ethos in the political culture is welfarism or liberalism (Ericson, Doyle, and Barry 2003). In the compensation-focused welfare approach 'provision for accidents is viewed as being a part of the welfare state in just the same way as the provision of health care and social security (Bowles 1995: 106-7). The insurance objective is to generate sufficient premium revenue to meet demand for services. The insurance system is underpinned by a sense of responsibility for collective solidarity, and risk is therefore spread across broad pools for the public good. If someone suffers from an accident, they should have resources to address the immediate health-related problems and to maintain their pre-accident standard of living in the longer term.

In contrast, liberalism espouses a deterrence-based market approach to accidents. It is assumed that 'only by requiring those who cause accidents to compensate their victims is it possible to create an incentive structure which will induce firms or individuals to the appropriate safety precautions' (ibid.). Deterrence is not only structured by charging the at-fault party for harms caused, but also by myriad threats and promises aimed at making all participants in the risky behaviour more aware of what appear to be unnecessary risks. Deterrence is additionally structured by having all participants in the insurance relationship – in particular, claimants, health professionals, and lawyers – appreciate that they must reduce their expectations for compensation. The insurance objective is to reverse premium inflation by emphasizing loss prevention and cracking down on claims. The principles of a liberal insurance system for disability are similar to those we described for life insurance in chapter 2. Prudence must be demonstrated with respect to loss prevention efforts and claims, and individuals must embrace more of the risk. If someone suffers from an accident, they should take responsibility for their contribution to it and the need to limit the costs of recovery.

The distinction between a welfarist and liberal model is not coincident with state versus private insurance arrangements. As previously noted, in 1997 the state vehicle insurance systems in four Canadian provinces varied enormously in whiplash claims, from a low of 70/100,000 in Quebec to high of 1,600/100,000 in British Columbia. Similarly, in the private vehicle insurance systems in the United States, in some jurisdictions (e.g., California) insurers experience extraordinarily high rates of whiplash claims, while in other jurisdictions (e.g., Wyoming, North Dakota) the rates are low. Malleson (2002: 26–7) argues that whiplash claims were not prevalent during the heyday of the National Health Service in the United Kingdom. Physicians were paid either a salary or on a patient per capita basis, and therefore had no incentive to promote whiplash-associated disorders. However, in the 1990s the National Health Service faltered and there was an expansion of private health insurance that pays on a per service basis. Whiplash became a lucrative source of work for the private health services and claims multiplied.

These data contradict the common view that disability claims are inevitably greater in welfare state public insurance arrangements compared to liberal state private insurance arrangements. Ironically, the advance of the strong neo-liberal state has fostered some disability claims catastrophes for insurers, because in such regimes significant segments of the population experience loss of socio-economic standing which accentuates psychosomatic disorders.

Private disability insurers we interviewed observed that claims vary substantially by political culture and economic conditions. The regional sales manager for a multinational company said that claims escalate during an economic recession as people lose jobs or have less income to meet their commitments. The stress that results from these conditions can cause serious disabilities, as well as the feigning of disabilities, and it is difficult to separate the two. 'A recession triggers stress, which is a huge claim area for us: mental and nervous disorders, family break-up, drug and alcohol abuse ... higher incidences of abuse of the policy. Your business is failing, you don't have any money. You go to your doctor, you say, "My back is sore." They can't prove it, what am I, the insurer to do? But your key motivation is to get money to pay your creditors ... If we're entering a period of recession, we might have a different rate class for occupations that are sensitive: stockbrokers, real estate agents ... [we might] adjust our rates to reflect the fact.'

Other private disability insurers concurred with this assessment. They gave particular examples of problems they faced with the rightsizing of both state bureaucracies and business enterprises in neo-liberal regimes. The vice-president of a large disability insurance brokerage described two social service agencies that saw their group disability premiums triple because of high claims rates by employees. He said the claims inflation was directly attributable to the state's neo-liberal regime, which had cut back resources for these agencies at a time when they were experiencing greater demands because of rightsizing in all sectors. 'Because they're facing government cutbacks, funding cutbacks, increased utilization, more clients ... mentally handicapped, physically challenged or underprivileged, or children's aid, all these groups are being tested to the maximum ... And they get downsizing in those organizations too because they don't have the budgets anymore. They've had no pay raises in some cases for four, five years. Stress in society, double incomes, chasing the Joneses, trying to make ends meet ... So people are either not coping with it or they don't see a favourable outcome and disability is their last straw so they jump at it.'

The claims manager for another disability insurer said that claims rates were especially high among working women with children. On relatively low employment incomes, this population seeks disability incomes as a temporary relief from work or as the answer to rightsizing. 'Females ... the ones from the east coast especially, I find them more difficult to deal with ... So if the job isn't there any more, or even if the job might be there, the person maybe tends to want to stay at home with their four little children. There isn't much to cause that person to want to go and get better, and they're going to have a bad back.'

These views are consistent with the fact that all types of health and well-being are related to distribution of wealth (Evans et al. 1994; Wilkinson 1996; Sullivan, Stainblum, and Frank 1997). When neoliberal regimes intensify wealth inequality, disadvantaged populations try to restore some equity by turning to insurance resources such as those available in state and private disability insurance systems. An executive with an occupational health and safety research organization observed, 'If you look at the Canada Pension Plan in the last decade, there's been a doubling of people who have long-term disabilities associated with soft tissue injuries. When you pull that apart demographically it turns out to be mainly older middle-aged men ... English-speaking origins, who are also the market casualties in the labour market. So it is one way of insuring. And I'm not trying to be cynical about this. People actually develop disabilities, there's a downward spiral in which if they didn't really have some patho-physiological process before, they're going to have one at the end of this. I think *the* big issue is all these mind-body conditions.'

The important consideration for both state and private insurers is how to manage loss ratios. If premium revenues can be increased substantially and regularly, insurers are of course delighted to receive them and have more scope to be generous with claims. If premiums are restricted – for example, because of competitive markets, regulatory requirements, or local politics – then a stronger emphasis on loss prevention and a crackdown on claims becomes necessary to manage loss ratios. In severe situations, insurers could exclude particular disabilities such as whiplash from their insurance policies. However, this solution is unlikely to be widespread because, as we have seen, insurers attract a large proportion of their vehicle insurance premiums from whiplash and other disability coverage.

Insurers have made many efforts to limit disability claims through public policy and underwriting criteria. There is considerable evidence that such efforts have substantial effects. For example, in Victoria, Australia, changes requiring claimants to report all accidents to the police, and the introduction of a special deductible for medical expenses, led to a dramatic reduction in whiplash claims (Awerbuch 1992). Cassidy and colleagues (2000) document how the change from a tort to no-fault auto insurance system in Saskatchewan in 1995 led to a substantial reduction in whiplash claims, especially with respect to pain and suffering. The Quebec provincial auto insurer claims that its 'no crash, no cash' policy – in other words, material damage to vehicles must be evident in order to process a personal injury claim – accounts in part for its lower rate of whiplash claims compared to other Canadian jurisdictions.

Insurers also manage the uncertainties of disability through micro-negotiation of what constitutes a disability in specific contexts. A work and health research specialist we interviewed said that, like whiplash, work-related back injuries, both bio-mechanical and psychosomatic, are predictable. 'We can predict as well as smoking and cancer ... But there is a bunch of serious insurance problems about how you make rules for what gets compensated for disability or what is considered to be work related. The determination of whether it is work related is all a matter of who says it is. There is no magic independent technology or device that would give you truth on this. So if somebody says it was caused by work, it was caused by work.'

The person at the forefront of this negotiation of causal attribution is the disability claims adjuster. She evaluates the assessments of health professionals who are diagnosing and treating a claimant's disability in terms of the structure and culture of the insurance company. Finnegan (1998: 6), an expert on claims management for vehicle insurers, describes the ways in which a disability claims adjuster handles a whiplash case in relation to the 'simultaneous strong and unconscious influence that corporate culture has on whiplash settlements.' For example, 'When she is having trouble meeting productivity goals or managing a high number of pending claims, she might have "fire sales," making quick settlements for higher than usual amounts. Similarly, her authority level – the amount she can pay without her supervisor's approval – influences her settlements. A surprisingly high percentage of whiplash claims are settled just below adjusters' authority levels. As a result, an adjuster with high average authority levels generally has higher payments than a company with lower levels' (ibid.).

Disability insurance adjusters we interviewed said that they were faced with a 'flavour of the month' problem. By this they meant that new disabilities are invented and magnified by health professionals, lawyers, and claimants in relation to the insurance framework with which they have to deal. The claims adjuster's task is not only to assist the claimant and those who serve him, but also to adjust the insurance definitions of disability to help maintain interinstitutional hegemony. We interviewed a member of a vehicle insurer's special claims team that was trying to adjust the definition of disabilities in this regard. 'We call them the description of the month. You'll hear about fibromyalgia claims ... TMJ, the temporomandibular joint issue where you have an auto accident and it affects your jaw ... Popularity, they're described for awhile and a year later no one is talking about them anymore. We've seen about twenty of those in the past ten years ... We have an insurance company with high liability limits and trends have developed that way.'

A manager of litigated claims for the same company also reviewed various 'popular' diagnoses used in personal injury cases to argue how 'arbitrary' they are and how he had to 'fight' the 'allegations' to protect company interests. For example, the company had about ten times the North American average for brain injury claims. His job was to hire neurologists, psychiatrists, and neuro-psychologists who could counter the experts used by plaintiffs in order to downplay claims of brain injury as a form of depression. He said that claimants 'believe that they have it, they really do ... because they've seen a ton of doctors.' The problem is accentuated among claimants with a history of 'emotional problems' or 'some abuse' who 'magnify and focus on this one incident as being a major cause and problem that they face on a daily basis.' Another special claims team adjuster for the company talked about variation in the ways in which other disabilities are accepted or not. 'The workers' compensation board in our province simply said there's no such thing as carpel tunnel, so you can't claim it. Well then what happened? No claims came in! So in my mind ... do we as an insurance corporation, we as a medical community, and we as a legal community develop these new types of injuries? Like fibromyalgia is a very controversial type thing. Is there such a thing? And you have very experienced doctors on each side who have really good cases for both, so you start to wonder.'

It is clear that all institutional players in the disability insurance relationship – insurers, various health professionals, and lawyers – understand that their collective micro-negotiations constitute the realities of disability. This fact is made starkly evident in the publication of two special issues of *Recovery, A Quarterly Journal on Roadway Causes, Injuries and Healing* (1998, 1999), published by ICBC. The first special issue is entitled 'Truth.' The opening editorial of this special issue declares what the truth is. 'Whiplash consumes more money and probably creates more frustrations over certainty than any other injury on BC's roadways ... [As] all of our authors in their own way suggest, the truth – the ultimate truth – is not knowable ... Perhaps humility in the face of the unknowable is exactly what's needed to enable us, separately and together, to step away from our fixed positions – our bastions of illusion – and communicate more effectively. Genuine dialogue can help us to function a little more practically (and truthfully) and work toward common solutions.'

The second special issue is titled 'The Uncertainty Principle' and opens with an editorial, 'Inexplicable Conditions.' Among the contributors to this special issue is Professor Hillel Sommer of the University of Manitoba, who also served as medical coordinator for Manitoba Public Insurance, the government vehicle insurer. He declares, 'Nowhere else in medicine is there as large a gap between what we think we know and what we can prove as in the area of musculoskeletal disorders' (Sommer 1999: 26). In fact, the gap is a chasm. Although whiplash claims form a multibillion dollar industry, 'There is no population-based study of WAD which provides an estimate of actual risk' (British Columbia Whiplash Initiative 1997: 8). A task force on WAD, established by the Quebec government auto insurer, documented that the voluminous medical literature 'has been polluted by the fashion to publish biographical papers – "what I do in my practice" – that offer no proof of either the reliability, validity or true efficiency of the practice' (Spitzer et al. 1995: 8). Similarly, Malleson, a psychiatrist with decades of experience seeing disability claimants in clinical settings, states in his excellent scholarly book on the subject, '[A]lthough these articles are often published in reputable medical journals, the extensive literature is filled with scientifically spurious studies. One misleading study after another shows how doctors and lawyers managed to finesse whiplash from a trifling injury into a permanent disability that keeps both doctors and lawyers gainfully employed. One Danish doctor, for example, titled his medical journal article, "With Whiplash, the Future Comes from Behind" [Durr 1994] ... Much medical whiplash literature is like medieval scholasticism. It matters more that a recognized authority has affirmed something to be true than that it actually is' (Malleson 2002: 5, 109).

The Quebec Task Force reviewed 10,382 medical publications and concluded that only sixty-two were of scientific merit. The few controlled studies with scientific rigour indicate that the rate of abnormal findings of whiplash claimants is the same as that found in non-claimant populations. The Quebec Task Force concluded that 'on the topic of whiplash, there is no decent epidemiology, nothing written on diagnosis, and barely any treatment discussed works' (Spitzer et al. 1995: 8).

Medical practitioners are evidently in a weak knowledge position in relation to neck and back injuries. The isolation of bio-mechanical causes of neck and back pain is rare: subjective complaints stand alone in 97 per cent or more of cases (Nachemson 1994; Frank et al. 1995). Insurers can seek interinstitutional hegemony over the definition, diagnosis, and treatment of disability not only because they control the money to pay insurance claims, but also because of the weakness of knowledge claims by health professionals. '[P]rofessions' classifications for diagnosis and treatment always leave considerable residual areas, filled with cases that are neither standard problems nor effectively classifiable along the various dimensions of professional knowledge. Since a profession exercises its weakest subjective jurisdiction over such cases, they should be the most easily poachable. But residuality is not the only aspect of subjective jurisdictional strength. Successful outcome, acceptability of treatments, and legitimization of cultural knowledge are all important' (Abbott 1988: 251).

Faced with the weakness of their knowledge claims, health practitioners must rely on their professional authority to declare that something is true. One context in which they make such declarations is expert panels that reach a consensus on classifications, diagnoses, and treatments. However, such contexts for expressing authoritative certainty pose contradictions. In particular, while expert panels are fully aware of the subjective nature of their enterprise and the way in which it must fit the practical exigencies of insurance, medical, and legal criteria, they nevertheless continue to represent their authority in scientific terms.

An example of this contradiction is found in the work of the Quebec Task Force. Having demonstrated the unscientific nature of the medical literature, the Quebec Task Force was still left with its mandate of developing guidelines for clinicians to diagnose and treat WAD. In order to pursue this mandate the expert panel had to forge a consensus, at least among themselves, on the state of existing knowledge. In doing so they provided a practical exemplification of Rorty's (1991) view that objectivity is consensus that is coerced. Ironically, like the researchers they criticized, the expert panel was compelled to use an approach that lacked methodological rigour yet conveyed a sense of scientific certainty and legitimacy. This irony is addressed by two professors of physical medicine and rehabilitation.

> Although studies were rejected based on rigorous scientific criteria, the consensus guidelines were adopted and promoted without the same rigor. The danger with such consensus guidelines is that, because they accompany an exhaustive best-evidence evaluation of treatments, they have acquired a false air of scientific truth.
>
> Thus the QTF's consensus guidelines were based on (in our view) flawed conclusions drawn from the QTF's cohort study regarding the natural history of whiplash injuries. The resulting classification scheme, WAD 0-IV, is therefore arbitrary, since there is little or no supporting evidence apart from the cohort studies conclusions.
>
> We believe that WAD management guidelines offered by the QTF are likely to create a false expectation that whiplash patients generally should do far better than they actually do. If this conclusion is not viewed critically, there is potential for misapplication of the guidelines by third parties in whiplash claims. We also find it disconcerting that a government no-fault insurance carrier funded these guidelines, and their wholesale adoption by the insurance industry as 'evidence-based' can be seen as particularly self-serving. (Teasell and Merskey 1999: 10)

We interviewed a research analyst for a vehicle insurer about his company's use of the Quebec Task Force WAD classification scheme and guidelines. He was fully conversant with the state of medical knowledge in this field and said that the Quebec expert panel only confirmed what insurers already faced in their everyday decisions: WAD is based on the subjective complaint of the injured claimant, as interpreted and framed by the lawyers and health professionals who make the case on the claimant's behalf. 'There are *no* proofs in there ... [The QTF] does not have *any* answers ... [It] does not produce recommendations that are based on some kind of factual analysis, or quantitative study ... [It is a] perpetuation of a model that is not as well founded as it should be ... [and simply] points to the lack of quantitative knowledge ... And that's very difficult to come by because basically you keep coming up again and again at the fact that the only site of soft tissue type injuries is the complaint of the individual who has it, so it's a very subjective area.'

Insurance compels experts to turn the subjective into the objective for the practical purpose of deciding whether, how, and how much to compensate a claimant. Objectivity is a warrant for action.

Physical medicine experts who diagnose and treat WAD do not operate with a consistent sense of what constitutes the 'normal.' As a physical medicine research and policy official told us in interview, the field of WAD diagnosis and treatment often lacks 'normalcy informa-tion ... what do we mean by normal function?' 'Normalcy' shifts according to the vagaries of the legal, political, cultural, and insurance system contexts within which physical medicine experts operate. Indeed, the field not only lacks a consistent sense of what is normal, it also lacks a consistent sense of what WAD is. 'Inconsistent definitions, descriptions and classifications used in reports of WAD and in com-mon clinical use make it impossible to compare and synthesize the findings of published studies' (Spitzer et al. 1995: 34). Such inconsis-tency is inevitable when WAD is largely invisible except for the verbal articulation of complainants.

The attributed causes of WAD are so multifactoral that it is impossi-ble to isolate and treat an identifiable cause. In one account, '"the sources of patient behaviour seem to be linked to psycho-affective development (personality), family background (modelling, operant conditioning), interpersonal dynamic state (couple in particular, family and relation with caregiver), social and medical support system (iatro-genic, social welfare system), gender (different meaning) and cultural influences (e.g., the expression of pain in various cultures)"' (Spitzer et al. 1995, cited in British Columbia Whiplash Initiative 1997: 38). This mosaic of factors leads Munglani (1999: 14) to state that WAD should not be considered 'a diagnosis in itself, but a symptom complex with multiple causes. The fact that so many possible factors can contribute to chronic pain also suggests that no single therapy is likely to be suc-cessful for all patients. Randomized controlled trials of single therapies are therefore unlikely to show significant results.' As Hacking (1990: 86) observes about the general problem of moving from multifactoral data on risk to the individual case, 'In practical medicine the facts are too few to enter into the calculus of probabilities *not* because we cannot get more data, but because obtaining more data about different indi-viduals is irrelevant to the particular case of the patient we wish to treat.'

As suggested in the reference above to the 'social and medical support system' as one of the sources of WAD, medical intervention itself has 'looping effects' (Hacking 1986, 1990). The rage to invent medical technologies sends practitioners in search of uses. Once in use a technology quickly becomes a normal part of medical procedures, including the insurance compensation of them. In the case of WAD procedures, '[t]echnology often goes through a trendy "fad phase" and is not always subjected to rigorous evaluation before it becomes widespread. The price paid by society for such shortcomings is aggravated by procedure-oriented fee-for-service reimbursement schemes that reward "doing" much more than thinking. Once such practices become part of the mainstream of clinical practice, it becomes very difficult to evaluate them because of legitimate ethical concerns about withholding accepted interventions from patients who might need them' (Spitzer et al. 1995: 10).

One pervasive technology used in whiplash treatment is drugs, which are often dispensed with no accepted knowledge of their effectiveness. 'Although oral medications such as painkillers and muscle relaxants are commonly used as part of the overall management of whiplash-associated disorders (WAD), no peer-reviewed studies of the effectiveness of these drugs have ever been published ... The QTF recommendations are fairly straightforward, but unfortunately they do not give the clinician any guidance about which agent to choose, what doses to prescribe and how long to treat' (McCormack 1999: 24).

We interviewed a personal injury adjuster for a vehicle insurance company whose experience led him to conclude that the dispensing of drugs and other therapies do have two known effects. The first is a looping effect that confirms people in their disabled identity. The second is a system effect that compensates health professionals for services of unknown benefits. 'The doctors mask these peoples' pains by medicines, therapies. People don't really know how bad they are, or how good they are, if they keep on going to these things ... "I believe that they are professionals, I trust you, so whatever you say I will do." And I think, unfortunately, doctors do take advantage of that, and the system.'

Workers' compensation insurers address the same uncertainties regarding spinal injuries. For example, back pain affects 80 per cent of adults at some point in their lives (Sullivan, Stainblum, and Frank 1997: 20). 'In the United States, it is the second most common reason for work absenteeism [and] the third leading cause of total work dis-

ability' (ibid.). The rate of low back pain is increasing substantially, yet
the etiology is uncertain. Typically there are

> no specific diagnoses, no constellation of reliable physical signs (i.e. objec-
> tive evidence of injury), and up until recently, little consensus on appro-
> priate care ... Back pain falls somewhere between an accident, injury and
> disease ... The absence of a specific causal event and the emphasis placed
> by adjudicators on 'objective' physical evidence of disease, often stands in
> the way of compensation, particularly with respect to soft tissue injuries
> ... [It is] multifactoral in origin ... and therefore the search for a specific,
> precipitating event may be fruitless in the majority of cases ... Dissatisfac-
> tion with job status, performance of repetitive, monotonous tasks and
> self-reported fatigue at the end of the day have also been associated with
> greater disability and absenteeism due to back pain. (ibid.: 20-1, 23; see
> also Sullivan 2000)

The history of workers' compensation is characterized by an increasing variety of disabilities that are invisible. Compensation schemes
were started largely in relation to visible physical injuries, but then
spread to soft tissue injuries, stress, and environmental exposures. As
the director of compensation services for a workers' compensation
board said in interview, 'the Board is challenged ever more to sort out
between "If I'm really not just feeling great, is it because my work is
not making me feel great? My boss? My relationship? Or the building?"' A claims department executive for a private disability insurer
said in interview that her company experienced the same challenge.
With a wider range of justifications for disability, claimants will use the
one that works in the situation, and are routinely backed up by health
professionals in doing so.

> What we see on our claims is somebody who's got a physical problem,
> maybe a back or something, if they're not covered by an insurance policy
> because it's pre-existing or something then they submit a stress claim.
> And the doctor will actually write in there, 'Stress due to the fact that the
> insurance company will not pay their claim!' That's a trend in the indus-
> try, and how do you deal with it? ... [We need] objective information [but]
> the line is moving ... At one time it was, 'Oh, that's silly, just get on with it
> dear.' Right? So that's where the line is moving. But as the line moves, we
> have to try and define that edge all the time ... We've seen more and more
> stress, burnout situations in the last few years as industry and bureau-
> cracy have downsized.

One reference for health practitioners in the workers' compensation field is the American Medical Association's *Guides to the Evaluation of Permanent Impairment* (fourth edition, 1993). This manual includes an introductory section, 'Are the Guides Criteria Objective and Authoritative?' (3). It proceeds by stating that there are many areas in which objective data are not available to calculate functional impairment and, therefore, standards must be set by consensual opinion among experts. Again, 'convincing' estimates are based on medical authority, not objective science. This is the only possibility because of uncertain knowledge, the looping effects of medical practice, and variability in interpretation throughout the medical estimation process.

> If the *Guides* contributors have been unable to identify objective data on the normal functioning of an organ system, they have estimated the extent of impairments on the basis of clinical experience, judgment and consensus.
>
> The estimates of the well qualified persons contributing to this book, most of them physicians, would be more convincing than those of most others in estimating the severity of people's impairments. It should be noted that the *Guides* does not and cannot provide answers about every type and degree of impairment, because of the considerations noted above and the infinite variety of human disease, and because the field of medicine and medical practice is characterized by constant change in understanding disease and its manifestations, diagnosis and treatment. Further, human functioning in everyday life is a highly dynamic process, one that presents a great challenge to those attempting to evaluate impairment.
>
> The physician's judgment and his or her experience, training, skill, and thoroughness in examining the patient and applying the findings to *Guides* criteria will be factors in estimating the degree of the patient's impairment. These attributes compose part of the 'art' of medicine, which, together with a foundation in science, constitute the essence of medical practice. The evaluation should understand that other considerations will also apply, such as the sensitivity, accuracy, reproducibility, and interpretation of laboratory tests and clinical procedures, and variability among observers' interpretation of the tests and procedures. (3)

The variable character of the calculus pointed to in this statement is evident throughout the AMA manual, and in comparing successive editions of it. For example, in a section on the valuation of psychiatric impairment (300*ff.*), four categories of functional limitation are identified. A five-point scale of impairment is constituted for each category, even though 'there is no specific medical test for any one of the categories' and 'current research finds little relationship between psychiatric signs and symptoms such as those identified during a mental status examination, and the ability to perform competitive work.'

The manual proceeds to indicate that percentage figures were used to calculate mental impairment in the second edition, but were dropped for subsequent editions because the Committee on Disability and Rehabilitation of the American Psychiatric Association advised *Guides'* contributors against the use of percentages in light of the fact that 'there are no precise measures of impairment in mental disorders' and 'the use of percentages implies a certainty that does not exist' (301). Moreover, efforts to express authoritative certainty about percentage calculations of mental impairment are too vulnerable to challenge in administrative hearings, and therefore pose a threat to professional credibility (ibid.).

The manual notes that removing the percentage calculation of mental impairment was an extraordinary step, since the sole purpose of the manual is to provide a basis for calculation of disability insurance claims. The use of the percentage calculation 'would be consistent with the *Guides* chapters for the other organ systems ... [V]arious systems for estimating disability have developed ranges of percentages ... If such estimates were not provided ... the material in the *Guides* on mental disorder might be ignored. This would increase the likelihood that estimates would be made inconsistently in the various jurisdictions' (301).

What is perhaps more extraordinary is the fact that many other impairments, and the subjective pain associated with them, are nevertheless subject to the apparent precision of percentage calculations. As we saw in the case of WAD, it is well established by the medical profession and by the insurance industry that they are not dealing with accepted scientific knowledge and the degree of certainty such knowledge promises. They operate on uncertainty. Nevertheless spinal injuries and associated disorders are subject to the counting practices of medical specialists of the invisible, while mental disorders are not, for fear of loss of professional credibility.

Legal practitioners also generate uncertainty in the disability insurance system. Just as medical practitioners are iatrogenic in amplifying the disability health care system, so legal practitioners are 'nomogenic' (Tyndel and Egit 1988) in amplifying the disability litigation system. Legal practitioners actively contribute to the creation of medical classifications, the legitimation of treatments, and the building of costly insurance claims. Thus, the way in which lawyers interact with the local medical and insurance cultures has a significant bearing on variability in rates of disability across jurisdictions.

We interviewed the manager of a special investigation team that was established by a vehicle insurer to reduce personal injury claims costs. In his view, the nomogenic effect of legal practice in personal injury cases is greater than the iatrogenic effect of medical practice. 'The lawyers certainly, most of them are a hindrance to their own client. They will propose, they'll say, "*This* is what you've got, and *this* is what it is worth, but to get it to be worth that you have got to be off work for six weeks. And you'd better go to the physiotherapist for ten weeks. And you'd better do this and this." And then in the psychology part, I would think that with claimants it is, "OK, I want to get this money, I'd better make sure it's worse." ... And then they get worse ... they're not going to get better because it's, "OK, I'm greedy, I want more money, to get there I have to do *this*."'

An insurance claims control expert with experience in many jurisdictions said that claims inflation for minor injuries was perpetuated by the legal system. She was hired by the attorney general's office in an American state jurisdiction to audit the claims of the top ten vehicle insurance companies operating in the jurisdiction.

> Eighty-five per cent of our whiplashes were third party ... All the whiplashes claimed on first party were major accidents ... [for which] the average number of treatments was three. The third party ... [was] running thirty or something ... We looked at the average cost per treatment; it's 50 per cent higher. We multiplied that out and we concluded 94 per cent of whiplash was 'tort somatic.' The tort system generated it. My number for British Columbia might be 97 per cent ... There *is* such a thing as whiplash, you can get it, but while all objective injuries are going down, whiplash has gone zooming up. The level of treatment has no medical basis whatsoever ... I mean is this *organized* fraud? ... Whiplash basically is the brain, there can be endless complications with it ... [This is] a multibillion dollar industry ... with no scientific basis at all ... [But] by and large I don't call that fraud because I think it is organized [systemic] I think people get [socialized] into it, I think it's *promoted* in a wide variety of ways. [After mentioning professionals advertising for disability clients during televised soap operas.] Anybody who needs to invent injuries to get the money has to make them.

A leading personal injury lawyer we interviewed was explicit in stating that he did indeed socialize clients into their disabilities for insurance claims purposes. In his view disability is an insurance-based category used to settle claims. As such it requires lawyers to fit clients to the category in order to achieve a just and justifiable outcome. He said that his 'brain injury' clients in particular are typically unaware of the ramifications of their condition, and thus benefit from his expertise in finding medical formulations that also meet legal requirements for lucrative and just settlements. 'So when I meet some of these people and I say, "How are you?" they say, "Oh I'm fine." "Any problems?" "No." ... If anything my clients underestimate or don't even recognize that they've got problems.'

In practice, lawyers do more than fit their clients into medical categories. Along with insurers and health practitioners, they create medical categories as well as the parameters of treatment and other forms of compensation. Malleson (2002: 211) documents how lawyers have successfully used the term 'post-traumatic' to advance the view that anything following an accident can be attributed to the accident. 'Plaintiff experts use it liberally – post-traumatic headache, post-traumatic depression, post-traumatic anxiety, post-traumatic fibromyalgia, post-traumatic neurosis. One Toronto psychiatrist, who makes a specialty of plaintiff whiplash reports, managed on one occasion to put ten different post-traumatic conditions in the same report' (ibid.). Currently, lawyers are quick to refer whiplash claimants to a psychologist and psychiatrist for a 'post-traumatic stress disorder' determination, and to a rheumatologist for certification of post-traumatic fibromyalgia.

The legal community is of course critically aware of its contribution to the enterprise. For example, Stone (1993) remarks that post-traumatic stress disorder has had the most pervasive influence on law and social justice of any diagnosis in the history of American psychiatry. This impact includes a 'cottage industry' for lawyers and health professionals. Referring to fibromyalgia, Madame Justice Rowlins of the Alberta Court of Queen's Bench concluded in *Mackie v. Wolfe* (1994) that this diagnosis is driven more by the litigation system than the health care system:

> The evidence here convinces me that the medical profession itself would not say that fibromyalgia, on the balance of probabilities, exists, much less is causally related to a motor vehicle accident. I am satisfied that fibromyalgia has become a court-driven ailment that has mushroomed into big

business for plaintiffs, particularly in British Columbia and Saskatchewan ... The evidence in this case satisfies me that the symptoms diagnosed as fibromyalgia are a relabelling of a condition by rheumatologists that has been with mankind for hundreds of years and represents a personality disorder. This particular disorder is often found in individuals who will not or cannot cope with everyday stresses of life and convert this inability into acceptable physical symptoms to avoid dealing with reality. (Quoted in Malleson 2002: 190; see Malleson chapter 13 for an analysis of this case.)

Ironically, Justice Rowlins used an alternative clinical diagnosis of 'personality disorder' to dismiss the diagnosis of 'fibromyalgia.' In doing so she further evidences the way in which medical and legal discourses are entwined in the ongoing negotiation of disability.

Legal practitioners move with scientific fashion, even when it is deemed 'junk science' (Huber 1991). They use medical experts to express authoritative certainty about what appears to be the case. Diagnoses that will work in a local medical, legal, and insurance context are advanced in the interest of claimant and professional compensation. Aggregate analysis of how what works varies within and across jurisdictions reveals the local practices involved. For example, we interviewed a fraudulant claims data analyst who undertook 'vulnerability assessments' for his insurance company clients. He compared claims costs across North American jurisdictions to reveal outliers and therefore potential sources of claims building and fraud. He referred to one insurance company that was the 'North American champion' in whiplash claims, and that was ten times the industry average on the specific diagnosis of brain injury. His quantitative analyses for this insurance company revealed an extremely high ratio of bodily injury to material damage claims, 'whereas the number of fatalities and objective injuries is very low. So anything you can see, it appears to be a fairly safe place, anything you can't see is very bad ... Subtle brain trauma ... you bang your head ... ten times the North American average ... Subtle brain injury is the whiplash of high limit insurance policies ... This corporation has got an 80 per cent chance of $1 million or more liability limit ... So rather than your neck hurting, it turns out your brains are scrambled, and you go for $1 million ... Absolutely organized around a limited number of law firms ... Are they well representing their clients or is it fraud?'

A perusal of professional magazines for lawyers, or of continuing education programs offered through bar associations, reveals the avail-

Table 3.2
Insurance Corporation of British Columbia Expenses, 1995

Expense	$M	%
Personal injury payments to claimants	945	38
Material damage payments to claimants	722	29
Direct and claims processing costs	298	12
Cost of legal services	223	9
Insurance operations	186	7
Premium tax	90	4
Other operations, including road safety	42	2
TOTAL	2,506	100

ability of constant training in the latest medical categories that are proving worthwhile for disability litigation. Malleson (2002: 255) cites a promotional brochure aimed at lawyers by Integrity Seminars Inc. of Eagles, Idaho. Entitled 'The Permanency of Whiplash,' the brochure promises training about 'plastic vs. elastic deformation, law of conservation of linear momentum, magnification of acceleration, and the effect of seatbelts and head restraints ... You will learn how soft tissue and closed head injuries occur, why over 50 per cent suffer a permanent impairment, and how to prove damages. The common myth that "minor vehicle accident damage means inconsequential injury" is completely refuted. Twenty-one checkpoints to determine a mild head injury are examined.'

The cost of legal services in the personal injury field is a major contributor to the magnitude of insurance premiums. Weintraub (1995) reports that chronic pain medical services and loss of employment or business opportunity costs account for 80 per cent of the awards from all lawsuits in the United States. Comparative studies across jurisdictions document that the higher the rate of legal representation in personal injury cases, the higher the claims costs (Insurance Research Council Inc. 1994, quoted by Malleson 2002: 260)

Table 3.2 documents that in 1995, ICBC's total expenses were $2.506 billion (Insurance Corporation of British Columbia 1996: 38). The largest single expense was $945 million for personal injury payments to claimants, followed by $722 million for material damage to vehicle payments to claimants. The cost of legal services was $223 million, and 'virtually all of the cost for legal services is attributable to personal injury claims' (ibid.: 38–9). The $223 million for legal services breaks down as follows. The legal bills of plaintiffs consumed $146 million (35 per cent of plaintiffs retained lawyers, who were paid out of the plaintiffs' settlements in accordance with negotiated agreements). Another $53 million went to legal counsel hired by ICBC to defend claims settlements, while $17 million was paid to legal services (e.g., expert reports, independent adjusters, private investigators) and $7 million to in-house counsel.

Spreading Risk

Given that disabilities arising from spinal injury are based on such limited and contested knowledge claims, the key question is how insurance is organized to spread disability risks. Workers' compensation insurance was developed to spread disability risks across broad pools to protect both parties in the employment relationship. Employees are protected from the effects of work-related injuries that threaten their livelihood and socio-economic standing. Employers are protected from costly litigation that is likely to arise in each case of serious injury without a workers' compensation scheme. Such litigation would pose constant uncertainty and in many cases threaten the viability of a business.

In Canada, the workers' compensation insurance system developed as a strong state responsibility in order to ensure the spreading of risk across broad pools. The responsibility is to promote solidarity among populations of workers in diverse employment situations and industries, and therefore among the state's population as a whole. The response ability is a welfare system that tries to ensure that everyone has sufficient health and well-being to work according to their productive capacities. Based on this ethos, workers' compensation coverage is generally provided on a group insurance basis paid for by employers. Where employers are involved in business enterprise, they in turn embed the cost of insurance in the price of the products they produce and sell. As a result, all consumers pay in effect a hidden sales tax for insurance covering the myriad workers who have produced and distributed the item they are purchasing. When such a system is functioning well, the state, employers, and insurers take risks on behalf of employee security, solidarity, and welfare.

Personal injury vehicle insurance was also developed to spread risks across very broad pools. All persons involved in a traffic accident are to be protected from the effects of personal injury that threaten their livelihoods and socio-economic standing. Where, in the eyes of government, private insurers cannot form adequate markets (e.g., in Canada, the provinces of British Columbia, Saskatchewan, Manitoba, and Quebec), the state forms its own vehicle insurance corporation to ensure broad pooling of risk and equitable rating criteria. Where private insurers do form an adequate market, the state is heavily involved in regulating the market. This involvement stems from the fact that vehicle insurance is made compulsory by the state precisely because of its risk-spreading properties for the overall health and well-being of the population. It is also justified on other solidaristic principles, including fair underwriting criteria and the need to provide special arrangements for high risk drivers and for victims of accidents involving uninsured drivers (for more detail, see Ericson, Doyle, and Barry 2003: chap. 7). When such systems are functioning well, it is the state and insurers who take risk on behalf of driver security, solidarity, and welfare.

In practice, disability insurance has proven difficult to underwrite because of the limits to knowledge and iatrogenic and nomogenic aspects of the medical and legal systems. Many private insurers have moved into disability markets with little or no experience in the field, experienced enormous problems with adverse selection and extraordinary claims, and been forced to leave the business with significant losses. In some markets – for example, workers' compensation in the United States – state governments have increased their role in insurance provision in response to such problems. The state becomes the insurer, at least as long as it takes to foster conditions to bring private insurers back into the market. Of course, the state can also experience great difficulty in managing loss ratios and spreading risk. The effort to raise premiums in tandem with high claims experience proves to be finite in political culture, as citizens resist further involuntary contributions to the broad pool and solidarity begins to splinter.

The uncertainties of disability mean that risks are often underwritten with a high degree of speculation. Lack of investment in underwriting investigations, and lack of control over iatrogenic and nomogenic system effects even when such investigations occur, leads to adverse selection, whereby those with a propensity to the disability being insured are more likely to want and acquire insurance. It also leads to related moral risks at the level of the insured, who may benefit as much or more from disability claims than from working. These circumstances have led to cases where there have been massive underwriting shortfalls and consequent financial crises for insurers. The chief actuary for a large underwriter of vehicle insurance described the problem at the level of claims management. 'The adjuster sees the injury on day one, it's in the leg, it's worth about $400,000 so you have to have $400,000 of reserve. Another month or two goes by, he is out of the hospital and it is not just a lost leg, something else has gone wrong as well and suddenly it becomes $1 million, and then some wise-guy lawyer gets involved and you have suddenly got a $2 million claim. And all that takes time, so claims grow, just as the claims numbers grow, the dollars grow even more rapidly and more and more dynamically and there's enormous variability in the dollars, shoot up and down all over the place.'

In the jurisdiction in which this company operated, the number of private disability insurance carriers had decreased from a high of thirteen to only five. Those that ceased operations in the jurisdiction had failed to underwrite disability insurance with enough stringency and ran into financial difficulties with excessive claims. An agent for a large disability insurance company informed us in interview that these departed companies had suffered heavy losses as a result of underwriting problematic illnesses such as fibromyalgia, stress, and chronic fatigue. He observed that it is extremely difficult to 'cement the claims' and thereby control loss ratios in relation to these illnesses.

The regional sales manager for a multinational disability insurer confirmed this point and said it signified a more general consolidation in private disability insurance markets internationally. He said that with his company in the United States in the 1980s, 'You could get $6,000 a month [income replacement coverage for a disability] without any income documentation! So we didn't know whether you were lying to us or not.' He went on to say that his company and the two other largest disability insurance carriers at the time 'all took our entire 1980s block of business and had to write it off.' In the case of his company, the write-off was $423 million pre-tax dollars in 1991 and 1992. Some other companies even offered to pay his company a 'premium' to take over some of their business. His company accepted some of these offers because it wanted to stay in the disability insurance field and the additional business would 'broaden our base of premiums and spread our risk out further.' In the late 1990s his company controlled 37 per cent of the individual disability insurance private market in the United States 'which is unheard of in a time where there's increased competition for insurance, for financial services ... The government has seen the same volatility too, it's a tough risk to manage.' He said that because of his company's expertise in disability insurance underwriting, it had many clients among large insurance companies that did not know how to underwrite disability coverage for their own employees.

Industry consolidation has been accompanied by several developments that tighten disability insurance coverage. These developments include more employers using alternative forms of insurance and greater control procedures over their private workers' compensation and group plans; more stringent underwriting, especially on individual policies; more stringent claims management; and the unpooling of risks by profession, socio-economic position, and other status criteria.

Group disability insurance is generally easier to underwrite. First, a sizeable group allows for more predictable claims experience and less possibility of adverse selection and associated moral risks. Second, group disability carriers can pool all of their premiums across groups, which further enhances predictable claims experience. Third, contracts are for a limited period, usually one year, so they can be renegotiated in the context of changing definitions of disability, claims service costs, premiums needed to improve loss ratios, and so on. In contrast individual contracts are usually bound and guaranteed for decades, leaving insurers exposed to the changing cultural, legal, medical, and political environments of disability. Therefore, according to our interviewees, private disability insurance became much more stringently underwritten over the 1990s, with restriction of eligibility to more serious and specifiable conditions. While group insurance contracts are more likely to be regulated regarding questions of fairness and discrimination, individual contracts may also exclude morbidity risks such as a medical history of back pain, complications arising from pregnancy, and mental or nervous disorders. For example, the regional sales manager of a large disability insurer in Canada said, 'We practise very sophisticated risk segmentation. We may have provinces that we put a specific exclusion or limitation of mental and nervous claims because they are higher, whereas other provinces you could obtain those standards [you need to underwrite profitably].'

As always, there is differentiation in underwriting for policyholders who are willing to pay higher premiums as a contribution to their insurer's loss ratio security. Higher status professional and wealthy clients can pay for favourable contract conditions that are unavailable to the less well ranked and well off. A leading disability insurance company we studied specialized in professional markets, for example, health professionals and lawyers. A sales agent who sold this company's products told us in interview that these professional clients had an 'own occupation' clause in their disability insurance contracts which allowed them to collect long-term disability payments even though they had moved to a new occupation. He gave the example of a client who had been a child psychologist and received disability payments for stress. This person eventually returned to work as an adult psychologist but continued to collect his disability payments on top of his salary.

Solidarity

The responsibility of disability insurance is to provide solidarity across broad pools of insured. When people suffer personal injury accidents, insurance premium contributions by all participants in the pool are to provide the resource base for health care and to remedy employment or business interruption losses that might lessen the accident victim's standard of living. Responsibility for solidarity is exemplified in the way spinal injuries and associated disorders have been addressed in various workers' compensation and vehicle insurance systems. Even when adequate professional knowledge is limited or absent, the insurance system remains sympathetic to subjective complaints of injury and provides generous compensation.

The enormous variation in rates of spinal injury claims and compensation across jurisdictions indicates that solidarity is relative. Some insurance regimes are exceptionally sympathetic to the culture of spinal injury claims on the principle that accident victims must be helped on their own terms. Fallibility rests with the institutions involved and, if anything, this fallibility should increase empathy for accident victims. Other insurance regimes are exceptionally unsympathetic to the culture of spinal injury claims on the principle that victims of accidents too often help themselves to resources in excess of what their circumstances require. Fallibility rests with the individuals involved and, if anything, this fallibility should increase the responsibility of accident victims to both contribute to their recovery and ensure that they make greater effort to prevent accidents in the future.

In these latter jurisdictions, solidarity breaks down as insurers try to force the insured to embrace more risk. Underwriting criteria become more selective and exclusive according to ability to pay. Instead of risk spreading there is risk unpooling into specialized insurance market segments, as well as depooling from the availability of any insurance. In vehicle insurance, for example, the unpooled pay extraordinarily high premium rates and receive very unfavourable contract conditions, while the depooled take the risk of driving without insurance (Ericson, Doyle, and Barry 2003: chap. 7). In Ontario, it is estimated that 10 to 15 per cent of all drivers, or about one million people on the roads, drive without insurance. In addition to the potential personal liability they face, this significant portion of the Ontario population is engaged in the criminal offence of driving without insurance on a daily basis. The government response is to punish this depooled population. 'In Ontario the government has just introduced fines of up to $50,000 for driving without insurance coverage, fines intended to discourage the million Ontario drivers who now either cannot afford their sizable premiums, or who optimistically hope to get by without paying. The whiplash lottery may be fun, but not, I expect, at the cost of no longer being able to afford to keep the family car on the road' (Malleson 2002: 264).

Many insurance regimes have broken up solidarity through efforts to transfer more of the risk to the insured and thereby protect their loss ratios. This trend is evident in changes to workers' compensation programs, especially in the United States (McClusky 2002). It is also evident in changes to vehicle insurance regimes in Canada, from which the following examples are drawn.

Faced with growing threats to loss ratios, vehicle insurers have eroded solidaristic features of their disability coverage and advanced the view that policyholders must take more individual responsibility for accident prevention and recovery. On the level of political culture, they attack what they call 'social inflation' as the cause of excessive disability claims. Social inflation refers to a culture of increasingly high expectations regarding both what insurers should compensate and what their responsibility should be for loss prevention. Social inflation is to be checked through measures that in effect blame the disabled victim and bring about her behaviour modification: more stringent insurance contract provisions, including loss prevention responsibilities, as well as an enforcement crackdown on exaggerated claims. Social inflation is also to be checked by mobilizing health service professionals in the loss prevention effort, and by cracking down on their contributions to exaggerated insurance claims. The problem of social inflation is said to be located not only in the culture of expectations among disabled claimants, but even more so among the health care professionals who are gatekeepers of disability. They are seen to often shut the gate behind those who have entered the system, and sometimes even lock it. Thus the Physical Medicine Research Foundation, funded by ICBC, makes the following declaration in its promotional mission document:

> The Canadian Centre for Occupational Health and Safety recently reported that the total cost of muscle and joint injuries in Canada has climbed to some eight billion dollars annually. This cost to our society extends beyond the financial aspect to the enormous losses in human terms. Consider the immense welfare and worker's compensation payments made just to people permanently disabled by back pain. Rather than helping people return to normal function, these payouts may be perpetuating their lives of miserable pain ... This lack of sharing, cooperation and coordination in the health care field has served to compound the problems, increasing the medical costs and the pain for millions of people.

A consultant's report to ICBC sets the terms of the issue in order to justify deterrence measures that are deflationary. 'We have noted that insurance costs have risen at an average rate of approximately 8 percent per year over the last several years. If the level of real inflation as measured by the Consumer Price Index (CPI) is 2 percent, the remaining 6 percent may be attributed to social inflation. Our goal (assuming no product change) would be to cut that social inflation by 50 percent over the next five years' (Insurance Corporation of British Columbia 1997a: 21).

The first manoeuvre in this process was to say that the social deflation initiative was simply carrying out the wishes of the people. Public surveys were conducted to show that the people are indeed strong on law and order approaches to disability insurance claims control. 'According to the public, the highest-rated feature of a motor-vehicle insurance system should be the ability to penalize reckless and at-fault drivers in order to prevent traffic accidents and injuries. The second highest-rated feature of a motor vehicle insurance system is seen to be guarding against fraud and misrepresentation. ICBC estimates that motor vehicle crime cost policyholders $134 million in 1995. In addition, fraudulent and exaggerated claims exceeded $150 million annually' (Insurance Corporation of British Columbia 1996: 49).

So construed, the public will can only lead in the direction of a breakdown in solidarity. The same survey evidence was invoked under the title of 'The Public Will' to declare that the new 'social responsibility' is to intensify surveillance and deterrence-based law enforcement in order to secure social deflation (Insurance Corporation of British Columbia 1997a: 3).

The report dramatized loss from traffic accidents. The first manoeuvre was to enforce a definition of accidents as 'crashes' to suggest that they are not accidents at all but attributable to a responsible party who acted intentionally, or at least negligently. The second tactic was to produce data to argue that about 90 per cent of all crashes are attributable to driver responsibility as opposed to vehicle standards, road engineering, road conditions, and so on. The third move was to say that traffic accidents cause more deaths and serious injury than crimes of violence in the Criminal Code. Indeed, many traffic accidents are the result of actual criminal violations: 'drinking drivers cost British Columbians about $358 million' annually (ibid.: 40); 'inappropriate speed and dangerous driving cost British Columbians approximately $604 million each year' (ibid.: 49). The fourth manoeuvre was to associate whiplash with the other 'criminal' dangers, and thereby justify its inclusion in efforts to carry out the public will through law enforcement crackdowns. In a table that attributes annual claims costs, the following are listed: whiplash $630 million, speed and dangerous driving $604 million, impaired driving $358 million, auto crime (theft of and from vehicles) $134 million, and road design/operation $134 million (ibid.: 6). The contextualization of whiplash with these other criminal sources of danger suggests or implies that it too might be a 'crime' perpetuated by claimants and professionals who inflate service fees and benefits.

This dramatization was transferred from the research studies and consultants reports into various forms of social advertising. For example, a brochure entitled 'The BI Story: Why Bodily Injury Costs So Much' was produced for distribution through insurance sales agents' offices as well as other public sources. This brochure explains the extent of whiplash claims and the limitations of knowledge about diagnosis, treatment, and financial management. It points to the moral risks posed by health service professionals: 'The number of visits to chiropractors, physiotherapists and massage therapists has increased on average 22 percent for each of the last six years. Compare this to an 8 percent increase in injury claims overall ... We are working on reducing medical costs by increasing our billing system controls. Plus, we are limiting the cost and reducing the number of doctors' and therapists' reports.' The brochure also declares a crackdown on claimants as a source of social inflation: 'where there has been minimal or no damage to the vehicle, we may refuse payment of an injury claim. We will resist any attempt to manufacture whiplash claims from minor traffic mishaps.'

In various documents, the success of a campaign in Victoria, Australia, was used to show that fatalities and personal injuries can be reduced through a combination of social advertising, extended surveillance, and punitive enforcement. '[W]ith sufficient political will and financial support, crash rates can be reduced' (ibid.: 9–12). Among the recommendations to foster less risky driving were mandatory recurrent testing of all drivers, raising the minimum age of eligibility to drive, graduated licensing, stricter enforcement of speed limits, stricter prosecution of reckless driving, photo radar, red light photo surveillance, and increased use of police random stop checks for impaired driving and other violations (Insurance Corporation of British Columbia1997a: 49–50).

Concomitant recommendations were made for the social deflation of claims. Reference was made to the Ontario Insurance Act, which makes 'it an offence to lie to an insurer to obtain benefits. Fines on conviction are large – up to $100,000 for the first offence and up to $200,000 for subsequent offences. ICBC is recommending legislative changes to define a specific charge of motor vehicle related fraud; to increase ICBC's powers to investigate and obtain evidence of fraud; to specify penalties and restitution; and to provide powers to enforce restitution' (ibid.).

These proposed legislative changes were to be accompanied by new special investigation units and claims coordination teams. An expert on claims management told us that in addition to more stringent surveillance and cost control measures, the task of these units and teams was to change the prevailing view of claimants that vehicle insurance is equivalent to government social programs that offer substantial support and long-term care. Claims managers 'try up front to deal with their [claimants'] expectations as much as possible, so that people coming into the process have a reasonable expectation what they're going to encounter.' At the same time, through initiatives such as the Physical Medicine Research Foundation (1997), health professionals were also to have their expectations brought in line with the insurer's bottom line.

Disability contracts are likewise written to make the insured more responsible. For example, basic vehicle insurance includes some mandatory coverage to compensate the innocent victim of an accident. However, the 'at fault' driver in a crash may not be compensated at the same level for the loss she suffers, and she must take out optional coverage at additional expense if she wants to be so compensated. This is evident in the following declaration of responsibility. Drivers are required 'to insure themselves against costs resulting from their own negligent driving (first party liability insurance). However, *they still must suffer the consequences of their actions* [emphasis added]. "At fault" drivers are compensated, but on a different basis from innocent accident victims. They remain eligible for medical, rehabilitation and wage loss benefits, but they are not entitled to receive compensation for non-financial (e.g., pain and suffering) loss and their compensation for financial losses (e.g., past and future wages, future care) varies, depending on the optional coverage purchased' (Insurance Corporation of British Columbia 1997b: 6).

Data indicate that the state vehicle insurance corporation in Quebec has been especially successful in limiting whiplash claim. Its success is attributed to ongoing resistance to the culture of spinal injury, for example, being stringent about evidence of material damage to vehicles before personal injury claims are entertained. One act of resistance was the commissioning of the Quebec Task Force on WAD. The Quebec Task Force was charged both with reviewing the available evidence on WAD and developing guidelines on diagnosis and treatment. Critics have argued that the Quebec Task Force was self-serving, asserting insurance institution hegemony over both accident victims and health professionals in the interest of better loss ratios.

The Quebec Task Force on WAD adopted a simple philosophy: 'prudence in the absence of evidence' (Spitzer et al. 1995: 40). Prudence means that both highly variable 'clinical judgment and individuality of patients ... should not be taken as excuses for a laissez-faire, highly variable approach to management' (ibid.: 38). The pragmatism of the Quebec Task Force extended to the point of conducting research in which recovery from WAD was deemed to occur when insurance compensation is terminated! As a physical medicine research specialist remarked in interview, since there is no clinical specification of normalcy 'they had to use something.' Using this definition, the Quebec Task Force was able to report that 97.1 per cent of claimants in a cohort study recovered from whiplash after one year. As critics point out,

One of the report's key conclusions – how long recovery takes – is misleading and places an unreasonable demand on people with whiplash: [T]he Quebec study may have excluded many patients who failed to recover, because the QTF defined 'recovered' patients as those who had stopped receiving compensation rather than those with resolved symptoms or even those who returned to work. Whether these people had actually returned to work, or were simply deemed able to do so by the insuring agency, is not clear. However, defining recovery this way overlooks people whose return to work was not successful because of continuing pain or disability ... [204/3,014 (6.8 percent) of people initially included in the cohort study] were excluded from the data set because they had suffered a recurrence. These were people who had been deemed at one point to have recovered but who continued to complain of symptoms. Amazingly, they were simply taken out of the final analysis ... Another group of people with recurring symptoms also may have been excluded because they had WAD combined with other injuries. (Teasell and Merskey 1999: 9)

Welfare

Disability insurance has been at the forefront of welfarism. In particular, workers' compensation schemes were conceived a century ago to spread risk and achieve solidarity among working populations (Sullivan 2000; O'Brien 2001). The welfare regimes of workers' compensation developed apace with medical science and technology, accommodating each new invention of health risk to its system of risk spreading and responsibility for solidarity. The response ability of these regimes is exemplified in the case of spinal injury associated disorders. As we have seen, all manner of complications arising from spinal injury have been addressed in workers' compensation insurance, as well as in vehicle personal injury insurance. Indeed, one can perhaps take a given jurisdiction's rate of spinal injury as a barometer of its commitment to a welfare regime.

Spinal injury is an important field for understanding the limits of welfare regimes. Because of the limitations of medical knowledge in diagnosis and treatment of spinal injury, it is not possible to say when enough is enough in medical terms. Indeed, on the basis of the medical evidence, including the iatrogenic effects of many treatments, it may be reasonable to contend that there should be little or no medical intervention in most cases (Malleson 2002). In any case, the response ability with respect to spinal injury reveals the fundamental dilemma of all jurisdictions with developed welfare regimes, namely, the problem of limits to consumption.

In this section, we demonstrate that disability insurers respond to the problem of limits to consumption by developing new regimes for handling spinal injury cases. In place of the uncertain knowledge of medical science, they substitute the more certain knowledge of surveillance systems that help them assess the credibility of insurance claims and control social inflation. They move from the welfarist tendency to manufacture victims to the neo-liberal tendency to blame victims. They adopt the deterrence-based approach of neo-liberal regimes in a concerted effort to reverse trends and effect social deflation.

In the first subsection, we analyse the enforcement crackdown on claimants. The neo-liberal regime of disability insurance is based on 'work hardening' the claimant. Work hardening is a regime for returning the claimant to work at the earliest possible stage. The claimant assumes responsibility as a collaborator in the struggle against an iatrogenic system that may be victimizing her even more than the accident itself. The work-hardening regime is coordinated by a new cadre of insurance inspectors who investigate every detail of the claimant's background, circumstances, and recovery. Medical policing is augmented, as health care professionals are mandated to detect fraud and malingering and circumscribe claims. There is also policing through the media, with advertising and publicity campaigns aimed at deterring disability insurance fraud and at cultivating informants to report on fellow workers or neighbours who may be cheating insurers. Private policing operations – for example, special investigation units within insurance companies charged with detection of major fraud and private investigation firms contracted to undertake photo surveillance in the hope of catching claimants in physical activity that would belie their disability claim – are also integral to the enforcement system. These various forms of policing include new surveillance technologies. We analyse one such technology which serves as a kind of lie detector of the body, trying to measure more accurately functional impairment and pain arising from accidental injuries.

In the second subsection, we analyse the enforcement crackdown on health professionals. Insurers are acutely aware of the iatrogenic dimensions of the medical response to spinal injury, and often attribute social inflation as much or more to health professionals as to clients. They do so by developing sophisticated auditing systems, for example, database surveillance of diagnosis, treatment, and billing practices. Further control is instituted by restricting assessment and treatment of disabilities to designated assessment centres and health professionals who have been vetted vigorously by insurers. Professional self-policing is also fostered, by means of special education programs and training manuals on the detection of malingering, pain management, and the iatrogenic effects of decisions. Compensation for professional services is altered to limit treatment and create incentives for medical policing efforts. There is also a tightening of the classifications and formats for diagnosis and treatment, an 'epidemiological surveillance' that tries to forge greater reliability in classifications. Finally, various control mechanisms are embedded in professional liability insurance contracts and their enforcement.

The combined effort to police claimants and health service providers heavily undercuts the welfare response on which the disability insurance system was founded. While there is variation across jurisdictions, where these policing mechanisms are strongly implemented, risk spreading gives way to risk unpooling and depooling, and solidarity to individual responsibility to pay for disability insurance programs.

The Enforcement Crackdown on Claimants

WORK HARDENING

Since disability is defined primarily as whatever interferes with a person's ability to return to work, the task is to discover the sources of interference and to resolve them in a collaborative relationship among insurers, employers, health professionals, and the claimant. Collaboration typically consists of having everyone agree that while the disability and associated pain may linger, the best approach is to have the claimant risk manage her problem at work rather than malinger. The core value is the Benthamite principle that good people work hard.

Work-hardening regimes support another equally simple principle of liberal regimes, namely, cost efficiency. In moral utilitarianism agreement that good people work hard dovetails with reducing claims costs for insurers and employment expenses for business enterprise. Indeed, the starting point for work-hardening programs is the fact that the majority of claims costs are attributable to the proportionately few who do not recover quickly from their disabilities. About one-half of whiplash claimants take no time off work (Malleson 2002: 257). In a study of whiplash claimants in the Quebec vehicle insurance plan, 'the 61.5 percent of subjects with only a whiplash injury whose absence [from work] lasted two months or less accounted for only 15.5 percent of the total costs, whereas the 26 percent whose absence lasted between two and six months accounted for 38.5 percent of the costs, and the 12.5 percent of patients still compensated 6 months after the collision accounted for 46 percent of the total costs' (Spitzer et al. 1995: 19).

In an article captioned 'New Approaches' and entitled 'Working Therapy,' Pimenthal (1999), 'author of several books on disability management and consultant with Milt Wright and Associates, Los Angeles,' offers an approach as old as Bentham's utilitarianism. Premised on the claim that disability 'direct costs (insurance and absenteeism) and the indirect ones (loss of production and worker replacement) are among the top five costs of doing business for any organization,' Pimenthal advocates that 'work should be part of therapy' (ibid.: 22). Consistent with all recommendations driven by efficiency imperatives, lack of adequate scientific knowledge does not get in the way of implementation. There is simply a call for future research that will better legitimate work-hardening decisions. 'We also need more research to develop work-as-therapy treatment protocols, return-to-work guidelines, and limited duty specifications, so that health care providers with whiplash patients have scientific back-up for their therapy decisions' (ibid.: 23).

An injury management specialist for a vehicle insurer confirmed in interview that work-hardening regimes are not evidence-based, but simply part of the company's efforts to improve loss ratios. 'We're looking at it with a lot of vested interest ... time is money in the insurance industry.' The interviewee said his company had no data on whether its new work-hardening regime was actually helpful to the disabled person or more cost efficient, 'but we can say that early intervention is definitely a commonsensical way to go.'

The lack of knowledge about recalcitrant disabilities such as whiplash is justification for work-hardening regimes. Instead of placing the onus on the insurance and health care systems to produce better knowledge for diagnosis and treatment, ignorance is confessed. This confession allows a shift to the production and distribution of surveillance knowledge useful in getting the person back to work quickly. Surveillance knowledge shifts responsibility onto health professionals to do their part in management of malingering, and onto the claimant to do her part in learning to risk manage her pain at work.

One licence to justify work hardening comes from the Quebec Task Force on WAD. '*Based on limited evidence and reasoning by analogy it is the Task Force consensus* [emphasis added] that ... prolonged use of soft collars, rest, or inactivity probably prolongs disability in WAD.' Insurers moved from this proclamation to work-hardening regimes in the hope that they would improve loss ratios. But as pointed out by many other experts, there is certainly no professional consensus on this matter, because evidence is lacking, and the aggregate data available do not allow the clinician to use it in any specific case before her. For example, a physiotherapist writing in a professional newsletter makes the following points: 'Having data, measurements and assessments does not give one enough information to direct care. Direction of health care for patients should rest principally with health care professionals. While management of loss costs, reduced prices, expanded market share, and making a profit do lie within the scope of the insurance industry, it's the practitioners who have to make the patients well ... It is not valid to take a mild whiplash injury personally suffered, and from it extrapolate that return to normal activity with pain is right. It may or may not be right depending on the pathology.'

Insurance companies' own experts sometimes accept this view, even if they nevertheless prescribe work-hardening regimes with reduced compensation.

> Because some studies have linked the prevalence of long-term disability to the level of compensation paid, some insurers have taken a very tough stance, withdrawing disability benefits to 'encourage' people to go back to work. But pain and disability are not the same thing; ending or refusing compensation may reduce disability but not pain.
>
> Obviously people without compensation will attempt to return to work, even if they are in a lot of pain. This clearly helps minimize the socioeconomic impact of the injury, but just because patients go back to work does not mean that they are pain-free.
>
> In fact, studies of patients' post-settlement pain and disability show that high levels of both persist, which reveals that compensation is not as significant in determining pain levels as suggested. (Munglani 1999: 14)

From Bentham to the Third Way, liberal regimes have focused on the moral responsibility to work hard. A contemporary slogan of the Third Way is 'no welfare without responsibility,' which means first and foremost the responsibility of finding work and keeping it (Giddens 1998, 1999). As we have seen in the case of soft tissue disability management, there is a very large industry dedicated to this task. This industry works hard to remobilize disabled people as workers and consumers (Miller and Rose 1997) in order to operate the insurance system more efficiently and profitably.

The same approach to work hardening is used in workers' compensation insurance regimes for lower back pain and other recalcitrant disabilities. In many jurisdictions, such as British Columbia, workers' compensation legislation requires that if the person is deemed able to return to work, she must do so even if she has not fully recovered. This is accompanied by a shift from a 'vocational rehabilitation' model, in which the person is given time and rehabilitation services before returning to work, to a 'disability management' model whereby the disability is risk managed at work. This approach involves a risk analysis of the claimant's task environment at work. For example, a 'functional capacity evaluation' ascertains whether the person can still do the work she was doing before, what might be altered egronomically to allow a return to full duties, and whether there should be lighter or alternative duties.

Are back strain and stress the result of work, inherited physiology, financial condition, family, or some other factors in combination? In workers' compensation, adjudicators determine the extent to which the problem is 'arising out of' the work situation compared to other situations. This determination inevitably requires broad discretion to allow adjudicators 'sufficient leeway to narrow or broaden coverage as they see fit, in keeping with whatever underlying policy objectives may have been identified' (Sullivan, Stainblum, and Frank 1997: 28). The discretion of adjudicators follows from the divergent expert opinions available from health professionals who are asked to diagnose and treat the invisible. As the director of compensation services for a workers' compensation board remarked in interview, 'You could probably get six or seven different opinions as to how disabled a person is, how long they should be off work, or what the limitations should be.'

In the face of such conundrums at the claims end, return to work can also be encouraged by building incentives into disability insurance contracts. A multinational disability insurance company we studied built a number of return-to-work incentives into its policies. The fundamental mechanism was to substantially underinsure the policyholder in order to control malingering. Income replacement levels for a person on a disability claim were kept to about half of the person's normal income on the experience that a higher level would severely affect loss ratios. A regional sales manager for this company said in interview,

We purposely underinsure an individual generally to around a 60 per cent income level to create a motivation to return to work ... If I was providing individuals with 100 per cent income replacement ... there's a certain percentage that would say, 'I can earn more by not working or as much by not working as working.' ... Some companies have sometimes in certain markets gone a few percentage points higher. But the reality here, or the mechanism that checks this behaviour is you're going to lose your shirt financially if you don't follow these models, these are pretty tried and true models ... If I raise my income replacement to 90 per cent, my claims loss ratio will go up correspondingly. And most companies try to govern a claims loss ratio ... at around 50 per cent, the soft variance 45 to 55 per cent ... maximal acceptance range probably in the low 60s.

This company also built a number of return-to-work conditions and incentives into the insurance contract. In keeping with the 'responsibilization' of the individual characteristic of liberal regimes, it called this package the 'enterprise claims system.' The package was designed to reward the enterprising disability claimant with a series of benefits for returning to work quickly, and it was combined with a more stringent surveillance of the claimant to ensure that she was indeed enterprising rather than malingering. A company official described this surveillance as a move from a 'paper audit' of paying a claim strictly on a reading of the contract to a 'clinical audit' involving ongoing claims management of the disabled person's condition and return-to-work process. To facilitate this move to clinical audit the company acquired another company with 3,500 employees who specialized in disability claims management.

INSURANCE INSPECTORS
Work-hardening programs have been accompanied by the establishment of case coordinator positions in insurance companies. Case coordinators are charged with inspecting the minutiae of the claimant's background and well-being at work and elsewhere. In practice, they are engaged in physiognomy, the 'ancient art or science of judging an interior reality by an external appearance ... color of the face ... passing expressions, bodily form or posture' (Graham 1979: 35; see also Rivers 1994). This practice is based on the view that disability claimants routinely express somatoform ailments that must be seen through in order to accelerate their return to work and deflate insurance claims costs. The task is to coordinate with health professionals and employers in 'building strong and healthy egos' in claimants on the view that acci-

dent victims have 'suffered more from the so-called emotional malad-justments or personality defects that accompanied their physical impairments than from the impairments themselves' (O'Brien 2001: 7). The following extract from an insurance company's manual for case coordinators reveals both the depth of inspection required and the way in which the facts discovered are to be valued with an eye on reducing claims costs.

> An accurate observation of the insured's environment, family dynamics as well as verbal and non-verbal behaviour will assist in developing the foundation for the insured's rehabilitation planning ... Listen to your clients and be attentive not only to what they say but even more so to what they do not say. Non-verbal clues, body language and voice tones often say more than words ... It is always important to ascertain the insured's family, social, employer, recreational, community and other networks, and the degree to which each network influences the insured ... The multicultural milieu of the province ... requires rehabilitation staff to be culturally competent ... [e.g.,] An insured who has limited English or none at all, will likely have less appreciation for the intent and the value of medical or rehabilitation services ... Some minority groups are disproportionately represented at the lower end of the economic spectrum and in the ranks of the unemployed. Their socioeconomic conditions, which may be characterized by poor housing, behavioural problems in children, dissatisfaction with social situation and health problems, may affect their medical and rehabilitation needs as well as service delivery ... An individual with a value system which puts an extraordinary emphasis on the medical model of care will be less likely to respond to active rehabilitation ... Family values of certain cultural groups may interfere, if not completely hinder the rehabilitation process. Independence, which is often the primary goal of most rehabilitation programs, may not necessarily be important to some cultural groups who may have a tendency to protect and care for an injured family member.

Work-hardening coordinators are also instructed to mobilize other experts. For example, 'neuropsychological assessment ... can also be used to weed out the relative contribution of any pre-injury factors such as learning disability, psychiatric disorder, malingering, or unconscious distortion of the effects of the injury.' However, the coordinator must be aware that 'scores on subtests can be affected/influenced by pain, medication, drug or alcohol use including caffeine, anxiety, poor

motivation, other personal issues ... [M]alingering or conversion reactions may alter performance consciously or unconsciously.' Moreover,
the testers themselves may not have been adequately tested. "Registered psychologists practicing in the area of neuropsychology have not
been tested by the College for their competency nor [is] their training
in this specialty validated.'

Having sorted through the maze of every conceivable factor that
could be related to tardiness in returning to work, the coordinator
must determine which support services might be offered to get the person back on the job. 'The process of vocational evaluation is accomplished using various techniques and incorporating the medical,
social, vocational, educational, cognitive, personality, and interest as
well as cultural information about the client and the economic data
predominant in the job market.' The coordinator's job is to put political, social, economic, and cultural frailties back into working order. In
doing so she 'must be fully aware of the insured's pre-accident work
history and performance. It is useful to have a complete summary of
the insured's employment, education, training as well as leisure activities and hobbies, which can provide some insight to any valuable skills
which might help in search for a new job. Factors such as absenteeism,
earnings, work history, career plans and time with any one employer
may project future attitudes toward returning to work. Consideration
must also be given to other factors likely to diminish the potential for
successful vocational rehabilitation, such as substance abuse, lawyer
and family influences, etc.'

The factors seen as likely to diminish success are revealed by a list-
ing of 'optional management strategies' for return to work. This list
appears in a consultant's document produced in collaboration with
the same insurance company. The ideal candidate for work hardening demonstrates the following characteristics and experience in the
system:

- shorter time out of work before rehabilitation
- satisfying job, better educated patient
- good work history
- younger patient
- few or no compensation benefits
- no pending litigation
- no substance abuse or self-destructive behaviour
- fewer psychotropic medications, few operations

- primary/secondary/tertiary gain factors not operative in perpetuating pain
- more directive 'return to work' approach in therapy

The case coordinator's manual instructs that there will be no vocational rehabilitation for those deemed employable. If the person is not employable by others, the next best option is to try to make her self-employable. With self-employment, 'in the event that this is the only viable option for the insured after going through the hierarchy of employment objectives, funding may be provided for required business courses only. No funding is provided toward the purchase of a business or start-up expenses.'

For those who are deemed employable, the work-hardening regime kicks in. 'Using real or simulated work activities, work hardening focuses on improving the injured person's physical tolerance, strength, stamina, and other behaviours related to employment ... It is important to note that work hardening is not the same as a fitness program.' The manual provides details on how the coordinator can facilitate work site modification, job search and placement assistance, on-the-job training, and formal training in educational institutions. Formal education must be 'marketable.' Moreover, the coordinator serves as an inspector by obtaining transcripts of results each term and verifying acceptable levels of 'motivation' such as school attendance.

On the job the claimant is expected to accept some pain and other personal sacrifices as part of the work-hardening process. As Baker (1996: 278) observes, 'Pain and other nonfinancial aspects of bodily injury, for example, can be understood in insurance terms as an ineluctable, nonmonetary deductible or coinsurance "payment."'

This approach to work hardening is exemplified by a soft tissue injury management program instituted by a vehicle insurance company. The company established a case coordinator system for the 25 per cent of claimants with soft tissue injury who do not return to work within thirty days. The manual for the case coordinators makes the program's rationale explicit: 'Focusing on pain tends to result in passive treatments which provide only temporary relief of symptoms, while making patients dependent on the welfare system.' A case coordinator was defined as the 'clinician who *rigorously* encourages early return to usual activities' [emphasis added]. As such, they had to be qualified occupational therapists whose mandate was to enforce 'the indemnification principle. That is, the client expects to be put back in

the same physical condition as before the loss (no better, no worse).'
This principle is the 'heads' or upside of the coin whose currency is
that the person will get no more than she deserves. The 'tails' or down-
side is the Benthamite principle of less eligibility: do not do anything
that would give the disabled person more than she would have
received if she had not been an accident victim. Above all, prevent
idleness when the person could be hard at work. 'Clients are obligated
by contractual obligation to mitigate or contain their loss. They must
take steps to make certain that their damages are reasonable and not
increased by failure to act with prudence. If, for example, their doctor
feels they should attempt to return to work but they fail to do so, any
additional claim for loss of earnings could be jeopardized.'

Acting with prudence entails first and foremost a return to work
even if it is painful. The emphasis is on the person's 'abilities' rather
than her disabilities, and on relative 'wellness' and 'best outcomes' (or
least worst outcomes) rather than full recovery in all cases. A leading
industry spokesperson for this new approach said in interview, 'We've
tried to be very clear that return [to work] function doesn't mean cessa-
tion of symptoms. It means that the person can continue working and
will have and may still have problems. In the same way that when we
look at the evidence we don't say that people have recovered, you
don't use that language.'

The claimant is socialized into managing her pain at work. Socializa-
tion includes moral lessons on how pain can be good for you because it
helps in achieving a higher moral value: the utilitarian principle that
good people work hard. Thus an injury management claims specialist
for a vehicle insurer said in interview, 'In a soft tissue injury it's very
subjective, everyone is affected a little differently, you can't see it, you
can't put your finger on it, so ... a lot of it is education ... If you, for
instance, sit at home and don't do anything, then the situation very
well could get worse ... Educate them to the point that – good pain and
bad pain – and in many cases pain is not a disabling thing, but rather
good pain could be good as well as assist in your recovery. So it's working through that pain to get back [to work].'

Industry internal documents and publications repeat this point,
while making its moral utilitarian underpinnings even more explicit.
Writing in a vehicle insurer's magazine, Rajesh Munglani (1999), MD, a
lecturer at the University of Cambridge Department of Medicine, and a
consultant in anesthesia and pain relief at Addenbrooke's Hospital,
Cambridge, writes on 'The Roots of Chronicity.' The article concludes

with the insurer's bottom line: 'Pain management programs and other rehabilitative approaches can help maximize the reduction in disability produced by effective pain relief. And – just in case – compensation awards could be limited so that patients aren't encouraged (consciously or subconsciously) to highlight their symptoms in order to qualify for such benefits' (ibid.: 15). The same message is conveyed in a vehicle insurer's manual for its soft tissue injury claims managers: 'Pain must be acknowledged but the insured needs to be encouraged to return to work through discomfort to improve function. This requires reassurance to keep the person focused on returning to work as this is a key factor in the recovery ... This program will be part of our strategy to restore public confidence in us as a high performance financially sound corporation.'

MEDICAL POLICING

Insurance inspectors mobilize health professionals in the enforcement crackdown on claimants. Physicians for insurers are to undertake fine-grained inspection of the claimant's background, accident, and efforts to return to work. For example, a vehicle insurer's manual for the management of whiplash claims constituted the physician as a claims investigator on behalf of the insurer. In the name of better medical knowledge about the injury received, the physician is instructed to obtain fine-grained detail as an accident investigator. 'Since there is a correlation between impact magnitude and the amount of energy applied to the body during a collision, it is worthwhile to ask the degree of impact, the amount of vehicle damage, the type of impact (rear-end, front-end, side-on, etc.), where patient was seated, position of headrest, use of seatbelt, etc.' These data can be compared to other accident reports for corroboration, possible violations, and signs of fraud. Physicians also serve as agents of surveillance in the patient's return-to-work plan. For example, they are instructed to 'be aware of patient's general home and work responsibilities' and to take these into account throughout the work-hardening process.

Medical policing is especially focused on the legitimacy of the claimants' injury, pain, and suffering. As Malleson (2002: chap. 11) documents, there is a long history in medicine of trying to delineate the nature of somatoform disorders, in which the psychological symptoms of a physical injury are judged to be authentic, and to distinguish them from illness that is feigned (Gavin 1843). Freud concerned himself with acting out through accidents, which he termed 'traumatophilic diathesis.' Sociologists have also conceptualized the 'sick role' and how it can become a central part of a person's identity over and above other aspects such as occupation (Parsons 1951). A person in a sick role typically engages in 'illness behaviors' (Mechanic 1961) that are exaggerated or feigned in order to confirm the identity, obtain sympathetic support, augment insurance compensation, and so on. The diagnosis 'compensation neurosis' was coined by Rigler (1879) to address the unseemly rush for insurance compensation following railway accidents.

Unable to make physical signs of spinal injury visible, health professionals in the employ of insurers try to make the signs of faking visible to ascertain whether there is substance to a claim. The simplest insurance-based definition of illness behaviour is whatever is 'dysfunctional' to the clinical eye as it is focused by the insurance system. An expert on the detection of deception and malingering advises that 'early recognition of dysfunctional emotions, beliefs, and behaviour will allow us to focus on psychosocial interventions that reflect the personal, social and cultural factors that affect pain perception' (Craig 1999: 19; see also Craig et al. 1999). A manual for clinicians dealing with whiplash claimants includes a subsection entitled 'illness behaviour.' It explicitly defines illness behaviour as any effort to seek compensation that is unwarranted. This undue compensation-seeking is referred to as 'secondary gain ... consciously or unconsciously using or maintaining symptoms to obtain psychological, social, or economic advantage expressed in behaviour that appears to seek sympathy, manipulate others, avoid work or responsibility, or save face when expectations are too high.'

In clinical shorthand, the claimant is said to suffer from 'compensationitis' (Munglani 1999: 14), 'dissimulation disorders' (Jonas and Pope 1985), or 'factitious disorder.' A manual for whiplash clinicians defines factitious disorder as 'A conscious or willful invention or distortion of symptoms to achieve secondary gain, usually a financial gain. It should be pointed out that it is not easy to detect malingering, as it can sometimes appear the same as previously discussed syndromes. The difference between malingering and the other psychological issues is that in malingering, the person knows that they are faking an illness or injury, and why – usually for money or to avoid traumatization or abuse.'

Another syndrome is 'pain disorder' where it is determined that pain is largely related to 'psychological factors.' In extreme form it becomes 'chronic pain syndrome' which is 'a condition of its own' and not just an acute pain that lasts longer. The manual instructs clinicians that they are not to 'think of chronic pain as either somatogenic or psychogenic. All pain is both. Patients' questions about the origins of pain are often really questions about the legitimacy of suffering. Restate questions about the origin of pain as questions about the nature of appropriate treatment.' Apparently a lot of suffering is illegitimate and the appropriate treatment is to restrict benefits. Lists of clinical symptoms for chronic pain syndrome indicate that it is not really distinguishable from malingering or factitious disorder. Among the symptoms listed in the manual are:

- Dysfunctional or maladaptive behaviour
- Reinforced by iatrogenic, and/or psycho-social stressors
- Often related to secondary gain (social, family, vocational or financial)
- Often provides the rationalization for quitting an unpleasant work situation, retirement, or breaking a workaholic pattern
- Pain may provide expectations for financial rewards through a legal and insurance or compensation system
- May result from complications arising from the involvement of various professions, such as medical, legal, insurance

Chronic pain syndrome is in turn construed as influencing diagnoses of fibromyalgia. The manual states that fibromyalgia may be caused or aggravated by malingering. An associated cause is 'litigation; the stress of having to "prove" one's dysfunction and to live with it could also be a factor.' The clinician is charged with the responsibility of trying 'to control the issues of secondary pain for gain behaviour. The rewards of pain and dysfunction can be powerful mediators for pain behaviour.'

These various clinical formulations for the governance of disability claims slip into 'red flag' indicators of fraud. Clinicians are directed to look for red flags of 'symptom magnification.' One manual for clinicians advised them to use indicators identified for low back examination and apply them to neck examination. It initially warned them that research findings in this area 'have *not* been scientifically validated as non-organic signs for the neck, and therefore can only serve as a guide to understanding the nature of clinical magnification complaints.' It then told them to ferret out signs of symptom magnification, for example,

- Instant symptoms after minor trauma exposure
- Disproportionate verbalizations, grimacing, tremors, collapse or crying
- Excessively slow, rigid or hesitant neck and general body motions
- Prolonged course of therapy with no apparent benefits
- Pain and dysfunction get steadily worse over time; patient does not report any 'good days'
- Pain and dysfunction spread to new areas as one improves
- Work avoidance, minor health excuses are used to avoid return to work
- Employer insists on 'pain-free' condition before return
- Distracted pain sites
- Discrepancy motions

'Distracted pain sites' and 'discrepancy motions' are examples of how the clinician can detect faking. Clinicians are to look for discrepancies between what movements the claimant can make during official testing and what movements she can make when she is 'distracted' and engaging in routine activities. For example, 'often as patients are routinely dressing or undressing, their movements are fluid and smooth and normal in range where previously they had been markedly limited. If a physical problem is limiting motion, it will be limiting in a consistent manner.' When the patient shows she has the range of motion to dress and undress normally, but not to perform the tests that will affect her disability claim, the clinician may treat the discrepancy as another clinical problem in need of reassurance rather than insurance. 'In a clinical therapeutic setting, when significant magnified findings are present, it may be helpful to politely bring these issues to the patient's attention. Such counseling has to be conducted in a supportive, empathetic and non-judgmental manner, with reassurance that help is available for this aspect of their problem. When significant non-organic problems are identified it is probably appropriate to seek a psychological or psychiatric referral. Patients have the right to be informed of all aspects of their problem, physical and emotional, and deserve our best care in attending to their needs.'

This clinical response to an excessive disability claim is one of several mechanisms used to make the claimant more responsible about her pain. Another mechanism is to threaten termination of benefits for non-compliance with a work- hardening plan. Thus a vehicle insurer's manual for rehabilitation coordinators instructed that 'The insured has a duty to mitigate his/her loss. When a rehabilitation plan, either medical or vocational, has been identified and recommended for the insured by the appropriate medical/vocational professionals, he/she has the responsibility to undertake such a plan ... If the insured's refusal to participate in a medical/vocational rehabilitation is due to lack of motivation or any reason other than a valid medical condition, advise the insured that his/her benefits ... will be terminated.' The manual does not elaborate on the meaning of valid medical conditions in this context. The authoritative certainty of medical science is needed at such decision points even if it is known that there is nothing but uncertainty. 'There have been no controlled studies of any form of conservative therapy for chronic neck pain after whiplash. No data, not even a simple audit, support any conventional intervention. Insurers and health-care systems are paying for guess-work in this arena ... Contrary to prevailing "wisdom" in this regard, formal studies and reviews have shown that neck pain is neither caused nor perpetuated by compensation neurosis or the pursuit of financial gain. These notions have arisen from physicians' reliance on disproven techniques to diagnose and treat whiplash' (Bogduk 1999: 13).

MEDIA POLICING

The enforcement crackdown on claimants incorporates policing efforts through the mass media (Ericson, Baranek, and Chan 1989). Media policing involves three related strategies. First, trend data are publicized to dramatize the scale of insurance fraud with respect to personal injury. The appeal is that any effort to cheat the system is victimizing all members of the insurance pool, not only the insurance company. In this context at least, insurers admit that their problems with claims handling are passed on to policyholders in the form of higher premiums and more stringent contract conditions. Just as the crackdown on recipients of state welfare is justified in the interests of the taxpayer, so the crackdown on private insurance disability claimants is justified in the interests of the policyholder. In the case of vehicle insurance, the fact is that the policyholder is paying hundreds, and in some cases thousands, of dollars annually for the damages lottery of personal injury claims, especially regarding whiplash. In the case of workers' compensation insurance, while employers and employees are paying substantially for the damages lottery of personal injury claims, every consumer is as well, because the cost of insurance is embedded in the price of goods and services.

The second strategy is to carefully select individual cases of major fraud for publicity (for more detail and case examples, see Ericson,

Doyle, and Barry 2003: chap. 9). While the criminal prosecution of disability claims fraud is extremely rare, the dramatization of individual cases of prosecution is presumed to have shock value. It is hoped that people will be shocked into more resentment of disability victims who appear to be overstaying their welcome in the treatment system. In turn, it is hoped that resentment will encourage more people to become informants in the policing effort.

The cultivation of informants is the third strategy in media policing. Through regular news stories about trends in insurance fraud and major prosecutions, backed up by advertising campaigns, insurers encourage all insured persons to join in the enforcement crackdown on claimants. Insurers operate their own informant tip lines, and also rely on informant system enterprises such as Crime Stoppers. Indeed, insurers are a major source of funding for Crime Stoppers; they also sit on its local franchise boards and provide various volunteer services (Carriere and Ericson 1989; Lippert 2002). They recognize the instrumental value of Crime Stoppers for solving not only insurance fraud cases, but also burglaries and the recovery of stolen property. They also recognize its symbolic value as a 'do good' organization that mobilizes community.

Apart from providing a means for detecting disability insurance fraud, informant tip lines serve to legitimate the broader enforcement crackdown system. Here too the insured population is called upon to protect the integrity of the risk pool. The appeal is to the common pool as commonwealth, ignoring the unpooling that often leads the insurance poor to fraud as a way of covering the steep premiums they have been paying. For example, a vehicle insurer we studied produced an informant recruitment brochure entitled, 'Fraudulent Claims Hit You in the Pocketbook.' The brochure declares that the company loses up to $320 million annually through fraudulent claims. While the company did not offer a bounty for tracking down fraudsters, the prospective informant is told that the reward derives from good insurance pool citizenship. 'Insurance fraud costs us and that costs you. If we can put a stop to this kind of fraud, we all win.'

The National Insurance Crime Bureau (NICB) in the United States runs various publicity and advertising campaigns to recruit insurance citizens as policing agents. For example, it ran a poster campaign to dramatize disability insurance fraud and the need for all insured to join in the informant effort against it. One such wanted poster shows a person grimacing in excruciating pain. Indeed, the pain is so severe that the eye, cheek, and side of the face are badly disfigured and have an inhuman texture. However, this person has not become badly disfigured and dehumanized by real pain and suffering, but rather by fraud. The word 'fraud' is repeated on several levels and with different sizes on the poster, indicating that this is a problem with many layers that need to be peeled back through investigation to achieve enforcement. Furthermore, each letter in the word 'fraud' is shot through with tiny holes to connote that deception must be seen through with microscopic inspection. This poster gives a new twist to the legendary State Farm Insurance slogan, 'Like a Good Neighbor.' The good insurance citizen is urged to see through the pain of fellow workers and neighbours in this way, and 'report the rip-off' to the NICB tip line. In keeping with the moral utilitarianism of insurance, good citizenship is given a cash value in the form of a reward up to $1,000.

PRIVATE POLICING

Private policing operatives are also dedicated to the crackdown on disability claimants. Insurers have greatly expanded their in-house private investigation departments, called Special Investigation Units, and much of this expansion is directed at disability claims fraud (Ericson and Doyle 2003b, 2004). Special Investigation Units undertake major fraud investigations, for example, of personal injury accident 'rings.' These rings stage fake accidents, and all occupants of the vehicles involved conspire with health professionals and lawyers to build fraudulent claims. Special Investigation Units also engage in sting operations in which they stage accidents themselves. For example, in a sting called 'Operation Bus Roulette,' bus accidents in New Jersey were staged by insurance investigators in order to catch 'jumpers' (people who jumped into a bus after a 'crash' to claim injury) and 'add-ons' (people who did not bother to jump on the bus but nevertheless filed a claim). A series of ten such staged bus accidents netted several dozen jumpers and add-ons, as well ten doctors and four lawyers who specialized in catering to the special needs of these claimants (Malleson 2002: 268–9).

We interviewed an investigator for a vehicle insurer's bodily injury claims investigation unit. The interviewee said that his newly created specialized unit received suspect cases from claims adjusters. He reported that only 13 per cent of the claims investigated by his unit were 'honest' and therefore paid in full. Another 26 per cent were deemed 'exaggerated' and claims payments were reduced accordingly.

The majority of claims, 61 per cent, were judged fraudulent and denied.

The complexities of trying to investigate the invisible nature of spinal injury claims are revealed in the efforts of a provincial government vehicle insurer we studied. This insurer created a new internal policy of 'no crash, no cash' in an effort to limit bodily injury claims. This policy made the visibility of material damage to a vehicle a precondition of making a claim for bodily injury. If there was minimal or no material damage to a vehicle in a reported crash, the insurer simply refused to process bodily injury claims. If the insured insisted on compensation, she was told to hire a lawyer and take the case to court. The cost of invoking legal process – both financially and in stress – was assumed to be a sufficient deterrent to claimants. The manager of a bodily injury claims unit explained the new policy during an interview. 'You've got a two-hour tab [repair bill] here, no damage to your vehicle, a person of your age and strength, it would be unlikely they'll be hurt. So we say, "If you are hurt, we just don't think it's compensable." We're not calling it a fraud, we're just arguing whether it's compensable injury or not ... Our position is, "We don't think you're due compensation, and if you want it, you're going to have to have a jury to say that you're entitled to it."'

Another claims official said in interview that this new policy had led some claimants to purposely damage their vehicle beyond what occurred in the accident in order to have enough material damage to justify the processing of a bodily injury claim. 'You rear-end me but it's not quite enough damage and I know that. I'll go out and smash it.' The interviewee described a case in which the claimant said there was substantial material damage and also filed a bodily injury claim. However, the driver of the vehicle that hit the claimant's vehicle from behind said there was no material damage. Material damage estimators matched up the two vehicles and decided that the $3,000 damage to the rear-ended vehicle was not a result of the crash.

We interviewed a personal injury lawyer about the no crash, no cash policy. She remarked that this policy

has nothing to do with statistical analysis or anything. It's just a policy: 'Where the damage to the vehicles is what *we've* described as minimal, we will take the position that you could not have been hurt. So we're not going to pay your medical benefits, and we will not pay you any compensation for your claim, and if you bring a claim, we will set it down for a five-day jury trial. No matter what the size of the claim – if it is a $2,000 claim, it is going to be a five-day jury trial' ... Cost saving ... nothing to do with the merits of the claims ... The same as saying to someone, 'Here is a carton of eggs. If I drop the carton, the carton looks OK, the eggs must be OK.'

This lawyer described the no crash, no cash policy as part of the insurer's fraud enforcement campaign, which was in turn related to its social deflation efforts. The purpose was 'to try and get that perception going ... relatively successfully ... convincing juries that [systemic fraud] must be the case ... Basically telling the jury you shouldn't believe this person ... their doctor ... their family.' A class action suit was organized against the no crash, no cash policy, but certification was denied at the appeal level because 'there's enough differences between the individual actions that they should be dealt with individually.' This lawyer said that the legal route around the policy was to take out a separate action against the insurer in each case under a specified section of the insurance contract regarding entitlement to medical and disability benefits.

Between 35 and 40 per cent of this insurer's bodily injury cases involved lawyers representing claimants. The insurer had a policy of encouraging claimants to settle without engaging a lawyer, in the hope of limiting the iatrogenic and nomogenic processes involved in personal injury claims. Claims investigators we interviewed said that claimants who agreed to settle on their own were offered particular interim benefits which would be cut off if they hired a lawyer. They were also offered better service in the claims process and sweeteners to a final settlement without the involvement of lawyers. When asked what lesser service meant in the case of claimants who hired lawyers, a claims investigator said it meant less positive attention because the time for such attention was needed to discourage other claimants from having lawyers. A colleague said that it also meant playing 'hardball.' 'We might not be as lenient with regards to paying something that we might on the front end ... Maybe a special damage that the person would be entitled to at the end of his claim we might pay that up front if they don't hire a lawyer versus if they do hire a lawyer ... [Maybe] a real proactive approach ... we might put some surveillance on the person.'

Another segment of private policing is dedicated to this proactive approach. Low-skilled, low-paid operatives contracted through private investigation firms spend long hours trying to capture disability claimants on camera doing things that seem to belie their claim. For example, Lowther (1996) reports that in 1995, ICBC used contract private investigations on 4,400 disability case surveillance assignments at a cost of $8 million. This custom accounted for the livelihood of about 80 per cent (n = 600) of registered private investigators in the province.

Private investigator photo surveillance assignments can be initiated at any point in the bodily injury claims process. If a claims operative finds the claimant suspicious, photo surveillance may be ordered to confirm the suspicions. An interviewee working as a bodily injury claims investigator gave a routine example. A painter who was on work leave after spinal injury came into the claims office to pick up his compensation cheque. The adjuster noticed paint on his hands, although he was supposed to have been off work for the previous two weeks. A private investigator was assigned and the claimant was captured on film at work.

Photo surveillance assignments are especially likely in litigated cases. A bodily injury adjuster for an auto insurer said in interview that up to 80 per cent of litigated cases involve such assignments. A private investigator for an insurance information services company said that surveillance assignments proliferate in the context of limitations in scientific and expert knowledge about disability claims. 'Doctors that do reports, it's their *opinions*. What the company is trying to confirm is that it *is* a fraud ... This guy is off for two months and I know he doesn't have a back problem, he's putting a roof on his house ... Surveillance is the easiest ... "You've got a back problem? How the heck do you explain that you're on the roof, building a roof here?" So usually the claimant says, "Oh God, I can't go to court on this, I'm OK." So the claim is settled.'

The methods that private investigators use to create a photo opportunity can be unsettling. Due process constraints on public police investigations are often absent in competitive environments of private investigation companies trying to secure more contracts. Reported cases of illegal entry to premises, collecting information extraneous to investigations, and collecting information for other investigative purposes beyond detection of disability claims fraud have been commonplace (Lowther 1996).

PRECISION

In this section, we analyse a new technology for the assessment of disability, which was created to address the limits to expert knowledge in assessing functional impairment and pain. This computer-based technology quantifies levels of functional impairment and associated pain, and promises to do so with much greater precision than individual physicians in traditional clinical settings. It uses the legitimacy of computer systems and trust in numbers to make the process of commodifying the body for insurance compensation appear objective. It thereby tries to make uncertainty seem as if it is risk. As Adams (1995: 25) remarks, the insurance ideal is 'that the odds be known, that numbers be attachable to the probabilities and magnitudes of possible outcomes. In practice, since such numbers are rarely available, they are usually assumed or invented, the alternative being to admit the formal treatments have nothing useful to say about the problem under discussion.'

We assign this new technology the fictional name, Precision. Precision is a word that describes the condition of being exact and accurate, especially through the refinement of measurement. According to the *Oxford English Dictionary*, being precise entails ensuring that something is 'accurately expressed' and that one is 'punctilious' and 'scrupulous in being exact, observing rules.' Precision technology is precisely that. It is a technology of expressive accuracy whose operators are to be agents of its formal properties: conscientious, over-attentive to details, and obsessive about procedural propriety. Precision exemplifies all of the pseudo-objectifying processes in the disability insurance system that we have analysed up to this point, and how they aim to control both professional service providers and clients.

A photograph of Precision at work is presented in figure 3.3. Here we can visualize a body being seen through by Precision and its punctilious and scrupulous operator. This photograph reveals that Precision is a computer-based technology for gauging a disability claimant's ability to perform various physical tasks. The only feature not made visible by this photograph is a hidden surveillance camera and audio recording system that can capture every gesture and word spoken by both the claimant and the technician.

We interviewed a physician employed by a workers' compensation insurer who was involved in the implementation of Precision on behalf of the insurer. He said the process of implementation was one of 'teaching the physicians and the external providers to be as consistent and fastidious with numbers as we need them to be for insurance purposes ... Every half a degree means a percentage perhaps in the pen-

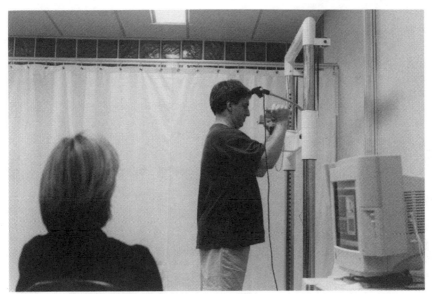

Figure 3.3   Precision at Work

sion over a lifetime.' During a demonstration of the technology, a physiotherapist operator described Precision as a 'data capture system' with respect to 'range of motion' capacity using 'calculation software.' It tests 'permanent functional impairment' of the 'medically pla-teaued,' meaning those whose 'situation medically will not change except maybe to get worse ... They've been through the wringer of rehab and everything seems to be staying the same, so now let's mea-sure what is left ... [regarding] the range of motion, as well as the strength loss and subjective considerations such as pain.' Precision was also introduced as a benchmarking tool in the process of work harden-ing for those not at the stage of being considered for permanent dis-ability pensions. A senior administrator for the same insurer said Precision fit 'the primary focus of this organization: return the individ-ual to productive employment.'

The claimant to be tested by Precision arrives at a designated assess-ment unit operated by a company on contract to the workers' compen-sation insurer. The claimant is required to complete a number of detailed questionnaires pertaining to her medical history, work history, the accident that led to the disability, self-assessment of functional abilities, and self-assessment of pain. She then warms up on the Precision machinery to gain familiarity and to become more comfortable with it. The warming-up process is accompanied by coaching from the attending clinician concerning procedures and how to perform the tests.

The testing entails a series of bodily movements in which the claimant is asked to lift, squat, grip, pinch, and so on. There are three trials for each movement interspersed throughout the testing process. Based on research literature pertaining to large samples of cases, the computer-based assessment of the trials for each movement is designed to predict, for example, that if the claimant lifts in a certain position, she has a certain amount of strength capacity. A physician explained in interview that, for example,

> You may have not lost it yet, and you may have a weakness in the range of motion, but you'd just had an entrophy at that point. And second, you may have a peculiarity of structural damage that allows you to exercise the muscles that form the contours of the surface anatomy, but some of the more functional muscles deeper are still in pain and not functioning properly. And the only way you can test that properly is by some kind of electronic dynamometer testing and repetitive testing, because theoretically if you had an anatomical problem at a certain point, you should have consistent weakness at that point. So because the way the Precision equipment makes these measurements function, you're able to predict, for instance, if you lift in *this* position you should have a certain amount of predictable drop in your strength to lifting in *this* position, whether you have injury or not. If you grip a dynamometer, like the Jaymar dynamometer, in five different positions, even if you have pain somewhere in your hand and wrist you should have a predictable curve of strength throughout the range of motion with your hand.

The computer software offers a series of real-time validity and reliability checks for the technician to monitor on the screen as the testing proceeds. A coefficient of variation is produced across all strength and functional tests as each movement is performed. The claimant's heart rate is automatically recorded at the beginning of testing and then used to compare with the ongoing recording of heart rate during the testing. A derived expected change is calculated and analysed. A sample case used to illustrate Precision's capability appears in the manual for technicians: 'The patient's heart rate was monitored during one or more of the ST tests in order to determine if the patient was performing at a maximal effort. Population studies [cited] indicate that an appropriate elevation in heart rate should follow a maximal whole-body execution. The table below shows average pre- and post-execution heart rates, the actual change and the *expected* (population average) and *minimum acceptable* (one standard deviation below average) increase. If the patient demonstrated *at least* the minimum increase, a valid effort is reported.'

During a demonstration of Precision, a technician told us that the heart rate checks were crucial in detecting the credibility of the claimant. 'After you start the next test, it gives you what your highest post-execution heart rate was afterward and at what time after the test, within the rest time period, it happened ... Now when we generate a report this comes out on a table showing an estimated increase that you would expect if someone gives minimal effort. So when you're generating force in this manner, using all your big muscle groups pushes the heart. You don't have to give it a lot to actually become valid in this test, so people who fail this are not trying.'

Each type of test has peculiar means by which claimants can 'become valid.' For example, in relation to grip strength a 'maximum voluntary effort' test places the claimant on a bell curve with respect to performance on five grip positions. Outliers are suspected of being liars. In the 'horizontal validity' test, the 'high-never' lift is performed at two different horizontal distances, ten inches and twenty inches. In a sample case provided in the operator's manual, technicians are advised that 'As an additional means of determining if the patient gave a full and consistent effort, certain tests were repeated with the patient being asked to move either 10 inches closer or 10 inches farther from the lifting handles. Population studies [cited] indicate that such a change should produce a 33 percent or greater *increase* in strength when moving farther away. When the expected change of at least 33 percent is *not* observed, an *Inappropriate Horizontal Strength Change* (IHSC) is reported by assigning a FAIL status to indicate inconsistent performance.' A technician demonstrating Precision to us said that this test had one purpose: 'purely just to determine someone's effort.'

The attempt to determine effort extends well beyond these and other validity and reliability checks on physical movements. Prior to testing on the Precision machinery, the claimant is required to complete detailed questionnaires on various specified health problems; medication history; work history; functional abilities; and difficulties experienced and pain with respect to balance, bending, carrying, climbing, driving, fatigue, handling, hearing, kneeling, lifting, memory, push/pull, sitting, standing, stooping, temperature, vision, and walking. The pain self-assessment also includes marking on the front and back of an illustration of a body where the claimant is experiencing pain and what type of pain it is. The claimant must sign and have witnessed the entire battery of questionnaires as a complete statement of confession about how her body works: 'I declare that all the information provided above is true to the best of my knowledge.'

In the functional abilities self-assessment, the claimant must assign each function specified a score from '0' (no change) to '10' (completely unable to perform function). If the claimant has difficulty describing her ability for a particular function, the technician assists with examples and figurative language. The self-assessment then becomes part of the computerized reliability and validity checks offered by Precision. For example, if the claimant assigns an '8' to her (in)ability to carry two grocery bags, this response is checked across a range of other indicators of her ability.

The pain self-assessment is also on a '0' (none) to '10' (unbearable) scale. The claimant has to repeat a pain self-report on this scale while engaged in the testing for each movement on the Precision machinery. The self-report questionnaire pain rating is then compared to the self-reported pain during Precision testing to check for consistency. At the end Precision commands all tests and prints out all inconsistencies at once against a plot of all pain response scales. If there is considerable inconsistency then the entire effort in all testing is suspect and open to further investigation. If there is consistency, it can be used as a basis for enhancing the compensation level for a particular disability. As a Precision program administrator said in interview, 'So if you have a 10 per cent functional impairment, and there's consistency in your pain argument ... I'm going to add an extra 2.5 per cent of pain for this particular case. That's an adjudicated decision.'

During a demonstration of Precision, a technician described the importance of the self-reported pain level questionnaire and the repetition of self-reported pain during testing as a key lie detection device.

> [It is] a cross-check for us, that this [questionnaire] gets sent on the [computer] file and if from what they typed in or what they actually put in, we can check that ... Unfortunately, we have to think that way ... The screen comes up after each test and we track the pain scale ... After each test we're going to be monitoring how your pain is doing throughout the test

... on a fixed scale of '0' is no pain, '10' is medical emergency ... Pain is a subjective, and a '9' to somebody is a '2' to somebody else ... The thing is though you can still determine, 'Is this consistent?' If it is a '9' to somebody ... [who] has chronic pain syndrome, this has become their life focus. This in itself is a disability now. So it is no longer the injury itself ... it's an '8,' '9' and it's a subjective thing. But what we've tried to do is standardize at least the way we capture that ... The testing will show that you can be somebody that has high pain responses but is still putting out a good effort and consistent effort. So, hey, maybe there is something to this person's pain. And the officers can weigh all to award something for that suffering in a sense ... [A] consistent dull ache ... '2, 2, 2, 2, 2,' ... [is] representative of their situation. It's when you have someone that starts at an 8 setting there and then they get up and do the static strength tests and forgotten and all of a sudden they're '0, 0, 0, 0.' ... Oh, it just got really painful at the end ... And then you see there's nothing on the graph, and it was an 8 but they didn't even generate any force [laughs]. You've got to cross-check.

A Precision program administrator said in interview that lie detection of the body is a key function of the testing process: 'the symptom magnification in someone that is minimally impaired trying to convince everybody that they're maximally, their impairment is 100 per cent disabling.' He gave an example of how a range of motion test on the Precision machine could be related to subjective pain scores to detect 'symptom magnification.' 'For instance in leg lifting if someone has less than twenty-three leg lift with back pain. You're not putting any stretch on the structures with the back – particularly the sciatic nerve and the nerve roots – until you get to about twenty degrees. So I think it is suspicious if you have a range of motion that is less than four or five degrees in any direction. Often you had that even with a surgical fusion, so it becomes suspicious if those things are correlated against the subjective pain in the performance during the functional testing.'

A senior administrator for the workers' compensation insurer also praised Precision as a device for calculating truth and trust. Believing that consistency through repetition builds reputation, he said tests may be repeated a dozen times if necessary. 'If you have a common knee injury ... we get you to do it twelve times. If you do it twelve times on the computer, and it's a physical problem every time you cross that particular point of angle, there will be a peak or a valley in the change of motor force that you have in that muscle. So if you try and simulate that injury it's very obvious, it's very inconsistent, it's all over the place ... This thing does detect simulation, but that's what we're here for, we're here to detect what's really going on. The reason that we're doing it is that we get an accurate measurement ... What differentiates a 5 per cent back disability from a 5.5 per cent back?'

The detection of simulation occurs through a number of additional investigative technologies and practices. The claimant is subject to being watched for tell-tale signs at every step of the way, both in approaching the testing centre and during the test. A Precision program administrator remarked in interview,

> You've never seen so many knee braces and wrist braces brought out of mothballs when you come in for an impairment rating. Everybody has got one. I mean you get people walking in with dual knee braces – and they've got blisters walking from their car to the building because they hadn't worn them for a year and a half – but they've got them on because a lot of people perceive this is a pot of gold at the end of the rainbow. The intent of the Precision system is not to catch the system magnifiers, it's to give a truly accurate reflection what the findings are on that particular day ... The clinician that actually conducts the test makes ongoing comments regarding the client's behaviour, from the moment of hitting the door until leaving. So, for instance, the patient was unable to bend over during the test, however, I noted that they had no difficulty bending to tie their shoes when they got dressed after their examination.

During a demonstration of Precision, a technician told us that she was constantly looking for signs of faking during tests. For example, during the hand-grip dynamometer testing she looks for 'whitening of the fingertips' as well as 'accessory muscles activating in the forearms, activation of musculage all the way up. Some people, all you see is a bit of gripping, and some people it is just hard to tell.' The technician can switch on a surveillance camera during testing to capture any subtleties.

Monitoring begins before a claimant even enters the clinic. Surveillance cameras are available in the clinic parking lot and corridors to capture bodily movements that do not match what the Precision testing records. The day of one of our observation sessions with Precision operators, a woman was detected as a 'symptom magnifier.' She claimed that she could not move her neck because of cervical injury, but three signs counteracted this claim: she drove her car a long distance to the clinic; she moved her neck considerably during the examination; and she was put under surveillance in the parking lot and again she displayed ample mobility with her neck.

The claimant may also be the target of photo surveillance in her everyday routines before and after the Precision testing day. A technician said she had recently tested a claimant who subsequently claimed that his disability had been aggravated further by the testing itself. Photo surveillance was used to belie this claim. 'The guy said he couldn't crawl out of bed the day after I examined him. Two days later, he was filmed coming in first in a Rambo-esque archery tournament, in which he travelled in camouflage fatigues and crawled across all kinds of terrain.'

The Precision process also involves efforts to validate what is already on the client's file. For example, prior to testing the claimant is required to describe in detail the accident that led to her disability. A technician told us that this requirement is 'just to determine if there is huge variation. I mean their history is well known and well documented throughout their file ... and if there's a huge discrepancy in information at least it is highlighted.' The entire Precision computer printout is reviewed by the physician responsible for the case to compare the data with the claimant's file.

In a special issue of *Recovery* magazine entitled 'Truth,' retired British Columbia Supreme Court Justice Lloyd McKenzie reflects on his involvement in personal injury cases and remarks, 'Apparently our medical predecessors took no heed of an accused's word or demeanour, preferring the non-verbal and objective tests available by trial by ordeal, water, fire or battle. I do not recommend a return to those forms of stern objectivity, but we can learn something from their disinclination to accept an accused's word at face value' (McKenzie 1998: 12). Apparently the architects and operators of Precision have learned a great deal about how to use trial by ordeal to produce 'stern objectivity.' Their objective is to provide authoritative criteria of rational acceptability that contribute to the disability insurance industry's efforts at improving loss ratios.

A Precision technician remarked during a demonstration that the problem of truth is created by the disability insurance system itself. 'The system definitely does not reward people for returning on their own integrity ... Most people have legitimate injuries, but then they get caught up and they have a lot of other pressures ... They may have a mortgage to pay, they're not working so hard, they're pushed to talk about this, and so "I'm owed." The world owes me.' The disability insurance industry responds by blaming the victim, using the power of technology to make the truth seem more visible, objective, and legitimate.

Precision assists in cracking down on exaggerated claims of functional impairment and pain. The crackdown is legitimated through the objectivity and neutrality which computers and quantification promise. However, as Precision operators readily admit, its science and technology are neither objective nor neutral.

First, Precision data are only precise according to the criteria of rational acceptability of the particular insurers who are using it. A senior executive with a workers' compensation insurer that used Precision said, 'I mean everything that goes into a computer has to be based first of all on a subjective statement of what the levels are – and we are not using the AMA *Guides*, we're using other measures. So there is some subjectivity error built into the beginning.' A physician involved in the administration of the Precision system for this insurer explained that the local political culture, including legal decisions, had to be included in the calculus, thus rendering the AMA *Guides* too rigid. Moreover, the AMA *Guides* are themselves based on the arbitrary standards of a panel of experts. As such they are debatable medically, politically, and legally. 'AMA standards are in as much controversy in the literature as anything else ... [so] there's no more logical reason for using them than our own.' He also said that in the jurisdictions where AMA guidelines are used to program Precision, there is a need 'to pick and choose different sections of different volumes ... So every edition has its best thing ... the best you can come up with to build your own system is the best approach.'

Second, subjectivity is introduced by testing procedures. As explained by a Precision administrator for a workers' compensation insurer, claimants 'have to be scripted properly. You have to be oriented properly with the equipment or it really isn't going to be reproducible.' He added that technicians 'have to really coach [claimants] as they go.' A technician explained in interview that coaching-in-process is necessary because it is not possible to standardize instructions and wording. 'There's interaction that takes place when you're trying to get the person to put out their best effort.'

Third, there is subjectivity in the technician's interpretations throughout the testing process. As we have seen, every gesture and word of the claimant as she approaches the clinic, participates in the test, and leaves the clinic is interpreted. How she ties her shoes, how her fingertips whiten and her muscles flex, how she reports pain verbally and through grimacing, are all indicative of her sincerity. Simultaneously, real-time data on the computer screen are interpreted in relation to the claimant's performances on the Precision machine. The overall test results and technician's observational notes are subject to further inferential leaps. During a demonstration of Precision, a technician observed,

> Determining somebody's effort is very difficult to do ... You must use a multitude of indicators ... The range of motion testing itself does not provide a coefficient of variation. And really it is a kind of inference from the remainder of the results as to how that is ... We standardize the ways the clinicians make comments in terms of these objectives, trying to identify what objective signs of effort should be seen. Doesn't mean that if they don't see them, that somebody didn't give an effort ... There [are] force curves generated, so that we know if somebody is giving full effort at a normal 'uninjured' position *this* is the form of the curve, and what we've seen is that people that even have injury and complaint still should generate the same sort of curvature, so you're looking at that sort of factor. You're watching for the objective signs, you listen to the pain response that they give and again it's all taken into consideration for the diagnosis.

We interviewed a leading specialist in occupational health and safety employed by a private research and policy institute. He viewed Precision as but another improbable effort to be objective and neutral about something that is inherently subjective and value-laden. Precision is

> a $100,000 device that measures frizzballs with micrometers ... It's quite a job to assess effort. Anything that is effort-dependent is difficult to measure. And a lot of standardization that is used ... is quite specious. So, Precision is used to deal with large-scale awards, but it's not a very precise thing. The fact that it's got some whiz-bang technology doesn't mean it's any better than anything else. The best way of measuring disability is to ask people what they can and cannot do. And I'm afraid that it turns out to be as reliable as anything else. So we rely on paper and pencil measures ... There is no device that accurately assesses deception. And there are some snake oil salesmen out there selling devices like this all the time –

there's a thing called 'spine-a-scope.' Anytime, when any of these devices have been subject to rigorous evaluation, it turns out to be a pile of hooey.

The Enforcement Crackdown on Health Professionals

AUDITING

The enforcement crackdown on health professionals is grounded in new technologies for surveillance and audit of their services and billing practices. Precision is one such technology, for it is aimed at control of health professionals as much as claimants.

Precision is a means of forging consistency and reliability in classification. As such, it does offer the potential of greater precision in the sense of more agreement among clinicians and therefore replicability. Towards this end, Precision technicians are coached in how to use and interpret the technology. The administrative head of Precision testing for a workers' compensation insurer said in interview that his primary responsibility was to ensure that health service professionals conform to the insurer's expectations. 'Every time you add a clinician it is retraining, getting the consistency, getting the accuracy ... Part of the trick in this business ... is you learn through repetition. So, for example, the more back claims you get the better you are at them. The better you get at asking the appropriate questions. The better you do in the examinations. The better you do at the calculations of the impairment. It's experience.' We interviewed one of this administrator's staff technicians on how she experienced this coaching in consistency. She remarked that Precision is 'only as good as the people that use it. So garbage in, garbage out ... So the better the training then definitely the better the accuracy ... What's more is that everyone is trained to do it in the same way ... We're bringing science to this really.'

Another dimension of the moral science of Precision is the limitation of testing to designated assessment units. In a workers' compensation insurance operation we studied, there were two designated assessment units for Precision testing. These units were private clinics on exclusive contracts to the insurer. A physician involved in administering the Precision testing program said that the contractual arrangement was advantageous to the insurer for several reasons. First, there was no capital cost to the insurer. Second, it reduces health professionals' incentive for bias and the perception of bias because the Precision technicians are just that, technicians who are not otherwise involved with the claimant. 'It is difficult for them to manipulate the results for anybody's benefit because they don't know what the impairment is going to be.' Third, it circumvents what the physician termed 'system doctors': those who have been a part of the workers' compensation system for years. System doctors work within the

> folklore of medicine, they're reticent to participate in changes that involve new technology. [With Precision] adhering to the art of medicine is going to be changed ... [System doctors do not have] a homogeneous medical background ... One physician might be very, very good at it, and another physician may not see that as a priority and just rush through it and give me whatever the hell you get ... Plus it is difficult to get people to adhere to something. They're smart organisms, they're very opportunistic, and they learn how to manipulate the system or they wouldn't survive medical education ... As soon as they're on their own in a new area, they will go back to the religion they were taught in their own medical school. And everybody has a different way, for instance, of measuring range of motion. Some people put a goniometer on the outside of the arm, some people try to align it up with what they think are the surface anatomy markers to actually line up with the bone. Some people take into account the concept of visual parallax, and the difference in their height from the patient's height, and other people don't ... If you were an emergency room physician or a trauma surgeon your concept of what was pain, and what was an emergency, was quite different from a general practitioner in a middle-class environment.

The assignment of testing to Precision technicians and technology signifies how previously entrenched experts lose jurisdiction in the system of professions (Abbott 1988: 45–6, 51–2). Workers' compensation 'system doctors' are losing jurisdiction in their disability assessments due to too absolute an association between diagnosis and treatment; lack of efficiency that includes iatrogenesis; problems in measurability; and problems of too much inference.

A fourth advantage of Precision testing through designated assessment units is the capacity to conduct direct surveillance of the technicians and to remove them from their positions if they are found wanting. According to an insurer's operational manual for Precision, the technicians are trained, evaluated, and inspected by the insurer's quality assurance team. In order to qualify to perform independent evaluations they must pass fifteen tests. The quality assurance team continues to scrutinize the initial evaluation reports prepared by the technician 'to ensure independent testing has not altered quality of reports.' A designated trainer coaches in consistency and inspects simultaneously. 'When a clinician has received "probationary sign-off" they have been deemed technically sound to perform the tests. Further experience in the actual testing situations with real clients is required to ensure that the technical knowledge can be applied appropriately. "Supervision" by the trainer is intended to provide support for troubleshooting which may come from experience and provide feedback of improving overall approach with clients.'

The quality assurance team 'reserves the right to renege the certification of a clinician should reports indicate the procedures are not being followed or that quality of reports decline.' However, assessment is not limited to the quality of reports or ongoing supervision by the trainer. The insurer also employs 'mystery shoppers' who pose as claimants to conduct first-hand undercover surveillance of technicians. As one Precision administrator explained to us, mystery shopping is necessary because the technician controls the clinic's surveillance cameras and the Precision machine itself and 'you could create any test you want in there.'

The elaboration and refinement of medical guidelines and procedures are also integral to auditing. For example, the *AMA Guides to the Evaluation of Permanent Impairment* (1993) states that quantifications of pain impairment can only be 'estimates' that 'are based on the physician's training, experience, skill and thoroughness' (304). These estimates are not objective in the sense of scientifically accurate, but they can be made objective through agreed-upon procedures. 'As with most medical care, the physician's judgment about pain represents a blend of the art and science of medicine, and the judgment must be characterized not so much by scientific accuracy as by procedural regularity' (304).

The AMA manual is a guide to objectivity as procedural regularity and propriety. 'Even though rating and estimating impairments cannot be totally objective, use of the *Guides* increases objectivity and enables physicians to evaluate and report medical impairment in a standardized manner, so that reports from different observers are more likely to be comparable in content and completeness. The *Guides* help minimize abuses and unrealistic verdicts that may arise from unjustified claims' (5). Here the manual makes clear that objectivity in the evaluation of disability is entwined with the objective of insurance claims control.

One recommendation for establishing objectivity is to have two physicians examine the same patient independently. This recommendation is based partly on the view that reliability exists when two observers agree on the same interpretation and classification. But it is also grounded in a concern that medical examiners themselves are a source of claims inflation. Having two physicians examine the same patient independently increases the prospect that each 'physician's participation in an employability determination will be independent of the individual's motivation to work' (6). It is also recommended that each physician repeat measurements as another check on the reliability of their assessments. 'Repeating measurements may increase their *credibility* [emphasis added] and therefore the authoritative certainty with which physicians can express their calculations of functional impairment' (9).

Insurance company case coordinators also audit the services of health professionals. In a vehicle insurance company we studied, the primary responsibility for auditing health service providers was assigned to case coordinators. A manual for these case coordinators was replete with instructions on how to enhance investigations of health services and to deny services when necessary.

Case coordinators were given detailed guidelines on contracting, monitoring, and evaluating service providers. They also had guidebooks on procedures and performance standards to give to their service providers. They were explicitly instructed to go beyond formal professional criteria. For example, they were urged to acquire and deploy knowledge of the local medical community to judge reputation and risks. 'Although registration, licensure, accreditation, certification, and professional affiliations are important in choosing service providers, experience, and "word-of-mouth" references are also effective in identifying reputable and competent practitioners.' In relation to some specializations, such as counselling, coordinators were asked to undertake thorough clinical evaluations of the clinicians they were contracting with. 'It has been said that a counsellor as a person and as a professional cannot be separated, therefore, when considering a counsellor, the Rehabilitation Coordinator must attempt to know as much about the counsellor's needs, values, motivations, and personality traits that could enhance or interfere with that counsellor's effectiveness.'

In dealing with general medical practitioners, coordinators were to scrutinize specific treatments prescribed and, if necessary, obtain another medical opinion to counter them. For example, coordinators were warned of 'occasions when a general practitioner recommends a specific treatment/intervention without carefully considering its benefits or potential contradictions,' and that the solution on such occasions is to mobilize more expert medical opinion.

Coordinators were given similarly detailed instructions about how to govern the use of medical technologies with iatrogenic potential. A section in their manual on this topic opened with a general rule that, 'When an equipment requested may result in medical contradictions, or further injury or damage to the insured, a medical opinion is required in order to consider the request for funding. An example of this is ... where the rehabilitative value has not been proven by appropriate research or studies.' No mention is made of the fact that, as we have seen, this would apply in the vast majority of cases, especially those involving spinal injuries. Coordinators are to become experts in prosthetics and orthotics and to be ever vigilant, because 'technology is continually coming up with newer and more expensive devices that may not necessarily be functionally beneficial or cost-effective.' There were seven pages on mobility equipment and aids alone, punctured with warnings such as 'the high cost of specialized power wheelchairs does not allow for mistakes in recommendation,' and if such equipment is classifiable as a vehicle, 'it is also important that the insured has the funds to pay for the vehicle insurance.'

Auditing is also focused on the billing practices of health professionals. There is particular concern about 'medical mills' that conspire in the building of spinal injury claims. 'Litigants often keep one set of doctors for their litigation problems and another for their illnesses about which they have genuine concern' (Malleson 2002: 279). But fraudulent billing is a more general problem across all health services. In Ontario, the estimated cost of medical fraud is about CDN$400 million annually, representing 10 per cent of all billing to the Ontario health service (ibid.: 336, citing Abbate 2000). Of course, such estimates lack precision because insurance billing fraud is extremely difficult to define, let alone enforce. An insurance fraud investigator who worked on contract to various insurers offered a simple example in this respect. A physician who has prescribed a series of medical tests for a patient may refuse to give the results over the telephone and insist on an office consultation. The consultation consists of four words, 'Your results are negative,' for which the physician collects a forty dollars office visit fee from the insurer. 'To me that is tantamount to fraud, that's all it is.'

Dataveillance auditing of billing across insurance companies is common. For example, in one Canadian province we studied, the provincial vehicle insurer had the capacity to match its personal injury database with the health care and workers' compensation databases to ascertain the treatment pattern of physicians involved in claims, including pharmaceutical practices.

In the same jurisdiction, all vehicle personal injury and workers' compensation claims were processed by the health care insurer. According to the health care insurer, this arrangement saved the vehicle insurer and workers' compensation insurer about $7 million annually. The health care insurer deemed this to be a reasonable price in exchange for centralized control over information that would enhance its capacity to build a more complete patient history for all residents of the province and to monitor the billing practices of health care providers. The claims billing system was electronic and under development to allow real-time auditing to identify problems immediately. An official involved in operating this system for the health care insurer said in interview that it was proving especially effective for

> physician audits ... It is pretty easy for physicians to do a double dip on one service, and I've seen examples of their charts where they would bill us, and on the bottom line you see a note 'bill the workers' compensation board,' and I've seen some where it also ... says 'bill the vehicle insurer.' So now what we have is one pipeline in where we distribute these claims out for approval to these other agencies and then process them and pay the physicians and recover them from other agencies ... The vehicle insurer is very concerned about 'fraud,' we are concerned about 'inappropriate billing' ... What we want to make sure is that the physician is rendering the appropriate services and billing is appropriate for it ... It's called the Billing Integrity Program.

'Billing integrity' is a major concern of all injury and health insurers. This health care insurer had approximately five thousand rules concerning the processing and adjudication of claims. Some rules were very clear about the extent to which the insurer was willing to compensate a physician. For example, 'aggressive doctors' were governed by a patient quota restriction that paid the full fee for services to forty-seven or less patients per day, only 50 per cent of the fee for services to the next thirteen patients, and nothing for in excess of sixty patients. If a physician was an outlier in terms of performing a particular procedure much more than other physicians, an investigation was initiated. Suspicious patterns were also the basis for other types of in-depth investigation, for example, into whether the billed procedure was the one actually executed, or whether the medial procedure executed was actually necessary.

A vehicle insurer we studied established several new investigation units as part of its crackdown on inflated claims. One unit was entirely dedicated to fraud investigations. A member of the unit said his work involved surveillance not only of injured claimants, but also of 'the doctors, lawyers, physios, and chiros' who make their living from the personal injury 'industry.' The surveillance of claimants and health professions is combined in the monitoring of billing practices. Billing practices can reveal that certain health service providers are associated with particular claimants: for example, all the claimants in a large-scale crash, or the same group of claimants in repeated cases. Moreover, the health service providers may bill for many more treatments than is usual for a crash of the type in question. An expert in billing pattern analysis for the insurer explained that in one case he ran, he found

> eleven patterns or something and then we had ten providers who stuck out in seven or more [patterns]. Their patients never got better ... The average number of treatments would be nine or so, but these guys are running forty for anybody who would go. We looked at the accidents and stuff involved and they were all minor. They were cross-referencing their people and running the bills up on it. They [the claimants] were all interconnected, most of them knew each other ... The more you looked at their files, the more they looked stamped out ... Their notes all looked identical, it just all comes down to one writer, they were all word processed and mass produced ... so these were clearly mills ... [One physiotherapist involved] even had his own disability claim against us for about $200,000! Totally disabled, where he was officially treating hundreds of patients! He was really on vacation ... while he was claiming workers' compensation and private insurance disability ... Cheating Revenue Canada, submitting false bills to the public health service provider, and running disability private policies.

DESIGNATED ASSESSMENT CENTRES

A second and related step in the enforcement crackdown on health professionals is the establishment of special clinics for assessing disability claims. We have already considered one such clinic in our analysis of Precision testing procedures. Designated assessment centres carefully select service providers and build in tight surveillance and audit procedures. In one jurisdiction we studied, such centres were established by a vehicle insurance industry committee working through the insurance commission regulator. A commission official told us in interview that these centres were explicitly designated to deal with the iatrogenic effects of health care provision for personal injury accident victims. She pointed to 'physician bias' as a major problem. She referred to some physicians as 'insured doctors' because they enjoy a comfortable life at the expense of insurance companies.

Some designated assessment centres have arisen on the assumption that they will be very stringent in suppressing the claims. The health professionals in these centres make their living by receiving a high volume of referrals from insurance companies that appreciate their stringency. This type of operation was evidenced in a Canadian Broadcasting Corporation (1998) documentary on *The Fifth Estate* entitled 'Prove It ... If You Can.' The documentary showed how new legislation governing automobile insurers in Ontario led to a more competitive insurance market, which in turn reduced premiums. Insurers then engaged in a crackdown on claims in order to compensate for the reduction in premium revenue. Part of this crackdown involved contracting out to designated assessment operators who obtained business by enforcing stringent criteria of disability.

In a case study presented in the documentary, a PhD candidate and part-time lecturer lost her student status and teaching position after suffering a brain injury in an auto accident. Her husband had to leave his job in order to care for her, and as a result they were living on welfare. As part of the humiliating process of obtaining financial consideration for her personal disability, the accident victim had to be assessed by five different medical review boards for government agencies: FB disability, Canada Pension Plan disability, Revenue Canada disability, Canada Student Loan forgiveness on the basis of disability, and Ontario Student Loan forgiveness on the basis of disability. While each of these boards concluded that she was permanently disabled, the medical assessor for the Economical Insurance Company did not. Moreover, he argued that she was exaggerating her injuries and was still able to perform her pre-accident occupation. The documentary quotes the head of the medical assessment operation that was being so economical on behalf of the insurance company: 'There's an honest belief in many of the claimants we see that they are disabled ... and they're not. They're self-deluding. The lawyers or rehabilitation counsellors may think for their good, "I'm going to get you money and this will solve your problem." People come to us now and say, "I was in a car accident, I was brain damaged." People have told me my brain is like Swiss cheese. The proof? I mislay my keys, I've mislaid my gloves. That may be evidence of a head injury, but it may also be evidence of just normal cognitive inefficiency.' The documentary then cites an article by this medical assessor in an industry magazine in which he claims that only 3 per cent of three thousand evaluations conducted by his company revealed the need for long-term disability benefits.

HEALTH PROFESSIONAL SELF-POLICING

Another tactic in the enforcement crackdown on health professionals is to foster self-policing. As we have seen, the field of whiplash-associated disorder is notorious for the invention of new diagnoses and technologies of treatment that are unproven and may even be detrimental. Health professionals are engaged by insurers to remind colleagues of the limitations of their craft and therefore of the need to limit their services. For example, writing in *Recovery*, the magazine of ICBC, Hillel Sommer, medical coordinator for Manitoba Public Insurance and assistant professor of medicine at the University of Manitoba, states that health professionals must reflect on the iatrogenic effects of their practices, and the fact that they often do more harm than good.

> Nowhere else in medicine is it acceptable to commence or prolong treatment without a clear diagnosis. Without clinically proven treatments, physicians fall back on non-specific results.
>
> Treatment attempts sometimes create new problems, such as side effects from drugs that are prescribed based on erroneous assumptions about the origin of the pain. Continued diagnostic testing may yield a false-positive result without a rational explanation, confusing the issue even more. This can set the stage for further investigations of ever-increasing evasiveness.
>
> Patients may be referred to other practitioners to undergo treatments such as electrical, thermal, or manual therapy. These passive treatments are often used well beyond their intended scope ...
>
> [T]he physician may end up acting as the injured person's ally. Even if an objective second look points out inappropriate management decisions, it's difficult for the original physician to change course. (Sommer 1999)

A public insurer of vehicles we studied funded a major initiative to educate health professionals on these issues. A curriculum was developed, along with practice guidelines, conferences, and training sessions. An official involved in this program told us that the purpose was to make service providers ask themselves, 'What do we do as physicians, clinicians, practitioners that iatrogenically causes pain ... and contributes to chronicity?' He observed that 'there is a medicalization that occurs and I think there [are] factors related to the systems that are out there that influence pain behaviour, that provide stress ... a major contributor to dysfunction.' A key factor was said to be a system in which the patient is forced to ask herself, '"How can I get better when I have to prove that I am sick?"'

One strategy in this initiative was to identify medical practitioners who would influence their colleagues to be more sensitive to their iatrogenic behaviour. An official of the company said in interview that the goal of the initiative was clear: 'educating physicians in proper diagnosis and treatment of whiplash injuries so that ultimately the length of recovery time will be reduced and our costs will be reduced.' Since there is no medical basis for proper diagnosis and treatment, it is the insurance basis of shorter recovery time and lower claims costs that should be operative. This required 'selecting high-profile influences in the medical community ... who [will] be able to demonstrate it to the people they come in contact with.' Physicians who remained recalcitrant were also to be reminded by their colleagues of their institutional loyalties. Another official for the company said in interview that, if someone is uncooperative, 'we'll seek to have another physician talk to that doctor ... to educate the doctor as to the benefits their patient could receive.' Needless to say, these 'benefits' were not the usual level of insurance benefits, but rather a new conception of what it means to be functional and back at work.

A manual to guide practitioners on how to be less iatrogenic offered various tips. Many of the tips urged avoidance of over-diagnosis and excessive treatments that might compound rather than correct problems. For example, there was a warning about over-prescription of drugs that might inure claimants to their disability rather than cure them. Pain killers and other drugs should only be prescribed where they support the moral utilitarianism of getting back into working order.

- Use time-contingent rather than pain-contingent schedules for medications and reactivation ... Pain-contingent schedules label pain as dangerous as well as aversive ... It is felt that pain-contingent analgesia

schedule has the potential to 'reward' pain, whereas the time-contingent dosing does not.
- Drugs should not be used to escape the drudgery of pain, but rather to facilitate functional recovery.
- Be cautious of a patient response whereby analgesia is used to facilitate opting out of responsibilities or activities. Be careful of the response: 'I have to take pain killers so I can rest (or feel good).' Rather the response should be: 'I use the pain medication so I can get things done.'

CHANGING PROFESSIONAL COMPENSATION INCENTIVES

The control of health services is also effected by changing compensation arrangements that affect diagnoses and treatments. For example, in the case of whiplash, a vehicle insurer we studied recommended a change in compensation of health service providers that would reward them for surveillance that identifies and checks claimants' chronicity rather than for practices that foster chronicity. In one jurisdiction we studied, physicians received higher levels of payment if they billed for an injury through the provincial workers' compensation scheme as opposed to the provincial health care plan. A workers' compensation official told us in interview that this led to some physicians 'saying it's work-related when it is not,' and a reform of this situation was initiated.

CHANGING PROFESSIONAL CLASSIFICATIONS

Another dimension of controlling health professionals involves revision of the forms on which they classify and report their medical activities. For example, since accounts of whiplash and what to do about it vary so widely, one control mechanism is to develop a new reporting format that will *formalize* consistency in what it means. The use of such a communication format of control for 'epidemiologic surveillance' was recommended by the Quebec Task Force on WAD. There was also a recommendation to enforce compliance through professional compensation incentives. 'Inconsistent definitions, descriptions and classifications used in reports of WAD and in common clinical use make it impossible to compare and synthesize the findings of published studies ... [A standardized form will] permit epidemiologic surveillance of the population and foster the pursuit of the research priorities set forth in this scientific monograph. Health professionals not reporting standardized data should not be reimbursed, and patients who do not provide information should be ineligible for benefits (Spitzer et al. 1995: 34).'

We interviewed a claims specialist for a vehicle insurer who elaborated on the rationale for this approach. What is important for insurers' management of their loss ratio is consistent classification, whether or not that classification is otherwise valid or reliable from the viewpoint of expert knowledge in the health sciences.

[The physician has] got to take his patient on good faith and he doesn't really want to get into issues of money and insurance. Through establishing a common approach to soft tissue injury it's possible for these doctors to say, 'Well, OK, based on the way that we look at this kind of injury here's how I would classify them.' Once classified, then you could pretty well leave it to anyone else, whether it's the insurance company or the legal community, to debate what that classification is worth ... We reached an agreement with the medical association on the format and style of medical reports for these kinds of injuries, so they complete them in a way that asks them questions about the injury so it can be classified ... It's a centralization and an attempt to describe or classify injuries of the subjective type because if we don't do it, they're all over the map. And what one doctor would describe as, let's say a mild soft tissue injury, another one would call it moderate. And in terms of pricing, the range of that could easily be $15,000. Maybe we're in dispute with possibly this person's lawyer because we don't even agree on the medical information, never mind on the value of the claim ... We're at the point that we would take any classification system as long as they would all agree to it.

PROFESSIONAL LIABILITY INSURANCE

Tighter control of health professionals is also effected through new professional liability insurance arrangements. All of the managed care mechanisms we have addressed to this point are creating a new array of professional liability exposures for health professionals and the organizations that employ them. Sensitive to these exposures, insurance companies underwriting this field place additional restrictions on professional practices. According to one major insurer in this field (Sedgwick 1997: 24–5), there is an improved environment for governing health service professionals through liability insurance which makes the underwriting conditions more favourable. Among the favourable elements is the fact that the number of physicians working as independent practitioners in the United States decreased from 75 per cent in 1983 to 50 per cent in 1996, making them more controllable through the centralized systems of managed care operations. Managed care operations have introduced new surveillance procedures, resulting in the 'mandatory nature of risk management and its consequent motivation as a discipline in most health care environments ... increasing effects of peer review pressures ... increasing oversight of both the cost and quality of care that is provided by managed care entities ... [and] increasing oversight by government and industry groups that focus on identifying marginal health care practitioners (e.g., the national practitioners data bank, state and national medical societies, etc.).'

Conclusion

In this chapter, we have addressed the conundrums faced by disability insurers in their efforts to spread risk, articulate solidarity, and effect welfare. Focusing in particular on whiplash-associated disorders following vehicle accidents and spinal injuries following work-related accidents, we have shown that insurers lack a solid foundation in medical science upon which to underwrite their disability insurance contracts and assess claims. In the vast majority of cases, health professionals are limited to interpreting claimants' subjective accounts of injury and pain, and insurers are therefore limited to interpreting these professional interpretations. Health professionals have a propensity to make inferential leaps in their interpretations, and to invent treatments that sometimes compound rather than correct the problem. Insurers are left with the uncertainties of an iatrogenic system.

Iatrogenesis in the health care system is entwined with nomogenesis in the legal system. Lawyers are business partners in the spinal injury enterprise, quick to engage new medical diagnoses and treatments and to build claims for compensation. Indeed, they are key participants in the process through which particular diagnoses and treatments become institutionalized and legitimate, and therefore a routine part of insurance compensation.

The medical-legal-insurance system with respect to whiplash and other spinal injuries is a multibillion-dollar enterprise. In jurisdictions with a strong commitment to spreading risk, articulating solidarity, and effecting welfare on behalf of disability claimants, the system is confronting its own limitations. At what point is it no longer possible to keep raising insurance premiums in order to cover the escalating costs of creative health care and legal care? At what juncture is it necessary to attack the credibility of health professionals and their medical diagnoses and treatments? Similarly, at what point is it necessary to attack the credibility of the lawyers who seem to be operating in professional self-interest over and above the well-being of disability claimants?

A serious assault on health and legal service provision has the effect of undermining the founding rationale for disability insurance systems. An enforcement crackdown means that broad risk pools begin to evaporate: Instead of risk spreading, we find more specialized insurance pools. These specialized insurance pools are market segmented according to ability to pay steep premiums, as well as the ability to be good risks who do not make disability insurance claims. Solidarity fractures as many are depooled from disability insurance entirely, while those remaining receive differential contract conditions and benefits based on their ability to pay. Human welfare responses to disability recede and liberal deterrence models ascend. Each insured and professional service provider is expected to do his or her part to prevent disabilities arising in the first place and to reduce expectations for compensation when disabilities cannot be suppressed. In this respect, disability insurance tries to incorporate the principles of the life insurance system as analysed in chapter 2. Embracing risk, prudence, and investment sit in an uneasy relation to spreading risk, solidarity, and welfare in contemporary disability insurance systems.

4 Uncertainties of Earthquakes: Absorbing Risk, Mitigation, and Infrastructure

Dangers, by being despised, grow great.
Edmond Burke, 'On the Petition of the Unitarians' (1792)

When tremendous dangers are involved, no one can be blamed for looking to his own interest.
Thucydides, *The Peloponnesion War* (c. 400 B.C.)

Life is the art of drawing sufficient conclusions from insufficient premises.
Samuel Butler, 'Lord, What Is Man?' *Note-Books* (1912)

Uncertainties of Earthquakes

The uncertainties of earthquakes pose a markedly different constellation of risk, responsibility, and response ability for the insurance industry. Fundamental conditions for insurance – ability to calculate the chances of the event occurring and the magnitude of the losses that may result – are extremely difficult to meet in underwriting earthquake coverage. The timing, location, and effects of earthquakes are unpredictable. Therefore, the only feasible approach is to try to absorb the impact of the risk.

Earthquake risk can be absorbed in two ways. First, the physical infrastructure of the built environment can be strengthened to offset property damage and, by extension, injury and death following an earthquake. Second, the insurance industry infrastructure can raise substantial capital to assist in recovery following an earthquake. The responsibility is to mitigate losses in these two ways. However, as we shall see, the construction of both a shock-resistant physical infrastructure and an insolvency-resistant insurance infrastructure entails additional uncertainties.

There are severe data limitations with respect to when and where a catastrophic earthquake will occur and the probable maximum loss (PML) that will result (Brun, Etkin, Low, Wallace, and White 1997; Munich Reinsurance 1992). Large magnitude earthquakes are rare and occur without warning, making data collection especially difficult. Canada has never had a catastrophic earthquake and, therefore, researchers must assume that data from other subduction zones are representative of, and applicable to, Canada. However, data from other zones are also very limited. Most seismic events occurred before the development of instrumentation to measure them. Moreover, the historical data available cannot be accurately translated into a specific contemporary setting. 'Therefore there is a high degree of uncertainty associated with any earthquake risk analysis' (Low 1997: 135). Wallace and White (1997: 5) observe that the unexpected earthquake in Northridge, California, in 1994 meant that 'reliance on the historical record for estimating the PML for a particular company, or the property-and-casualty industry as a whole, became obsolete.' The 1995 earthquake in Kobe, Japan, occurred along a previously unknown fault and thus was unexpected.

Even in the limited contexts where there is scientific infrastructure to measure seismic activity, the data collection process is subjective. The data necessary to establish a PML are based on human observations beyond technological instrumentation. Moreover, the technical measurements of the magnitude of an earthquake are open to competing interpretations.

The Guttenberg-Richter Scale is the scale most commonly used to measure a seismic event. It describes the 'total energy of the seismic waves radiating outwards from an earthquake as recorded by the amplitude of ground motion traces on seismographs at a normalized distance of 100 km from the source' (Smith 1996) ... The Guttenberg-Richter scale does not include ground shaking intensity, duration, or frequency, which are necessary to infer potential damages. Accordingly, the M is usually converted in a seismic module to a Modified Mercalli Index (MMI). MMI provides a measure of seismic ground shaking intensity by assigning a numerical value to the human observations of felt ground motion and the extent of physical damage to buildings and undeveloped land. The experienced individual will rate the intensity of an earthquake from MMI=I, not felt except by a very few under exceptionally favourable circumstances, to MMI-XII, total destruction ... Though MMI is extremely subjective, it can be argued that it is no less scientific than Guttenberg-Richter Scale measurements since seismologists can disagree on the exact rating of the magnitude of an event ... For international comparison of seismic shaking intensity, MMI is highly uncertain. However, within a given jurisdiction, MMI provides a common forum. Seismic measurement is still limited. That is:

- Not all seismic parameters are confidently measurable yet, such as depth to hypocentre
- Not all seismically active areas are equipped with instrumentation, and
- Often, in areas that are equipped, the instruments are either not triggered, or not immediately triggered, during an event. (Low 1997: 139–40, 144)

The available data are debated by experts. Within the scientific literature there is a 'West Coast' debate about seismic activity in the Cascadia subduction zone 150 kilometres off Vancouver in the Pacific Ocean (ibid.: 129–32). One side of the debate argues subduction is occurring aseismically and may stop entirely within a century. There is no historical record of major seismic activity in this area, and at most a few moderate earthquakes will be experienced over the coming centuries. The other side of the debate contends that a similar plate to the one in the Cascadia zone was the source of the largest recorded earthquake in history, which occurred in Chile in 1960. This side also contends there was a major earthquake along the Cascadia subduction zone three centuries ago. Compression and bulging along the coastline suggest two plates are locking, building energy for another major earthquake.

Problems with data collection and interpretation have led to imaginative analytical techniques and models. Lammare and associates (1992) have devised a statistical approach that tries to overcome incomplete datasets. Attempting to 'quantify uncertainty,' they refer to their approach as the 'bootstrap method' (Low 1997: 144–5)!

Following the unexpected earthquakes at Northridge and Kobe, computer simulation models have become popular. However, at best 'seismic risk modelling is to be used as a diagnostic tool to aid in decision making and management of risk. Alone, it does not provide solutions' (ibid.: 126). Indeed, the available models all have fundamental problems with respect to unknowns, assumptions, uncertainties, and validation (ibid.: 157–62). As a result Wallace and White (1997: 5) ask, 'How were risk managers in the insurance industry to assess the reliability of the estimates produced by these models?'

We interviewed risk managers in both state emergency planning programs and the insurance industry about their capacity to act on expert knowledge about earthquakes. A state official responsible for emergency planning observed that unlike California, British Columbia has no surface faulting to provide some observable evidence.

> Earthquakes are potentially extremely large and they're totally unexpected in terms of an accurate prediction of when they'll occur ... Whether you're a *believer* in one in five hundred [years] catastrophic earthquake or one that occurs every twenty to thirty years and is moderately damaging ... Scientists can't even watch to see what is going on. So to quote our seismologist, he says that the next earthquake that causes damage will probably be from a fault that he doesn't even know exists and it could be under Victoria, it could be under Vancouver ... Planning is being done in the absence of experience ... Planning an earthquake ... people don't know what they're dealing with. It's essentially working off a piece of paper in your mind.

A commercial underwriter for a large and conservative insurance company said that his firm undertook its own geological survey of the Vancouver region. The region was mapped into precise zones based on MMI analysis of a Guttenberg-Richter scale 7 earthquake. The mapping was so fine-grained that in the interviewee's former high-rise residence, 'I know that my building was probably going to be pretty safe, but I was going to be able to go fishing off my balcony, because right around [the corner] was just going to disappear, because that's reclaimed land.' In his present home, 'according to our maps, my living room is in one Mercalli zone and my bedroom is in another. So who knows what is going to happen there?' When asked about the apparent precision of this mapping and his company's expense in producing it, this commercial underwriter said, 'We've got so many different experts talking about different things – there is no true answer. But – we're a security industry ... if we're too conservative, that's better than being too loose. We should *assume* there's sound evidence that there's going to be a quake in Vancouver. Now, how do we handle it?'

This interviewee expresses a common sentiment about underwriting earthquake catastrophe insurance and, indeed, insurance more generally. One has to act as if the evidence is solid in order to act at all. Underwriting, like life itself, is the art of drawing sufficient conclusions from insufficient premises. Earthquake underwriters must create a sense of objective knowledge out of their incomplete, subjective, and differently interpreted data. While science provides indispensable knowledge upon which to act, it also produces uncertainty and makes the world unstable and mutable. As Porter (1995: 7–8) observes, 'Quantitative estimates sometimes are given considerable weight when nobody defends their validity with real conviction ... Quantification is a way of making decisions without seeming to decide. Objectivity lends authority to officials who have little of their own.'

Absorbing Risk

Insurers respond to the uncertainties of earthquakes by absorbing risk in two ways. First, they participate in programs that try to make the built environment more resistant to catastrophic loss from earthquakes. Second, they try to absorb risk through their loss ratio practices. In particular, they participate in elaborate reinsurance arrangements to ensure that the enormous capital that is required to fund a catastrophic loss is available across the industry. They also underwrite earthquake insurance in creative ways in order to generate premiums for investment and, hopefully, capital accumulation that can be used to offset catastrophic loss claims.

Major efforts to address earthquake risk through physical infrastructure usually involve the state in partnership with the private sector, including the insurance industry. One of the many ways in which the state serves as the ultimate insurer (Moss 2002) is through fostering civil engineering solutions to building, bridge, and road infrastructures and to vital supply lines such as gas and water that can reduce losses in the event of a large magnitude earthquake.

The state also develops building code standards for earthquake resistance. Buildings that do not meet earthquake resistance code standards bear high costs in the event of a catastrophe. However, it is expensive to build or renovate up to code standards. It is also sometimes a guessing game as to what natural hazard building code standards one should try to meet. The city of Kobe, Japan, was built to withstand very heavy winds and storms, which requires light walls and heavy roofs. Light walls and heavy roofs are disastrous in an earthquake. When Kobe experienced an earthquake along an un-known fault line, heavy roofs collapsed, accounting for most of the property damage as well as an estimated 90 per cent of 5,470 deaths (Wallace and White 1997: 9). Another consideration is that buildings which are better at protecting people because they are constructed to collapse gradually can also increase the overall cost of structural prop-erty damage (ibid.: 10).

In California the reality of recent earthquake catastrophes encour-aged the government and insurance industry to provide incentives for loss prevention. For example, 300 companies that together underwrite more than one-half of the business established the Insurance Institute for Property Loss Reduction. One project involved collaboration with city and state officials in Los Angeles to assist policyholders in retrofit-ting their homes for earthquake resistance (Brun et al. 1997). There is also a United States Insurance Services Office that rates the effective-ness of local enforcement of building codes so that insurers can rate properties and vary premiums according to local enforcement (ibid.).

In Canada there are no such financial incentive schemes and build-ing code-rating systems. The industry has asked all levels of govern-ment to increase spending on making the built environment more earthquake resistant. An impetus for government expenditure was provided by a study of the Vancouver lower mainland area funded by Munich Reinsurance (1992). Following this study, a new emergency operations and communications centre was built to withstand an 8.5 magnitude earthquake on the Richter scale. The hope is that it will still be standing even if little else is. Building codes are unevenly devel-oped, legislated, and enforced and there is 'buck passing' among levels of government and the insurance industry. '[T]he incentive for one level to minimize hazard is reduced if another level ultimately pays for that loss. One such example is building codes, which are researched and recommended nationally, legislated by the provinces, and en-forced at the municipal level. If building codes are not enforced, funds for repairing avoidable damage come from private insurance compa-nies or the federal and provincial governments' (Wallace and White 1997: 8).

The insurance industry focuses more on claims management after the fact than on prevention. In Canada the property and casualty insur-ance industry has established a claims emergency response plan for each province to address all major natural disasters. The plan includes a sharing of claims specialists across member companies, who in turn coordinate with emergency response officials. An important reason for this organization is the minimization of losses through exaggerated insurance claims, a common problem after catastrophes. The problem is not only with claimants themselves, but with suppliers such as building contractors who price gouge in a high-demand, low-supply situation (Baker 1994; Baker and McElrath 1997). Following Hurricane Andrew, in Florida, for example, the cost of building materials was inflated by as much as 300 per cent.

In some contexts, insurers do foster physical infrastructure measures among their policyholders. We observed an insurer's loss control specialist on an inspection of a commercial client's premises. Following his detailed inspection of the premises, he had a meeting with the chief financial officer of the company. About twenty minutes of this meeting was devoted to business interruption problems in the event of an earthquake. The chief financial officer was told that he should have a disaster control plan and that models could be supplied. He was informed that it would be wise to obtain electrical generators and make other supplementary arrangements because the municipality might be unable to supply electrical power for an extended period. He was informed of the possible need to outsource company operations to other facilities in the event of a catastrophe. Computer and data system back-ups were recommended, as were new storage racks in the warehouse that would meet earthquake-shaking standards.

Individual homeowners can also take loss prevention measures (Brun et al. 1997: 170). Structurally they can strengthen and anchor the foundation of their homes and brace walls, posts, and chimneys. Within the home they can arrange for the shutting off of utilities, brace the water heater, and secure heavy furniture, pictures, and cupboard latches. However, these measures are not requirements of the home insurance policy contract.

The primary means through which insurers absorb earthquake risk is their loss ratio practices. In particular, they focus on developing an elaborate network of reinsurance partners to absorb the catastrophic losses that might result from a substantial earthquake. We interviewed the vice-president in charge of reinsurance for a large property and casualty insurance company. He said that his company had catastrophe reinsurance at different layers with seventy reinsurers and that total coverage was $400 million, for which annual premiums totalled $12 million. The main reason for having this hefty annual premium over several decades – with only minor claims for a couple of hailstorms – was the risk of an earthquake in British Columbia. The decision about reinsurance levels was not based on expert assessments of earthquake risk. To the contrary, the expertise available is so uncertain that the company could only speculate on what might be adequate coverage for an earthquake catastrophe.

> [We have problems with] quality of data ... garbage in, garbage out ... I'm uncomfortable with this black box side where you put all your stuff in and these numbers come out and, my gosh, there's the answer! It's not real ... There [are] changes in the model as well, like year over year, which could drive out some pretty significant variations in terms of output ... We had a number that was sort of here, and, gosh, there's a new version that's come out suddenly, our number is here now. I mean if I was trying to assess your exposure based on the output of that, you'd drive yourself crazy ... Do you pick a one-hundred-year return period or two hundred and fifty or five hundred or a thousand or ten thousand, like what number do you pick? Beyond a certain point you, say, 'Well, gee, we might have to buy reinsurance for every single nickel of property value that we have out in British Columbia,' which is obviously ridiculous and not even doable ... So we have to pick a cut-off point saying, 'Here's the range of probability, we're dealing with a five-hundred-year return period or whatever,' and work to that. But that generates about $100 million [PML], and indexed for inflation [e.g, in relation to building replacement costs] $125 million or maybe $150 million. So we buy $400 million ... We know there's a whole lot we don't know about earthquake faults in British Columbia compared to California ... And even in California where they think they know a whole lot about where it is, they have Northridge which was in the area where they didn't even know they could have an earthquake. They didn't even know there was a fault there ... How could we say, 'Well, gosh, this lovely model has come up with this number and that's got to be the right number so we'll buy to that level?' We buy more than double that level because we *feel* we need to. Because there's a whole lot we don't know and we don't want to be caught in a situation. Our first obligation is to make sure we can pay our policyholders.

Similar concerns were expressed by other insurance executives we interviewed. The CEO of a large property and casualty insurance company also said that his company took a conservative approach in 'picking a number' and gambling on levels of catastrophe reinsurance. Although he concurred that the data and models used to ascertain

PML are highly problematic, he also criticized companies that choose to be less conservative in their estimates or, worse still, do not bother with data or models at all.

> [An earthquake of high magnitude is] a phantom event. We know it's going to happen. It might be five hundred years away. You know there's competing models. One model says it's going to be forthcoming, it'll be a $200 million event [for our company] and the next one says it'll be a $400 million event. I mean you might as well blind yourself and get dizzy before you throw the dart in terms of picking a number. There are companies out there, if there was an event tomorrow, haven't got the capacity to handle it. They're making a promise, they can't keep it ... [We use] latest science ... in favour of the more conservative. Whereas many people have only picked the model that produces the lowest results. Some aren't using any models at all, whereas we're dealing predominately with licensed reinsurers, all our reinsurers are high quality ... There's *nobody* that can stand up and say for certain that they can keep the promise because we don't know.

The generation of premium revenues for investment and capital accumulation is also crucial for loss ratios. Premium setting involves the insurer in determining 'how much coverage to offer and what premium to charge so as to make a reasonable profit while not subjecting itself to an unacceptably high chance of a catastrophic loss' (Kunreuther 2002: 4). But premium setting is extremely difficult in the case of earthquake insurance because both the chance of the event and the estimation of loss are beyond the capacity for reasonable calculations. Kunreuther et al. (1995) argue that in highly ambiguous situations such as earthquake underwriting, insurers tend to inflate premiums. They support this contention through a survey of 896 underwriters in which respondents were asked to determine premiums required to insure a factory against property damage from an earthquake. In the judgment of the researchers, respondents tended to propose inflated premiums. However, this judgment is problematic since it seems impossible establish a reasonable premium because the risk and its probable effects are so unpredictable. Furthermore, insurers typically set premiums more in relation to competitive market conditions than to fanciful data on risk.

Our interviewees made it clear that insurers underwrite and price earthquake insurance largely in terms of local markets rather than in relation to expert knowledge on PML and the possible insolvency of their company in the event of a catastrophe. An earthquake underwriter we interviewed said that his work entailed reading the market to make 'an educated guess and a bit of a hopeful bet, which is after all the fundamentals of insurance.' A state regulator we interviewed agreed that reading the market in these terms is what earthquake underwriters do. The 'expected experience' with earthquakes is always related to the 'public's willingness to accept particular premium rates. And there's always some company in the market that is willing to drive down the premiums just to maintain your client base.'

At the time of our research there was a highly competitive or 'soft' market for earthquake insurance coverage in British Columbia. Limits of coverage were increasing and premiums and deductibles were decreasing. The marketing manager of a large commercial insurance broker said in interview, 'The exposure hasn't changed, we can still have a significant earthquake ... They [insurers] want money, they want to invest that money, they want to use that money. So they're prepared to give some things to allow themselves to write business.'

For many insurers earthquake coverage is simply an extra made available with a bundle of coverages on the general commercial or home policies of their clients. If a client wants earthquake coverage, it is added largely because it is necessary to close the deal for the general policy. A CEO said in interview, 'we're not trying to sell earthquake, sometimes you have to supply some earthquake capacity to underwrite a whole account.' He said that his company was very conservative in this regard. '[I]f there's a bad one, some of those insurance companies are going to go under. And we're convinced that we will not, we'll forego business today rather than put on more earthquake capacity.' When asked about less conservative companies, he said they were driven by a greater need to generate premiums for investment in a soft market and, therefore, often included earthquake coverage as a 'loss leader ... You'll have a company that will start giving away the earthquake for free, I mean they're not even charging for it: Earthquake has gotten very cheap again and very abundant, that's mainly due to competitive pressure.'

A commercial underwriter working in this soft market concurred that earthquake coverage was being thrown in as an incentive by most insurers, often regardless of their ability to pay in the event of a catastrophe. 'They're not charging for it, they're providing full earthquake limits on their policies, they've lowered their deductibles ... [Brokers] go to any number of insurers who will give them full quake with no initial premium and low deductible, which we won't do that. But if a quake ever happens, we'll be in a position where we will financially be able to pay the claims that we will experience whereas the other insurers, I am not sure they will. So it is something that we contend with the brokers a lot.'

This underwriter's contention was that she lost commercial insurance business to competitors because they offered cheap or free earthquake insurance even if unable to pay claims. She was restricted from competing on these terms because her company was more prudent. 'Earthquake has impaired and restricted our underwriting in Vancouver. A company with our capacity could go hog wild out here. Probably even make money, even in the depressed prices of this market.'

Earthquake coverage itself is a means of generating some premium revenue for investment profits. However, the main function of earthquake coverage is to attract consumers to broader homeowner and commercial insurance packages. In the opinion of a federal government regulator of insurance company solvency, in British Columbia it is 'unusual to find 60 per cent of homeowners have actually got earthquake insurance. You know why it is? Well, gee whiz, we find that their premium rates are ridiculously low. Caution flags start to go up. If you look at it, and you find also that the way they've managed that risk is to close their eyes to it, then I don't have prudent management here. It's way too low. People wouldn't pay the kind of insurance premium that you typically should be paying.'

Another peculiarity of earthquake insurance underwriting is the lack of differentiation among policyholders in terms of the degree to which they are presumed to be exposed to risk of an earthquake. For example, in British Columbia there is a legislated contract provision in the homeowner's insurance policy that provides coverage for any damage caused by a fire following an earthquake. This provision creates a moral risk at the level of the policyholder. As articulated in interview by an insurance company's disaster planning specialist, 'If you don't have earthquake insurance and the house is hit, toss a match in it.' A solvency regulator made the same point. 'If there's an earthquake and you're still standing, you toss the match so the gas is all over the place. There's a moral hazard.' In her view the fire insurance premium should vary by earthquake risk. 'The idea that it's totally socialized by being a flat thing across a whole bunch of regions is bananas from my perspective.'

This particular provision of homeowner insurance policies makes underwriting of these basic policies difficult. Somehow underwriting should include estimates of potential loss resulting from fires after earthquakes, but such estimates are largely guesswork. Wallace and White (1997: 12) feel that the 'distribution of quake-related fire protection may be inciting insurance firms, under competitive market conditions, to underestimate further, or ignore, earthquake-related fire losses in computing prices for basic coverage ... [and] disadvantage firms that attempt to price fire damage properly.' They also note that fire coverage in the basic homeowner's policy is 'more generous and less costly' than earthquake coverage, for example, carrying a much lower deductible. As a result even those with earthquake coverage added to their homeowner's policy 'could commit arson in order to benefit from a lower fire deductible and this could greatly compound damage resulting from fire following a quake' (ibid.). In addition 'an insured with no earthquake shake damage coverage, but whose building was damaged by the shaking, could also be tempted to commit arson as the fire damage would be covered and it could be very difficult at the time of a major quake to determine which damage was fire and which arose from the shake.'

Some insurers have tried to address this moral risk by devising policies that they hope will escape the legislated requirement. A vice-president of one company we studied said that 85 per cent of its policyholders had earthquake coverage on their home policies, well above the industry average. The reason for this high level was that earthquake coverage was included in the basic homeowner's policy rather than as an additional coverage rider, which is the usual practice. Responsibility for not having earthquake coverage is placed on the client, who must exercise the option to remove it. However, removal also includes removal of fire following earthquake coverage, which is the pricing key. He said that his company was able to obtain lower rates from reinsurers because the fire following earthquake moral risk was dealt with in this manner.

Earthquake risk is also socialized among property and casualty insurance policyholders who live in regions of Canada where there is no earthquake risk. An earthquake underwriting specialist for an insurance company said in interview that policyholders of all lines of property and casualty insurance across Canada are unwittingly 'on the risk' of an earthquake in British Columbia. 'The quake problem has always been recognized in British Columbia, quantified in British

Columbia, not necessarily charged for in British Columbia. In essence using property fire rates, which were barely sufficient to fund for the eventuality of a quake. When you're improperly funding for a quake in British Columbia, you're in essence degrading the rates you have here and saying to Alberta risks and Manitoba risks and Ontario risks, "Well, you're funding this risk as well ..." People have been looking on a book basis and saying, "Do we have enough money to sustain a quake?"'

An insurance company solvency regulator for a state agency expressed his worries about how an earthquake in British Columbia could result in a failure to meet different types of insurance claims across the country. 'When everything is lying on the ground, broken up, who are they going to call? They can't call their private insurer because it's not there anymore! And, by the way, people are going to call them for their auto accident in Ontario. They can't call them either [laughs] 'cause they're not there anymore! Who are people going to look to? This is the idea of preferring that the private sector step up ... to these things and for individuals too.'

Mitigation

Since it is impossible to prevent an earthquake from occurring through direct intervention, the responsibility is to mitigate the effects should a 'big one' occur. As we have already seen, the risk can be absorbed through the engineering logic of earthquake resistant physical infrastructures and the economic logic of insolvency resistant insurance infrastructures. However, it is extremely difficult to make people responsible in these ways.

The uncertainties of earthquakes make people highly equivocal about investing in physical infrastructure that will mitigate loss. How does one estimate the probability of a catastrophe in the specific case of property one owns and therefore decide the level of earthquake resistant construction and at what cost? If the risk is perceived as too remote in time and specific place there is little incentive for such loss prevention measures. If the risk is perceived as too immediate, then preventive efforts may also be seen as not worth the investment. It may be preferable to walk away from the property and declare bankruptcy in the event of a catastrophe.

Compared to other types of property insurance (Ericson, Doyle, and Barry 2003: chap. 8), it is difficult to enforce loss prevention efforts as part of earthquake coverage. An official involved in emergency preparedness programs for a state agency said that effective enforcement of earthquake loss mitigation standards would only be possible if insurance was mandatory. When insurance is mandatory – for example, in the case of vehicle insurance – the state and industry can write sanctions into the insurance contract that 'responsibilize' the property holder to take preventive action. When insurance is not mandatory, an escalation of costly sanctions against a policyholder will lead her to seek an insurer with less stringent requirements or simply to drop the coverage.

Insurance companies are especially reluctant to get tough in earthquake loss prevention requirements if they are operating in a soft market. A tough approach to loss prevention in this circumstance will entail a loss of customers to competitors.

The insurance industry tries to make state agencies take more responsibility for loss prevention, but in a jurisdiction where there has never been a catastrophic earthquake, this too is difficult. Referring to a specific earthquake loss mitigation program, our emergency preparedness interviewee said, 'the people who don't like it the most are the politicians' because they are more focused on 'the priorities of the moment.' He and a second emergency preparedness official then expressed their frustration at trying to involve the public in earthquake loss prevention programs.

First official: [People] haven't experienced it. You can't paint a picture that is accurate enough to convince them and even if you do there is a certain gambling aspect in every citizen.

Second official: It's a large unknown ... [The public believes] they're going to have to pay for it at the end ... [in] tax dollars.

First official: In recorded history in British Columbia there's never been a casualty in an earthquake.

Second official: There was one dead fellow that was rowing his boat.

First official: Rowing his boat, he had a heart attack. Given that, are people going to take it seriously? ... [We're not even prepared for floods] Dyking systems over there, it's in dreadful shape. It has not been maintained for years.

Second official: A year ago the water was that far [hand gesture] from the top of the dyke. Everybody saw it. Did that have any effect? They said, 'It didn't go over, the dykes held.'

First official: [referring to an 'emergency preparedness week' radio and television media blitz] We want to terrify them. [But] we've learned here that you don't try to terrify senior citizens ... They don't do anything because they're not afraid of dying today ... It doesn't take much imagination to visualize these horror scenarios, but that's not motivational ... The common man has a lot of common sense. What is the probability? Not news. No one can confirm it.

The general lack of interest in earthquake loss prevention is another reason why it may not be feasible to require it as a condition of insurance contracts. We interviewed an earthquake specialist for a multinational insurance company that specialized in commercial underwriting. He said that earthquake loss prevention requirements were not written into his company's policies. Rather, recommendations were made as part of on-site inspections by company loss control experts. He said these experts often appealed to human injury or death risks posed by inadequate prevention measures, more than to property damage, as a means of securing compliance.

A loss control inspector for the same company said in interview that if the company contractually mandated an earthquake prevention and recovery plan from a commercial client, 'we'd probably be laughed out and rightfully so because it's not ... very generic.' He said that all he could do is 'to get the thought process going ... the "what if" scenarios, "Well, what if the press goes down? ... What if your raw materials supplier in Japan can't get this?" and if we get a blank look back, we know that we could have a problem here and that's what we try and work with.'

People also ignore earthquake preparedness in the form of insurance coverage because the risk is remote in time and unspecified in place. People in earthquake-prone areas may not buy earthquake insurance because they see a catastrophe as improbable or an act of God. Even when a significant earthquake has occurred in the region they may adopt the 'gambler's fallacy' that one hazardous event means there will not be another (Petak and Anderson 1982; Palm 1990; Insurance Bureau of Canada 1995).

In a survey conducted by the Insurance Bureau of Canada (1995), most people said they would turn to insurance companies (70 per cent) rather than the state (17 per cent) in the event of an earthquake. However, many of these people did not even have earthquake insurance coverage. Indeed, 60 per cent of people interviewed had no home or tenant insurance at all, but said they would look to insurance companies for support after an earthquake, while only 23 per cent of this group said they would look to the state! Evidently their faith in the private insurance market was so great they thought it would help them even if they were not part of it. Wallace and White (1997: 13) make an understated observation that, 'These results point to the need for increased public education about risks related to natural hazards and ways of reducing vulnerability, such as insurance coverage.'

The public does respond when there is a significant earthquake elsewhere in the world, especially one that is closer to home culturally and geographically. For example, after the significant earthquakes in California in 1989 and 1994, property owners in British Columbia increased their demand for earthquake coverage. Underwriters we interviewed pointed to this tendency and said that they had to be careful under this circumstance not to use the opportunity to sell too much coverage, which would lead to unfavourable exposure. They also said that the effect is short-lived. After the initial shock demand dissipates and the market softens. An interviewee observed, 'It gets calmer and people [insurers] start giving the endorsements away ... I'll throw in earthquake for no extra fee ... same with hurricanes ... In this industry memory tends to lapse over a year or two period. Over five years, everyone forgets it.'

The cultural economy of earthquake underwriting is revealed in comparing British Columbia with Quebec. While Vancouver and Montreal have similar risks of catastrophic earthquake, only 5 per cent of homeowners in Montreal purchase earthquake insurance compared to 60 per cent of homeowners in Vancouver (Wallace and White 1997: 13). In the province of Quebec, less than 1 per cent of homeowners purchase earthquake insurance, while in British Columbia 33 per cent of homeowners purchase it (Insurance Bureau of Canada 1996: 16). Among commercial insurance policyholders 30 per cent of those in Quebec have earthquake coverage compared to 80 per cent in British Columbia (ibid.).

We interviewed an earthquake underwriting specialist for a multinational insurance company. His assessment was that Quebec 'has areas that are as bad and a few that are worse than most of Vancouver. It's just not as active a seismic zone.' He attributed the huge discrepancy in coverage between the two jurisdictions to cultural factors. In particular, he felt that the proximity of British Columbia to California led to more 'hype' in the media and attendant fear about a major earthquake. When asked why the insurance industry does not promote the risk and need for coverage in Quebec, he replied that the main barrier was negative 'public relations, because the peoples' first reaction probably would be, "Here comes the insurance industry to try and get more money out of us. They're just trying scare tactics. There really isn't an earthquake exposure and they want us to think there is."'

As we document in the following section on infrastructures, responsibility for mitigation is negotiated among state agencies and private insurance companies. For individual property holders, earthquake preparedness is viewed as a market choice rather than a socialized responsibility requiring compulsory insurance. We interviewed a state official responsible for emergency planning who stated emphatically, 'If the individual knows it is going to happen eventually, surely the individual has the responsibility to do something ... You can't expect the government to do everything. At least you have to be prepared to be on your own for 72 hours; [build] up to seismic code when you're renovating ... [or] if you build [something] new ... insure.'

The problem for the individual consumer is acquiring knowledge upon which to act. As we have seen, the insurance industry itself is aware of the uncertainty of scientific knowledge and therefore speculates. Indeed, many companies underwrite earthquake coverage knowing that they are unlikely to meet their promise to pay in the event of a catastrophe. Knowledge of this moral risk posed by insurance companies is also something about which many consumers remain ignorant. The CEO of a major property and casualty insurance company said in interview that the industry as a whole was irresponsible in keeping the consumer uninformed about both earthquake risk and the risk of companies that insure it.

> If we were forced to provide the protection as an industry that we should in behind our promise, which not everybody is doing, we are going to find that the economics of providing this stuff are a lot less [attractive]. And the consumer at some point in time should be able to say, 'Well maybe I really don't want all that coverage, or maybe I have a deductible, or maybe I could do some form of co-insurance, or maybe I don't want to buy it from this company at all because you won't be there.' The consumer can't make any of these decisions because that information isn't there. Nobody is educating them and nobody is giving them the information to be educated. And that's fundamentally wrong.

Infrastructure

The comments of this CEO indicate significant problems with the insurance infrastructure for earthquake risk. These problems coalesce around the possibility that an earthquake catastrophe might be of such magnitude that many insurance companies in Canada would become insolvent. This insolvency would ramify throughout the industry and affect policyholders in other lines of property and casualty insurance. Nevertheless insurers still underwrite earthquake risk as a means of generating extra premium dollars and selling their commercial and home insurance packages.

In this section, we begin by examining the risks to policyholders posed by insurance companies that routinely underwrite earthquake insurance despite the prospect of insolvency. We then consider how insurance companies create risks among themselves (Bohn and Hall 1999). This occurs because all property and casualty insurance companies are required to pay into the Property and Casualty Insurance Compensation Corporation [PACICC] compensation scheme for policyholders of failed companies. If several companies that underwrite earthquake insurance fail after a catastrophe, more prudent companies will have to pay substantial sums into the compensation scheme, which may cause some of them to fail as well. The reinsurance market is another source of risk. Many reinsurers are outside Canadian regulatory jurisdiction and they may have exposure of which the primary insurer is unaware. In the event of a catastrophe a reinsurer may also not be in a financial position to meet its promises. Finally, we examine state and industry surveillance efforts to manage these risks of insolvency. These efforts suffer from the same limits to knowledge, market constraints, and loss prevention problems faced by the insurers themselves. Moreover, once the state involves itself in catastrophe insurance additional uncertainties emerge.

It must be kept in mind that the situation described here pertained during our field research in the late 1990s. Changes to insurance markets, industry practices, and government regulation have taken place since then. Nevertheless, insolvencies always loom with regard to major catastrophic risks such as earthquakes (Froot 1999).

Insurance company officials and state regulators we interviewed were unanimous in declaring that the property and casualty insurance industry in Canada routinely underwrites earthquake insurance in the face of insolvency if a large magnitude earthquake occurs. A state regulator said that the only certainty is uncertainty: the consumer and her agent must put their faith in what appears to be a strong company because no one really knows what will occur and what the impact will be. 'An earthquake that is eight [on the Richter scale] or something like that, flattens every place: will every company be able to pay up? No ... When they had the big hurricane [Andrew] down in Florida, a lot of insurance companies just walked away and said, "Well, we can't pay" ... That could occur here. You look at your company, it looks pretty strong, your broker *hopes* it's strong, and at the end of the day you don't really know.'

Wallace and White (1997) provide some dramatic figures to express the enormity of the problem. If there is a large magnitude earthquake shock in the Vancouver region, the risks posed by insurance infrastructure will create economic shocks in the future. In 1994, while the PML of a large magnitude earthquake in Vancouver was between $9.7 and $12 billion, the estimated capacity of the insurance industry to cover claims was $2.3 billion (ibid.: 12). By 1997, it was estimated that a sizeable earthquake

> could now cost $30 billion, or one-third of the province's GDP. Such an event could cause an economic shock 10 times greater than the most recent recession, and less than half of this loss would be covered by insurance (IBC, 1994a). If current trends continue, the economic vulnerability of Canadians to an earthquake in British Columbia will increase ... The Canadian insurance industry is at risk ... The IBC has estimated that roughly one-quarter of companies writing property insurance in British Columbia would become insolvent following an earthquake in Vancouver (IBC 1994). Furthermore, these insolvencies would be felt throughout the Canadian insurance market, which might not be able to meet claims from other areas of the country. A contagion effect could occur if policyholders cancelled policies with companies that they felt might become insolvent, making insolvency a self-fulfilling prophecy for many firms. (Ibid.: 8, 12–13)

We interviewed an underwriter for a multinational company that sells commercial earthquake coverage in British Columbia. He said that his company took a pragmatic approach to underwriting earthquake insurance. 'Well, if I really thought we were going to have one, I wouldn't live here. We looked at this [company office] building and we decided it's going to sway and snap off on the fifteenth floor. So, we haven't moved.' He continued with his pragmatism. 'The earthquake rate is generating premium, it's going into the general pool. It's not like anyone is setting it aside [in an earthquake reserve pool]. Frankly, our company isn't.' This interviewee also readily admitted that the company's pragmatic approach was a gamble and might not pay off. 'If a major quake happens in Vancouver, it probably is going to fry the industry ... I don't know how the industry would recover from it. Are we capitalized at this moment to say, "Yep, we've got the liquid cash ready to roll?" Tough to say ... Whether we're capitalized or not has too many variables to say yes, or no.'

We also interviewed the earthquake-underwriting specialist for the same company. He made it clear that while earthquake insurance underwriting is routine, it would result in a catastrophe for the insurance industry if a significant earthquake occurs. 'A subduction quake off Vancouver Island that caused a major event in Vancouver, I believe that last figure was $34 billion in anticipated damage. Our industry cannot at its current rates sustain $34 billion in any catastrophe. You would see a number of companies liquidate, a number of companies would be bankrupt, a number of companies ... would probably have to rely on parents ... Reinsurers would be fairly hard hit.'

There is considerable variation in how companies address this threat of insolvency. More prudent companies that restrict their underwriting and have substantial reinsurance identify less prudent companies as the source of greatest risk. An earthquake underwriting specialist for a multinational company complained about smaller company 'mavericks ... who don't really seem to care about earthquake ... I say that more as a consumer who doesn't want the insurance industry to collapse due to a quake because I'm going to have claims too and I want them paid for.' The vice-president of reinsurance for another large company talked at length about the irresponsibility of many companies that was affecting his company as well as the industry as a whole. 'We're saying the insurance industry can't afford to pay for earthquake in British Columbia. There's all this promise to pay in the policies that have been issued, but we as an industry don't have the resources to pay that ... even if ... you use modelling ... and double that just in case ... For the expected loss of like $15 billion or $16 billion – after you take off deductibles and the fact that some people don't buy earthquake insurance – our industry will probably need to pay close to $10 billion. And we can't pay anywhere near that ... even with reinsurance.'

A major concern for these interviewees was their compulsory participation in PACICC, which requires still solvent companies to compensate policyholders whose insurers have become insolvent. PACICC was established primarily as a means of protecting policyholders from isolated insolvencies that arise occasionally from insurance risks and operations. At the time of our research a policyholder with an insolvent company could claim from PACICC up to 70 per cent of unearned premiums ($1,000 maximum) and $250,000 in respect of claims arising from each policy issued by the now insolvent company. These arrangements are manageable in the event of single company failures that occur from time to time. However, there are potentially catastrophic consequences if several companies collapse at once, because the claims against remaining companies will be so large that some might fail also in a house-of-cards effect. An official involved in the compensation scheme said that in the event of a large magnitude earthquake 'a lot of companies would go bankrupt ... [This] could have a house-of-cards effect back in Toronto because there's fewer healthy companies to assess the bailout, and at $250,000 a claim that can add up pretty damn quick ... Some of our members have said we should exclude any claims participation types that have to do with earthquakes. That's not our role. I don't insure types of coverages ... We protect policyholders of bankrupt insurance companies. I don't care whether it is fire or earthquake or volcanoes.'

We studied a large insurance company whose executives were very concerned about other companies that posed risks in the context of PACICC arrangements. This company was conservative in both its approach to underwriting earthquake insurance in British Columbia and its level of reinsurance to cover a catastrophic loss. It developed its own network of expertise in earthquake modelling, PML estimates, and reinsurance and shared this expertise with insurance solvency regulators for the state. The vice-president for reinsurance said that training sessions were offered to regulators as an additional way to convince them that even strong companies like his own could fail because of the risks posed in PACICC arrangements.

> Our concern is that our industry could be brought down by something like an earthquake happening or that we ourselves could be brought down ... [Under PACICC obligations we would] have to ante up for the company that went down. And we're saying that in an extreme event like an earthquake, that kind of mechanism wasn't meant to deal with that. If we have a lot of companies disappear, as we think they will, the few companies that are remaining, if they are assessed and they have to pay the losses for all

those companies that went down, it's going to pull us down ... even though we're doing all the right things and doing everything we can to make sure we can pay.

The vice-president for distribution of the same company said that while the company did everything possible to cover its own exposure to earthquake catastrophe, it still faced the potentially catastrophic risks of other insurance companies and PACICC.

> Our exposure to earthquake is our largest single concern. And we are not actually big players in that whole market ... But one of the things that we've been really vocal about over the past few years is the extent to which the industry is prepared for a major earthquake in British Columbia. And frankly it is not. We think we are, but we think we are in a minority ... People have a right to expect to have their claims paid ... We're vulnerable because ... PACICC ... has agreed to indemnify claimants if insurance companies go under. And we think many, many insurance companies will go under if there is a major earthquake in British Columbia ... The only thing that will save us in the short run is that there's a maximum assessment that can be made against us in any one year.

The CEO of another large insurance company said in interview that he preferred not to underwrite earthquake insurance, but he was forced to do so to be competitive. Nevertheless, he restricted earthquake underwriting to the point where it was having a detrimental effect on his overall business. Competitors were underwriting earthquake insurance to gain market share, but in a catastrophe his company would have to pay for his competitor's irresponsibility through PACICC.

> Richmond-Delta – which all the theorists say will disappear like jelly in the ocean – if I restrict my writings on what otherwise looks like a good piece of business, I lose. And then if somebody else doesn't restrict but they don't have the where-with-all when the event takes place to do it [cover the claims] and I have to contribute to PACICC as part of the industry – and I will – I basically pay twice rather than once ... And I just got myself on the board of PACICC because I've had no luck at resolving this issue going at it one way. I'm about to go at it another way ... We've actually curtailed our business – of *any* business in certain areas – so that the amount of exposure we're taking is manageable with the resources we've got. That gives you

problems in the marketplace and, in the short term, as long as that event hasn't happened, I'm losing money, falsely, but losing.

Concern about PACICC was not limited to large companies watching small companies steal business from them through irresponsible underwriting. Some small companies were also concerned that their better lines of property and casualty business were jeopardized by other companies that decided to gamble on earthquakes. The CEO of a company that specialized in a vehicle insurance niche market outside British Columbia complained vehemently about how his company was jeopardized by others who speculated on earthquakes in British Columbia.

In many cases, insurance companies will not have sufficient reinsurance to cover them ... For example, the [name] Insurance Company is out there with a minimal amount of capital, writing a lot of business in British Columbia. Now if they happened to become insolvent because of an earthquake and they had $2 or $3 billion in losses that they couldn't cover, then suddenly the rest of the industry would have to cover that. And then if we had a share in proportion to our premium rates in the country and we had to take $3 billion of capital out of the insurance industry, a number of other insurance companies would suddenly become insolvent as well. As they become insolvent, then all of their policyholders would be into PACICC as well ... a chain reaction until the final few would also go broke ... A situation like that would be very detrimental to Canada itself. Because you destroy the insurance industry here, how could everyone driving a car, owning a house, industry, they're all dependent upon insurance. You can't expose the insurance industry to such a disaster through a fund that was set up with a totally different intention.

The primary underwriters of earthquake insurance face similar problems in relation to reinsurers. Most earthquake risk is laid off with reinsurance companies, some of whom may also gamble irresponsibly and become insolvent in the event of a catastrophe. If insolvencies occur, other reinsurance partners have to cover the losses and a house-of-cards effect results. An earthquake-underwriting expert for a multinational company explained in interview that

if you have any given reinsurer on too many of those buildings, there is where your real problem lies. Because an earthquake [is] ... going to pierce those reinsurance dollars very quickly ... If you had a reinsurer who was not cognizant of earthquake exposures, they could run hog wild in a market like this. Where competition is fierce and rates are low, they could gobble up business by simply undercutting all the competition ... tending to pick up the lower layers of the excess, where all the money is. So they're going to be the first reinsurer burned, they're going to be the first reinsurer to lose all of their funds, they're going to be the first reinsurer to go bankrupt. That is going to start a chain reaction where other reinsurers have to start dropping down because that's the nature of reinsurance: if you can't collect from one, the ones above will drop down. And what you've done there is taken somebody who had put themselves higher up for a reason, collected less money in return, all of a sudden dropping down to pay a layer they did not expect to pay so, in essence, shifting the burden where it wasn't expected to be shifted.

Both the institution of privacy and the multinational dimensions of the reinsurance business mean that neither a primary insurer nor the solvency regulator in its country of origin can obtain full disclosure regarding the risks posed by reinsurance pacts. An earthquake-underwriting specialist for a multinational insurance company we studied said that solvency regulators for the state are very disadvantaged in accessing relevant information about reinsurers. As a consequence regulators rely on the primary insurers to assess insolvency risks in the reinsurance relationship. He said that his company bound reinsurance in the United States and, therefore, Canadian regulators had no direct jurisdiction over them.

So they have to shift certain onus to us because they can't go after the reinsurers, they can't even find out who we're using in some cases ... They haven't got time to call all 300 companies [we use] ... wherever they may be – France, England, United States – and find out every treaty reinsurer and then in turn investigate them ... So to a degree they do shift the onus onto us and make us responsible for reporting who is there and some details about them ... Red flag system, if they saw particular reinsurers popping up ... or unknown reinsurers popping up again and again ... [or a reinsurer is driving] business down, down, down in terms of price and up in terms of exposure.

This interviewee said his company was so well capitalized and so well endowed with its own expertise internationally that it handled its natural catastrophe exposures in Canada, including earthquake risk, largely outside of reinsurance arrangements. A significant reason for this approach was the company's belief that reinsurers pose substantial risks. '[Our PML is] calculated pretty much outside of reinsurance ... reinsurers may have exposure out there of which we're not aware either, so we can't necessarily count on them.'

We interviewed an underwriter for a multinational company that underwrites earthquake insurance in both British Columbia and California. She said the surveillance and regulatory regime in California was stricter and more intrusive, whereas in British Columbia she was allowed to underwrite earthquake insurance at whatever price would attract business in a soft market. The company's California office had just been fined $1 million

> for deviating too much from the EPA's rating that we have on our system, whereas I've got files that are 20 per cent of what the low end of the range is because that's the market and you either write it or you don't. Whereas in the States they get fined for that kind of stuff. So from my standpoint I'm happy, just leave the regulators out of it, let the competitive market environment detail what the best thing is for that client. If the client can get $12 grand [premium from a competitor] and we're going to have to charge them $16 or $20 grand, but the [regulator's] range is telling me I have to do $30 or $40 grand, well who is that benefiting? Just because I put in some filed rates [with the regulator]? I'm a big believer in free enterprise. Stay out of our way, just let us do our thing.

Some of the insurers underwriting earthquakes in British Columbia met on a regular basis to discuss their underwriting practices and use moral suasion with each other. They circulated a list of each company's practices, such as policy conditions (e.g., deductibles) and specific geographic areas that should not be underwritten. However, this effort at collective self-regulation did not include all companies, in particular, those seen as posing the greatest risks of insolvency. One member of the group said that the joint declaration of reasonable deductible levels, excluded areas, and so on was at least a signal to others about their degrees of irresponsibility.

The responsibility of an individual company for self-regulation varied by the capital it could access to gamble on earthquakes. For example, interviewees told us that the time-line standards an individual company chose to estimate PML varied by its practical underwriting capacity and access to capital rather than scientific assessment or prudence with respect to solvency. The vice-president for reinsurance of a more conservative company complained that the solvency regulator only required models based on a 250–year projection. He said that the regulator's response was that 'there's a lot of companies that perhaps can't make that 250 level first, so let's get everybody there and then look at the next step.'

The Office of the Superintendent of Financial Institutions (OSFI) established a task force in 1995 to address earthquake insurance issues and problems. The main impetus for the task force was the insurance industry's desire to increase the involvement of OSFI because companies were experiencing too many problems trying to regulate each other. A solvency regulator described the situation as 'a bit unusual' and motivated by the fact that 'they don't like somebody getting an advantage in any way if they can help it ... some feeling that people were not pricing for this risk appropriately.' An industry association official concurred. She said that the industry was pressing the state by arguing that all three levels of government were also exposed to the risk of irresponsible underwriters. 'So what we're saying is, if the insurance industry for whatever reason is unable to meet its obligations, then the government is going to be on the hook. So better you talk to us now so that we can together ensure the viability of this product and of the insurance companies to respond, than to wait and find out after the fact.'

A state solvency regulator said that his agency was especially keen to avoid having the Government of Canada become the deep pocket following an earthquake catastrophe. He referred to the Florida hurricane catastrophe risk, where state involvement in the insurance constellation creates a significant moral risk at the level of the insured. 'You virtually have people who double and triple the size of their houses ... And you know that every five years they're going to get wiped out but they couldn't give a hoot. And private coverage has gone way down ... They think governments have deep pockets and there's no pricing mechanism for pricing it properly.'

Another state solvency regulator said that it is imperative to emphasize that governments are not the ultimate insurer of earthquake risks. The way to reinforce this is to emphasize continually an individual choice and responsibility model. Each insurance company is responsible for underwriting earthquake risk prudently and the key to doing so is to make individual policyholders pay differentially for whatever risks they face.

Do something. Don't sit around and pontificate about it ... that doesn't advance us at all ... The government should not be the bearer of costs of earthquakes. I mean if people want to live in Richmond [a suburb of Vancouver], which is a huge earthquake risk area, that is one of the costs of living in Richmond, which should be reflected in their choice of living there, to be one of the economic signals to perhaps move people out of there ... The premiums will be higher in Richmond ... And people can make choices, rather than having the taxpayer in Penticton, who has no earthquake risks, footing the bill for the guy who wants to live in Richmond.

In 1994, it was estimated that a catastrophic earthquake in British Columbia could require $12 billion in federal assistance, not counting compensation to policyholders whose insurers become insolvent (Wallace 1997: 200). Two state officials responsible for catastrophe emergency programs said in interview that their responsibility was to spread risks among individuals and institutions, including moral risks. In the process, the state should not contribute to moral risk itself by giving the impression that it is the ultimate deep pocket in the event of a catastrophe. However, this is largely a smoke and mirrors dance, where 'insurance' is to be provided by private industry and 'disaster relief' is at the discretion of government after the fact.

First official: [We seek] a way of spreading the responsibility for a potential risk throughout society ... an individual and a corporate responsibility to manage that risk financially by insurance ... And the government's disaster assistance plan is based on that premise. It is not available for insurable risks ... [which are judged] largely on the advice of, and in conjunction with, the insurance industry itself.
Second official: That's not to say that immediately following a disaster earthquake, the government changes its mind – which is not stated policy of course ... We don't plan on it. And we certainly don't advise people not to get insurance because that might happen.
First official: Government policy is that disaster assistance is not provided for reasonably and readily insurable risks ... It's moral hazard in that aspect. But disaster financial assistance isn't insurance anyway. It's relief ... If you had a government policy, and enumerate in that policy that indeed assistance in this instance would be available, then indeed you are ... undercutting the rationale for buying insurance and for assigning a degree of responsibility that indeed government feels is appropriate for individuals

and corporations to manage their own risks ... [It would be] political death to say no [to disaster relief] in most circumstances of course, but it would be financially irresponsible for government in effect to write a blank cheque.

The state experiences particular difficulty in displacing responsibility for earthquake risk management because the threat is so remote. It is especially problematic to govern at a distance when the danger is at a distance. A state regulator of insurance company insolvency said in interview that the remoteness of the possibility of a catastrophic earthquake and the fact that there has never been one in Canada makes it politically impossible to make insurance compulsory. Agreeing with this assessment, one of his colleagues said that the remoteness of a possible earthquake catastrophe also means that no one is happy about giving up much of their capital in long-term planning for it. Just like the insured who is reluctant to pay substantial earthquake insurance premiums, insurance companies themselves have difficulty thinking that they should be reserving substantial capital for something that is modelled to occur centuries into the future. This regulator said that he has to convince insurance companies that 'once every 500 years you might have a huge claim, but in between you're going to be collecting some premiums. Hold it guys, it isn't your money yet! Five hundred years from now you might need it!'

In contrast to the Canadian situation, jurisdictions that have experienced a major earthquake actively involve the state in insurance markets. For example, in California, since 1985, insurers have been legally required to provide earthquake coverage to anyone who has a homeowner's policy with them. Following the Northridge earthquake in 1994, about 90 per cent of insurers severely restricted the sale of new homeowners' policies or stopped selling them altogether. In 1996, the State of California stepped in with an earthquake-specific insurance company, the California Earthquake Authority. The California Earthquake Authority offers earthquake coverage to homeowners in collaboration with private sector primary insurers and reinsurers (Kleindorfer and Kunreuther 1999: 153).

In Canada, the federal solvency regulator is not in a position to govern insurance company practices more directly. It cannot gain sufficient access to knowledge of company practices in solvency risk management. Moreover, most of the knowledge it does obtain must be kept confidential for fear of undermining public confidence in vulnerable individual companies. Any actions which upset the regulator's compliance relationship with companies are likely to further restrict access to knowledge. A regulator said in interview that all his agency could do was articulate standards in a best practices guideline, require insurance company managers to report regularly on compliance with the guideline, and hope that managers themselves are able to govern their own earthquake risk loss ratio practices effectively. The 'responsibilization' of managers includes having them 'demonstrate that you have appropriate reinsurance coverage, and/or capital and/or reserves, dedicated reserves, to meet the 250-year-return period event ... What we can do is check that the company management is going through the right kind of processes, that their data is being captured in the right kind of ways, some of these kinds of things, so we can have more *faith* in the estimates that they're developing ... This involves some reliance on the fact that appointed actuaries, auditors and boards, directors, and their committees are doing what they're supposed to be doing under the Insurance Companies Act.'

In the mid-1990s the property and casualty insurance industry pressured Canadian governments for special tax considerations on money earmarked for earthquake catastrophe management (Brun et al. 1997: 172; see generally Bradford and Logue 1999). The proposals were made in the context of awareness that the industry itself would face a catastrophe following a large magnitude earthquake. The industry requested: 1) relief from paying income tax on earthquake insurance premium income; 2) segregated investments on capital reserved for earthquake-related claims and tax exemption on those investments; 3) a credit facility from the British Columbia and Quebec governments for an interim period of twenty-four years in order to build sufficient reserves; and 4) more government spending on earthquake-resistant physical infrastructure, including tax incentives to encourage individuals to invest in this form of absorbing risk.

The federal government initially resisted the tax concessions requested, especially the tax exemption on reserve investments. We interviewed a federal cabinet minister who strongly opposed either tax exemption or tax deferral because it would deprive the government of assets it might need for disaster relief. He argued that the government is in effect the main 'insurer' of such catastrophic loss, a fact made all the more evident by the admission of some insurance companies that they did not have assets to cover an earthquake catastrophe. He also said that this admission raised serious questions about why these companies were even selling earthquake insurance. He was adamant that the government not give insurance companies the institutional equivalent of the Registered Retirement Savings Plan scheme for their long-term corporate benefit.

On the other hand, federal solvency regulators we interviewed were in favour of tax concessions. One said in interview, 'As a regulator I would like to see very low taxes, so I can get as much capital and surplus in the companies as I possibly can. Taxes draw down capital, and surplus pulls back earnings, so our objectives and Revenue Canada's objectives are a tad different here.' A colleague emphasized that private insurance arrangements for catastrophes help to absorb if not dissipate risks to the economy. Part of the calculus may be tax-based support, but this element intersects with everything from what pricing is reasonable for consumers to the ways in which international reinsurance markets can absorb risks. The regulatory objective is the most liberal regime possible to reduce the extent to which the state 'insures' through disaster relief.

[We examine whether] better private arrangements for catastrophes are advantageous, and that therefore the state ought to offer some kind of guarantee for contingency funds as a potentially cheaper way of sharing that risk around in a societal sense than being on the hook for the disaster relief ... The safety and soundness of the institutions we regulate is only a small part of the considerations that are part of that determination ... Suppose that we say there is no ultimate back-stop contingency underwritten by government ... Suppose that we tighten up the rules on how much you can write without adequately funding it, reserving against it ... or adequately pricing it ... The response is going to be essentially some combination of less insurance, or higher prices for that insurance company, to consumers. And in that, we can through those kinds of techniques make sure that there's not a catastrophe in the insurance industry by virtue of insurance companies having written business that is fundamentally unsound business. The cost of that will be shifting more of the cost of the earthquake onto private sector participants: From a pure risk sharing point of view, is it more efficient to share these risks within Canada, with governments being part of the sharing, or is it more efficient to share those risks around the world, through the international insurance market? ... It's better risk diversification to share those risks internationally, and in fact you'll end up with an overall cheaper product ... because the likelihood of separate events that can be negatively correlated in Canada is probably a hell of a lot lower than it is having those trends of separate events negatively correlated around the world that you might share risks across.

In 1998 the federal government initiated some tax concessions to help the private insurance industry build reserves to meet earthquake catastrophe claims. We interviewed two officials responsible for provincial-level emergency planning and relief programs. They saw these concessions as simply the latest move in the ongoing negotiation of earthquake insurance infrastructure between the insurance industry and the state.

First official: [Before the soft market the industry was] making earthquake insurance so high that nobody got it, as a way of blackmailing the government. They tend to talk in worst case terms, [to] say this could bankrupt the industry if we don't do this. The fact is they haven't had an earthquake that comes close to bankrupting the industry, and now [with the tax concessions] they can save up for it, the answer is in their hands, provided that the earthquake doesn't happen for the next fifty years. If it does happen then they're bankrupt, and if it doesn't then they're not. But that's what insurance is about.
Second official: Well, that's what the claim is about. There's a lot of poker playing going on there.
First official: But insurance is a gamble.
Second official: Or, as they say, 'risk management' [laughs].
First official: Another model is catastrophe bonds. It's like reverse insurance. If there is no disaster your return is greater. If there does happen to be one and they have to use funds or spend the bonds, you are out of luck.
Second official: It can be looked at as a form of lottery. It's a voluntary tax. If you're lucky, you'll make money.

Tax concessions that allow insurance companies to build reserves for earthquake-related claims were granted in exchange for more stringent auditing and reporting requirements. Among the risks being scrutinized in this more stringent regime is the moral one that some companies might be falsely claiming tax exemptions for earthquake reserves absent earthquake exposure. In the words of an earthquake underwriting specialist for a multinational company, there is a mandatory requirement to report 'actual earthquake exposure ... to ensure that insurers who have no earthquake exposure aren't tucking away earthquake dollars and protecting them from income tax and things like that.'

Conclusion

In many respects, no one in the earthquake insurance relationship is fulfilling their responsibilities to mitigate the potential for catastrophic losses. Individuals are reluctant to take action to improve the earthquake-resistant features of their built environment. They are also reluctant to pay earthquake insurance premiums, except temporarily when a significant earthquake in a culturally close jurisdiction gives them cause for concern, or when the earthquake coverage is cheap or simply given away in a bundle of property and casualty insurance coverage. Insurers have little capacity within their insurance contract incentives or powers of moral suasion to lead policyholders to improve their physical infrastructures for risk absorption. They also appear to have little capacity to persuade each other about the need for greater responsibility in gambling on earthquakes. The state ends up as the ultimate risk manager (Moss 2002), both through spearheading the strengthening of the physical infrastructure and by being left on the hook for insurers' inability to meet promises to pay. Indeed, based on the evidence presented in this chapter, in the event of a major earthquake the state may be left with an economic shock as great as the physical shock to the built environment and those who inhabit it. While state officials bravely espouse a liberal view that it is up to individuals to make market choices about how they want to absorb earthquake risk, and up to the insurance industry to help them mitigate it responsibly, they know that this model is precarious. In efforts to construct a shock-resistant physical infrastructure and an insolvency-resistant insurance infrastructure, uncertainties proliferate.

5 Uncertainties of Terrorism: Pre-Empting Risk, Precaution, and Vigilance

There is no terror in a bang, only in the anticipation of it.

A. Hitchcock (1984)

Terror ... often arises from a pervasive sense of disestablishment, that things are in the unmaking.

S. King, *Danse Macabre* (1981)

In this chapter, we examine how the insurance industry addressed the terrorist attacks on 11 September 2001 (hereafter referred to as 9/11), especially the attack on the World Trade Center (WTC) in New York. These attacks not only led to catastrophic losses for the industry, but also precipitated radical changes to underwriting and loss prevention practices. The sharing of risk and responsibility among the insured, primary insurers, reinsurers, and governments was de-stabilized, as each party struggled to pass on its exposure to the uncertainties of terrorism. The 'pass the exposure express' among these parties was one of the most significant aftershocks of 9/11.

A new configuration of risk and uncertainty emerged. Insurers pre-empted the risk of financial exposure to terrorism by either refusing to insure it or insuring it on terms that were extremely difficult for the insured to bear. Pre-emption was also effected through new approaches to preventive security based on the precautionary principle (Ewald 2002; Baker 2002a). Although catastrophic terrorism in North America remains a low probability event, its potential consequences are of such magnitude that extreme vigilance is called for. Governments, insurers, and the insured intensify surveillance through legal, military, police, and technological resources that far exceed the cost of 9/11.

Uncertainties of Terrorism

Terrorism as Intentional Catastrophe

There is an extensive academic literature on terrorism, with exhaustive debates over definitions and meanings. However, we are primarily concerned with how terrorism is conceived and responded to by insurers. Following 9/11, insurers rewrote definitions of terrorism in order to exclude or change coverage of it. As we consider in more detail in the next section, these definitions varied depending on whether the particular insurance company wished to participate in underwriting terrorism coverage, and if so, how it wanted to limit its exposure.

In insurance terms, a catastrophe is a large-magnitude loss. Whether an individual insurance company experiences a large-magnitude loss is not simply a matter of the level of claims it must pay but also depends on its financial condition. A loss of several hundred million dollars may be a catastrophe to one company and indeed spell insolvency. Another company can absorb such a large loss in the normal course of business and not experience it as a catastrophe.

Catastrophic loss is attributable to both natural hazards and human behaviour. Among natural hazards, some, such as earthquakes, are not subject to direct human intervention. While insurers' earthquake risk is human-made to the extent that humans inhabit an earthquake zone at all and build expensive infrastructures there, the actual hazard is not of their own making. As we learned in chapter 4, the only thing that can be done in relation to earthquakes is mitigation of harmful effects through attention to how the human environment is constructed, how people are trained in disaster preparedness, and how insurance is organized.

Other natural hazards, such as storms, are subject to more direct human intervention to prevent a loss. For example, insurers in Canada have experimented with the chemical seeding of storm clouds to lessen the impact of hail storms on damage to vehicles and the built environment (Ericson, Doyle, and Barry 2003: 296–7). A more effective policy on emissions that contribute to global warming could influence hurricane and other storm patterns which, in turn, might reduce the risk of catastrophic loss.

The issue of global warming indicates that many catastrophes are more human-made than natural, or indeed result from complex interactions between humans and nature. The 'manufactured uncertainties' (Beck 1999, Giddens 1990, 1994) of contemporary society result from advances in science and technology that have unintended side effects with catastrophic consequences. Chernobyl, Bhopal, asbestosis, sinking oil tankers, and many other recent disasters exemplify Perrow's (1984) point that accidents with catastrophic consequences have become normal in the complex technological systems of modern society.

While questions of intentionality are sometimes at issue in such normal accidents, in the case of terrorism intentionality is explicit. For insurers, terrorism is intentional catastrophe. Terrorists are explicitly in the business of uncertainty. They play on randomness to keep whole populations in fear, anticipation, and disestablishment. They precipitate the urge for more certainty, expressed through escalating security measures. At the same time they are adept at grasping the rationality of each new security system in order to subvert it and induce more uncertainty.

The terrorist power of uncertainty is especially strong because we live in a risk society that is characterized by a cultural desire to tame chance and effect security. Terrorism strikes at the cultural foundation of risk society because it is a stark reminder of the limits to risk assessment and management. Human beings can always subvert rational systems by manipulating their rationality. The terrorists involved in the 9/11 events managed to organize their attack without police intervention, pass through airport security on the day of the event, and turn airplanes into bombs to create catastrophic loss. They displayed in the most spectacular fashion imaginable a new form of power, the power of catastrophe. They hit home as never before the 'ungovernability of modern societies' (Stehr and Ericson 2000): how those with little power can work cheaply and efficiently against powerful institutions to destroy, and to create 'a pervasive sense of disestablishment, that things are in the unmaking.'

Risk and Uncertainty Prior to 9/11

Of course, terrorism was known to insurers prior to 9/11. They had suffered significant losses in terrorist attacks over the previous decade (Swiss Re *Sigma* No. 1/2002: 17). For example, an IRA bomb in London's financial district in 1992 resulted in an insured loss of $671 million, and another one in the same district the following year cost $907 million. An IRA bombing in Manchester in 1996 cost $744 million. The 1993 bombing of the WTC by al-Qaeda resulted in an insured loss of $725 million. Following these previous losses, insurers took measures to limit their exposure to terrorism-related losses. After the bombings in the London financial district, insurers and reinsurers moved quickly to exclude terrorism coverage. However, they were brought back into the market through the establishment of a pool, known as Pool Re, among over two hundred companies, and the involvement of the British government above pool limits (Walker and McGuiness 1997). After the 1993 WTC bombing, one of the major reinsurance companies revised some underwriting criteria and the insured limits on its WTC contracts. These decisions saved this company from even greater losses in the 9/11 event. Another leading reinsurance company produced a document after the 1993 WTC event stating the need to fundamentally restructure the underwriting of insurance and reinsurance coverage for terrorism. However, as we shall see, such advice was not taken up. It took the 9/11 insured loss of $55 billion to precipitate significant change.

Some insurance executives were aware of the literature on new forms of terrorism prior to 9/11. For example, a reinsurance company executive said that he was aware of the 1999 Rand Corporation publication in which there is considerable detail on religiously motivated terrorism, including reference to the continuing goal of total destruction of the WTC twin towers (Lesser et al. 1999). This publication and others (e.g., Stern 1999) mapped the rise of a new 'religious terrorism' over the 1980s and 1990s. They emphasized the peculiar dimensions of this terrorism that make it especially difficult to predict and control. Its support base is spread geographically rather than being concentrated in a particular jurisdiction. It has amorphous constituencies beyond specific state governments, which free it to use weapons of mass destruction without alienating a state-based political constituency. Its strategy is irregular attacks, playing on randomness and the uncertainty and fear it fosters.

There was also evidence beyond specialized reports. Journalists had traced the evolution of al-Qaeda terrorism in regular reports, including interviews with Osama bin Laden and other major figures in which terrorist activity was threatened (for a retrospective account, see Miller, Stone, and Mitchell 2002). For example, they identified Ramzi Yousef as the mastermind behind the 1993 WTC attack, and his subsequent unexecuted plot to explode twelve jumbo jets simultaneously. Yousef was connected with bin Laden and others in the U.S. embassies in Africa plot, the USS Cole bombing, and 9/11 (ibid.). These patterns were also under active investigation by the FBI (Public Broadcasting System, *Frontline* 2002).

In the context of this prior knowledge, an obvious question arises: why did insurers and reinsurers not severely limit or entirely exclude terrorist activity from their insurance contracts? If the new terrorism is so uncertain, and it has such potential for catastrophic loss, why not leave the responsibility for risk management and loss entirely to governments and/or to organizations and individuals? Myriad risks are not insured in private markets, and are left to government schemes or no insurance capacity at all (Moss 2002).

There are several reasons why full terrorism insurance coverage was sustained prior to 9/11. First, interviewees said that a large-magnitude terrorism loss was simply not on their 'radar screen.' Indeed, as one interviewee observed, if someone had imagined a total loss of the WTC he would have been deemed crazy and dismissed. It would also have been impossible to sell insurance to clients based on a total loss scenario, because they too did not perceive such a risk. Prior to 9/11, probable maximum loss scenarios for the WTC imagined the destruction of two floors. The WTC terrorist attack of 1993 had failed, and resulted in a contained loss of well under $1 billion. As an interviewee observed, 'The magnitude of the loss in the 1993 bombing was not that great ... It caused injury and it caused physical damage to the property, but it didn't bring the building down. And so again they said, well, "What was our loss? How many millions of dollars? That's not so bad. Keep on going."'

Typical comments were offered by a leading risk management consultant to financial services companies. 'The probability was so small that people thought they would easily ignore it ... It is not that they mispriced it [terrorism risk], it is that they didn't even think it existed ... [9/11] was a shock to the information system. It's new information that this risk is much higher than we thought, *a priori*. Or we could think that it is a new kind of event that we did not anticipate that it could happen here before.' A senior executive in life insurance said, 'Terrorism has simply not been contemplated in the pricing and actuarial analysis of group life insurance. We simply have no pricing model.'

Second, some insurers said that they were abreast of patterns in the new religious terrorism but did not include it in their portfolio of catastrophic risks. A reinsurance executive said, 'An international reinsurer is supposed to have a certain experience with catastrophes. But the question is ... given the diversity of liability scenarios, how can we meaningfully process such experience? This is scarcely possible using actuarial methods alone. It calls for professional methods that are probably more akin to those of a social historian than those of an actuarial scientist or a legal expert.' He went on to say that his company had losses in previous terrorist attacks in different parts of the world, and that he was aware from the RAND (Lesser et al. 1999) study and other sources that collapse of the WTC twin towers had been a goal. 'So the problem is not know or not to know, the problem is ... what you should consider ... This is a sophisticated game, obviously, but this sophisticated game is based on the selection of four, five, six catastrophes out of twenty, thirty, forty, fifty. And this selection is absolutely dependent on, I don't know what, *casual* developments. And so the whole basis of this sophisticated and rational game is not so sophisticated.'

According to some interviewees, cyber-risk failure of computer-based information systems because of technical problems or intentional sabotage ('hacking' or 'cyber-terrorism') was *the* insurance industry issue prior to 9/11. The concern was not only the immediate consequences of system failure, but also the long-tail risk perceptions of customers who might refuse to conduct further business with the affected enterprise. Indeed, these long-tail consequences are so serious that enterprises usually keep their cyber-risk losses secret and pay their own losses. A reinsurance executive explained in interview that while catastrophic violent physical attacks by terrorists were not on the industry's radar screen prior to 9/11, cyber risk was at the centre of the risk portfolio.

> The financial damage [in cyber risk loss] was I guess much higher [than 9/11], but nobody claimed. There was no secure basis on the policy because it was just silent. And to prove there is non-excluded coverage is always difficult. On the other side, there is a secrecy issue ... If you expose to the media, to the public, that you actually have a damage, it might actually affect your business, as you do on-line business, for example. And so a lot of [companies] nowadays still don't go to the public. Nevertheless, there is high exposure and that's the reason why everybody [every insurer] goes for some exclusions worldwide.

Third, there were insurance conventions and legal restrictions on excluding terrorism in different lines of insurance. For example, most employees who lost their lives in the WTC had group life insurance policies through their employers. These policies generally have few, if any, exclusions, and not ones that would apply to death arising from terrorist activity. Employees who were injured were covered by compulsory workers' compensation insurance policies. State regulations for such policies require coverage for injuries arising from anything that happens at work, including terrorist activity. Again terrorism coverage was simply embedded in policies without a thought. In the commercial property line, terrorism was part of 'all risk' coverage. Insurers were legally obligated to offer a limited, but significant, amount of terrorism coverage for property losses in any U.S. jurisdiction with a statutory fire insurance policy. Indeed, even if a given state's Department of Insurance approved a terrorism exclusion, any loss from terrorist activity involving fire would still be covered under a statutory terrorism exclusion (see Baker 2003b: chap. 4, and in particular his discussion of *Watson v. USAA*, 566 N.W. 2d 683 (Minn. 1997)). Thus a fire loss precipitated by terrorist activity would be covered in the same way as fire loss precipitated by careless smoking, faulty wiring, arson by a third party, and so on.

Fourth, in most lines of insurance, especially commercial property and casualty lines, there was a highly competitive soft market throughout the 1990s. Insurance companies were chasing premium dollars and were not keen to make stringent contracts for fear of losing business. Although some insurers, and especially reinsurers, would have preferred 'named perils' contracts – for example, naming terrorist activity as a peril and either charging more for it or excluding it – the soft market would not allow that to happen.

9/11 Insured Losses

As of August 2002, the estimated insured loss for 9/11 was $55 billion. This was the first insured loss from terrorist activity that exceeded $1 billion (Swiss Re *Sigma* No. 1/2002: 17). According to the estimate of a reinsurance company in March 2002, there was also $50 billion uninsured economic damage arising from 9/11, making the total loss more than $100 billion. The previous highs for any type of event-specific catastrophic insured loss in insurance history were $21 billion for Hurricane Andrew and $15 billion for the Northridge earthquake.

Table 5.1
Estimates of the Insured Loss (All Lines) from the 911 Terrorist Attack

Line of business	Range, in USD bn
Property	10.0–12.0
Business interruption	3.6– 7.0
Workers' compensation	3.0– 5.0
Aviation	3.0– 6.0
Liability	5.0–20.0
Other non-life	1.0– 2.0
Life & health	4.5– 6.0
Total	30.0–58.0

Source: Swiss Re Sigma No. 1/2002, Citing Tillinghast Towers Perrin,
Status on 31 January 2002

Table 5.1 provides a range of estimates for 9/11 insured losses across lines of insurance. Each line experienced multibillion dollar claims, in many cases at record levels for a single catastrophe.

Individual insurance companies suffered heavy insured losses arising from 9/11 claims. Preliminary estimates of losses suffered by the top fifteen groups (pre-tax, net of reinsurance) as of 31 December 2001 are presented in figure 5.1. These figures are of course very rough estimates at an early stage of claims processing. However, they do give an indication of the significant impact on large companies. For example, Lloyds' alone experienced an estimated $9 billion in claims, although $6–7 billion was recoverable from reinsurers they themselves went out to. Swiss Re's loss is now known to be greater than the figure given here, and for the first time in their history they reported an overall loss for the fiscal year.

The tragic loss of life from the 9/11 terrorist attacks also far exceeded any previous terrorist event. While 3,212 lost their lives from the terrorist attacks on 9/11, the next nine most deadly terrorist attacks each involved between 100 and 300 victims (Swiss Re Sigma No. 1/2002: 17).

Risk and Uncertainty after 9/11

From an actuarial perspective, the terrorist attacks of 9/11 posed many conundrums. There was a perceived inability to work from the basic parameters of insurance risk assessment: probability and severity of loss calculations. Regarding probability, there were no data on fre-

Figure 5.1
Insured Loss Estimates* (updated through 31 Dec. 2001)

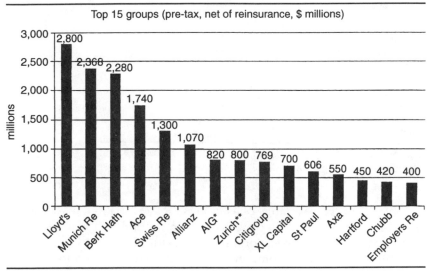

Top 15 groups (pre-tax, net of reinsurance, $ millions)

*Midpoint if company has announced range
**Includes $289MM for Converium
Source: AM Best, III

quency – for example, similar to the data available for natural hazards such as hurricanes – upon which some assessment of risk over time and place could be made. Regarding severity, the data available from past terrorist events gave no indication of the 9/11 insured loss. Indeed, previous loss magnitudes suggested that the maximum terrorist activity loss would be in the millions rather than billions of dollars. As one insurance executive summarized the assessibility problem, 'How many $1 billion, $5 billion, $20 billion terrorist events will there be in one year, five years, ten years? That's actually at the heart of why our business has become very conservative relative to terrorist activity. There's just no real knowledge of the type of event which could occur, how large an event, how frequent.'

While industry officials began to feel that a terrorist attack on a given location may be a low probability event, there was considerable unease about the potential severity of further losses through terrorist activity. The first step was to change probable maximum loss (PML) estimates on major commercial complexes from partial loss to total loss. The pre-9/11 catastrophic imagination envisaged a major accident that would cause significant but containable damage. The post-9/11 catastrophic imagination refers to the WTC site as 'ground zero,' language drawn from nuclear war, and assumes the worst. A senior industry official said that pre-9/11,

> The worst case scenario that major reinsurers thought of was, hey, a small plane going into the WTC, taking out a couple of floors, a fire ensuing that would be put out and they would call it a day. They never, ever, contemplated the two towers coming down on the same day. Now they are doing that, now the PML's include complete destruction of the building, any building ... that is being written. The insurer's PML is that another plane is going to go into it and completely destroy the building. Or a nuclear attack which is completely going to render the building useless for the next fifty years.

The dread of nuclear, biological, and/or chemical terrorist attacks moved to the forefront of arguments about the inability to estimate severity of loss. This dread was expressed in policy documents, for example an Organization on Economic Cooperation and Development (OECD) report on 'Economic Consequences of Terrorism' which includes a feature box, 'How to prepare for the risk of mega-terrorism' (OECD 2002: 120). This feature provides detail on how 'security specialists' imagine 'terrorists could at some stage attempt to explode a nuclear device or release contagious viruses in a populous metropolitan area.' One scenario draws on familiar fear about Russian sources of external threat to envisage all of Manhattan as ground zero.

> During the Cold War, the Soviet Union developed 'suitcase' nuclear bombs that could be carried by a single person. Although the Russian authorities have taken steps to protect nuclear material from theft, it is not clear that all devices can be accounted for. Even a crude nuclear device could create an explosive force of 20,000 tons of TNT, demolishing an area of about three square miles. If detonated in Lower Manhattan, the whole of Wall Street and the financial district would be destroyed. Hundreds of thousands of people would die suddenly. Assessing the economic impact of such a terrorist attack is really impossible ... An attack against, for instance, New York City using a nuclear weapon could leave most of the metropolitan area uninhabitable for years. The direct impact would

reduce the country's production potential by about 3 per cent, that is, the equivalent of a small OECD country's GDP. (ibid.)

Similar exercises in catastrophic imagination were engaged in by industry executives we interviewed. One executive whose company had suffered catastrophic losses in the WTC said that event raised the spectre of nuclear, biological, and chemical attacks to come.

> If you think about that in the context of insurance and reinsurance, the WTC is not, probably, the worst case scenario. So it's not knowing what capability people have, the extent to which they have types of other weapons, and how they might use them ... You put a nuclear bomb over New York City and you're going to see an economic condition like you've never seen here ... Just the magnitude of this stuff. I call it a randomness, just a complete unknown of what might happen. Not only in frequency, but scope and severity.

This interviewee's reference to 'randomness' points to another peculiarity in terrorist activity insurance. Although terrorist attacks may be experienced as random by victims, they are intentional on the part of perpetrators. Indeed, terrorists intentionally induce the uncertainty of randomness not only in the lives of their actual victims, but also in those who fear becoming victims. The psychological effects of terrorism as a business of uncertainty are seen as having additional economic effects beyond the direct costs of recovery from a terrorist attack. Thus, an insurance company interviewee said that if terrorist strategy turns to regular bombings in shopping malls in different regions of the United States, 'it would have a tremendous psychological impact on the U.S. public. And so there are just so many different variations, and ultimately because there are so many variations without predictability, we may become very concerned relative to application.' The fact that terrorist activity can happen anywhere means that it cannot be 'walled off' by geographic region and allocation of specific capital in the same way as natural catastrophe risks.

The 9/11 attack also created new uncertainties for insurers regarding aggregation risk: the over-concentration of insured loss exposure in a particular location. Prior to 9/11, high-rise commercial buildings with established business tenants were generally perceived as ideal risks. On the property side, a building with contemporary construction standards and a sprinkler system was viewed as an easily assessible and lucrative insurance risk. For group life, health, and workers' compensation insurers, well-paid professionals working in such buildings were also among the best risks. As one insurance executive expressed it, 9/11 'turned the nature of risk on its head.' The prime commercial property in a downtown location was now looked at as a potentially bad risk. What is the total loss estimate? Is it a symbolic 'trophy' target for terrorists? What exclusions, lower insured limits, and increased prices should be imposed by any single insurer or reinsurer in the name of prudence?

Group life insurers with concentrations of professional employees depend on reinsurance to address both the problem of concentration and the fact that their product is based on the law of large numbers with limited scrutiny of each individual in the group. However, the severe hardening of reinsurance markets after 9/11, and in many cases total exclusion of terrorist activity coverage, made it difficult for primary group life companies to offer coverage in concentrated commercial sites.

U.S. health insurance plans are based in local areas and do not normally carry reinsurance. Therefore, if the primary insurer covers a large number of employees on expensive health plans concentrated in particular commercial properties vulnerable to terrorist attacks, it faces catastrophic insured losses it may not be able to cover.

Workers' compensation primary insurers in the United States are legally prohibited from excluding terrorist activity, and rely on reinsurance. However, after 9/11 reinsurers variously failed to renew contracts, or offered to renew them with more stringent conditions and higher premiums, leaving the primary insurers with greater threat of aggregation risk exposure.

As the New York Superintendent of Insurance testified before a U.S. House of Representatives committee, 'Large buyers of insurance are no longer reaping the benefits of scale because the very characteristics – large number of employees, vehicle fleets, valuable real estate – that made them attractive to "cash-flow" underwriters prior to September 11th, are now making them undesirable to "risk-oriented" underwriters concerned especially with single-location concentrations of risk' (Serio, 2002: 3).

As we analyse in detail in the following section, aggregation issues were at the centre of industry efforts to exclude or limit terrorist activity coverage. A reinsurance specialist for an insurance group addressed the topic in a speech to colleagues in the spring of 2002. He emphasized that aggregation risk is a problem of knowledge in all fields of catastrophe management. Primary insurers have difficulty enough ascertaining their aggregation risk; reinsurers, removed from first-hand analysis, know even less; and, retrocessionaires (reinsurers of reinsurers) can know so little that they must make decisions on the basis of trusting their partners and their sense of good bets.

> Think about the difficulty that [each individual insurance company] has in determining the aggregation of risk in various locations around the country. And then picture yourself as a reinsurer who picks up a part or all of these companies' exposures as well, and so the aggregation of risk is compounded and the knowledge level is at least once if not twice, removed. As a result, until the middle of September [2001], I don't know that the reinsurance community had ever evaluated the kind of hazard that was demonstrated in a multiple explosion event in the heart of the financial district in New York. That became very clear to the reinsurance industry during the months that followed ... The reinsurance community globally is unregulated in most ways and is free to move quickly in and out of markets and in and out of coverages ... As a result the reinsurance community began, as I said in October [2001], to exclude terrorism from most kinds of aggregate covers. By the time we got to January 1 [2002], there was essentially no meaningful reinsurance available for terrorism for catastrophic loss. There is reinsurance available for individual risks, but in terms of aggregation of loss ... things which take multiple policies and put them into one event, there is very little if any reinsurance capacity for those kinds of events if they're driven by terrorism ... Retrocession-aires are so far removed from risk that there is no capacity for terrorism reinsurance in the retro market today. As a result reinsurers ... if they want any kind of exposure to terrorism are taking this net from their own account and therefore have very little capacity or appetite for it.

Various reinsurance executives we interviewed made the same point. One said that the 'aggregation or accumulation issue – essentially is the business that we're in, and that's our biggest concern whether it be from a hurricane, from an earthquake, or from a terrorist event.' Another said that 'Big reinsurance companies, as a result of being so big, they deal with so many customers that cede volatility to them ... So if the only thing you take in all day is volatility, you can imagine what your volatility is. It's huge, potentially. So you need to have controls ... [because] we're in the volatility assumption business.'

The 9/11 losses also made insurers aware of correlation risks across lines of insurance business. As documented in table 5.1, there were multibillion dollar losses in each of property, business interruption, workers' compensation, aviation, liability, and life and health insurance. The problem for large insurance groups, and especially reinsurers, was exposure across several of these lines arising from the same incident in ways they had not previously appreciated. An executive of a major reinsurance group stressed in interview that 9/11 'highlighted for the industry the tremendous correlation risk that exists within our business, from different lines of business, that we never thought would correlate to a single event. With that awareness now, we are looking at all of our business with that as a primary focal point. Trying to identify how many times we are exposed to the same risk, the same potential loss from any number of different places within our organization.' A colleague added that 'if you had the right scenario, or call it the wrong scenario, you could truly, severely impair even our company with all of the risk they have accumulated worldwide. So the whole concept of risk management has I think been taken to a whole different level as a result of ... realizing correlation risk [in] the WTC [event]. Realizing that, we have just so much risk as an entity, that maybe wasn't appreciated beforehand. Maybe this is a wake-up call to the industry.'

New forms of correlation between the underwriting, investment, and credit risk sides of insurance also emerged. The 9/11 insured losses interacted with the broader capital market downturn and low interest rate environment to provide new understanding of how such correlation can develop in an actual case. A reinsurance executive said in interview that this knowledge was in turn used to amplify uncertainties about the magnitude of future losses. She referred to this as 'enterprise risk' and offered the following assessment:

It's not only the unintended, unrealized correlations within insurance lines, but there's also a correlation between what happens in terms of our insurance liabilities and what might happen with regard to the asset side of our balance sheet. For example, suppose there is a dirty bomb in New York City, in the financial area, what do you think the impact would be on stock market performance? Ultimately, that trickles through into the balance sheet of insurance and reinsurance companies. In other words, that's basically affecting their ability and their financial strength. So there's a correlation not only in terms of insurance products that we provide, but also relative to the financial strength and the foundation for providing those products. So there's absolutely a correlation there ... enterprise risk, a whole-risk evaluation.

As we document in the following section, 9/11 insured loss experience led to a reconfiguration of insurance relations and practices, as each party struggled to pre-empt their own risk and pass exposure on to other parties. But the uncertainties have not led the industry to assert that terrorism is completely uninsurable. As a reinsurance executive declared at an industry conference, 'We love ambiguity. We know how to handle uncertainty. And I think that we know it much better than the average consumer or the buyer of our products. Risk has always two dimensions. It is a threat, a peril, but it also contains the aspect of opportunity. And the art is to balance these two, threat and opportunity, in a smart and conscious way.'

In an effort to be smart and conscious, insurers searched for new knowledge that might help them to model terrorism risk and thereby make more vigorous decisions about underwriting or exclusion. Not surprisingly, on a formal level this search has been squarely within the established analytical frameworks through which insurers try to turn uncertainty into risk. For example, in its publication, *Sigma* (No. 1/ 2002: 20), Swiss Re offers the following advice to the industry:

> Terrorism risk must be treated on the basis of the established principles of risk assessment and management: identify threats, accurately define perils and covers, limit exposures, quantify risks, price risks adequately, grant cover separately or exclude terrorism risk altogether, if these criteria cannot be fulfilled ... Insurers and reinsurers who are willing to assume terrorism risk must re-implement or revise some established insurance principles and tackle a new set of topical issues.
>
> 1. Coverage conditions, wordings and clauses: update the definition of risk, covered perils, excluded perils. Apply sublimits and specify named perils to restrict the scope of cover.
> 2. Pricing and underwriting: develop more refined pricing methods and procedures, adjusted to risk type, country, region, loss experience and expectancy.
> 3. Risk and capital management. For example: extend scenarios and capacity management procedures to make allowance for possible terrorist attacks, enhance analysis for correlations between lines of business and between underwriting/investment/credit/operational risks,

develop alternative risk transfer products and systems addressing terrorist risk.

Immediately following 9/11, three companies with expertise in natural catastrophe modelling – AIR Worldwide Corporation, Risk Management Solutions and Equecat Incorporated – developed terrorism risk models for insurers (Green 2002; Treaster 2002b; *Business Wire* 2002). The modellers claimed that they could provide insurers with more certainty about their terrorism coverage decisions. For example, a *Business Wire* (2002) announcement of the AIR Terrorism Loss Estimation Model (TLEM) quotes the president and CEO of AIR as saying, '"The problem is the current uncertainty about coverage, exclusions and price."' The solution is TLEM, which 'analyzes various threats posed by domestic extremists, formal international and state sponsored terrorist organizations, and loosely affiliated networks ... It considers frequency and severity of attacks, likely targets and the impacts on both the intended targets and on surrounding structures – all within a fully probabilistic framework.' Perhaps anticipating scepticism that the uncertainties of terrorism can be converted into 'a fully probabilistic framework' of risk, the news release invokes the authoritative certainty of Buck Revell, a former associate deputy director at the FBI responsible for criminal investigations, counterterrorism and counterintelligence, who served on an expert panel to help develop TLEM: '"The evaluation process that AIR has undertaken regarding terrorism is extremely important ... The first and most important element of being prepared is to understand the true nature of the risk and the consequences of not being prepared for a terrorist attack."'

The terrorism models draw upon conventions developed in modelling natural hazard catastrophic loss. Indeed, one model even claims to take weather conditions into account because winds could affect the dispersal of chemical and biological agents. A primary focus is the diversification of geographic and concentration risk. Knowledge for diversification is provided through data on urban aggregates and zonal distributions of insurance written. Risk Management Solutions catalogued a thousand buildings across the United States as prime targets of terrorism and made them the subject of various terrorist activity simulations involving different types of weapons (e.g., airplanes, bomb blasts, nuclear, biological, chemical). AIR did the same for 330,000 properties, ranging from the Empire State Building in New York to the Capital building in Carson City, Nevada. AIR also analysed properties for concentration risk exposure in property and workers' compensation insurance lines, and for multiple lines of insurance exposure.

Severity estimates are based on various types and capacities of weapons and their projected impact. Risk Management Solutions used about two dozen different weapons in its scenarios, for example, airplanes of different designs and capacities, trucks loaded with explosives, cake boxes loaded with explosives, and so on. The AIR TLEM modellers 'figuratively triggered different sizes of explosives, sometimes at more than one location on the site. Then they calculated the damage to the landmark and the surroundings. The program can also detonate blasts at each property in an insurance company's portfolio.' AIR is a division of Insurance Services Organization, the mega-provider of information to the industry. As such, AIR has access to that organization's Specific Property Information database on two million properties in the United States to help assess its terrorism target buildings regarding size, construction, occupancy, and preventive security protection.

In spite of claims about 'a fully probabilistic framework' and an understanding of 'the true nature of the risk,' terrorism loss estimate models are heavily dependent upon the subjective opinions of selected experts. Both AIR and Risk Management Solutions hired former FBI and CIA counterterrorism operatives to make educated guesses about landmark buildings that might be the targets of terrorism. AIR also used its experts to estimate frequency. As the TLEM product manager declared, '"There's no physical science behind [frequency estimates]. You can't extrapolate from past history, so we use expert opinion and codify that"' (Green 2002). The AIR experts used the Delphi Method of estimating frequency and severity as developed by the RAND corporation during the Cold War (*Business Wire* 2002). This approach 'turns educated guesses into numerical rankings that are cranked into a computer to determine risk' (Treaster 2002b). Of course, the developers of TLEM, including the experts themselves, realized the limits to this form of knowledge. According to the president and CEO of AIR, at one juncture 'her team considered leaving it up to clients to come up with a frequency estimate. But she said she was convinced that clients wanted her to set down a marker. "They want to have some kind of default," she said' (ibid.). Her counterpart at Risk Management Solutions was more reticent to sell uncertainty as if it is a risk. He said, 'it might be six months before his team figures out an estimate of the frequency of attacks. He may just give up. "This is very speculative," he said. "It requires a level of insight into what they [terrorists] are thinking that right now is not there"' (ibid.).

Appreciating the limits of such models, insurance companies struggled with alternative ways of gaining insight into what terrorists are thinking. One reinsurance company we studied formed its own panel of experts consisting of senior company executives. Their main source of knowledge was news reports of the 'war on terrorism,' which were used to inform their underwriting guidelines and decisions. One executive observed in interview:

> I don't think we have much of anything right now ... How big is terrorism? How many terrorists are on U.S. soil right now? These are all questions that are completely unknown at this point. We get information, we file all the trade journals, we get a lot of information on what's found in the caves of Afghanistan and so we know all that. And we actually build underwriting guidelines somewhat around those types of information ... to try to avoid a second event [insured loss for the company] of this magnitude ... limitation on limits that we put out, sub-limits potentially, different classes of business that we think might be more susceptible to a terrorist act than others. We kind of got in a room and just tried to theorize, tried to get in the head of a terrorist ... Probably thinking about the mega-events where there [are] a lot of people affected. So we said, OK, what types of risks might have a lot of people in them ... We've been trying ... unsuccessfully so far, to get the FBI in ... [We want them] to share knowledge, to either validate our underwriting approach, or to add to it, or maybe invalidate it, based on what they found through interrogation of people that have been captured, based on some information that comes out publicly ... This is coincidental, but everything that had come out as a targeted either property or class within the caves of Afghanistan had already been addressed in our underwriting guidelines.

Executives of the same company related that their other approach to underwriting terrorism was based on a geographic risk-spreading model for natural perils. In this model, aggregations were identified in thirty-seven regions of the world and underwriting limits were set at $1 billion per event. It was the responsibility of the local member of the company group in a given region to assess natural peril aggregation risk in relation to the $1 billion limit. An interviewee who outlined this approach said that it was going to be applied to terrorist activity underwriting.

That's the most scientific form of that within our company group ... We are putting together a similar, in concept, budget for terrorism for our company group. We will have our own budget, but we will have a group budget as well. And that will be – we haven't decided on the level of it – but that will be, in a similar fashion, a number that drives decision making in particular areas of the world. And once you reach that budget [limit] you will not be able to sub-limit any more risk in that area of the world. It's kind of classic spread risk theory: you take so much risk, and you take it to a certain level, and you have it in thirty-seven different areas, not all thirty-seven hopefully are going to get hit at the same time, hopefully you've collected enough premium to cover it when it does. That's a second form of risk management, call it global risk management.

Of course, this 'most scientific form' of underwriting simply establishes limits to gambling on catastrophic losses. Beyond the house limit lies uncertainty. Even the promoters of terrorism loss estimation models admit to the uncertainty of time and place of terrorist attacks. Green (2002) quotes the president of Equecat as saying, 'We don't know where and we don't know when, but we know it's going to happen.' Treaster (2002b) cites the president of AIR as saying that while TLEM is only 'a first step in imposing rational measurement on what has been totally unquantifiable,' it is 'better than anything else our clients have to use.'

As we learned in chapter 4, natural peril catastrophic loss models are very limited. However, there is at least some accumulated experience relevant to frequency and severity, creating a capacity to gauge especially vulnerable regions (e.g., Florida for hurricanes, California for earthquakes) and total loss scenarios. As emphasized previously, most industry officials do not perceive a parallel with respect to terrorism. Addressing an industry conference, an executive of a reinsurance group compared terrorism to natural peril modelling.

I don't think it's [terrorism insurance coverage] capable of being priced with the knowledge we have today. When we do windstorm evaluations, we do computerized modelling of 10,000 iterations. The actual event of an Andrew, of a Floyd, of an earthquake, will always be different from the model that's used to predict it, but the deviation around that model is shrinking all the time because of the experience that we have. We have very little experience in this [terrorism] arena, some of it we didn't even recognize. And so I think it will take a great deal of time for us to be able to model the kind of exposure that we have. And we do not know how to model some of the things that we fear the most.

While it is difficult to create reasonable loss estimation models for terrorism, insurers' experiences with 9/11 led them to revise natural catastrophe models. First, the new 100 per cent probable maximum loss estimates for large commercial properties that followed 9/11 were applied to all types of losses, however caused. Second, the concentration risk exposure revealed in the World Trade Center loss, especially regarding workers' compensation, was applied to underwriting hurricanes and earthquakes that might hit a city centre. Third, the correlation risk across insurance lines that was discovered through 9/11 was also applied to natural catastrophe underwriting.

There is another temporal dimension to the uncertainties of terrorism compared to other sources of catastrophic loss. On the surface, terrorism appears to be a short-tail catastrophe similar to windstorms and earthquakes. The event is sudden and has direct impact, making losses immediately evident. In contrast, liability catastrophes such as asbestosis, tobacco, toxins, medical malpractice, corporate wrongdoing, global warming, and historical injustices are long-tail. They are catastrophes because of the claims dollars involved: in 2002 the estimate for asbestosis insured losses in the United States was $65 billion, and the estimate for the Enron debacle was $5 billion. These catastrophes are long-tail because they emerge through years of scientific, legal, and political discovery of harms. The process is an emerging one of 'name, blame, and claim': vocalizing, dramatizing, and scandalizing through the mass media in order to shape risk perception and make the case for extraordinary compensation (Lahnstein 2002).

Terrorism has both short- and long-tail dimensions. With reference to the Hitchcock quotation at the beginning of the chapter, terrorism begins with an immediate 'bang' and enormous loss. However, terror persists through continuous fear of another bang while not knowing when or where it will come. To the extent that terrorism is rooted in fundamental cultural and religious beliefs, as well as issues of political economy, it is long-tailed. Risk perception emerges through socializing, dramatizing, and scandalizing in political culture, for example, creating the view that terrorist activity signals a new kind of 'war' that is indeterminate and indefinite.

Pre-Empting Risk

The Pass the Exposure Express

In the aftermath of 9/11, insurers moved quickly to pre-empt risk. Pre-emption involved several interrelated strategies. First, a large number of primary insurers and reinsurers cancelled or failed to renew contracts where they perceived significant exposure to terrorism risk. Here the pre-emptive strategy was to pass terrorism exposure to another party: from reinsurers to primary insurers, from primary insurers to insured organizations and individuals, and from both insurers and the insured to governments.

Second, if they were legally required to underwrite terrorism insurance, or decided that they wanted to do so in the hope of profiting from it, insurers engaged in various pre-emptive measures to anticipate and appropriate the nature of their exposure. They each developed definitions of terrorism to bring to the table in negotiations over contract terms and exclusions. They also used the opportunity for substantial premium increases in an already hardening insurance market. In this context they evoked another, historic meaning of pre-emption: dealing in goods in order to profit by an enhanced price (*Concise Oxford Dictionary*, 8th ed. 1990).

Third, those with continuing stakes in the terrorism insurance market also tried to pre-empt risk through preventive security measures. As we shall learn in the final two sections of the chapter, they joined governments in espousing the new responsibility of extreme precaution. Since terrorism is a risk of such high consequence, the responsibility is to do everything possible in advance in order to prevent it. The response ability is vigilance: more intrusive surveillance, enabled through dropping due process standards of procedural justice, in frantic efforts to make people more visible and their actions more certain.

In this section we explore how each party in the insurance relationship – primary insurers, reinsurers, the insured, and governments – tried to pre-empt terrorism risk by passing exposure to the other parties. This is a story of how, in conditions of extreme uncertainty, insurers have difficulty forming a market, and seek the help of governments as the insurers of last resort. Governments, meanwhile, seek both the capital and preventive security capabilities of the insurance industry to spread at least some of the risk. Insured organizations and individuals are especially vulnerable, as they face being uninsured, underinsured, and/or paying substantial premium increases to insurers and governments scrambling for more capital.

Insurers' first pre-emptive reaction to 9/11 was exclusion of terrorism coverage in insurance contracts scheduled for renewal. This pre-emptive strike is a common response to catastrophic loss. For example, after the Mount St Helens' volcanic eruption in 1980, Hurricane Andrew in 1992, and the Northridge earthquake in 1993, insurance coverage that was previously 'given away' as part of standard all perils contracts was suddenly pre-empted through exclusions. As an insurance official remarked about reported losses in the months following 9/11, 'It was like playing, "Can You Top This?" because every day you read another figure. It started out at $25 billion, 30, 40, 50, 70, 80 – nobody really knew how big the loss was going to be. And it was in that climate the insurance industry said, wait a minute, no, we cannot take a chance on that happening again ... I mean the wholesale, we are not going to cover anybody for terrorism anywhere under any circumstance, was kind of a knee-jerk reaction, it was an emotional reaction.'

The rush by reinsurers and, in turn, primary insurers, to exclude terrorism coverage was described by the Superintendent of the New York State Insurance Department as the 'pass the exposure express' (Serio, 2002: 12). As we analyse in more detail below, reinsurers are relatively free to exclude terrorism coverage from their agreements with primary insurers. Primary insurers have some latitude to exclude terrorism coverage also, although their degrees of freedom vary substantially across lines of insurance and the regulatory regime of each state jurisdiction. Without terrorism reinsurance, primary insurers are vulnerable and try to pass the exposure to the insured through exclusions. If governments fail to step in to provide some form of backstop terrorism coverage, the insured and the political economy in general are left to suffer.

In the absence of an appropriate federal response to the issue of terrorism, consumers or their primary insurers will be ultimately left to assume and address the terrorism exposure. Carriers, already reeling from the record-setting losses attributable to the World Trade Center attack, will see a further deterioration of the industry's capital base in the event of a disaster – be it manmade or natural disaster – that results in even a fraction of the expected total loss from September 11th. Businesses and individuals will be forced to make economic choices when faced with suddenly higher premiums for less coverages or faced more dramatically with the notion of going without insurance for terrorist risk, i.e., covering the risk with their own resources. Many may well have to reconsider expansion plans in the works just months ago, consider reducing employee benefits, such as health insurance, consider the likelihood of securing lending without the availability of all-risk coverages, or consider amending the amount of insurance they carry in order to be able to afford the premium increases. A more drastic measure could be a decision to 'go bare' and operate without insurance coverage, something many commercial entities have already decided as their only course of action. Some may even decide to adopt the risk management technique of 'avoidance' by disengaging themselves from otherwise economically sound activities that may be subject to the peril of terrorism. (Ibid.: 6–7)

The exclusion of terrorism risk by insurers is a declaration of failure of the insurance institution. To the extent that terrorism risk is passed to organizations and individuals, insurance undercuts its claims to being a modern technology capable of spreading risk. Instead of cushioning disasters through universal compensation of loss, it redirects the impact of catastrophic loss to the level of individual suffering. It admits that it cannot convert uncertainty into risk, and thereby reinforces the profound sense of disestablishment that it is supposed to alleviate.

Of course, terrorism coverage was never entirely removed from the insurance market. First, after 9/11 some multi-year contracts with terrorism included remained in force. Second, some terrorism coverage remained compulsory. Workers' compensation schemes in every state require coverage for injury at work however caused, including acts of terrorism. The U.S. National Association of Insurance Commissioners voted to ensure that personal lines of property and casualty insurance continued to include terrorism coverage in all states. Regulators in five states – New York, Florida, California, Texas, and Georgia – ruled that terrorism coverage must be made available in commercial lines of property and casualty insurance. These five states constituted about 38 per cent of the U.S. commercial market at the time. Third, some insurers decided to take advantage of the opportunity for selling terrorism insurance on the view that terrorist activity is a low probability, high profit risk.

As we have already seen, industry executives and officials repeatedly emphasized the uncertainties of terrorism and concluded that it is impossible to price insurance for terrorist activity on an actuarially sound basis. A reinsurer's publication on terrorism insurance in the wake of 9/11 stresses that 'economic feasibility' is one requirement for insurability, and observes that in the case of terrorism coverage 'the evident uncertainties regarding risk quantification make the economic feasibility of the business extremely doubtful' (Swiss Re *Sigma* No. 1/2002: 18). A senior industry official remarked in interview, 'When you're dealing with terrorism, it's completely outside the realm of predictability. And there's really no way of pricing it or calculating it. I don't know what the answer is. Does this mean then that this is an exposure which each property owner must bear entirely onto him or herself or itself?'

Given such emphatic statements about the uninsurability of terrorism, how does the insurance industry continue to provide coverage? The short answer is that insurers gamble. As we learned in the case of earthquake insurance, the limits of knowledge provide insurance opportunities as well as fear of failure. The risk calculus of frequency and severity is replaced by the uncertainty calculus of threat and opportunity. In the words of an insurance company executive addressing an industry conference, 'Of course, from the perspective of the private insurance company, we can only insure terrorism if we have a fair chance to get the right price and even make a profit from that ... It is not completely uninsurable but it is not insurable as more conventional perils, we are somewhere in between which calls for a differentiated position.'

The reality is that many perils have been insured when the source of catastrophic loss was not even known at the time of underwriting (e.g., asbestos), the science is shaky (e.g., earthquake), or the insured losses are largely shaped by the interinstitutional culture of claims (e.g., disability and medico-legal inflation). Insurance is a business of uncertainties and the key question is which party becomes more averse to the uncertainties and decides to withdraw from the contractual relationship or to seek more enabling conditions of participation. Thus, the official quoted above who declared an inability to calculate and price terrorism insurance and confessed, 'I don't know what the answer is,' proceeded to provide the answer. Referring to the history of marine insurance contracts, he observed, 'Insurance was not always as scientific as they would like you to think it is today ... At some point in the beginning it was somebody simply saying, "You're asking me to put up £50,000, yeah, I'll do it." It was as simple as that. And some of that enters into insurance today.'

In this spirit, the question is who is willing to embrace what risk at what price? Where insurers perceive a potential for bearing too much of the burden themselves – for example, because severity is too extreme (a nuclear, biological, or chemical attack in an urban area) or because government, reinsurance, or other partners are unavailable to share the risk – they will try to eliminate or at least severely limit their participation and pass the exposure on. Where insurers still provide limited coverage in such contexts, the price of insurance will be exceptionally high and those who need it may not be able to form a large enough pool to make it affordable. Furthermore, those who perceive low risk – for example, those outside of urban areas and without symbolic targets of terrorism – will not be interested in terrorism coverage at any price, creating further limits to risk sharing. In other words, the mutuality required for insurability begins to unravel. There is not enough diversification to form risk communities for insurance purposes, and insurers accelerate the 'pass the exposure express.'

To the extent they are able to offload more extreme threats – either to the organizations and individuals who face them, or to governments as insurers of last resort – insurance companies are willing to take on some terrorism coverage as profitable. Their appetite for risk will be whetted further if they can negotiate their preferred definitions of terrorism in contracts, manage their concentration risk in each locale, and obtain enhanced premium revenue because of higher demand in a climate of uncertainty. As an insurance company executive related in interview, 'The challenge is really not to just walk away from the experience but ... to underwrite it ... Even though we are not offering a specific terrorism product per se, we know that we have embedded in our business, in our portfolio, a lot of terrorism exposure. And that's the exposure that we are trying to manage, and contain, and budget for, such that we can still participate in what is now – all odds equal – a very attractive marketplace with rising prices.'

An executive in another company said that the key to underwriting terrorism coverage in this environment is selective exclusion. A year after 9/11, 'exclusions are being applied to make sure that we are not just picking up any type of terrorism ... It's the uncertainty factor. If you are uncertain, it's very tough to price a product, and come up with an accurate pricing for it. Then you should try to exclude it in some form or fashion, or control it ... We don't exclude terrorism on everything ... [for example], we do exclude terrorism on the liability side on a target risk basis. That means a directors and officers liability on an airport or on a large office building that contains, for example, a stock exchange, we would exclude terrorism there.'

The key to a given insurer's exclusion and inclusion strategy is negotiating the meaning of terrorism with participants in the industry. As a reinsurance executive stated pithily in interview, 'We need to define it in order to exclude it.' There was a marketplace of definitions open to negotiation depending on how the reinsurer or primary insurer wished to participate in a specific terrorism risk.

A detailed definition of terrorism was developed by a reinsurance company we studied. The company's intention was to create a very broad definition in order to negotiate terrorist activity exclusions in reinsurance contracts with ceding companies (primary insurers) where desirable. The definition of terrorism was drafted with reference to some wording in codified government sources, but additional wording reflected the reinsurer's specific concerns.

This definition of terrorist activity had several notable features. First, terrorist activity is simply what is deemed to be terrorist activity by any authorized government official. The voice of constituted authority is invoked over and above anything else. Second, terrorist activity can be identified by harms to people, tangible property (e.g., buildings), intangible property (e.g., business documents, cyber documents), the environment, or natural resources. Third, a wide range of motives, mixed with imagined harms, are identified. These include political, ideological, philosophical, racial, ethnic, social or religious opposition; influencing government; frightening the public; and interfering with the economy. Fourth, specific human behaviours are identified, for example, threatened or actual hijacking, sabotaging, kidnapping, release of contaminants, bombing, interfering with systems and infrastructures, and assaults on government officials, employees, properties, and processes. Fifth, the only exception offered occurs when any of the threatened or actual behaviours are shown to be motivated by personal objectives unrelated in any way to the terrorist activity motives listed above.

A reinsurance executive involved in contract negotiations with primary insurers said that 'We might throw out these words, someone else may throw out another set of words to define terrorism, and we work through it ... Everybody usually has a different point of view on things, which are guided by maybe corporate risk appetites and such.' A colleague added, 'There are as many terrorism exclusions in the marketplace as there are ceding companies. So at last count I think we were up above 250 [companies]. So there's probably 250 some-odd wordings for terrorism exclusion in the current marketplace.' He stated that the final definition of terrorism settled on for a given insurance contract depends on terms of the contract. 'There's a lot of negotiation that goes back and forth with the companies depending upon our participation in the program, limits offered, attachment points, whatever, where we may come off some of those [definitions that exclude terrorism] objectives ... Sublimits are one of the ways to obviously reduce your exposures, to reduce your limits, then maybe we can give a little bit on the wording.'

Primary Insurers

The pre-emptive actions of reinsurers to exclude, limit, and redefine terrorism coverage posed serious consequences for primary insurers. For example, the group life insurance industry was not generally in favour of excluding terrorism, but could only reasonably maintain it with the participation of reinsurers. Without reinsurance, primary insurers would have to embrace the risk of terrorism and face possible insolvency in the event of another catastrophe. This threat could only be relieved if government regulators allowed primary insurers to exclude terrorism, but in several state jurisdictions, including New York, regulators did not allow exclusion. If exclusion was permitted, the burden of terrorism would be shifted to the level of the individual and both the insurance industry and the regulators who are supposed to protect the consumer would in effect be admitting the failure of their respective institutions.

A life insurance executive emphasized that 'reinsurance ... is a critical risk spreading mechanism for the group business. We work in the law of large numbers, we have very minimal underwriting, and disasters would tend to have a huge impact on us because of the clustering of employees. So reinsurance enables a life carrier to spread that risk to maintain some stability and favourable pricing.' He said that, as of March 2002, approximately one-half of his company's reinsurance partners were not offering terrorism coverage upon renewal of contracts. Moreover, those who were offering coverage introduced new exclusions, for example, nuclear, biological or chemical acts of terrorism. He also said that upon renewal of contracts, reinsurance rates were rising exponentially. With terrorism excluded, the increases ranged from 700 per cent to 1300 per cent. With terrorism included, the increase was another 250 per cent.

Property insurers also felt the impact of pre-emptive measures by reinsurers. According to Standard and Poor's (2002b: 1), 'Reinsurers, which operate on a global scale and face much less regulation, notified primary insurers soon after September 11 that they would drop terrorism coverage when policies came up for renewal. About two-thirds of property insurers lost their terrorism reinsurance coverage on January 1, and the remainder will lose it on July 1. While a majority of state regulators have agreed to let primary insurers in the U.S. follow suit and drop terrorism coverage for corporate clients, the corporate policy renewals occur throughout 2002 ... This gap, coupled with steep price increases for the little reinsurance still available, means that primary insurers have dramatically increased their retention of risk, even if only on a temporary basis.'

Faced with increased exposure to the uncertainties of terrorism, many primary insurers in turn passed exposure to the insured. A Prudential Securities survey in the first quarter of 2002 reported that one-half of U.S. commercial property insurance buyers had no terrorism coverage, 26 per cent had limited coverage, 6 per cent had stand-alone coverage, and only 18 per cent had full coverage (Hartwig 2002: 4).

As mentioned previously, regulators in five states, including New York, did not allow primary insurers blanket exclusion of terrorism coverage on commercial properties. At the same time, these regulators appreciated that, without reinsurance, primary insurers were left over-exposed to the catastrophic consequences of another terrorist attack. Unable to force reinsurers to participate, the regulators' choice was to make either primary insurers or consumers bear the burden of terrorism. Forty-five states chose consumers, five states chose primary insurers. A regulator in one of the latter states said in interview that the decision was taken not to let the consumer

be the last stop in the pass the exposure express ... Where does this end? Should we eventually let the consumer bear the terrorism risk? And we do not believe so. We are saying the consumer should have coverage for terrorism exclusions in primary policies. So the consumer now has the coverage, the insurance companies are providing that coverage, but now the reinsurance companies are not providing them with reinsurance for their exposure. And *that* is why we support some sort of federal intervention to eliminate the gap that currently exists because of the actions of reinsurers ... Even forcing insurers to cover this risk does not make sense to some extent because they do not have the ability to rate, and we know that ... [Without government intervention] the alternative is to completely eliminate coverage: let the reinsurers eliminate coverage because they can't rate it, let the primary insurers eliminate coverage because they can't rate it, eventually we will all bear this risk ourselves. And that in our opinion is not a good outcome.

An additional concern was how debt-rating agencies were scrutinizing the publicly traded insurance companies. The decline in capital markets at the time resulted in significantly lower returns on the investment side of insurance company operations. As a result, rating agencies were paying more attention to the underwriting side. If the insurance company's underwriting was seen as problematic – for example, because it had terrorism exposure without reinsurance – it faced the possibility of a rating agency downgrade, with implications for its equity price and financing capacities. In the autumn of 2001, Standard and Poor's put twenty-two insurers and reinsurers on 'Credit Watch' and lowered the ratings on fourteen companies, commenting, 'The continuing uncertainty accounts for some of this' (Standard and Poor's 2002b: 2–3). The managing director of insurance company ratings for Standard and Poor's declared, 'If regulators force the industry to accept risk without a [federal government backstop], then there will be ratings consequences' (ibid.).

The difficulties of property insurers were compounded by the fact that they had been operating in a soft market throughout the 1990s. Highly competitive markets meant that they were using low pricing and lax underwriting to attract business, and there was concern about capital adequacy throughout the industry (Standard and Poor's 2002a: 2–3). Indeed, the industry had experienced losses on the underwriting side (premium revenue minus claims and administrative expenses) in every year since 1979, culminating in the biggest loss ever in 2001, estimated at $50 billion (Insurance Information Institute website, www.iii.org, 2002). It was the strong investment markets of the 1990s that buoyed their overall profitability, and indeed encouraged further competitive pricing and lack of vigilance on the underwriting side. As a senior official observed in interview, throughout the 1990s 'companies were subsidizing their insurance side because of good returns. They were buying market share, underpricing their insurance because they were getting so much money from their investments. Now it is the reverse.'

In the jurisdictions we studied, property and casualty insurance companies are legally required to take into account their investment income in determining their insurance rates. According to one interviewee, in the late 1990s the investment return assumptions were as high as 15 per cent, whereas by 2002, they were at 5 per cent. The downturn in investment returns, especially in equity markets, thus contributed to a hardening of the market and premium increases. A capital markets specialist informed us that while insurance regulators may be concerned about heavy investment-side subsidization of premiums during a soft market, they more or less go along with it because it is unpopular to suggest that consumers should be paying more. 'It's hard to deal with a really long-term problem in the short term if things are going well.' He added that even in the height of the equity market bubble in 2000, regulators' 'stress testing' of a company's loss ratios would use a worst case scenario of a 20 per cent correction of the NASDAQ index, not an 80 per cent downturn as was experienced by 2002. During a soft market, everyone is compelled to go with competitive underpricing, reduced vigilance in loss prevention, and aggressive investment. 'The problem is that if the companies and the people would assume scenarios which with hindsight would happen, then nobody would be in business. Because, if you would have known with certainty, or forced companies to estimate that the stock market would do what they did, that would have driven an awful lot of companies out of business! The permanent optimism ... Especially if your peers are doing much better, you have to, to a certain extent, go with the flow because the investors would abandon you if you don't perform. As well as your competitors, even if they perform for the wrong reasons.'

As we document in more detail below, 9/11 was only one of several catastrophic losses that took significant capital out of insurance company operations. Medical cost inflation, medical malpractice claims, the continuing costs of asbestos liability, Enron and Worldcom corporate crime liabilities, and toxic mold liabilities each constituted multibillion dollar insurance catastrophes. Standard and Poor's (2002c: 4) records that the State Farm group of companies, for example, was an aggressive soft market player in the 1990s. Into 2001 it had about $38 billion in surplus capital and 20 per cent of the U.S. market. However, 9/11 and other catastrophes accounted for underwriting losses of $9.3 billion in 2001. 'State Farm posted a combined [loss] ratio of 120 per cent for its auto insurance business in 2001, and 135 per cent for its homeowners line, but it was the Texas homeowners business, written by its State Farm Lloyds affiliate, that carried the most shock value. For every premium dollar the company earned in 2001, it paid out 1.56 in losses, of which exposure to toxic mold accounted for 62 cents.'

It was the combination of lower investment returns, long-tailed liabilities, new catastrophes, and retraction of reinsurance, and not just 9/11 losses, that significantly hardened the primary insurance market into 2002. Significant capital taken out of the industry, a capacity shortfall, and a new sense of risk aversion all led to demand exceeding supply, driving up premiums. In the words of the New York State Insurance Department Superintendent, 'Unfortunately, September 11th has changed what might have been a gradual hard-market "curve" into a disaster-driven " hair-pin" bend. The combination of lack of terrorism coverage and rising insurance rates is likely to create availability and affordability problems for consumers in the short run' (Serio 2001b: 9). In an analysis by the research department of Swiss Re, 9/11 accounted for about one-half of the aggregate equity decline in the global insurance industry:

> The international insurance industry is currently in a phase of steeply rising prices, known as a 'hard market.' The terrorist attack of September 11 triggered the largest loss ever for the insurance industry, with the cost to direct insurance companies and reinsurers being estimated at between USD 35 and 55 bn. Together with other large insurance claims and losses on investments in the order of about USD 50 bn due to the downturn on the capital markets, this caused the aggregate equity of the global insurance industry to decline by about USD 100 bn. The relative shortage of insurance capacity, especially for large risks and in reinsurance, in conjunction with the need to re-assess many risks, has led to the current hardening of the market. But September 11 has accelerated and drastically intensified a trend that had already been underway since the year 2000. After a long soft-market phase, prices had bottomed out and were starting to rise again. (Swiss Re *Sigma* No. 3/2002: 11)

The reference to reassessment of risks is also significant in accounting for the hardening market. As we have already considered, 9/11 led insurers to re-examine their probable maximum loss estimates on commercial properties, and to project total loss rather than a small percentage. There was also a reassessment of the amount of risk capital needed to support the insurance institution, and of liquidity needs in the event of another major catastrophe. Considerations such as these

Figure 5.2
Growth in Net Premiums Written (All P/C Lines)

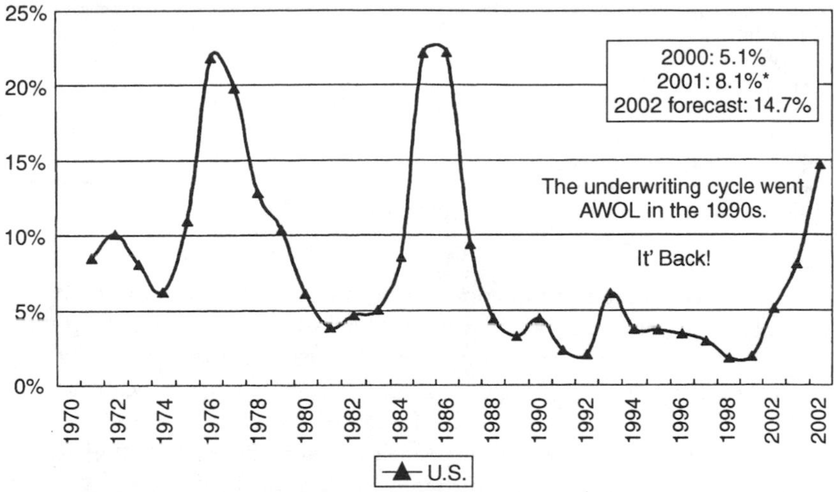

2000: 5.1%
2001: 8.1%*
2002 forecast: 14.7%

The underwriting cycle went
AWOL in the 1990s.

It' Back!

*Estimate from I.I.I. Groundhog Survey
Source: AM Best, Insurance Information Institute

led to new underwriting standards and the establishment of lower limits on a given risk, forcing many insured to seek higher priced policies
from multiple carriers.

As indicated in figure 5.2, the soft market in U.S. property and casualty insurance throughout the 1990s, as measured by net premiums
written, was hardening significantly between 1999 and 2001, and was
projected to take a 14.7 per cent leap in 2002, reaching levels not seen
since the mid-1980s. Table 5.2 documents rate increases in the fourth
quarter of 2001 by line of business. There were substantial increases
across all lines, but especially in commercial coverage. According to the
OECD, 'The hikes in insurance premiums have hit several industries.
The strongest impact has been on aviation, but other sectors, including
transportation, construction, tourism, and energy generation have also
been affected. Overall, it is estimated that commercial property and liability insurance rates have been raised by 30 per cent on average, with
"target" structures such as chemical and power plants and "iconic"
office buildings seeing steeper increases' (OECD 2002: 125).

Table 5.2
Rate Survey, Fourth Quarter 2001

	Rate increases by line of business				
	No change	Up 1–10%	Up 10–30%	Up 30–50%	Up > 50%
Commercial auto	1%	5%	51%	36%	5%
Workers' comp	1%	20%	46%	24%	3%
General liability	0%	7%	64%	22%	5%
Commercial umbrella	1%	2%	21%	34%	41%
Commercial property	0%	2%	28%	38%	31%
Business interruption	1%	8%	53%	25%	10%

Source: Council of Insurance Agents and Brokers

While there were myriad contributors to the hardening property and casualty insurance market, opportunism after 9/11 must be considered. By law, insurers are not permitted to recoup past losses through higher premiums. The insurance premium rate is supposed to be prospective. To rate retrospectively, for example, with respect to 9/11 losses, would obviously skew premiums significantly. Nevertheless, various interviewees observed that 9/11 was used by company agents and brokers to justify higher rates. For example, a senior executive of an insurance company took the view that while he personally 'would not peg' the sharp premium increases on 9/11, 'sometimes I view it as a broker's easy way of selling a rate increase to a client ... pegging it on 9/11 as opposed to understanding the economics behind it, to explain it to a client better.' He proceeded to explain the 'economics behind it' with reference to small commercial firms that were experiencing 25 to 30 per cent increases upon renewal of contract,

which is well in line with what was received on the hard markets of the past as well. The ones that enjoyed the benefit of, let's say, naïve underwriting over a number of years are probably seeing multiples. Losses that were not taken into consideration in pricing in the past because of the soft market are being corrected for that in the future. To sum it all up to 9/11, as I said a number of times before, I think that that's in most instances a cop out. I think it's more of a correction which 9/11 just accelerated a lot quicker than we anticipated because it took a lot of capital out of the market ... Some large companies on the financial 500 side saw multiples ... they may see multiples again ... [Previously] insurers thought this [hard] market was going to last a year and a half ... If that's the case the insurers only have one opportunity to get it correct once, so the accounts that were very lowly rated, that should have received proper technical rating, received it.

Reinsurers

Reinsurance is an essential component of a catastrophe insurance program. Its most important feature is a global capacity to spread risk efficiently over time and place. In this capacity it provides protection to primary insurance companies with a local domicile, which in turn protect the insured and relieve government of full responsibility for disaster relief.

As we have already learned, following 9/11 reinsurers pulled back dramatically from their participation in terrorism coverage. From their perspective, this was a responsible act of precaution while insurance markets were rethought and reinvigorated to address the new dimensions of terrorism. Compared to the primary insurance industry, the reinsurance industry had far less surplus capital to cover another catastrophic loss. Its losses from 9/11 were disproportionate, estimated by some interviewees at 60 per cent or more of the $55 billion total. Too much exposure to the uncertainties of terrorism could threaten the solvency of some reinsurance companies, which in turn would affect the recoveries of primary insurance companies and perhaps their solvency as well. Insolvent primary insurers would mean that the insured might not recover through an insurance claim.

While other parties to a catastrophe insurance program need reinsurers, reinsurers have the greatest ability to withdraw from participation when the uncertainties become too great. Operating globally, a reinsurance company can escape most forms of direct regulation – including mandatory participation in certain coverages such as terrorism – to which primary insurers must comply. Of course, reinsurers are not entirely free in this regard. They must consider their relationships with primary insurers and governments in jurisdictions where they place a great deal of their business. For example, 35 per cent of all insurance company capacity in the world is based in the United States. Reinsurers are not likely to withdraw unilaterally from an area of coverage important to the U.S. government and primary insurers. Partnerships with the U.S. government and primary insurers were especially compelling in the wake of 9/11. Partnerships were at once instrumental and symbolic in value. Reinsurers had much to gain from business relations that would help form new markets for terrorism coverage as a low probability, high profit enterprise. They also recognized the symbolic value – moral and political – of being seen as integral participants in the 'war on terrorism.'

Following 9/11, the reinsurance industry engaged in efforts to involve primary insurers and governments in terrorism insurance programs. In particular, it sought the participation of the U.S. federal government to serve as the reinsurer of last resort in a backstop program. Such programs had been negotiated in other countries, for example, France (Standard and Poor's 2002b: 3–4). According to senior executives in the reinsurance industry we interviewed, the initial withdrawal of reinsurers from terrorism coverage was in part an exercise in prudent responsibility about the capacity of their industry, and in part a political strategy to force government participation as reinsurers of last resort. As one interviewee explained,

Some of the restriction on the reinsurance side is actually meant to initiate the creation of governmental facilities ... [That intention is] specifically expressed at least in some of the external memos. So both bodies – the governmental bodies and the reinsurers and insurers – they are talking to each other. So their representatives meet and there is no ivory tower with the reinsurers. *They* decide what to do, and *that* is the reality. Every step is very controlled I would say. There is a social responsibility, as any other business player, but there is an economical limit to everything. That's the same as providing unlimited coverage in certain areas. Who can, from an economical standpoint? The social responsibility as well comes into play when you think of actually maintaining the ability to pay claims ... So when you reach that limit then, and you are not able to provide coverage to that extent, to your understanding, that goes beyond your economical abilities, then it's your social responsibility as well to say no ... There is a social responsibility of governments as well. There hasn't been a lack of effort by the insurance industry ... to try and achieve some type of pooling arrangement to satisfy all parties. I've heard a number of times this terrorism is an attack on the state, an attack on the corporation, the state has an obligation to step up and try to find something that will satisfy all of its corporate citizens. And it doesn't seem to be doing that ... At one point, social responsibility can become social irresponsibility because, if we did go bankrupt as a company, it would affect a larger scope of people. We've been criticized for this as well. Part of that pullout was to *force* some action and some response on the part of the government.

A colleague who was also present at the same interview added, 'It's a power play, it's balance of power. There's always some market forces that come into play.' Interviewees in other contexts made the same point. Reinsurers are perhaps the purest representatives of market fundamentalism as the cornerstone of political economies. Therefore in negotiating the meaning of terrorist activity, and how they will participate in variously excluding or including it in insurance programs, reinsurers operate from the perspective of 'the market forces that come into play.' A senior insurance industry official observed that just as the market contracts in the uncertainties created by a catastrophic event, so it expands in the opportunities of profiting from terrorism insurance.

> Largely the nature of the coverage in the reinsurance market, the price of the coverage in the reinsurance market, is established by the market itself; I hate to put it this way, but this is an industry that doesn't always have the longest memory. And what it will ultimately take is somebody to decide, wait a minute, there is a lot of money to be made in providing reinsurance for terrorism ... The appetite for terrorism coverage [will eventually increase] ... The fear of what a terrorism event could possibly do is going to somehow diminish over time. Right immediately following 9/11, that was the definitive terrorist event, and that's what everybody was thinking in their minds when they sat down to negotiate these contracts. If the terrorist event had been instead twenty or thirty people killed in a suicide bombing, would the market have said no, we cannot insure any property anywhere in the world for a terrorist event?

Reinsurers faced the same market conditions we have documented for primary insurers. The soft market in the 1990s meant that low premiums and favourable contract conditions were on offer to primary insurers seeking reinsurance. Indeed, this market condition was one reason why broad terrorism coverage was included in reinsurance contracts rather than excluded or treated as a special coverage with higher premium. The market was so soft that low-priced, multi-year reinsurance contracts were written, although the preferred practice is annual contracts. This meant that some contracts still included broad terrorism coverage well beyond the normal renewal time of January 2002. This continuing exposure provided another reason for reinsurers to be hesitant about including terrorism coverage where contractual agreements allowed them choice.

The competitive pressure over the 1990s was to obtain reinsurance premiums to invest. The hope was to make significant investment returns without a major catastrophic loss that would undercut profits. Into the autumn of 2001, hopes were dashed by the combination of poor investment markets, 9/11, and various long-term liability problems.

The long-term liability problems paralleled those facing primary insurers, albeit with differential impact. Senior executives of reinsurance companies singled out medical claims inflation as a particular problem. For example, one executive observed that in the 1990s soft market there was 'systematic underpricing of product, and maybe a lack of realization of how substantial medical inflation had become. And medical inflation disproportionately affects reinsurance entities. This was way before the World Trade Center, way before corporate scandals, and cost the industry billions, and maybe billions to come.' Some of the medical inflation problems were concentrated in the area of personal injury claims to auto insurers (see chapter 3). This area of claims inflation was a source of catastrophic loss for both primary insurers and reinsurers. It had become a particular concern in New York State. According to the Superintendent of the New York State Insurance Department,

> The private passenger automobile market in New York is being strained almost to the breaking point. Overutilization and outright fraud by some insureds, medical practitioners and attorneys have resulted in double-digit increases in the personal injury protection [premiums] ... We've already experienced the insolvency of two small New York insurers, largely as a result of fraud and abuse ... The situation was compounded by the September 11th disaster in which 878 vehicles were totalled costing the industry an additional $11 million. Now, as insurers reassess how they will allocate their diminished capital base, private passenger automobile insurance may become an unintended victim of the attacks. Having a destabilized auto market discourages insurers from committing scarce resources. (Serio 2001b: 8–9)

Scandals at Enron, Worldcom, and other major corporations were also percolating. These scandals constituted a multibillion dollar catastrophe for the insurance industry not only as a result of enormous surety claims and directors and officers' liability claims, but also because of heavy loss of insurance company investments in these entities.

Continuing problems at Lloyd's were another source of uncertainty for the reinsurance industry. The 1990s soft market and severe losses in

9/11 compounded an already weak environment in London. Lloyd's syndicates (private investors with unlimited liability) experienced enormous losses in the early 1990s, primarily arising from their exposure to the Piper Alpha catastrophe (Luessenhop and Mayer 1995). They did not recover, and have become displaced by the admission of limited corporate capital into the London market. 'In recent years, the Lloyd's market-place has been highly unprofitable: between 1998 and 2001 the accumulated loss totalled more than GBP 6 bn! This is equivalent to about 60 per cent of the average underwriting capacity. At a solvency margin of around 50 per cent, this means that over 100 per cent of the equity committed has been lost within the past four years!' (Swiss Re *Sigma* 3/2002: 4).

The weakness in the London market was significant because it constituted about 15 per cent of reinsurance capacity worldwide and was *the* international trading centre for 'reinsurance covers that are large, unusual and complex ... [I]f difficult risks are going to find capacity at all, this is where they will find it' (ibid: 4). The limited corporate capital that has come into Lloyds' is organized, in effect, through insurance companies that have formed within Lloyd's structures, half of which are actually from the United States and Bermuda. Both capital and insurance operations are increasingly offshore, making the London market resemble an e-business virtual outstation (ibid: 23).

The global and virtual features of insurance capacity were also evident in the new capital that flowed into the business after 911. A \$30 billion influx of capital had occurred by the early summer of 2002 (OECD 2002: 3; Swiss Re *Sigma* 3/2002: 15). Lloyd's had at most a 7 per cent share of this equity, again limiting its ability to build capacity in a hardening market. Almost half of the new capacity was created in Bermuda, mostly in new companies. The new capital was opportunistic 'hot' money rather than 'committed' money, venture capital in search of short-term gains from insurance market conditions.

Capital gains were possible for several reasons. First, the market was hardening and there was opportunity for high premiums and reduced limits across a range of coverages, not only for terrorism. Second, where 'admitted' companies in a given jurisdiction such as New York cannot provide insurance at regulated rates, 'non-admitted' companies are able to offer coverage at exceptional rates. Because of all of the capacity problems we have described, including the lack of reinsurance, many admitted companies were not offering coverage and this created a gap for non-admitted carriers to step in and profit from extraordinary premiums. Third, with respect to terrorism coverage in particular, 'trophy' or symbolic buildings presumed to be targets could only be placed on the non-admitted market where prices are whatever the market imagines is reasonable. Fourth, the new companies that formed in these market niches did not carry the liabilities of 9/11. Nor did they bear any of the previous investment decline and catastrophic liabilities we have outlined. They could simply gamble that there would not be another major catastrophic loss from terrorism in the short term, and make a lot of money if their guess proved correct.

On one level the newly capitalized companies were not so much competing as offering needed capacity to the marketplace. Such companies typically fill a void for awhile and then are bought or dissolve when the market softens. On another level, they competed in certain areas, for example, on higher layers of reinsurance for terrorism or other special risks. To the extent that they have a competitive effect, it may help to contain further rate increases (OECD 2002: 127). However, if the new companies use their competitive advantage of no past liabilities to undercut prices too much, that choice can negatively affect existing companies who have liabilities from the past and want the hard market to continue for awhile to bolster their capacity. A senior executive of a reinsurance company observed that the reinsurance industry is very easy to get into and out of, and this has implications for the major companies that are willing to manage catastrophic losses in the long term.

New capital has gushed into the business ... And that in itself dampens the effects of the replenishment of those [companies] ... that have been in business historically, that were in business on September 11th, and suffered those losses, and suffered underpricing in the soft market prior to that, directors and officers scandals and corporate scandals and so on ... [The newly capitalized companies] serve as additional supply. That in and of itself dampens our ability to get better prices or replenish our capital ... They start up without existing liability, without an existing book of business. We have the book of business to protect, whereas they don't ... a book of business that has risk attached to it already, where they don't. A *big* difference. And I would say they're into most of the things we're into ... They've been competitive because we have to build into our price past liabilities as well as future liabilities, they only have to worry about future liabilities. So if our price vis-à-vis renewal was increased by 50 per cent, they might only come in at 45 per cent, that's still 5 per cent cheaper. They're still making all that margin but still being able to take all that business from us because they're 5 per cent cheaper. And in the past the facilities would have come in and maybe be 50 per cent cheaper. That's what we're not seeing now. They're being very smart about how they're competing with us.

Established reinsurers were also opportunistic. Indeed, some of them were involved in generating the new capital that flowed into the industry, and in underwriting terrorism as a potentially profitable means of recovering from their 9/11 losses.

Other established reinsurers were more conservative in their approach. However, they too seized the opportunity for higher prices across lines of reinsurance that was presented by 9/11 and the already hardening market. 9/11 not only created further need to recover from past losses, it also created the opportunity to immediately raise premiums and to sustain the duration of the hard market. A reinsurance company executive said in interview that the 1990s soft market and unforeseen liabilities created

a necessity to improve the returns. Has 9/11 given further impetus to that? Definitely! ... They've gotta make money. This is not a non-profit organization. So when they have losses, they have to pass them through, and they pass them through to all the insureds to different degrees ... Unfortunately, our costs are very difficult sometimes to determine. And it takes years, many times, to determine the cost of the products that we sold. And that's what happened even before the World Trade Center [WTC]. We underestimated the cost of the products that were sold. When we found out what the cost was, we needed to pass through that cost. And the hard market was going to occur, I'm firmly convinced, regardless of whether the WTC occurred or not. I think what the WTC will do, will probably elongate it for several years.

Hard markets also give reinsurers an opportunity to engage in hard bargaining with ceding primary insurance companies. They can command higher prices for reinsurance that primary insurers pass along to the insured. They can redefine the meaning of risks covered, such as terrorism activity. They can require more stringent loss prevention enforcement by primary insurers. A reinsurance company executive observed in interview, 'The questions that we're now asking are as important in a soft market as they are in a hard market. Only now that it is a hard market, we're in the driver's seat. So we're taking advantage ... of the situation. You can perform better underwriting in a hard market than you can in a soft one.' He said that his main problem was with staff underwriters who had only experienced the occupational culture of the soft market over the previous decade. In this culture, ceding companies and their brokers dictated contract terms to reinsurers. Now the situation was reversed. 'We have brought up underwriters in this [soft] market who are used to being *told* what to do by a broker ... So that is ten years of an underwriter who is reduced to having a broker say, "This is what I need," [and] "I give it to you" is the only response [by the underwriter].' During those years very little information was passed back and forth. Now what we are saying, time has stopped, we are going back to the basics ... make sure that the underwriter and the other side understand that *these* are the questions that need to be asked.'

The Insured

The efforts of primary insurers and reinsurers to pre-empt risk following 9/11 had the greatest impact on insured commercial organizations. The withdrawal of terrorism coverages left many organizations 'bare.' In effect, trillions of dollars of exposure was pre-emptively transferred to business enterprise. Moreover, as insurance contracts became due for renewal, there were huge price increases, often with much lower insured limits on a given contract. This sharp increase is captured in figure 5.3, which shows the 'cost of risk' (largely insurance and related instruments) to American corporations between 1990 and 2002 (estimated). It portrays the decreasing costs through the 1990s soft market, and the projected sharp increase following 9/11. The estimated increase is attributed equally to 9/11 and to a market that was already hardening.

In the months following 9/11, the New York State Insurance Department documented the impact of the pre-emption of risk on the insured. It held public hearings across the state to learn more about the experiences of the insured. Reports of commercial insurance premium increases between 100 and 300 per cent were commonplace. While the problems were especially acute in New York City, and in Lower Manhattan in particular, they extended to business enterprise across the state. For example, at a forum in Albany

Figure 5.3
Cost of Risk per $1,000 of Revenues: 1990–2002E

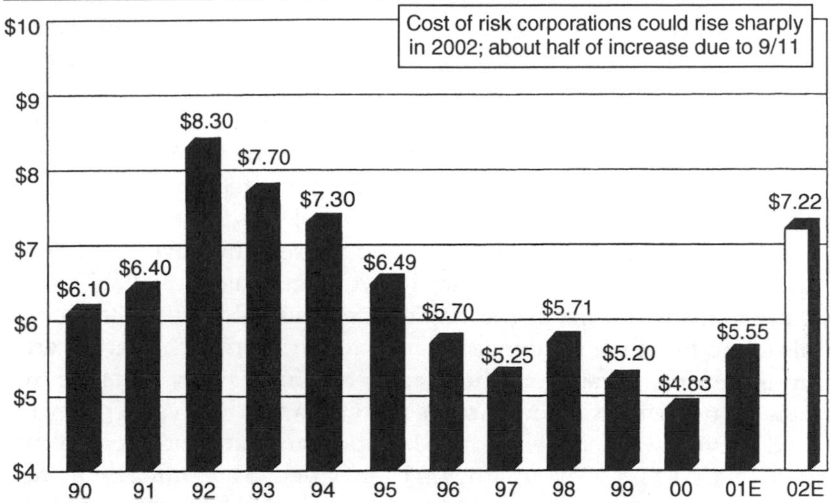

Source: 2001 RIMS Benchmark Survey; Insurance Information Institute estimates

the Department heard from a steel merchant and fabricator in the Capital district; his story is representative of the concerns faced by businesses throughout the state. The company's general liability premiums skyrocketed from $8,000 last year to $75,000 upon renewal this year; the premiums for their automobile coverage jumped from $31,000 to $56,000; and the umbrella policy premiums increased from $6,000 to $34,000. In all, this company's insurance bill for these coverages increased from $45,000 in 2001 to $165,000 in 2002, a 267 per cent increase! To add insult to injury, the president of the company complained that while they began shopping around for these coverages months before they were due to expire, they were able to obtain only two quotations from the market just four days before the expiration date of their current policies. In 2001, they had the luxury to choose insurers and coverages from over a dozen quotations. In order to stay in business and fund this exorbitant increase in premiums, the company is contemplating raising costs to its fabrication customers by 10 per cent. The company also considered lowering their insurance bill by getting out of the fabrication business entirely and focusing only on selling steel. (Serio 2002: 17–18)

News reports about spectacular premium increases, lower insured limits, and excluded coverages became commonplace. An insurance executive in Canada said in interview that apart from the obvious terrorism target risks, the commercial insurance increases were attributable to the hardening market. He blamed brokers for using 9/11 as an easy handle with which to justify price hikes. 'That's where I get annoyed sometimes when brokers go out and sell it, especially to a small little commercial risk in Saskatchewan, and saying that he's been affected by 9/11, that's the reason why he's getting a 65 per cent increase ... It's not, it's a reflection of the market.'

In the year following 9/11, various non-profit and government organizations in New York City faced severe insurance availability and affordability problems. For example, one group of twenty-three hospitals found that their insurance premiums almost tripled, their coverage limits were cut in half, and they had to obtain this new coverage from more than twenty different carriers rather than the one carrier they had used previously. The New York Metropolitan Transportation Authority's (NYMTA) policy up to 9/11 provided $1.5 billion coverage, including terrorism, for an annual premium of $6 million. Upon renewal, coverage was cut in half, terrorism was excluded, and the price was increased 300 per cent. Separate terrorism insurance was underwritten for just $70 million coverage, with a $30 million deductible and $7.5 million premium! In other words, this modest terrorism coverage alone was now costing the NYMTA 25 per cent more than its entire property coverage, including terrorism, had cost before 9/11 (Standard and Poor's 2002c: 3).

Jewish organizations in New York – synagogues, schools, and charitable foundations – complained that they were being singled out for termination of insurance or steep premium increases. Termination or higher pricing on their properties may have been based on location (e.g., Lower Manhattan) or the fact that these properties were deemed to be especially vulnerable to terrorist activity. Termination of an insurance agreement on the basis of the religious affiliation of the insured was prohibited by state regulators. However, the ability to detect actual discrimination by insurers was difficult because of the range of factors taken into account in underwriting a particular property and the hard market conditions prevailing at the time.

In a study of the economic consequences of 9/11 on New York City, Thompson (2002: 6) argues that it is wrong to think of insurance claims payments as offsetting the economic impact. He observes that 'a major disaster affects future premiums so that it [insurance] is best seen, in economic terms, as a loan to the affected economy, to be paid out of an ongoing differential in premiums that reflects the loss that insurers and reinsurers have sustained' (ibid.). Furthermore, the increased spending on both public and private security following 9/11 also contributed to ongoing insurance operations to the extent that it helped reduce future claims payments.

The insurance availability and affordability problem had the potential to affect investment – for example, in new construction projects – and therefore growth. '[The] existence of instruments to share and limit risk – which help reduce uncertainty – are often associated with increased investment. These instruments have included over time the creation of limited liability corporate structures, the development of hedging instruments in financial markets and the growth of the insurance industry, the size of which is positively correlated with GDP. To the extent that it increases uncertainty related to investment decisions, reduced insurance coverage may thus have a negative impact on growth' (OECD 2002: 125).

In the year following 9/11, organizations coped with availability and affordability problems in different ways. Some simply went without insurance coverage they previously held, although they did not necessarily reveal their exposure to parties that would be concerned about it, such as creditors. In some contexts, banks amended loan agreements to allow commercial real estate construction and project developers to operate without terrorism insurance coverage. There was also some flexibility in the energy, utility, and power sectors, as lenders made decisions about requiring terrorism insurance coverage on a case-by-case basis. In some instances, lenders allowed such facilities to go without terrorism coverage on a temporary basis (Standard and Poor's 2002b: 6).

Companies in particular sectors also formed their own 'captives' or self-insurance pools, usually in collaboration with insurers and governments. This practice was already growing, but it took on new dimensions following 9/11. For example, firms in the energy, utility, and power sectors find market-based insurance very expensive and it is often advantageous to form self-insurance pools. Power companies, for example, can pay between 1 and 10 per cent of the insurance limits they cover. This means that $50 million of coverage could cost up to $5 million annual premium (ibid.: 5). Following 9/11, the airlines faced an insurance capacity crisis and tried to form their own industry insurance company with the help of a U.S. federal government backstop (Treaster 2002a).

With respect to the exclusion of terrorism from insurance contracts, individual insureds in the United States experienced less of a direct impact than did organizations. As noted previously, the National Association of Insurance Commissioners voted not to allow exclusion of terrorism coverage from personal lines and casualty insurance. (Canadian insurers, in contrast, did invoke terrorism exclusion provisions in home insurance policies). Terrorism coverage remained compulsory in workers' compensation insurance, and group life insurers generally managed to maintain terrorism coverage in their plans.

Individual insureds were not as fortunate on the matter of premium increases. The hard market, stiffened considerably by 9/11, meant that personal lines, workers' compensation, and group life policies were typically renewed with price hikes. Even where the premium costs are borne by the employer – for example, in workers' compensation and group life and health plans – they inevitably trickle down to employees in the overall salary and benefits package.

The insured were highly vulnerable to insurance companies riding the 'pass the exposure express.' Insurers are eager to gamble on uncertainties as long as they continue to reap profitable returns. However, a catastrophic loss leads them to seek refuge until they can restructure the market and gain confidence that they will again be on the winning side. The refuge is provided by governments, who help underwrite faltering insurance markets. This socialism for business enterprise can supersede any socializing effects on behalf of the insured.

Government

Government can be defined with respect to its risk management functions and activities. As Moss (2002) has shown, government is 'the ultimate risk manager' because it has unique capacities to intervene in imperfect markets in order to shift, spread, and reduce the direct impact of risks. For example, through its legal powers government can *shift* the risk of corporate limited liability from shareholders onto creditors, or the risk of product liability from consumers onto manufacturers. It can *spread* risk among citizens by establishing a compulsory social insurance scheme, or by requiring banks to contribute to deposit insurance schemes. It can deal with the immediate impact of a catastrophe through direct disaster relief (this is the usual approach for dealing with floods). Even apparently anti-statist governments such as the United States must invest heavily in each of these areas of risk management because markets in risk are imperfect. 'Perhaps one of the strongest criticisms of a system of freely competitive markets is that the inherent difficulty in establishing certain markets for insurance brings about a sub-optimal allocation of resources' (Arrow and Lind 1970: 374, cited by Moss 2002: 3). This difficulty must be addressed by government, whose responsibility it is to 'undertake insurance in these cases where [a private market for insurance], for whatever reason, has failed to emerge' (Arrow 1963: 961, cited by Moss 2002: 3).

There are a number of reasons why private insurance markets are imperfect or difficult to establish at all. First, there is the problem of adverse selection (Baker 2003). The best risks may leave the pool because they feel they do not need insurance or can manage to self-insure. Those left in the pool are the worst risks, and insurers then increase premiums to the point that there are affordability problems, or terminate coverage to the point of availability problems. For example, owners of commercial properties in a small prairie town may opt out of terrorism coverage, while owners of commercial properties in Lower Manhattan may want special terrorism coverage but experience affordability and availability problems.

Second, there is the problem of moral risk (Heimer 1985; Baker 1996; Ericson, Doyle, and Barry 2003). For example, owners of insured commercial properties may be less vigilant about possible sources of loss in the knowledge they are insured against loss. Thus, a commercial property owner insured for terrorism may invest less in private security officers and surveillance technologies in the knowledge that he will be compensated in the event of terrorist activity.

Third, people misperceive risk. Moss (2002) documents that in legislative debates in the United States from the early nineteenth century onwards, misperception of risk was the primary justification for government involvement in risk management. For example, there was an argument that people do not think they will be injured at work, therefore, they are unlikely to purchase workers' compensation insurance policies in the private market, and worker protection must be made compulsory by government. In the present case of terrorism, organizations and individuals might decide it is a low probability risk and therefore be reluctant to pay a special premium for terrorism insurance. This reluctance may turn into unwillingness when insurance premiums are rising across the board in a hard market.

Fourth, some risks may be either so frequent, or so severe in their consequences, that private entities cannot manage them on their own. For example, inhabited areas prone to extensive floods have proven too risky for private insurance markets. If human habitation and economic development is still deemed desirable in such areas, government backstop insurance and/or disaster relief programs are necessary. Similarly, commercial entities signified as symbolic targets of terrorism may prove too risky for private insurers to cover on their own and government involvement is in order.

As a consequence of such factors, there is a broad range of risks that simply cannot be addressed through private insurance markets. One indicator of this fact is the broad exclusions that have been standardized in insurance contracts, for example, regarding acts of war. Another sign is forms of insurance that have been tried but failed, for example, private market unemployment insurance. Insurance to protect against the devaluation of personal property is another example of something that private industry would not underwrite. In many such fields, if there is to be any guarantee against loss at all, it must come from government. But in some of these areas the government decides that the risk management problem is so great that it too will stay out of the equation.

Government has a number of advantages in risk management compared to the private sector (Moss 2002). First, it has the legal power to compel insurance coverage. This power is exercised, for example, regarding workers' compensation, and the use of motor vehicles. Mandatory insurance forces broad risk pooling to take advantage of the law of large numbers and fosters innovative special pool arrangements ('facilities') for exceptional risks. As such, it can overcome some aspects of adverse selection and risk misperception.

Second, government has the power to compel revenue. It can tax to raise money and spread risk across an entire population of taxpayers. It can also print money. As a consequence, government has exceptionally deep pockets to handle risks that are too much for the private market to bear.

Third, government has power over temporal risk. Both its power to compel insurance and its power to compel revenue give it the capacity to force future generations to participate in risk spreading over time. For example, the U.S. government handled the Savings and Loans crisis in the 1980s through deposit insurance payments of hundreds of billions of dollars paid for through taxation that mortgaged the future of the next generation (Zimring and Hawkins 1993).

In the immediate aftermath of 9/11, the U.S. government took extraordinary measures. The Federal Reserve made a large, temporary injection of liquidity to safeguard the financial system. It declared that it was prepared to inject further amounts to whatever degree was necessary to avoid payment failures and defaults. The OECD subsequently judged the Federal Reserve response to be highly effective, concluding that 'One lesson of this crisis is that when policymakers have to take rapid decisions in an environment of deep uncertainty and imperfect information, priority ought to be given to liquidity management' (OECD 2002: 117–18).

The federal government also took extraordinary steps to protect the airline industry, which was already in difficulty before 9/11. In addition to the four airplanes destroyed and lives lost in the 9/11 attack, the industry suffered further through airplanes being grounded for several days after 9/11, and through a huge decrease in passenger traffic. The Air Transportation Safety and System Stabilization Act (ATSSSA) provided a number of measures to bail out and stabilize the industry (Campbell 2002). Five billion dollars in direct compensation and $10 billion in loan guarantees were provided for 9/11 and promised for any subsequent terrorist attack. There was a $100 million liability cap on airlines for a given terrorist attack to 21 March 2002. Provision was made for federal reimbursement of airline insurance premium increases to 1 October 2002, subject to the secretary of transportation's discretion regarding the nature of these increases and insurance provided. The secretary of transportation was also given the capacity to reinsure any aspect of airline insurance coverage.

According to Standard and Poor's (2002b: 4), the Federal Aviation Administration developed a temporary insurance program that was extended several times after 9/11 until a more permanent scheme could be put in place. This program collected a premium of $7.50 per flight for coverage that began at the $100 million claims layer. Meanwhile, a more permanent airline insurance program with a federal backstop was under development. Against the complaints of American Insurance Group, which wanted to provide private market terrorism insurance for airlines at a higher premium, the industry worked with the federal government to develop a self-insurance pool. In one proposal at the time, there would be '$1.5 billion of coverage for each event, with costs estimated at 50 cents to 70 cents per passenger, which is significantly lower than what private insurers are offering. Beginning with about $300 million in capital plus premiums from participating carriers, the pool would still initially need support from the government, but any subsidy paid out would steadily decline over five years. While this arrangement would increase airlines' insurance costs, it would, more importantly, provide the needed coverage and avoid a threat to credit quality from liability risk' (ibid.; see also Treaster 2002a).

The most extraordinary provision of the ATSSSA was the Victims Compensation Fund (VCF). This provision was designed to compensate victims in a direct and timely manner, as an alternative to the tort liability system. Anyone who suffered personal injury in the terrorist attacks of 9/11, or beneficiaries of those who experienced wrongful death, could apply to the VCF. The victims included all those involved at the WTC, Pentagon, and Shanksville, Pennsylvania, including flight crews and passengers as well as rescue workers. Since the claim was payable by the U.S. Treasury, the VCF was not really a 'fund' or insurance but simply a contribution to disaster relief. The VCF payment was reduced by any collateral sources such as life and health insurance, pension benefits, and specified charitable donations the victim received from sources such as the Liberty Fund.

If the victim or beneficiary decided to opt for the VCF, they were required to relinquish any right to sue through the tort liability system. The events of 9/11 precipitated the mass tort of all time, and the VCF provided an alternative that would short-circuit the extraordinary legal, time, and psychic costs of litigation. In the legal opinion of some, the fact that the VCF option pre-empted the right to sue made it unconstitutional. In the words of a government official we interviewed, some 'victims are very upset with that provision ... if the person was well insured, they could receive basically nothing from the fund, and in return they have to give up the right to sue anybody, they're giving up their legal rights.' The VCF arrangement was consistent with many other legal enactments following 9/11 that short-circuited legal process or avoided it altogether.

The VCF component of the ATSSSA was the 'purest' no-fault statute ever adopted in the United States. The statute was drafted by leading representatives of the plaintiffs' bar, a group that would benefit enormously from litigation. The plaintiffs' bar cooperated in the VCF process because they felt they had no choice but to do so. Indeed, they not only helped to develop the VCF alternative to the tort system but offered free legal services to victims and their families as a gesture of solidarity.

The VCF was intended to protect victims from the 'damages lottery' (Atiyah 1997) of the tort system. If litigation was pursued, victims might be further victimized by the tortuous legal system. Already dealing with the pain of uncertainty, victims with a case before the courts over several years would experience prolonged anxiety and an unknown outcome. The fact that all cases would be assigned to one court, the Southern District of New York, ensured an enormous backlog of cases. Indeed, cases from the 1993 terrorist attack at the WTC were still pending in this court when the 9/11 attack occurred.

On one view the VCF was 'an unprecedented government social welfare relief program' (Campbell 2002: 211). It was social assistance offered by the U.S. Treasury after the event, based on the expression of solidarity. It was the first direct obligation federal bill since medicare thirty-six years earlier. Social security was the only other direct obligation provision in U.S. history. The VCF was in no way a tort remedy, but rather the government stepping in in lieu of a tort feasor at a propitious moment. In a statement announcing the regulations for the VCF, the official in charge of the program called it an '"unprecedented expression of compassion on the part of the American people to the victims and their families ... designed to bring some measure of financial relief to those most devastated by the events of September 11 ... [and] an example of how Americans rally around the less fortunate"' (ibid. 2002: 15–16).

The VCF was also an example of how Americans rally around their less fortunate industries. The VCF was a crucial ingredient in efforts to bail out the airline industry following 9/11. That industry would also have experienced the pains of the tortuous legal system, to the point of being crippled. The ATSSA capped airline liability for 9/11 to their insurance coverage at the time. In effect, the VCF would cover any excess that the airlines would have been compelled to pay as a result of litigation. Through this mechanism, the VCF provided a federal immunity to commercial entities (airlines) for state-based tort claims, dispossessing the state of jurisdiction. Speaking at an insurance industry conference, a legal expert who had been close to the ATSSA legislative process made the following observations:

> When this bill originally came up in Congress it started as purely a bailout for the airline industry ... The airline industry ... is not a well managed industry. They are surprisingly a cash poor industry, [and] their insurance was about to be cancelled across the board by all insurance carriers for all

airline companies. They could not renew their lines of credit, and they operate on very, very short windows of time. And essentially the airline industry in this country was going to collapse, and take down the U.S. economy with it. That was the context [in which] everything happened, the day after [9/11] ... Congress had no choice. The airline industry was going to be bailed out one way or the other ... [The argument was made] you cannot bail out the industry and leave the victims behind. That caught on like wildfire ... Congress was going to limit the liability of the airline industry. They could not allow lawsuits to mount against the industry that ultimately would bankrupt the industry, but more importantly would destroy the industry *the next week* if lawsuits had started flying because they wouldn't have been able to get the lines of credit, their insurance would have been cancelled, and the industry would have collapsed. There was no choice. So the government responded and stepped up to the plate to protect the citizens from harm as being the only alternative that was available at that time ... What the government really has done here is spread the risk over all of the taxpayers of the United States.

Government bailouts of industries are selective. As mentioned previously, there was a massive bailout of deposit-taking institutions following the Savings and Loans crisis in the 1980s. On the other hand, there was no bailout of industries affected by the asbestos liability crisis, which by 2002 cost an estimated $65 billion and dozens of bankruptcies. Candidates for special protection vary by what is central to the government's risk portfolio at the time, as well as situational exigencies.

There were also efforts by state governments to address the situational exigencies of 9/11. We focus on New York State because it was most directly affected by the World Trade Center catastrophe. Immediately following 9/11, the New York State Insurance Department (NYSID) established an emergency claims-handling process with representatives of major insurance companies. Its capital markets bureau conducted stress tests of insurance companies to ensure their ability to pay claims and solvency. A memorandum was issued to insurers reminding them of the superintendent's 'ability to exercise his emergency authority to declare a moratorium precluding the termination or suspension of policies or other adjustments to cancellations or non-renewals' (Serio 2001a: 23). As insurance company filings for exclusion of terrorism coverages mounted, the NYSID resisted within its general policy of prohibiting such exclusions. At the same time, it mobilized its complaint system, public hearings, and systematic audits to address 9/11-related claims and contract problems.

Rate regulation was more difficult. As we have stressed throughout this book and in previous research (Ericson, Doyle, and Barry 2003), insurance is an uncertain business in which prices are based on complex judgments beyond the quantitative precision of actuarial science. A regulator observed in interview, 'Actuarial science ... is a misnomer ... it's an art more than a science, if the presumptions are reasonable we approve them for the rates ... Two actuaries could use the same data and come up with completely different sets of rate level indicators. We try our level best to ensure that whatever we are approving is reasonable.'

The degrees of regulatory freedom vary by market conditions. For example, in highly competitive soft markets insurers may be allowed to deviate downward from the established rate. The deviation may be as much as 15 per cent, especially if the insurer can show it has lower administrative expenses and/or higher investment returns than the regulator's assumptions. When the market hardens, the downward deviation allowed for competitive purposes is narrowed or disappears altogether. After 9/11, regulators were underpinning the hardening market by limiting downward deviation in prices. Moreover, in some cases, such as workers' compensation insurance filings, they allowed for the first time a 3 per cent extra loading on price for catastrophic risk.

Some of the extraordinary price increases for commercial insurance following 9/11 were possible because the more risky properties were underwritten by 'non-admitted' or 'surplus lines' insurers and therefore not subject to the rate regulation mandated for 'admitted' insurers. When admitted insurers domiciled in the state are not willing to offer coverage – for example, because they do not have reinsurance for terrorism and yet the regulator requires them to include terrorism coverage – non-admitted insurers are allowed to fill the void at whatever price the market will bear. There are only two basic requirements. First, insurance brokers must show that they have made a diligent but unsuccessful effort to place the business with three admitted market companies that could conceivably underwrite the risk concerned. Second, the non-admitted insurer must provide standard fire coverage without the exclusion of terrorism.

Regulators have limited ability to control reinsurance pricing. They can do so indirectly through the rate filings of primary insurers. If a reinsurance price increase is one of many components taken into account in a rate filing by a primary insurer, it may be accepted. However, if a rate increase is predicated solely on an increase in reinsurance prices, it is likely to be rejected. A regulator said that he had turned down some recent filings in which primary insurers said, '"The reinsurer just raised its price 50 per cent, so I·have to raise my price by 50 per cent" ... In some cases what they'll do is they'll go back into the reinsurance market and find other [reinsurers], or buy less reinsurance from that company and go to someplace else for higher limits ... or not get reinsurance, or not write. And some companies are doing combinations of all those things. There is a hard market.'

Another form of indirect regulation is a requirement that a licensed primary insurer wishing to take credit for amounts it will collect from reinsurers must use reinsurers that are also licensed or accredited by the state regulators. Alternatively, if an unlicensed or unaccredited reinsurer is used, the ceding company can only take credit if the reinsurer has posted collateral or established a trust fund to guarantee money that is claimed as collectible.

In the year following 9/11, there were efforts to involve the federal government in a terrorism insurance program. Various proposals were made in which the government would be responsible for insured losses from terrorism above certain layers covered by the insurance industry. The arguments for a federal backstop program were as follows.

First, there were strong arguments from primary insurers, reinsurers, and insurance regulators that the industry simply did not have the capacity to underwrite terrorism on its own. This incapacity was evidenced by all of the uncertainties of terrorism outlined previously. To summarize, from an insurance industry perspective, terrorism exposure cannot be adequately measured, monitored, or predicted, and therefore it was difficult to allocate specific insurance capacity to terrorism coverage or to obtain reinsurance. Without sufficient reinsurance to limit their exposure, primary insurers were left vulnerable and tried to exclude coverage. Their vulnerability was compounded by the fact that regulators in some states, including New York, continued to require primary insurers to maintain terrorism coverage in various lines of insurance, leaving them exposed in ways that made insurance markets dysfunctional and with potential for insolvency. The spectre of further terrorism catastrophes, especially if they involved nuclear, biological, or chemical devices, inevitably led individual insurance companies as well as the industry as a whole to want to limit their exposure. The uncertainties of terrorism were infinite, while industry capacity was finite. The solution was government involvement above specified industry limits, which would allow insurers and reinsurers to know their exposure and therefore help them to price the coverage they offered with more certainty.

Second, it was clearly unfair for the insured to be forced to embrace the risk of terrorism. Placing the onus on innocent victims to deal with the consequences of terrorism was politically unacceptable. Yet the 'pass the exposure express' was heading swiftly in that direction. Where there was no coverage, businesses were left vulnerable to not being able to maintain lines of credit, their expansion plans and other forms of risk taking were inhibited, their employee benefit programs were threatened, and they were exposed to total loss in the event of another terrorist attack. Where there was some coverage, it was at a price that many could not afford, leaving them with the 'choice' of going without coverage or reorganizing the financial management and other aspects of their enterprise.

The third line of argument was that government is in the best position to insure against terrorism. As discussed above, government can help forge risk pools and a certain solidarity through its formidable legal and economic powers. It alone can create and enforce legal rules to overcome insurance capacity problems. It has the deepest pockets, and can tailor their depth through the power to tax ex post and to finance indemnity over time. This power gives government greater creditworthiness than industry and allows it to spread risk over time and place. Government participation as a reinsurer of last resort would provide premium revenue. If another terrorism catastrophe did not occur for a considerable period, this revenue could be used to build a substantial reserve and/or to fund anti-terrorist security measures that might further reduce the risk. Government also has the greatest information resources about terrorism; consequently its participation in an insurance program is vital to both underwriting and preventive security measures in an overall protection package for both insurers and insured.

The fourth argument pointed to the government's *duty* of security and protection in conditions of uncertainty. For example, in a submission to a U.S. House of Representatives Committee, the Superintendent of Insurance for New York concluded by stating, 'The private sector, by itself, does not have the capability to develop a solution to this problem ... Government participation is necessary because the nature of the risk has the potential to disrupt our national economy and presents a significant hurdle to recovery from the current recession ... [M]any of the issues driving the current market, such as the public uncertainty about the security measures implemented to thwart future terrorist attacks and a general sense of insecurity prevailing in the civil aviation industry since September 11th, are not within the realm of insurance regulation and can only be tackled at the national level' (Serio 2002: 26–7).

Fifth, a federal government backstop would limit the exposure of insurers to a known degree, thereby addressing the severity of terrorism exposure. Federal government military and police security measures are designed to prevent terrorist attacks, thereby addressing the frequency side of the equation. As an insurance official argued in interview, 'The government is responsible for protecting us from terrorism. Doesn't it psychologically go hand-in-hand to say we're going to protect you, and in the event we are unable to protect you, we will help financially to fix the problem?' A senior insurance executive we interviewed underscored the uncertainties of terrorism and its 'warlike' qualities to argue that long-term government participation in a terrorism insurance program was essential and at the very heart of its security mandate. 'The randomness of the [terrorism] acts, the unpredictability, the inability to have empirical data to price the products, the potential effect not only on our business but on the economy – we *better* have funds there, otherwise the economy could come to a screeching halt ... The terrorism that we're talking about today is really just a new form of warfare. And for all intents and purposes we are in fact at war. I don't think any government should expect private enterprise to finance the economics of the effects of war.'

There were protracted debates about models for a backstop program, or whether the government should participate at all. Some took the view that the government should not participate because the insurance industry would eventually return to adequate capacity for terrorism coverage. The insurance system worked remarkably well in the case of 9/11, and over half of the losses were covered by reinsurers and capital outside the United States. New capital was flowing into the industry, and hopefully the insurance system would work again in the event of another catastrophe.

Others expressed caution about a government backstop program because they perceived moral risk problems at the level of insurance companies (Bohn and Hall 1999). Some took the view that primary insurers might use the backstop protection to take questionable risks in other lines of business and as a general form of solvency protection. Others contended that a backstop program would lead insurers to inflate claims beyond their limits in order to collect from government. It would also entail administrative expenses for government audits of insurers to address these moral risk problems. Some concluded that these moral risk problems were significant enough to justify making government the sole insurer of terrorism risk, or as simply there to provide disaster relief when necessary.

Another view was that private insurers are in the best position to establish and monitor anti-terrorism loss prevention measures. Therefore government should not absorb all of the risk, but rather partner with the insurance industry and devolve to them the task of overseeing the control of terrorism risk by insured organizations. Through contract incentives and auditing by insurers, the insured could be mobilized to hire private security personnel and purchase surveillance technologies that might prevent terrorism. The federal backstop would simply be a general incentive to insurers in this regard.

The U.S. House of Representatives eventually passed a bill entitled The Terrorism Risk Protection Act and sent it on to the Senate. This bill would have provided federal loans to primary commercial insurers to cover claims for terrorist activity. 'The Secretary of Treasury would make a formal determination that an act of terrorism has occurred where aggregate insured losses industrywide are greater than $1 billion and, for an individual commercial carrier, a threshold of total losses plus its losses must exceed specific levels of capital surplus and net premiums at that time. There are both industrywide and individual carrier triggers to determine assessments for repayment. Assessment and surcharge plans would apply to municipal self-insurance programs as well. The bill also limits damages for lawsuits arising from a federally designated act of terrorism' (Standard and Poor's 2002c: 6).

The insurance industry did not regard this proposal as very helpful. While a loan would provide liquidity to the insurance system at the time of a catastrophe, it would do nothing to alleviate insurers' exposure to terrorist activity and therefore they would continue to be reluctant to sell terrorism coverage. A substantial loan might also increase the credit risk of a primary insurer.

The insurance industry preferred government involvement in an excess-of-loss reinsurance program, and a proposal to this effect was introduced in the Senate. In a program of this type, the insurance industry is responsible for claims to a specified level, after which the government acts as a reinsurer and pays any excess. For example, in the late autumn of 2001, the Senate Banking Committee proposed a two-year program, with a possibility of a one-year extension, in which the industry would retain the first $10 billion in catastrophic loss from each terrorist attack, and above this amount the federal government would cover 90 per cent and the industry 10 per cent.

There were continuing debates about the length of time the government should be involved in such a program, and about what was an appropriate retention level for the industry. For example, we interviewed a senior executive of a reinsurance company who argued that the government program should be permanent and the retention level $1 billion 'to change risk appetite. A $10 billion retention on the part of the industry might not because it is still a $10 billion loss. And I think that what these [programs] are all intended to do is change the availability of insurance.' In contrast, a risk management consultant to financial institutions took the view that there should be a high level of industry retention, at least $10 billion but perhaps $20 billion or even $30 billion. Moreover, even when the government's layer is triggered, there should still be a 'quota share' industry participation at, say, 20 per cent.

> A material share. That means that the private sector institutions, their risk is aligned with the risk up and down the entire layer of loss. They're going to price that appropriately. For the government, you're providing real capacity, but you're providing it at private market rates, which allows the private market to work *with* the federal government. You're facilitating the private reinsurance markets, you're not replacing them. To the extent that the private reinsurance markets can take a larger share, they can actually crowd you out of the market provided that you price it correctly ... Technically this should be a revenue-raiser for the federal government ... Why is there no subsidy? Because you are charging private market rates at a federal government funding cost ... The spread is in effect profit for the federal government that can be used to fund homeland security ... It is internalizing the risk with the party that can control it. The federal government taking these resources, ploughing them into measures that can control the risk, reduce the overall risk exposure of the country. So what you have done is create a program that facilitates private sector institutions generating revenue that can be ploughed back into reducing the overall societal risk exposure.

The U.S. federal government finally passed the Terrorism Risk Insurance Act on 26 November 2002 (Bumiller 2002). This bill only covers terrorist activity by foreign groups or governments, not Americans. It includes a provision that allows victims of terrorist activity to sue corporations for punitive damages, thereby providing an incentive for corporations to intensify preventive security of their properties and operations. It requires all insurers of commercial properties to offer terrorism coverage. The most significant government backstop layer begins at an insured loss of $10 billion and is capped at $100 billion for a given terrorist event. In this range the government program pays 90 per cent of insured loss. Below $10 billion the government program pays a lesser proportion.

Various models for government participation in terrorism insurance coverage were available in other countries (OECD 2002: 127). The French government responded swiftly to the insurance capacity problems following 9/11 through its state-owned reinsurance company. Caisse Centrale de Réassurance covers physical and property damage caused by terrorist attacks above a $1.32 billion industry retention level. The industry manages its share through a pooling arrangement involving primary insurers and reinsurers.

Countries with ongoing problems of terrorist activity have more long-standing insurance arrangements. For example, Spain created a state insurance compensation fund in 1928, Consorico de Compensación de Seguros, to cover extraordinary risks including terrorism. Following 9/11, this fund provided third party liability reinsurance for air transportation catastrophes resulting from war and terrorism risks. Israel has a Property Tax and Compensation Fund – funded through property tax – to cover property and casualty losses arising from terrorist activity. The U.K. government helped establish Pool Re after IRA attacks in urban centres in the early 1990s. This scheme covers property losses, but not injury, death, or third party liability. Pool Re is a reinsurance company composed of more than two hundred voluntary insurance company members. The U.K. government in turn participates in reinsurance with Pool Re. Primary insurers cover terrorist activity losses up to £100,000, after which Pool Re is involved. Pool Re losses are limited to what has been reserved from earmarked premium revenue, plus an additional call on members of 10 per cent of annual premium if needed. Above that level, government reinsurance is triggered.

Governments and the insurance industry have the capacity to compel many additional requirements in conjunction with backstop programs. In its publication *Sigma* (No. 1/2002: 19–20), Swiss Re suggests the possibility of mandatory insurance and premium surcharges to help generate capital more quickly and thereby make participation more attractive to reinsurance companies. In a mandatory program, all property risks would be covered against terrorism, helping to provide more affordable coverage for high risk properties. In a surcharge program, dedicated capital could be accumulated to help address further terrorist attacks. Various provisions to share the loss are also proposed, including significant deductibles carried by the insured; a terrorism pool composed of insurers and reinsurers; and reinsurance of the pool 'on a non-proportional, per event basis by private reinsurers, and in excess of that amount jointly by reinsurers, capital markets, and the government.'

Insurance risks can be transferred to capital markets through catastrophe bonds (OECD 2002: 126). The investor buys a bond carrying a specified return and collects if the catastrophic loss does not occur during the period the bond is in force. Launched in 1996 in relation to natural catastrophe risks, the market in these bonds was thin because investors had little knowledge of the frequency and severity of the catastrophes concerned, and because the soft market for reinsurance meant that the offered return on such bonds was not competitive with reinsurance. The hardening market into 2001 had the potential to make catastrophe bonds more attractive to investors as an alternative to reinsurance, and various groups were exploring this instrument with respect to terrorism catastrophe. A capital markets specialist we interviewed explained that catastrophe bonds 'widen the audience who take risks because some of the investors ... are not insurance companies. So it is just a way to sell risk ... [Although] its hard for me to understand how you would model earthquakes ... there are ways to limit the risk for investors with earthquake bonds. The bonds can be structured so that the investor only takes a limited risk and ... only gets a certain percentage back or loses the coupon. So there is no reason why that could not be done with terrorism issues as well ... I think it is just a question of price, and historically it has been cheaper to get rid of your risk with reinsurance rather than selling it off in capital markets.'

Precaution

Responsibility for dealing with the uncertainties of terrorism is based on the precautionary principle. This principle implores everyone to pre-empt risk by heeding warnings, being suspicious, and embedding security measures in everyday life. For example, in its report on the economic consequences of terrorism, the OECD describes the worst case scenario of a nuclear attack on an urban centre and then declares, 'In view of this, preparedness should be seen as essential, even if the possibility of such an attack is considered as remote' (OECD 2002: 120).

Baker (2002a) observes that 9/11 crystallized a societal trend towards precaution regarding various types of risk, especially those that are low in probability but high in severity (see also Ewald 2002, Haggerty 2003). There is a retreat from the belief that harm can be subject to precise risk analyses and thereby predicted and controlled in advance. This retreat threatens the insurance system, which is based on the belief that one can predict both the efficient level of prevention that will minimize harm and the future cost of harm. To be responsible within the dictates of the precautionary principle, one must engage in prevention at all costs and appreciate that the future cost of the harm is immeasurable. The only response is extreme vigilance, a kind of pre-caution. One should even exercise caution about how one is being cautious.

The insurance system regularly confronts limits to knowledge in ascertaining the efficient level of vigilance and future cost of harm. As we have documented, there was industrywide confession of ignorance about terrorism risk after 9/11. Perceptions of threat led insurers to pre-empt risk by transferring it to other parties in the insurance relationship, especially to the insured and governments. In the words of the New York State Superintendent of Insurance, 'In the insurance world, perceptions of a threat could be just as important as a real threat' (Serio 2002: 8).

Some industry insiders described 9/11 as a classic exemplification of the 'insurance curse.' Risks that were unimaginable before a catastrophic loss have two impacts after the loss. The first is the immediate cost of indemnity payments. The second is the effort to learn about the previously unknown risks, but as knowledge accumulates uncertainty magnifies. These two impacts combine to make underwriters precautionary. The precautionary approach is compounded by the organizational culture in which underwriting decisions are made. Underwriters often get into trouble and sometimes lose their jobs for accepting an insurance risk that proves undesirable and costly *ex post*. In contrast, they are less likely to be in jeopardy for rejecting what proves, in retrospect, to be a desirable risk because that decision is much less visible.

The precautionary approach of insurers after 9/11 shifted responsibility for precaution onto other entities. Testimony to the NYSID indicated extraordinary precaution among commercial entities. For example, the NYSID Superintendent said, 'We know of individuals and businesses vacating the upper floors of high rise buildings not only because they are unable to obtain appropriate insurance coverage but out of additional concern for personal safety' (Serio 2002: 7). A survey of chief executive officers of major commercial entities conducted in November and December 2001 asked them to identify security issues that were of greater concern after 9/11 (Insurance Information Institute,www.iii.org, 25 April 2002). Among the matters specified were mail processing (86 per cent), travel (85 per cent), employee protection (79 per cent), infrastructure protection (75 per cent), risk assessment capabilities (71 per cent), office/plant protection (69 per cent), employee morale (69 per cent), supply-chain distribution (51 per cent), customer security (50 per cent), and productivity (47 per cent).

Vigilance

Response ability for the uncertainties of terrorism is based on vigilance. Vigilance is watchfulness against danger. It is effected through surveillance technologies, security personnel, and circumspection. It is driven by fear: the anticipation of the next bang, and the feeling that things are in the unmaking. Fear is valorized as an important component of the 'pre-rational warning system' (Haggerty 2003: 206; De Becker 1997) that hopefully makes everyone intuitively aware of terrorist threats.

The new vigilance about terrorism meant that reinsurers undertook more stringent investigations of primary insurers, who in turn were pressured to conduct more thorough investigations of the insured. A senior executive of a reinsurance company explained how 9/11 changed the commercial risk underwriting environment in this regard.

> Its impacted our whole underwriting process, where, before we renew reinsurance contracts, we ask for a lot more information from our clients in terms of concentration [risk] ... How many employees do you have at any one location? How many people in one building? Stuff that before nobody would care to find out or ask about. Now it's being asked by the reinsurer, and in turn the insurance company needs to find out from the insured and make sure that information is kept up to date. Absolutely, it has affected the underwriting process in general, the transparency of

information, the way we have looked at it accumulating ... You are also
dealing with a very 'live' market. This [9/11] came at the end of a very
soft market. Typically in a soft market people don't dare ask a lot of questions. If you ask many questions, the client goes somewhere else. You
have to superimpose market conditions now. Since 9/11 – the market
started turning before 9/11 – 9/11 really pushed it up in a much more
dramatic fashion. Now it's OK to ask ten, twenty, thirty questions before
you renew your account, and get that information.

A reinsurance executive said that his company was questioning ceding insurers about their clients' preventive security arrangements with
respect to terrorism. This new vigilance was exercised in relation to all
commercial reinsurance under consideration, but intensified if the
buildings involved were deemed symbolic targets of terrorism.

One of the first questions we ask our underwriters toward their clients is,
'What do your clients do about the terrorism exposure?'... There's things
you can do on an underwriting basis, on a loss prevention basis ... to
avoid a terrorist act. For example, you own a building and you have a
security guard at the entrance, that will prevent a lot of unwanted people
from wandering around the building. The WTC, the top door to the roof
had been locked for some reason. A good loss control person, had she or
he done a review, would have noticed that door probably should not have
been locked, lives would have been saved ... We have developed a number of very detailed questionnaires ... [regarding] accessibility, security,
after-event evacuation procedures, those types of things ... And this tar-
get-class list ... main targets of terrorism, many of those [questionnaires]
have to do with the security ... precautions that are taken. We're just trying to limit the accessibility of these major targets to outsiders, to people
that we don't want in there. Inside concerns, how are you monitoring the
inside of your plant?

In direct underwriting situations, some insurers sent loss control
engineers to field sites with detailed questionnaires addressing terrorism-related security arrangements. This assessment was used to decide
whether terrorism coverage should be excluded entirely, or included at
particular sublimits and prices. Agreed levels of surveillance personnel and technologies were negotiated in this process.

Interviewees offered various examples of increased vigilance about
commercial operations. A reinsurance company executive used the

example of a trucking company and said that before 9/11 the drivers' licences may have been checked annually for authenticity, but now 'we may come up with a recommendation that if you want us to reinsure your business, we want you to *insist* on having drivers' records checked on a quarterly basis. Because there is turnover and you never know who is going to drive a truck on a particular day. So in those cases, we would make a proactive check that they do so, we would come back and follow up ... We can certainly get off that business, or break the contract, if we don't like what we see.' Another interviewee illustrated the point with 'the courier company that couriers packages, or a small airlines company, I wouldn't necessarily exclude terrorism but I would ask questions. "What have you done since 9/11 to increase your security? Do you check what's in the packages before they board the plane? How are your pilots trained? How do you screen people?"'

Some interviewees observed that this increased vigilance between reinsurers and primary insurers, and in turn, between primary insurers and insured, signified a decline in trust in insurance relationships. Each party to the relationships was now more concerned about whether they could 'transfer trust' regarding the responsibility for precaution and response ability of vigilance. A reinsurance executive described the new underwriting emphasis on preventing terrorism and asked,

> How much do you trust a client to control his portfolio in this way? ... The extent to which you are actually willing to trust is I think reduced. You ask for more information, you ask for more data of experience ... Is it trusting the people or is it trusting the data that you get? ... There is another key word which is called transparency. Transparency is now the main goal that you want to achieve in your portfolio ... It's not necessarily risk averse now, but you look closer at risk, you look closer at accumulation, and you look closer at your managers who reinsure ... I would compare it to let's say, a hanging bridge in the jungle. You see the first steps and it might be solid wood, but you don't know what's in the middle, and you don't know what the ropes are on that bridge now, after that [9/11] happened. And the analysts [rating agencies] are very carefully watching your steps on that bridge ... You have to demonstrate that you are able to transfer your trust ... Basically you give someone else the pen to write certain risks for you which come in your books. So as a reinsurer you have to make sure that this pen is used accurately. As a consequence, at last renewal of treaties, we came off certain treaties because we didn't want to be, let's say, more patient in some contexts than we had been in the past.

There is no doubt that business enterprise became more vigilant after 9/11. In a survey of chief executive officers asking them to identify 'post 9/11 precautions,' the following were mentioned most frequently: review of disaster plan (90 per cent), background checks on contractors (51 per cent), background checks on employees (39 per cent), limiting staff on a single flight (36 per cent), and considering alternative office space (35 per cent) (Insurance Information Institute www.iii.org, 25 April 2002). It is not known whether these changes were made as common sense measures within the business enterprises concerned, or as a result of pressure from insurers or governments. It is likely that the impetus derived from a combination of these sources.

Organizations were urged to examine building infrastructures regarding their physical security features. With visions of the Titanic as *the* infallible technology that failed in mind, commentators pointed out that the WTC had once been touted as 'collapse proof.' Those contemplating future high rise construction were implored to take note of total loss risks, while those responsible for existing buildings were asked to address remedial measures that might reduce such risks. On a mundane level, advice flowed on the need for target hardening. 'For instance, installing a film across windows can reduce the risk of injuries from flying glass. By putting a barrier around a building, a company can keep potentially dangerous cars and trucks away' (Green 2002). Caught in the marketing of (in)security following 9/11, organizations bought into an array of surveillance technologies aimed at monitoring people and lethal weapons. According to the publisher of the new *Homeland Defence Journal*, '"The Sept.11 attacks will be the biggest catalyst for U.S. technological innovation since the Soviets launched their Sputnik satellite in 1957, spurring the competing U.S. space program' (Krane 2002: D16).

Private security was a fast-growing and substantial part of the U.S. economy prior to 9/11. One estimate (Anderson 1999) of private security spending is about $40 billion annually, with almost half devoted to private police staff and the remainder to preventive security technologies. The OECD (2002: 136) projects that private security will expand considerably in the wake of 9/11, with possible effects on economic growth and productivity: 'A doubling of private security might reduce the level of potential output by 0.6 per cent after five years and the level of private sector productivity by 0.8 per cent.' In a report on 'The Fiscal Impact of 9/11 on New York City,' the City Comptroller documents that

The percentage of all workers [in New York City] who are security guards rose from 0.88 per cent in 1993 to about 1.07 per cent in 2001, an increase of 21.6 per cent in the share ... [T]he impact of the 1993 [World Trade Center] bombing appears to have been a 22–3 per cent increase in security spending over four years, followed by little net change. The average salary for a security guard is about $20,000, costing the employer about $30,000 with benefits, supervision and other costs, so another 21.6 per cent increase in the number of guards from a base of 37,159 in 2000 would mean a cost increase of $241 million per year, or $964 million over four years. Security-related spending, however, is a cost that may be seen as an investment because it helps to narrow the future property/casualty [insurance] premium between NYC and other cities. (Thompson 2002: 22)

The vigilance of insurers was underpinned by governments. On the state level, insurance regulators increased their involvement in preventive security initiatives. For example, the Superintendent of the New York State Insurance Department declared, 'The current environment of insecurity and the distinct threats of possible additional events require the Department to go well beyond its traditional role and activities to assist and protect consumers and the industry as they deal with the September 11th losses and the new challenges that lie ahead' (Serio 2001b: 45).

The NYSID was represented on the state disaster preparedness committee. This committee addressed various aspects of 'target hardening,' for example, improvement of construction standards to make buildings more resistant to the impact of explosives. One initiative in this regard was 'Fire Wise New York,' a program that focused on fire safety through improvements in construction techniques. The NYSID also formed its own 'Disaster Preparedness and Response Unit' to institutionalize the regulation of preventive security and oversee the development of disaster plans it required of each insurance company. Through its approval process for insurance rates, NYSID was also in a position to support insurance company programs whereby the insured receive a premium reduction if they have specific preventive security measures in place. As one insurance official explained, 'In hard markets it's very easy, you simply say if you're not doing these things we are not going to insure you. But most markets are not that hard, so what we'll try to do is say, "Listen, if you do these things, we'll give you a lower price." And that's where [the regulator becomes] involved because they have to approve the rates ... Often there is no data, but intuitively you know that these things work.'

Insurance regulators also helped to establish communication links between insurance companies and government agencies regarding terrorism intelligence. In one model, the regulator was to be the hub of an insurance company intelligence network. In describing this model, two insurance officials said that multinational insurance companies are an excellent source of intelligence.

> *First official:* Before they invest more in a global area, I'm sure they want to see what the stability of the government is, because they're going to deal with the government. I don't know what the potential for corruption is in those countries, but certainly it's got to be present. And what comes to mind is last week I watched 'The Godfather,' and they were down in Cuba and investing money and then Castro came in and the money went. And I am sure the [insurance] industry is doing the same thing, they're making assessments on the ground as to the stability of the area. So they do pay attention to those kinds of things.
>
> *Second Official:* And they're [insurers] directly involved in assessing that in many respects, especially if they write kidnap and ransom coverage, directors and officers, ocean marine ... Although that business is not regulated, insurers are well aware of the political and other risks that are present in different parts of the world, and explicitly take that into account in underwriting and rating.

We previously considered insurance industry arguments for a federal government backstop program. By functioning as a reinsurer of last resort, the government would help the industry to address the severity side of insurability. The industry recognized that the federal government had the lead role in preventive security. By functioning as an insurer of first resort in preventive security, the government would help to address the frequency side of insurability. Indeed, both aspects of federal government involvement were viewed as crucial to the stability of the insurance industry in the short term and the underwriting of terrorism coverage in the long term.

The federal government was seen as the only institution that could coordinate effective preventive security because of its fiscal, legislative, military, and police powers. For example, speaking at an industry conference, a consultant to the industry emphasized that 'The U.S. government is actually already a risk manager in this event. The amount of money that is being spent ... on the war against terrorism is akin to just loss control that an insurance company would undertake in evaluating what it is going to charge. And that is a component that the government is taking on now, and according to the President, is going to continue to take on forever ... That might help reinsurers and the private insurers in pricing down the road when they know that that component is being addressed and there is more information about terrorism out there'

Similar views were expressed by industry officials in other contexts. For example, an interviewee underscored the importance of effective security measures in restoring public and industry confidence that they could return to business as usual.

> The longer we go without another terrorist event, the more success that our government has in fighting and uncovering terrorist cells and arresting people and fouling plots, the longer that happens, the more comfortable people get, the more comfortable the industry will get ... Perception is a very big part of the insurance industry. They are lemming-like. You don't have to talk about conspiracies. All it takes is one person to do so, and then they hear it on the news and everybody is doing it ... I see the government involvement as almost a psychological support more than financial.

It is well known that the U.S. government – as well as governments elsewhere, including Canada (Daniels, Macklem, and Roach 2001) – moved quickly to legislate vigilance. The U.S. 'Patriots Act' in particular provided for new surveillance, investigative, and detention powers (Cavoukian 2003). But there were other legislative moves, for example, the ATSSSA and subsequent Security Act, which provided extraordi- · nary powers of surveillance, information sharing, and law enforcement with respect to all modes of transportation (Campbell 2002). Unlike enabling legislation in earlier times of crisis, these measures are likely to be long lasting, even permanent in one form or another. They reinforce the legislative hardening of the preventive security market that was already underway prior to 9/11: a shift from individual due process rights towards system rights to access knowledge useful in administration of populations and targeted law enforcement (Ericson 1994a, 1994b; Ericson and Haggerty 1997, 2002).

The legislative inflation was accompanied by an expansion of military and police expenditure (OECD 2002: 132–3). In the proposed budget for fiscal year 2003, the U.S. President asked Congress for $48 billion additional spending on national defence, a 14 per cent increase over the previous year. The President also sought an appropriation of $38 billion for 'homeland security,' an increase of 90 per cent over the previous year. The homeland security appropriations were supposed 'to improve the preparedness of "first responders" (firemen, police, rescue workers), enhance defences against biological attacks, secure borders, and improve information sharing, and includes $8 billion for domestic defence spending' (ibid: 134). In addition, in March 2002, there was a $27 billion request for emergency funding, of which $19 billion was earmarked for defence and homeland security. All of this additional spending was to be financed through government borrowing. Other countries followed suit, albeit with less formidable resources. For example, 'Canada has started to implement a five-year programme to fight terrorism, costing 0.7 per cent of GDP,' while the U.K. military 'requested an additional 0.7 per cent of GDP to meet the requirements of the war against terrorism' (ibid.).

As exemplified by the formulation of the U.S. 'defence' and 'homeland security' appropriation requests, military and police roles were brought closer together following 9/11, especially regarding the development of surveillance technology and systems (Kraska 2001; Haggerty and Ericson 2001). One proposal advanced by the newly appointed Director of Homeland Security was to amend the Posse Comitatus Act, which prohibits the military from directly engaging in domestic police work, to allow them to do so (MacArthur 2002: A15).

A substantial part of the government's resource allocation was earmarked for anti-terrorist science and technology. In an article entitled 'Terrorism Worries Bring Big Business: Pitch the Product the Right Way and "You'd Be Amazed What You Can Sell,"' Associated Press journalist Jim Krane (2002) observes that in the year following 9/11, technology companies opened sales offices in Washington and staffed them with retired military and security officials. The big players included Microsoft, IBM, Dell Computers, and Oracle Corporation, which proposed a national identity card and database. Smaller firms also saw the opportunity for expansion. For example, 'Visage Technology Inc., a small Massachusetts company that makes drivers' licences, used a post-Sept. 11 investment of $25 million to purchase a biometrics firm, open an office with a view of the U.S. Capitol and recruit John Gannon, a former deputy director for intelligence at the CIA, as a board member. The company hopes to sell face-recognition kiosks to government.'

Krane observes that 'The market is also beholden to the terrorists that spawned it.' He concludes by quoting Loren Thompson, a military analyst with the Lexington Institute think tank, suggesting that the marketing of (in)security is driven by uncertainty. '"No one knows whether there will be another attack," Thomson said, "or what form it will take."'

The same sense of business opportunity based on uncertainty was evident in other quarters. For example, in a communication to faculty about a new $170 million anti-terrorism science and technology program funded by the Government of Canada, a Canadian university research office stressed opportunism. '[A]pplication might be a profitable exercise ... It sounds like virtually any area that could be relevant to potential terrorist activity would be fair game, which covers a wide variety of fields.'

The expansion of legislative, military, policing, and technological mandates for vigilance has led to a new politics of surveillance and visibility (Haggerty and Ericson, forthcoming). While the insurance industry is a major interinstitutional player and beneficiary in the effort to target undesirable people and exclude them from full participation in social and economic life, it remains very much in the background, subtly influencing security practices and leaving the coercion and visible politics to government. One year after 9/11, John Mac-Arthur (2002), publisher of *Harper's Magazine*, said that 'In recent weeks, police-state-style vigilance has intensified alarmingly.' He offered case illustrations of system rights trumping individual due process rights. For example, a U.S. citizen was declared an 'enemy combatant' and subjected to investigative detention for an unlimited period. MacArthur also describes spectacles of discrimination, for example, the case of a dark-skinned family that aroused suspicion as a flight from Chicago approached New York. The flight was escorted by two U.S. fighter jets because the family 'apparently displayed too much enthusiasm about seeing Manhattan from the air. A citizen spy reported their behavior to the crew. When they landed the Joint Terrorism Task Force was waiting with guns. A few hours of interrogation established that the [family] were Hindus from Southern India.'

The act of the citizen spy in this case cannot be assumed to be the aberrant behaviour of a redneck. More likely, she or he had been socialized into the new responsibility of precaution and response ability of vigilance. Indeed, the civic duty of vigilance was being mobilized by government. The U.S. Justice Department proposed Operation TIPS:

the Terrorism Information and Prevention System. Part of a new 'Citizen Corps' program, Operation TIPS aimed to recruit 'millions of American workers who, in the daily course of their work, are in a unique position to see potentially unusual or suspicious activity in public places ... All it will take is a telephone or access to the Internet as tips can be reported on the toll-free hotline or online. Information received will be entered into the national database and referred electronically to a point of contact in each state as appropriate' (Citizen Corps Operation TIPS 2002). There was to be particular emphasis on recruiting volunteers among workers with access to private spaces in homes, businesses, and transportation systems. For example, postal service workers, utility employees, truck drivers, and train conductors were identified as desirable recruits. Here at least, system rights to knowledge were eventually trumped by privacy concerns as the U.S. Congress prohibited the further development of Operation TIPS in November 2002 (Cavoukian 2003: 4).

Civic duty was also promoted through Pentagon-supported films and television series. For example, ABC-TV developed *Profiles from the Front Lines*, a 'reality' series that depicted the war against al-Qaeda in the mountains of Afghanistan.

Individual citizens were also the targets of marketing efforts aimed at making patriotism and vigilance blend into one. 'The sales pitch for Du Pont EI's EVAC-V8 personal hood, which allows a person to breathe while escaping a burning building, declares, "Here's an effective, inexpensive way to increase Homeland Security for you and your family." Another company markets home radiation detectors under the banner "Homeland Protection," while warning of the potential for a "dirty bomb." Other copycat products include an $18.95 "Department of Homeland Security" doormat and a Bally Casino "Homeland Defence" gaming token' (Krane 2002).

Many of the communications on vigilance-as-citizenship prepared citizens for the new reality of being watched as well as watchers, and the bearers of their own control. For example, the Government of Canada circulated a brochure, 'Protecting Our Borders and Skies: Information from the Government of Canada for Travellers.' The cover page of this brochure features a picture of a young Asian child holding a large Canadian flag, below which are pictures of ships, a train, an airplane, and cars at a border crossing. Inside, there is a declaration of intensified surveillance, followed by advice on self-policing. The declaration of surveillance is promoted as a public good. It serves as both reassurance about security and a deterrent to those with designs on breaching security.

Canada welcomes visitors, immigrants and refugees who want to live peacefully in this country. But the Government recognizes that authorities must be able to identify and exclude people who pose a risk to Canada and the rest of the world – and has taken steps to do so

- enhanced screening measures overseas for people en route to Canada;
- more resources for detentions and removals;
- new fraud-resistant Permanent Resident Cards; and
- the new *Immigration and Refugee Protection Act* and regulations to update the federal immigration and refugee system

Making Travel More Secure ...

- enhanced background checks
- additional reference and documentation requirements
- electronic verification processes ...
- armed undercover police officers on Canadian aircraft and enhanced policing at airports
- new state-of-the-art explosives detection systems at Canadian airports.

These reassurances/warnings are followed by instructions on self-policing. For example, even though passports were redesigned to be more foolproof, travellers should carry multiple forms of identification. Six tips under the heading 'Fly Smart, Fly Secure' tell the traveller how to prepare for various security checks.

Unlike the other approaches to uncertainty we have studied, this one appears to have no limits. It is impossible to argue there is too much (or too little) security when precautionary measures are taken in such high drama of uncertainty. Nevertheless, much of the multibillion dollar expenditures for vigilance – which far exceed the economic losses from 9/11 – seem to be misdirected. The risk of terrorist attack on the purchaser of the Homeland Security doormat is low. Going to war to depose leaders of terrorist activity does not stop or even stem that activity (Lesser et al. 1999). And, while death and injury to innocent victims must be prevented, 'fighting terrorism without dealing at the same time with problems of human rights or economic development is a self-defeating proposition' (Caryl 2002: 30; see also Rashid 2002).

Extreme vigilance promoted indefinitely also victimizes. In particular, it victimizes those who are unfairly incarcerated, transported, or more subtly, excluded. It also victimizes each and everyone through invasion of privacy, restriction of liberty, and compulsory spending on a 'security' that is more within us as a yearning than outside us as a fact. As English dramatist William Congreve wrote in *Love for Love* three centuries ago, 'Security is an insipid thing, and the overtaking and possessing of a wish, discovers the folly of the chase.'

6 Uncertain Business

As it will be in the future, it was at the birth of Man – There are only four things certain since Social Progress began: – That the dog returns to his Vomit and the Sow returns to her Mire, And the burnt Fool's bandaged finger goes wabbling back to the Fire.

Rudyard Kipling, 'The Gods of the Copybook Headings' (1927)

If a little knowledge is dangerous, where is the man who has so much as to be out of danger?

T.H. Huxley, *Collected Essays*, Vol. 3 (1895)

What is all knowledge too but recorded experience, and a product of history; of which, therefore, reasoning and belief, no less than action and passion, are essential materials?

Thomas Carlyle, *Critical and Miscellaneous Essays on History* (1838)

Where is the wisdom we have lost in knowledge? Where is the knowledge we have lost in information?

T.S. Eliot, *The Rock*, pt. 1 (1934)

Risk society is also an uncertain society. In addition to the natural hazards that have always plagued human settlements, we must now contend with unintended and intended catastrophes that are products of modernity. The complex systems of science and technology are producers of new risks with catastrophic potential, such as accidents at nuclear energy and chemical plants. At the core of relentless economic development, these systems are also embedded in conflicts of civilizations and cultures. These conflicts too have catastrophic potential, as evidenced by the new terrorism and the warfare responses to it.

Such apparently non-distributable risks are brought to the centre of Western political cultures and treated as uncertainties that must be dealt with at all costs. They confront societies with the limitations of modernity and its conceptions of progress, especially those associated with the rational management of risk through science and technology. Insurance as a modern institution and technology of risk does not escape this radical doubt. Its progress over most of the twentieth century as a lubricant of social integration and moral community is now viewed by many as receding in the face of unprecedented uncertainties.

Insurers are the first to stress that theirs is an uncertain business. From the origins of life insurance well before actuarial tables were invented through to current liabilities for hazards, such as asbestosis, which they did not know existed at the time of underwriting, insurers have operated with little or no systematic knowledge of risk. Indeed, uncertainty is embedded in the organization of insurance and its technologies. As such, it is part of the products which insurers sell. Insurers market themselves as experts in uncertainty who take risks on behalf of those who want their unique forms of protection.

Insurers thrive on risk taking in conditions of uncertainty because it offers the promise of profits. In this respect, they have always embraced risk. Of course, they take risks skilfully, cushioning the effects of loss in ways that serve their profit-making interests. Insurance technology allows them to convert a risky event, process, or state of affairs into the logic of capital risk and its distribution. The uncertainties of scientific experts about the nature of a risk, and of the insured in search of protection from the risk, are reconfigured into capital against whose loss insurers offer a guarantee. Certainty is re-presented in the form of capital that will be available to compensate for harms suffered. In the moneyed cultures of the Western world, this form of certainty is compelling. Insureds buy into it to protect their capital from risk and feel secure. Insurers buy into it by putting their capital at risk and to seek profits.

We have presented case studies of how risk and uncertainty are addressed in four different fields of insurance. These fields were chosen because they each pose different conundrums for insurers about how to assess risk and deal with uncertainty. Each field presents unique problems with respect to the scientific knowledge available, underwriting decisions, administration, loss prevention, claims management, reinsurance, and investment. As a result, each field involves a different approach to risk, which in turn entails variation in conceptions of responsibility for addressing the risk as well as response ability in dealing with it. The distinctive approaches in each field reveal that insurance is a diverse industry with multiple capacities. They also show why social theorists must take into account different manifestations of risk and uncertainty, and how each manifestation entails different logics and practices.

The insurance model for dealing with the uncertainties of life is embracing risk, prudence, and investment. As we have seen, the life insurance industry is now focused on life course management more than compensation for death. As such, it has become a core institution of neo-liberalism, which emphasizes the responsibility of individuals to embrace risk through prudent investments that allow one to build, protect, and selectively use financial assets over the life course. This focus is fraught with uncertainties and is a producer of new risks. New financial products and features have proliferated without a prior history of underwriting and pricing, leaving both the insured and insurers exposed to unforeseen investment market risks. At the same time, a refinement in medical criteria for underwriting life insurance has also produced new products and features without a prior history of data, again leaving the insured and insurers with unforeseen and costly exposures.

The investment focus of life insurance means that the insured is also involved in risk taking for profit and exposed to capital loss. As the insured joins insurers in putting capital at risk, life insurance is revealed to be much more than a technology for spreading risk. Moreover, risk shifts from a negative logic of danger and harm to something that is positively valued, at least for those willing to play with it. The complexities of new life insurance products, which are often beyond the comprehension not only of the insured but also the agents who sell them, indicate that risk is embraced for reasons well beyond the technical calculation of probabilities.

The uncertainties of disability are managed through a model that emphasizes spreading risk, solidarity, and welfare. Disability insurance is an important institution for addressing the uncertainties of routine engagement with science and technology, especially while at work or driving. Seen as an unfortunate by-product of modern technological progress, personal injury accidents are met with compassionate compensation to the victim to maintain her standard of living and personal sense of worth.

The disability insurance system has peculiar uncertainties and is a perpetual source of new risks. Many personal injuries cannot be assessed on the basis of observable evidence, and there is little consensus on what constitutes successful medical treatment. The meaning of disability is negotiated in each local insurance-medical-legal context, and uncertainty is based not simply in limited knowledge but in an environment that is changing and erratic. Medical practitioners, underpinned by personal injury lawyers, invent new disabilities that are easy to imagine but impossible to prove. An iatrogenic system is compounded by adverse selection and moral risk problems among the insured. The loss ratios of insurers are threatened, as escalating premiums cannot keep up with accelerating claims.

This situation results in a shift towards embracing risk. The insured is made more responsible for accident prevention, and held more responsible for the consequences of an accident because she has failed to prevent it. When costs escalate and experts do not have accepted knowledge to diagnose and treat disabilities, insurers try to gain the upper hand in determining knowledge requirements and insurance capacity. There is a crackdown on insurance terms and conditions, health care services available, and on what constitutes a legitimate claim. The disabled are 'work-hardened' back into their usual routines on the view that too much insurance protection can be harmful, forcing the injured claimant into dependency and compounding the iatrogenic tendencies of the helping professions. In the new disability insurance environment, surveillance and suspicion loosen solidarity and welfare, and there is a re-emergence of age-old principles that good people work hard and are responsible for their own (mis)fortunes.

The uncertainties of earthquakes are modelled on the basis of absorbing risk, mitigation, and infrastructure. Earthquakes affecting built environments are known risks, but unpredictable as to timing, location, duration, and effects. While earthquakes are very low in probability, they can be catastrophic in severity. But severity is also extremely difficult to assess. Probable maximum loss models are based on dubious assumptions and highly subjective criteria. Earthquakes have the additional feature that they are embedded in natural processes in which it is impossible to intervene to alter the course of events. If there is a desire to construct human habitats in earthquake zones, the only possibility is to absorb risk.

Earthquake risk can be absorbed through the capital logic of insurance: the insured seeks protection of assets from the remote possibility of catastrophic loss, and the insurer seeks to build capital over the long term through a combination of premium revenue, investment returns, reinsurance, and government participation. Earthquake risk can also be absorbed through making the built environment more shake-resistant and teaching people survival techniques. However, all of the above measures are difficult to mobilize because the risk is remote. People are unresponsive to the usual range of insurance contract sanctions that encourage responsibility. Furthermore, insurers often have difficulty organizing the formation of capital specific to earthquake risk. This difficulty means that the solvency of some insurers may be threatened if a major earthquake occurs. As a result of all of these considerations, governments inevitably participate in absorbing earthquake risk. They do so through some combination of improving the shake-resistant features of the built environment, granting tax concessions to help insurers build capital reserves, participating in reinsurance programs, and providing disaster relief after-the-fact.

Insurance deals with terrorism through a model of pre-empting risk, precaution, and vigilance. Terrorism is intentional catastrophe, aimed not only at severe destruction of property and loss of life but also at disestablishment of broader social, cultural, political, and economic infrastructures. Terrorists are also in the business of uncertainty, thriving on randomness, the culture of fear, and the intensification of (in)security.

Terrorism challenges the insurance system because it is difficult to provide estimates of frequency and severity and to spread risk. The insurance system responds by pre-empting risk: passing more exposure to the insured and governments, and fostering vigilance through a precautionary attitude and intensification of surveillance. Pre-emption displaces compensation as the primary goal of the insurance system, as risk society's population of riskophiles becomes the uncertain society's population of riskophobes. Ironically, the greater the effort to pre-empt risk, intensify precaution, and sustain vigilance, the greater the uncertainty. New risks and uncertainties arise around issues of discrimination and exclusion, restrictions on liberty, invasion of privacy, reduction in public accountability, inequitable security protection, and consumption of massive resources for security, all of which yield more terror.

The four models of uncertainty, risk, responsibility, and response ability are not exclusive to the insurance industry. These models draw upon the political culture of risk society, and their implementation in turn helps to produce that culture and society. Insurance is one institution among many that use these models to address uncertainties and to redress failures of risk management. At the same time we are not suggesting that all institutions are equal. Insurance is a dominant institution in advancing these models, and is often hegemonic in forming practices around them.

Insurance is at the forefront for a number of reasons. It is an originating institution of how risk and uncertainty have been understood and addressed. It is one of the lead institutions of science and technology. Over the course of the twentieth century insurance protected increasing numbers of people against an expanding range of risks with greater levels of compensation. The insurance industry not only keeps abreast of knowledge of risk but actively participates in production of that knowledge. It assesses scientific knowledge of risk as it is relevant to insurance logics, helps manage the impact of science and technology on society, and participates in the creation and legitimization of new risks. The insurance industry struggles to make the seemingly incalculable subject to calculation, and thereby to produce risks and find ways of insuring what had previously been thought to be uninsurable. As we have seen, this tireless effort requires ingenuity in relation to each field of uncertainty, resulting in distinctive approaches to risk, responsibility, and response ability.

The insurance industry is central to the coordination of social institutions in other respects. It is a key innovator and participant in communication systems that produce and distribute knowledge of risk. It takes an active role in the development and implementation of loss prevention infrastructures. It is an important cultural institution, in particular through its use of risk analysis to variously promote and ameliorate the culture of fear. Last, but not least, insurance is at the core of political economy, underpinning and shaping the liberal state.

The four models are ideal types and not entirely discrete. Our case studies have revealed the ways in which the models are continuous. In the messy detail of how the insurance industry actually engages risk and uncertainty, the impurity of the models is revealed.

Risk society is not static. A model that is more salient in one time and place is less so in another. This point is evident when we consider how the uncertainties of life and disability have been dealt with in many Western countries over the past fifty years. For a brief period between the 1960s and the 1980s, the uncertainties of life were addressed more in terms of a model of spreading risk, solidarity, and welfare. The welfare state promised ample social security, pensions, and even death benefits to all citizens. This model has receded somewhat in the past two decades in favour of what we have documented in chapter 2. The neo-liberal citizen is to deal with the uncertainties of life by embracing risk, prudence, and investment. The uncertainties of disabilities suffered at work or in traffic accidents are still primarily engaged through a model of spreading risk, solidarity, and welfare. However, social, cultural, political, and economic changes have also compromised this model. As we learned in chapter 3, disability insurance programs increasingly force the insured to embrace risk, for example, through returning to work and other routines quickly even if it is painful. Pain is now extracted as a co-insurance payment. The person at risk of disability – which in effect is everyone who works and/or travels in vehicles – is also made responsible for preventive safety, and encouraged to prudently invest in a fit body and financial instruments in case they are needed as a brace against a future disability.

There are elements of each approach to risk in the implementation of each of the four models. This blurring of approaches is most obvious with respect to risk spreading. Spreading risk is an objective of all insurance. In particular, the capital and loss ratio logics of insurance offer a unique capacity to spread risk. For example, although the uncertainties of catastrophic loss from earthquakes primarily entail absorbing risk, and the uncertainties of catastrophic loss from terrorism primarily entail pre-empting risk, both of these fields also involve efforts, however difficult, of capital risk spreading through reinsurance and government participation in prevention, co-insurance, taxation, and disaster relief arrangements.

Our case studies reveal that risk society experiences increasing difficulty in spreading risk. New sources of catastrophic loss make risk appear less distributable. These include both the disastrous 'normal accidents' in complex systems of science and technology and the intentional misuses of these systems by terrorists and other saboteurs. Other sources of catastrophic loss – natural hazards such as storms and earthquakes – are now more dangerous and costly because of the expanding infrastructures and populations concentrated in urban areas. There is now the spectre of an unprecedented insurance capacity crisis resulting from one super catastrophe, or from a combination of major catastrophes occurring over a short period. The extreme difficulties in spreading risk, and the realization of insurance system capacity limits, have also appeared in health and welfare insurance systems. The potential ungovernability of modern societies through risk and insurance is painfully revealed in each case.

The limits to risk spreading in each field of insurance create pressures to embrace more risk. In the case of earthquake coverage, to the extent there is inadequate capacity in the insurance system to cover a catastrophic loss, the burden will fall on those directly affected. If the government offers disaster relief to those affected, the costs will be borne by taxpayers into the future. They will have embraced the risk without knowing it. In the case of terrorism, to the extent there is inadequate capacity in the insurance system exposure is passed to organizations and individuals. They must brace for the risk through their own forms of precaution and vigilance, and embrace the consequences of any catastrophic loss. Again, the only possible source of additional relief is at the discretion of governments.

It is also clear from our case studies that some risk must be absorbed in each arena of uncertainty. Health, well-being, longevity, and a civilized death are based on investment in a range of financial instruments, fitness regimes, and lifestyle choices beyond life insurance products. Disability risk must also be absorbed in other ways. Beyond whatever insurance compensation is provided in services and cash, the disabled person, and usually family and friends as well, must absorb pain and suffering. In the case of terrorism, we have seen how everyone must absorb some combination of higher insurance costs, invasion of privacy, restrictions on liberty, and living in apprehension if not fear.

Some risk in each field is also subject to pre-emption. The only exception is earthquake, in relation to which proactive intervention in the course of natural forces is simply not possible. In relation to the uncertainties of life, some aspects of the life course are increasingly subject to an emphasis on safety that entails pre-emption, precaution, and vigilance. The extreme sensitivity to child safety is a case in point, as is the more general cultural preoccupation with crime and public safety. In such cases a precautionary attitude and vigilance to the point of self-restriction have become commonplace. The lack of knowledge for diagnosis and treatment of some disabilities, combined with an iatrogenic system, has also led to the introduction of pre-emptive measures. These measures include more exclusions and limits in disability insurance contracts, as well as a strong precautionary emphasis on safety education and accident prevention. There is also a strong emphasis on vigilance in the claims process, as surveillance expands to make visible the excessive claims of the disabled as well as those who provide legal and medical services to them.

The nexus between responsibility and response ability is a crucial determinant of who is held accountable for risk and uncertainty. A capacity to respond to a risk through knowledge, technologies, and financial resources inevitably shapes conceptions of responsibility and who is deemed accountable. Each of our case studies raises the question of who should be accountable for putting in place adequate protection from risk and uncertainty. If insurance is to be a viable form of protection, there must be mutual forms of accountability among insurers, reinsurers, governments, and the insured. Insurance can be viewed as an elaborate game in which the parties try to hold each other accountable, especially when things go wrong.

Since insurance is an uncertain business, there is always the potential that one or more parties will become averse to the uncertainty and decide to withdraw from the relationship or to seek more enabling conditions of participation. The process of withdrawal and changed conditions is an everyday routine, as insurance contracts are negotiated, cancelled, and altered to make uncertainty more tolerable. But in an uncertain society an escalating sense of adversity changes the climate of insurance and accountability. As we have seen, in many fields of insurance, the insured are held more accountable by insurers through restrictions on the terms and conditions of insurance contracts, intensified scrutiny of claims, and the threat of depooling into a less favourable market segment or unpooling from insurance entirely. The hardening insurance market is social, cultural, and political, as well as economic.

Concurrently, insurers pursue less accountability for risk spreading that is in the public interest. In life insurance they place more onus on the individual to design an investment portfolio that meets her particular needs. This approach includes 'feature creep,' the development of highly specialized products sold to fine-grained market segments and based on little or no actuarial experience for risk spreading. In disability lines, insurers compel the insured to take more responsibility for preventive safety and painful recovery in order to suppress claims costs. A welfarist ethos of solidarity and risk spreading begins to unravel in favour of a neo-liberal ethos of individualism and risk dreading. In earthquake coverage, insurers sell the product in the knowledge that they cannot properly spread the risk. If there is a major earthquake, many insurers would become insolvent and unable to meet their obligations to the insured. In terrorism coverage after 9/11, insurers immediately shifted from a broad spreading of risk to systematic exclusion of coverage, or underwriting terrorism as a special coverage with exorbitant terms and conditions.

As we learned from the earthquake and terrorism case studies in particular, reinsurers are crucial to the capital risk spreading capacities of the insurance industry. The reinsurance industry has a global capacity to spread capital risk efficiently over time and place, providing protection to primary insurance companies which in turn protect the insured and relieve government from accountability as the ultimate insurer. But reinsurers also have the greatest ability to withdraw from an insurance relationship when uncertainties become too frightening. While they must be careful not to threaten their overall relationship with major primary insurers and governments, reinsurers can withdraw from particular risks and markets with relative impunity. Indeed, they may do so as part of a strategy to force more accountability from their partners, for example, to have their primary insurance partners assume more of the risk or to involve governments in reinsurance programs. Reinsurers are also part of uncertain societies that now seem to be preoccupied with pre-empting risk, precaution, and vigilance. There is a point at which a reinsurer will decide it is being accountable by withdrawing from a risk in relation to which it feels overexposed. If everyone else is committed to new forms of accountability within the precautionary approach, reinsurers will also claim to be accountable in this way.

Governments are typically left accountable for failures in civil society to spread risks or to contain exaggerated uncertainties. Government is the ultimate source of accountability because it has unique capacities to intervene in imperfect markets in order to shift, spread, and reduce the direct impact of risk and uncertainty. As we have documented extensively in both this book and *Insurance as Governance*, insurance markets are not easy to establish. Among the more prominent difficulties are some combination of adverse selection, moral risk, risk misperceptions, inability to gauge probabilities, and the potential for severe catastrophic loss beyond insurance industry capacity.

Governments have unique capacities to handle these difficulties. They have very deep pockets because they can both print money and tax heavily. They have time on their side because heavy losses from today's calamities can be paid by future generations of taxpayers and investors in government bonds. Governments also have enormous insurance capacities. They have the power to create their own compulsory insurance schemes. These schemes force broad risk pooling that takes advantage of the law of large numbers and eliminates problems such as adverse selection, depooling, and unpooling. Governments can also make private insurance compulsory, a measure that not only broadens insurance participation but also offers greater scope for government regulation.

Governments can partner with reinsurers and primary insurers. As happened in the case of terrorism coverage after 9/11, they can serve as a backstop in reinsurance programs by providing coverage above limits established for private market insurance. They can also mobilize special pools or 'facilities' for exceptional risks such as nuclear power plants. Last, and by no means least, governments have an enormous health, welfare, education, military, and policing capacity to effect preventive security that protects all parties from some forms of insured loss.

It is always problematic to assert that either private industry or government should be the insurance provider in a given field. The problems solved and raised by government involvement depend on the type of uncertainties being addressed and the specifics of insurance markets in local contexts. For example, in chapter 3 we showed that the moral risks of inflated whiplash claims are not necessarily greater if there is a government insurance scheme. Under the previous, more government-centred National Health Service in the United Kingdom there were comparatively few claims for whiplash; with the subsequent increase in scope for private medicine paid by private insurance, whiplash claims ballooned. In Canada, there is enormous variation in whiplash claims across the provinces. Among the four provinces with government vehicle insurance schemes, Quebec is very low on whiplash claims, Manitoba and Saskatchewan are much higher, and British Columbia is exceptionally high. Whiplash claims in Quebec are also very low in comparison to the provinces with private vehicle insurance markets. There is similarly enormous variation in rates of whiplash claims across American states with comparable legal environments. These findings testify to the fact that insurance conundrums posed by moral risk and iatrogenic systems are not easily attributable to whether or not government is heavily involved in the insurance scheme.

If a government does not participate in an insurance scheme, it may nevertheless be held accountable for compensation if a catastrophe occurs. In cases such as earthquake or terrorist attacks, the question of accountability becomes whether government should be involved in insurance programs or simply provide disaster relief if a catastrophe occurs. Regardless of the approach taken, the government faces serious questions of accountability and even legitimacy. Among the more prominent issues is whether the insurance or disaster relief program may perforate the government's deep pockets and cost everyone too dearly. As we saw in the case of earthquake insurance in British Columbia, the government may try to mobilize some capital by encouraging a private insurance market with its model of individual choice and responsibility. At the same time, the government recognizes that it will be accountable for disaster relief in excess of whatever loss the insurance industry can bear.

Governments also have insurance limits. They can only select into their portfolio a few major non-distributable risks that are especially salient in political culture. As we noted in chapter 5, the U.S. federal government has participated in some spectacular bailouts of business enterprise, most notably following the Savings and Loans crisis in the 1980s and in relation to the airline industry following 9/11. But it did not respond to other catastrophes, such as the asbestos liability crisis, which over time has formed the largest insured loss in history. Governments do not insure everything, and a great deal of risk and uncertainty is left to other mechanisms of civil society.

Insurance has many imperfections. Among the most prominent sources of imperfection are limits to knowledge, limits to capacity, and profit-seeking that compromises its potential for risk spreading, welfare provision, human compassion, and moral community. Nevertheless, insurance remains a central institution for making the risk society a civil society. It uniquely blends state and civil society efforts to organize in the face of uncertainties. Life insurance does help to organize personal provision for the life course. Disability insurance does help to organize benevolence when someone suffers an accident that limits his or her full productive capacities. Earthquake insurance does help to organize the absorption of a literal shock to the built environment. And terrorism insurance does help to organize the preclusion of intentional shocks to the foundation of risk society and an even more precipitous fall into the uncertain society.

While the insurance business is a bulwark against the uncertain society, it can also foster it. To the extent that pre-emption of risk, precaution, and vigilance permeate different fields of insurance, the industry undercuts its role as a cementing institution of civil society. A model of pre-emption, precaution, and vigilance sustained indefinitely victimizes populations on a selective basis, and eventually tears the fabric of society. It forces costly preventive security measures that detract from human rights and economic development as sources of greater certainty. It leads to radical depooling and unpooling of insurance risks that fuel more uncertainty. It spawns an unsavoury market in (in)security, a market beholden to exaggerated sources of human suffering that provide business opportunities for profit. It threatens to reverse the real progress made by the insurance institution over the twentieth century. If it continues to lessen coverage for more populations in more fields of risk, the insurance industry will help to make the uncertain society a reality.

References

Abbate, G. 2000. 'College Panel Delays Crackdown on Fraud by MDS.' *Globe and Mail*, November, A15

Abbott, A. 1988. *The System of Professions: An Essay on the Division of Expert Labor.* Chicago: University of Chicago Press

Adams, J. 1995. *Risk.* London: UCL Press

– 2003. 'Risk and Morality: Three Framing Devices.' In R. Ericson and A. Doyle, eds., *Risk and Morality*, 87–103. Toronto: University of Toronto Press

Allan, S. 2002. *Media, Risk and Science.* Buckingham: Open University Press

Altheide, D. 1995 *An Ecology of Communication: Cultural Formats of Control.* New York: Aldine de Gruyter

Altheide, D. 2002. *Creating Fear.* New York: Aldine de Gruyter

American Medical Association. 1993. *Guides to the Evaluation of Permanent Impairment.* 4th ed. Chicago: American Medical Association

Anderson, D. 1999. 'The Aggregate Burden of Crime.' *Journal of Law and Economics* 42: 611–42

Arrow, K., 1963. 'Uncertainty and the Welfare Economics of Medical Care.' *American Economic Review* 53: 941–73

Arrow, K., and R. Lind. 1970. 'Uncertainty and the Evaluation of Public Investment Decisions.' *American Economic Review* 60: 364–78

Atiyah, P. 1997. *The Damages Lottery.* Oxford: Hart Publishing

Atkinson, A. 1999. *The Economic Consequences of Rolling Back the Welfare State.* Cambridge, MA: MIT Press

– 2000. 'Can Welfare States Compete in a Global Economy?' In R. Ericson and N. Stehr, eds., *Governing Modern Societies*, 259–75. Toronto: University of Toronto Press

Awerbuch, M. 1992. 'Whiplash in Australia: Illness or Injury?' *Medical Journal Aust* 157: 193–6

Baker, T. 1994. 'Constructing the Insurance Relationship: Sales Stories, Claims Stories, and Insurance Contract Damages.' *Texas Law Review* 72: 1395–1434

– 1996. 'On the Genealogy of Moral Hazard.' *Texas Law Review* 75: 237–92

– 2002a. 'Liability and Insurance after September 11th: Embracing Risk Meets the Precautionary Principle.' *The Geneva Papers on Risk and Insurance* 27: 349–57

– 2002b. 'Risk, Insurance and the Social Construction of Responsibility.' In T. Baker and J. Simon, eds., *Embracing Risk: The Changing Culture of Insurance and Responsibility*, 33–51. Chicago: University of Chicago Press

– 2003a. 'Containing the Promise of Insurance: Adverse Selection and Risk Classification.' In R. Ericson and A. Doyle, eds., *Risk and Morality*, 258–83. Toronto: University of Toronto Press

– 2003b. *Insurance Law and Policy: Cases, Materials and Problems*. New York: Aspen Publishers

Baker, T., and K. McElrath. 1997. 'Insurance Claims Discrimination.' In G. Squires, ed., *Insurance Redlining: Disinvestment, Reinvestment, and the Evolving Role of Financial Institutions*, 144–56. Washington: Urban Institute Press

Baker, T., and J. Simon, eds. 2002. *Embracing Risk: The Changing Culture of Insurance and Responsibility*. Chicago: University of Chicago Press

Barbalet, J. 1996. 'Social Emotions: Confidence, Trust and Loyalty.' *International Journal of Sociology and Social Policy* 16: 75–96.

– 1998. *Emotion, Social Theory and Social Structure*. Cambridge: Cambridge University Press

Beck, U. 1992a. *Risk Society: Towards a New Modernity*. London: Sage

– 1992b. 'Modern Society as a Risk Society.' In N. Stehr and R. Ericson, eds., *The Culture and Power of Knowledge: Inquiries into Contemporary Societies*, 199–214. Berlin and New York: Walter de Gruyter

– 1999. *World Risk Society*. Cambridge: Polity Press

– 2002. 'The Terrorist Threat: World Risk Society Revisited.' *Theory, Culture and Society* 19: 39–55

Beck, U., A. Giddens, and S. Lash. 1994. *Reflexive Modernization: Politics, Tradition and Aesthetics in the Modern Social Order*. Cambridge: Polity Press

Best, J., and G. Horiuchi. 1985. 'The Razor Blade in the Apple: The Social Construction of Urban Legends.' *Social Problems* 32: 488–99

Bogduk, N. 1999. 'Fact vs. Fiction.' *Recovery* 10 (2): 11–13

Bohn, J., and B. Hall. 1999. 'The Moral Hazard of Insuring the Insurers.' In K. Froot, ed., *The Financing of Catastrophe Risk*, 363–89. Chicago: University of Chicago Press

Bourdieu, P. 1984. *Distinction: A Social Critique of the Judgment of Taste*. London: Routledge and Kegan Paul

– 1990. *In Other Words: Essay Towards a Reflexive Sociology.* Cambridge: Polity Press

Bourdieu, P., and L. Wacquant. 1992. *An Invitation to Reflexive Sociology.* Cambridge: Polity Press

Bowles, R. 1995. 'Accidental Damage and Personal Injury.' In *Association of British Insurers: The Balance Between Public and Private Protection.* London: Association of British Insurers

Bradford, D., and K. Logue. 1999. 'The Influence of Income Tax Rules on Insurance Reserves.' In K. Froot, ed., *The Financing of Catastrophe Risk,* 275–306. Chicago: University of Chicago Press

British Columbia Whiplash Initiative. 1997. *Whiplash-Associated Disorders: A Comprehensive Syllabus.* Vancouver: Physical Medicine Research Foundation

Broadbent, E., ed. 2001. *Democratic Equality: What Went Wrong?* Toronto: University of Toronto Press

Brun, S., D. Etkin, D. Low, L. Wallace, and R. White. 1997. *Coping with Natural Disasters in Canada: Scientific, Government and Insurance Industry Perspectives.* Toronto: Institute for Environmental Studies, University of Toronto

Bumiller, E. 2002. 'Government to Cover Most Costs of Insurance Losses in Terrorism: Bush Signs Bill Seen as Aid to Building Industry.' *New York Times,* 27 November.

Business Wire. 2002. 'AIR Worldwide Releases Terrorism Loss Estimation Model to Analyze Financial Impact of Terrorist Attacks on Insurers, Reinsurers and Corporations.' 3 September

Butler, G. 2002. 'Getting the Tough Cases Back to Work.' *Risk Management Magazine* (November): 28–32

Butler, R., et al. 1997. 'HMOS, Moral Hazard and Cost Shifting in Workers Compensation.' *Journal of Health and Economics* 16: 191–206

Campbell, R. 2002. 'America Acts: The Swift Legislative Response to the September 11th Attack on America.' Paper to the conference, Liability and Insurance after September 11th, Insurance Law Center, University of Connecticut School of Law, 21–2 March

Canadian Life and Health Insurance Association. 1996. *Canadian Life and Health Insurance Facts.* Toronto: CLHIA

Carriere, K., and R. Ericson. 1989. *Crime Stoppers: A Study in the Organization of Community Policing.* Toronto: Centre of Criminology, University of Toronto

Caryl, C. 2002. 'Tyrants on the Take.' *New York Review of Books,* 11 April, 27–30

Cassidy, D., et al. 2000. 'Effect of Eliminating Compensation for Pain and Suffering on the Outcome of Insurance Claims for Whiplash Injury.' *New England Journal of Medicine* 342: 179–86

Cavoukian, A. 2003. 'National Security in a Post 9/11 World: The Rise of

Surveillance, the Demise of Privacy.' Paper to the conference, The New Politics of Surveillance and Visibility, Green College, University of British Columbia, 23–5 May

Citizen Corps, Operation TIPS. 2002. http://www.citizencorps.gov/tips.html, 19 July 2002

Clark, G. 1999. *Betting on Lives: The Culture of Life Insurance in England 1695–1775*. Manchester: University of Manchester Press

– 2002. 'Embracing Fatality through Life Insurance in Eighteenth-Century England.' In T. Baker and J. Simon, eds., *Embracing Risk: The Changing Culture of Insurance and Responsibility*, 80–96. Chicago: University of Chicago Press

Clarke, M. 1999. *Citizens Financial Futures: The Regulation of Retail Financial Services in Britain*. Aldershot: Gower

Collins, R. 1993. 'Emotional Energy as the Common Denominator of Rational Action.' *Rationality and Society* 5: 203–30

Craig, K. 1999. 'A Personal Puzzle.' *Recovery* 10 (2): 18–19

Craig, K., et al. 1999. 'Detecting Deception and Malingering.' In A. Block et al., eds., *Handbook of Pain Syndromes: Biopsychosocial Perspectives*, 41–58. Mahwah, NJ: Lawrence Erlbaum Associates

Daniels, R., P. Macklem, and K. Roach, eds. 2001. *The Security of Freedom: Essays on Canada's Anti-Terrorism Bill*. Toronto: University of Toronto Press

De Becker, G. 1997. *The Gift of Fear: Survival Signals that Protect Us from Violence*. Boston: Little Brown

Defert, D. 1991. '"Popular Life" and Insurance Technology.' In G. Burchell, C. Gordon, and P. Miller, eds., *The Foucault Effect: Studies in Governmentality*, 211–33. Chicago: University of Chicago Press

Descartes, R. [1641] 1992. *Meditations on First Philosophy*. Ed. and trans. G. Hefferman. South Bend, IN. University of Notre Dame Press

Dishman, C. 1999. 'Review Article: Trends in Modern Terrorism.' *Studies in Conflict and Terrorism* 22: 357–62

Doob, A., and G. Macdonald. 1979. 'Television Viewing and Fear of Victimization: Is the Relationship Causal?' *Journal of Personality and Social Psychology* 37: 170–9

Douglas, M. 1985. *Risk Acceptability According to the Social Sciences*. London: Routledge and Kegan Paul

– 1986. *How Institutions Think*. Syracuse: Syracuse University Press

– 1990. 'Risk as a Forensic Resource.' *Daedalus* 119: 1–16

– 1992. *Risk and Blame: Essays in Cultural Theory*. London: Routledge

Douglas, M., and A. Wildavsky. 1982. *Risk and Culture: An Essay on the Selection of Technical and Environmental Dangers*. Berkeley: University of California Press

Durr, E. 1994. 'With Whiplash, The Future Comes from Behind.' *Sygeplejersken* 94: 34–6

Ericson, R. 1994a. 'The Decline of Innocence.' *University of British Columbia Law Review* 28: 367–83

– 1994b. 'The Royal Commission on Criminal Justice System Surveillance.' In M. McConville and L. Bridges, eds., *Criminal Justice in Crisis*, 113–40. Aldershot: Edward Elgar

Ericson, R., P. Baranek, and J. Chan. 1989. *Negotiating Control: A Study of News Sources*. Toronto: University of Toronto Press; Milton Keynes: Open University Press

Ericson, R., D. Barry, and A. Doyle. 2000. 'The Moral Hazards of Neoliberalism: Lessons from the Private Insurance Industry.' *Economy and Society* 29: 532–58

Ericson, R., and A. Doyle, eds. 2003a. *Risk and Morality*. Toronto: University of Toronto Press

– 2003b. 'The Moral Risks of Private Justice: The Case of Insurance Fraud.' In R. Ericson and A. Doyle, eds., *Risk and Morality*, 317–63. Toronto: University of Toronto Press

– 2004. 'Criminalization in Private: The Case of Insurance Fraud.' In N. Desroshers, ed., *What Is Crime?* Vancouver: UBC Press; Quebec City: Laval University Press

Ericson, R., A. Doyle, and D. Barry. 2003. *Insurance as Governance*. Toronto: University of Toronto Press

Ericson, R., and K. Haggerty. 1997. *Policing the Risk Society*. Toronto: University of Toronto Press; Oxford: Clarendon Press

– 2002. 'The Policing of Risk.' In T. Baker and J. Simon, eds., *Embracing Risk: The Changing Culture of Insurance and Responsibility*, 238–72. Chicago: University of Chicago Press

Ericson, R., and N. Stehr, eds. 2000. *Governing Modern Societies*. Toronto: University of Toronto Press

Esposito, J. 2002. *Unholy War: Terror in the Name of Islam*. Oxford: Oxford University Press

Evans, R., et al. 1994. *Why Are Some People Healthy and Others Not? The Determinants of Health of Populations*. New York: Aldine de Gruyter

Ewald, F. 2002. 'The Return of Descartes's Malicious Demon: An Outline of a Philosophy of Precaution.' In T. Baker and J. Simon, eds., *Embracing Risk: The Changing Culture of Insurance and Responsibility*, 273–301. Chicago: University of Chicago Press

Finnegan, D. 1998. 'Shades of Grey.' *Recovery* 9 (4): 6–8

Foucault, M. 1988. 'Social Security.' In L. Kritzman, ed., *Politics, Philosophy, Culture*. London: Routledge

Frank, J., et al. 1995. 'Occupational Back Pain: An Unhelpful Polemic.' *Scandinavian Journal of Work Environment Health* 21: 3–14

Froot, K., ed. 1999. *The Financing of Catastrophe Risk.* Chicago: University of Chicago Press

Garland, D. 2003. 'The Rise of Risk.' In R. Ericson and A. Doyle, eds., *Risk and Morality*, 48–86. Toronto: University of Toronto Press

Gavin, H. 1843. *On Feigned and Factitious Diseases Chiefly of Soldiers and Seamen.* London: Churchill

Geneva Association. 2001. 'Managing World Security.' *Geneva Association Information Newsletter* 34: 3–4, editorial

Giddens, A. 1990. *The Consequences of Modernity.* Cambridge: Polity

– 1991. *Modernity and Self-Identity: Self and Society in the Late Modern Age.* Stanford: Stanford University Press

– 1994. *Beyond Left and Right.* Stanford: Stanford University Press

– 1998. *The Third Way: The Renewal of Social Democracy.* Cambridge: Polity Press

– 1999. *The Third Way and Its Critics.* Cambridge: Polity Press

Gilliom, J. 2001. *Overseers of the Poor: Surveillance, Resistance, and the Limits of Privacy.* Chicago: University of Chicago Press

Glassner, B. 1999. *The Culture of Fear: Why Americans Are Afraid of the Wrong Things.* New York: Basic Books

Glenn, B. 2000. 'The Shifting Rhetoric of Insurance Denial.' *Law and Society Review* 34: 779–808

Gowri, A. 1997. 'The Irony of Insurance: Community and Commodity.' PhD dissertation, University of Southern California

Graham, J. 1979. *Lavater, Essays on Physiognomy: A Study in the History of Ideas.* Berne: Peter Lang

Green, J. 1997. *Risk and Misfortune: The Social Construction of Accidents.* London: UCL Press

Green, M. 2002. 'Cat Models Look to Predict Losses from Future Attacks.' *Best Wire*, 29 August

Gunter, B. 1987. *Television and the Fear of Crime.* London: John Libbey

Ha, Tu Thanh. 2002. 'Big Picture Missed in Run-Up to Terror.' *Globe and Mail*, 25 May, A4

Hacking, I. 1975. *The Emergence of Probability: A Philosophical Study of Early Ideas about Probability, Induction and Statistical Inference.* Cambridge: Cambridge University Press

– 1986. 'Making up People.' In T. Heller et al., eds., *Reconstructing Individualism*, 222–36. Stanford: Stanford University Press

– 1990. *The Taming of Chance.* Cambridge: Cambridge University Press

– 1999. *The Social Construction of What?* Harvard: Harvard University Press

- 2003. 'Risk and Dirt.' In R. Ericson and A. Doyle, eds., *Risk and Morality*, 22–47. Toronto: University of Toronto Press

Hadler, N. 1997. 'Fibromyalgia, Chronic Fatigue, and Other Iatrogenic Diagnostic Algorithms: Do Some Labels Escalate Illness in Vulnerable Patients?' *Postgrad Med* 102: 162–77

Haggerty, K. 2003. 'From Risk to Precaution: The Rationalities of Personal Crime Prevention.' In R. Ericson and A. Doyle, eds., *Risk and Morality*, 193–214. Toronto: University of Toronto Press

Haggerty, K., and R. Ericson. 2001. 'The Military Technostructures of Policing.' In P. Kraska, ed., *Militarizing the American Criminal Justice System: The Changing Roles of the Armed Forces and the Police*, 43–64. Boston: Northeastern University Press

Haggerty, K., and R. Ericson, eds. Forthcoming. *The New Politics of Surveillance and Visibility*

Hartwig, R. 2002. 'Industry Financials and Outlook.' *Insurance Information Institute Media*, 26 June

Hawking, S. 1988. *A Brief History of Time*. New York: Bantam Press

Heimer, C. 1985. *Reactive Risk and Rational Action: Managing Moral Hazard in Insurance Contracts*. Berkeley: University of California Press

Huber, O., R. Wider, and O. Huber. 1997. 'Active Information Search and Complete Information Presentation in Naturalistic Risky Decision Tasks.' *Acta Psychologica* 95: 15–29

Huber, P. 1991. *Galileo's Revenge: Junk Science in the Courtroom*. New York: Basic Books

Illich, I., I. Zola, J. McKnight, J. Caplan, and H. Shaiken. 1977. *Disabling Professions*. Toronto: Burns and MacEachern

Insurance Bureau of Canada. 1995. *Public Opinion Environment*. Toronto: Insurance Bureau of Canada

Insurance Corporation of British Columbia. 1996. *Motor Vehicle Insurance in British Columbia at the Cross Roads: Vol. 1: The Case for Change*. Report prepared by KPMG, Exactor Insurance Services Inc., Eikler Partners Ltd. (19 December)

- 1997a. *Loss Prevention: Road Safety and Auto Crime Five Year Plan*. Vancouver: ICBC

- 1997b. *Automobile Insurance Review*. Report to the B.C. Minister of Finance and Corporate Relations, and Minister Responsible for ICBC. (March)

Insurance Research Council. 1994. *Auto Injuries: Claiming Behavior and Its Impact on Insurance Claims*. Oak Brook, IL: Insurance Research Council Inc.

Jonas, H. 1984. *The Imperative of Responsibility*. Chicago: University of Chicago Press

Jonas, J., and H. Pope. 1985. 'The Dissimulation Disorders: A Single Diagnostic Entity?' *Comparative Psychiatry* 26: 58–62

Keynes, J.M. 1937. 'The General Theory of Employment.' *Quarterly Journal of Economics* 51: 209–33

Kleindorfer, P., and H. Kunreuther. 1999. 'Challenges Facing the Insurance Industry in Managing Catastrophic Risks.' In K. Froot, ed., *The Financing of Catastrophe Risk*, 149–94. Chicago: University of Chicago Press

Knight, F. 1964 [1921]. *Risk, Uncertainty and Profit*. New York: A.M. Kelley

Krane, J. 2002. 'Terrorism Worries Bring Big Business: Pitch the Product the Right Way and "You'd be Amazed What You Can Sell".' *Toronto Star*, 29 August, D16

Kraska, P., ed. 2001. *Militarizing the American Criminal Justice System: The Changing Roles of the Armed Forces and the Police*. Boston: Northeastern University Press

Kunreuther, H. 2001. 'Risk Analysis and Risk Management in an Uncertain World.' Paper to the Society for Risk Analysis Annual Meeting, Seattle, 4 December

– 2002. 'The Role of Insurance in Managing Extreme Events: Implications for Terrorism Coverage.' Draft manuscript

Kunreuther, H., J. Meszaros, R. Hogarth, and M. Sprania. 1995. 'Ambiguity and Underwriter Decision Processes.' *Journal of Economic Behavior and Organization* 26: 337–52

Lahnstein, C. 2002. 'Liability and Insurance in Large Loss Scenarios.' Paper to the conference, Liability and Insurance after September 11th. Insurance Law Center, University of Connecticut School of Law, 21–2 March

Lammare, M., B. Townshend, and H. Shah. 1992. 'Application of the Bootstrap Method to Quantify Uncertainty in Seismic Hazard Estimates.' *Bulletin of the Seismological Society of America* 82: 104–19

Lash, S. 1993. 'Reflexive Modernization: The Aesthetic Dimension.' *Theory, Culture and Society* 10: 1–23

– 1994. 'Reflexivity and its Doubles: Structure, Aesthetics, Community.' In U. Beck, A. Giddens, and S. Lash, eds., *Reflexive Modernization: Politics, Tradition and Aesthetics*, 110–73. Cambridge: Polity Press

Leiss, W. 2001. *In the Chamber of Risks: Understanding Risk Controversies*. Montreal and Kingston: McGill-Queen's University Press

– 2002. 'The Concept of Risk.' *Horizons* 5: 4–6

Lesser, I., B. Hoffman, J. Arguilla, D. Ponfellt, and M. Zanini. 1999. *Countering the New Terrorism*. Washington: RAND

Lewis, J., and A. Weigart. 1985. 'Trust as Social Reality.' *Social Forces* 63: 967–85

LIMRA. 1997. *The Buyer Study Canada: A Market Study of New Insureds and the*

Ordinary Life Insurance Purchased. Hartford: Life Insurance Marketing
Research Association

Lippert, R. 2002. 'Policing Property and Moral Risk through Promotions,
Anonymization, and Rewards: Revisiting Crime Stoppers.' *Social and Legal
Studies* 11: 478–502

Livingston, M. 1998. *Common Whiplash Injury: A Modern Epidemic.* Springfield,
IL: Charles C. Thomas

Lo Pucki, L. 1996. 'The Death of Liability.' *Yale Law Journal* 106: 1–42

Low, D. 1997. 'Seismic Risk Models.' In S. Brun et al., *Coping with Natural
Hazards in Canada: Scientific, Government and Insurance Industry Perspectives,*
121–64. Toronto: Institute for Environmental Studies, University of Toronto

Lowi, T. 1990. 'Risks and Rights in the History of American Governments.'
Daedalus 119: 17–40

Lowther, B. 1996. 'Maximum Coverage.' *Monday Magazine* 22 (46): 1, 6–7

Luessenhop, E., and M. Mayer. 1995. *Risky Business: An Insider's Account of the
Disaster at Lloyd's of London.* New York: Scribner

Lupton, D. 1999. *Risk.* London: Routledge

MacArthur, J. 2002. 'Friends Tell it Like it is.' *Globe and Mail,* 5 September, A15

Malleson, A. 2002. *Whiplash and Other Useful Illnesses.* Montreal and Kingston:
McGill-Queen's University Press

Mangon, S. 1995. 'Catastrophe Insurance System in France.' *Geneva Papers on
Risk and Insurance* 20: 474–80

Maticka-Tyndale, E. 1992. 'Social Construction of HIV Transmission and
Prevention among Heterosexual Young Adults.' *Social Problems* 39: 238–52

McClusky, M. 2002. 'Rhetoric of Risk and the Redistribution of Social Insurance.' In T. Baker and J. Simon, eds., *Embracing Risk: The Changing Culture of
Insurance and Responsibility,* 146–70. Chicago: University of Chicago Press

McCormack, J. 1999. 'A Prescription Quandary.' *Recovery* 10 (2): 24–5

McKenzie, L. 1998. 'Rarely Pure, Never Simple.' *Recovery* 9 (4): 9–12

McQueen, R. 1996. *Who Killed Confederation Life?* Toronto: McClelland and
Stewart

Mechanic, D. 1961. 'The Concept of Illness Behavior.' *Journal of Chronic Disabilities* 15: 189–94

Merleau-Ponty, M. 1962. *Phenomenology of Perception.* London: Routledge and
Kegan Paul

Merskey, H. 1997. 'Whiplash in Lithuania.' *Pain Research Management* 2: 13

Miles, M., and M. Huberman. 1994. *Qualitative Data Analysis: An Expanded
Sourcebook.* Thousand Oaks: Sage

Miller, J., M. Stone, and C. Mitchell. 2002. *The Cell: Inside the 9/11 Plot and Why
the FBI and CIA Failed to Stop It.* New York: Hyperion

Miller, P., and N. Rose. 1997. 'Mobilizing the Consumer: Assembling the Sub-
ject of Consumption.' *Theory, Culture and Society* 14: 1–36
Mills, H., and G. Horne. 1986. 'Whiplash: Manmade Disease?' *New Zealand
Medical Journal* 99: 373–4
Moss, D. 2002. *When All Else Fails: Government as the Ultimate Risk Manager.*
Cambridge: Harvard University Press
Munglani, R. 1999. 'The Roots of Chronicity.' *Recovery* 10 (2): 14–15
Munich Reinsurance Company of Canada. 1992. *Earthquake Economic Impact
Study: A Study of the Economic Impact of a Severe Earthquake in the Lower Main-
land of British Columbia.* Toronto: Munich Reinsurance Company of Canada
Nachemson, A. 1994. 'Chronic Pain: The End of the Welfare State?' *Qual Life
Research* 3: 511–17
O'Brien, R. 2001. *Crippled Justice: The History of Modern Disability Policy in the
Workplace.* Chicago: University of Chicago Press
O'Conner, J. 1973. *The Fiscal Crisis of the State.* New York: St Martin's
O'Malley, P. 2002. 'Imagining Insurance: Risk, Thrift, and Life Insurance in
Britain.' In T. Baker and J. Simon, eds., *Embracing Risk: The Changing Culture
of Insurance and Responsibility,* 97–115. Chicago: University of Chicago Press
– 2003. 'Moral Uncertainties: Contract Law and Distinctions Between Specula-
tion, Gambling, and Insurance.' In R. Ericson and A. Doyle, eds., *Risk and
Morality,* 231–57. Toronto: University of Toronto Press
Organisation for Economic Cooperation and Development. 2002. 'Economic
Consequences of Terrorism.' *OECD Economic Outlook* 71: 117–40
Palm, R. 1990. *Natural Hazards: An Integrative Framework for Research and Plan-
ning.* Baltimore: Johns Hopkins University Press
Parsons, T. 1951. *The Social System.* Glencoe, IL: Free Press
Perrow, C. 1984. *Normal Accidents: Living with High-Risk Technologies.* New York:
Basic Books
Petak, W., and A. Anderson. 1982. *Natural Hazard Risk Assessment and Public
Policy: Anticipating the Unexpected.* New York: Springer-Verlag
Physical Medicine Research Foundation. 1997. *Our Mission.* Vancouver: PMRF
Pimenthal, R. 1999. 'Working Therapy.' *Recovery* 10 (2): 22–3
Pixley, J. 2002. 'Finance Organizations, Decisions and Emotions.' *British Journal
of Sociology* 53: 41–65
Porter, T. 1995. *Trust in Numbers: The Pursuit of Objectivity in Science and Public
Life.* Princeton: Princeton University Press
Power, M. 2003. 'Risk Management and the Responsible Organization.' In R.
Ericson and A. Doyle, eds., *Risk and Morality,* 145–64. Toronto: University of
Toronto Press
Priest, G. 1990. 'The New Legal Structure of Risk Control.' *Daedalus* 119: 207–27

Public Broadcasting System. *Frontline*. 2002. *The Man Who Knew*. Broadcast Video, October

Rashid, A. 2001. *Jihad: The Rise of Militant Islam in Central Asia*. New Haven: Yale University Press

Recovery. 1998. 'Special Issue, *Truth*.' *Recovery: A Quarterly Journal on Roadway Causes, Injuries and Healing* 9 (4)

Recovery. 1999. 'Special Issue, *The Uncertainty Principle*.' *Recovery: A Quarterly Journal on Roadway Causes, Injuries and Healing* 10 (2)

Rigler, C. 1879. *Über die Foglen der Verletzungem auf Eisenbahen*. Berlin: Reimer

Rivers, C. 1994. *Face Value: Physiognomical Thought and the Legible Body in Marivault, Lavater, Balzac, Gautier and Zola*. Madison: University of Wisconsin Press

Rorty, R. 1991. 'Solidarity or Objectivity.' In *Objectivity, Relativism, and Truth*, 21–34. Cambridge: Cambridge University Press

Rose, N. 1999. *Powers of Freedom: Reframing Political Thought*. Cambridge: Cambridge University Press

Roussel, V. 2000. 'Scandales Politiques et Transformation des Rapports entre Magistrature et Politique.' *Droit et Société* 44–5: 19–39

– 2002. *Affaires de Juges: Les Magistrats dans les Scandales Politiques en France*. Paris: La Découverte

– 2003. 'New Moralities of Risk and Political Responsibility.' In R. Ericson and A. Doyle, eds., *Risk and Morality*, 117–44. Toronto: University of Toronto Press

Schrader, H., et al. 1996. 'Natural Evolution of Late Whiplash Syndrome Outside the Medicolegal Context.' *Lancet* 347: 1207–11

Sedgwick Insurance. 1997. *Insurance Market Trends and Development*.

Serio, G. 2001a. *Testimony of New York State Insurance Department Before U.S. House Committee on Financial Services*, 26 September

– 2001b. *Testimony of New State Insurance Department Before Assembly Speaker Sheldon Silver and Assembly Standing Committee on Insurance*, 12 December

– 2002. *Testimony of New York State Insurance Department Before U.S. House of Representatives Committee of Financial Services, Subcommittee on Oversight and Investigations*, 27 February

Shapiro, S. 1987. 'The Social Control of Impersonal Trust.' *American Journal of Sociology* 93: 623–58

Shiller, R. 2000. *Irrational Exuberance*. Princeton: Princeton University Press

Shorter, E. 1992. *From Paralysis to Fatigue: A History of Psychosomatic Illness in the Modern Era*. Toronto: Macmillan

– 1994. *From the Mind into the Body: The Cultural Origins of Psychosomatic Symptoms*. New York: Free Press

Simon, J. 2002. 'Taking Risks: Extreme Sports and the Embrace of Risk in

Advanced Liberal Societies.' In T. Baker and J. Simon, eds., *Embracing Risk: The Changing Culture of Insurance and Responsibility*, 177–208. Chicago: University of Chicago Press
- 2003. 'Risking Rescue: Mountain Rescue as Moral Risk and Opportunity.' In R. Ericson and A. Doyle, eds., *Risk and Morality*, 375–406. Toronto: University of Toronto Press
Sommer, H. 1999. 'Patients in Peril.' *Recovery* 10 (2): 26–7
Sontag, S. 1979. *Illness as Metaphor*. London: Allen Lane
- 1989. *AIDS and its Metaphors*. London: Allen Lane
Soros, G. 1998. *The Crisis of Global Capitalism*. London: Little, Brown and Company
Sparks, R. 1992. *Television and the Drama of Crime: Moral Tales and the Place of Crime in Public Life*. Milton Keynes: Open University Press
Spitzer, W., et al. 1987. 'Scientific Approach to the Assessment and Management of Activity-Related Spinal Disorders.' *Spine* 12 (Supplement): 1–42
Spitzer, W., M. Skovion, L. Salmi, D. Cassidy, J. Duranceau, S. Suissa, and E. Zeiss. 1995. *Scientific Monograph of the Quebec Task Force on Whiplash-Associated Disorders: Redefining 'Whiplash' and its Management. Spine* 20 (Supplement): 2–68
Squires, G., ed. 1997. *Insurance Redlining: Disinvestment, Reinvestment and the Evolving Role of Financial Institutions*. Washington: Urban Institute Press
Standard and Poor's. 2002a. 'U.S. Insurer Failures Decline by Almost 40% in 2001 Dispute Adverse Economic Conditions.' *Standard and Poor's Insurance*, 27 March
- 2002b. 'Terrorism Coverage Remains in Doubt.' *Standard and Poor's Insurance*, 15 April
- 2002c. 'U.S. Property/Casualty Insurance Midyear Outlook 2002: Negative Fundamentals Outweigh Higher Pricing.' *Standard and Poor's Insurance*, 28 May
Stehr, N. 1992. *Practical Knowledge: Applying the Social Sciences*. London: Sage
- 1994. *Knowledge Societies*. London: Sage
- 2002. *Knowledge and Economic Conduct: The Social Foundations of the Modern Economy*. Toronto: University of Toronto Press
Stehr, N., and G. Böhme, eds. 1986. *Knowledge Societies: The Growing Impact of Scientific Knowledge on Social Relations*. Dordrecht: Reidel
Stehr, N., and R. Ericson. 1992. *The Culture and Power of Knowledge: Inquiries into Contemporary Societies*. Berlin and New York: de Gruyter
- 2000. 'The Ungovernability of Modern Societies: States, Democracies, Markets, Participation, and Citizens.' In R. Ericson and N. Stehr, eds., *Governing Modern Societies*, 3–25. Toronto: University of Toronto Press

Stern, J. 1999. *The Ultimate Terrorists*. Cambridge: Harvard University Press

Stone, A. 1993. 'PTSD and the Law: Critical Review of the New Frontier.' *Bulletin of the American Academy of Psychiatry and Law* 21: 23–36

Sullivan, T. ed. 2000. *Injury and the New World of Work*. Vancouver: UBC Press

Sullivan, T., and P. Baranek. 2003. *First Do No Harm: Making Sense of Health Reform Possibilities*. Vancouver: UBC Press

Sullivan, T., E. Stainblum, and J. Frank. 1997. 'Multicausality and the Future of Workers' Compensation.' Paper to the Third International Congress on Medical-Legal Aspects of Work Injury

Swerdlow, B. 1998. *Whiplash and Related Headaches*. Boca Raton: CRC Press

Swiss Re *Sigma* No. 1. 2002. *Natural Catastrophes and Man-Made Disasters in 2001: Man-Made Losses Take on a New Dimension*. Zurich: Swiss Reinsurance Company

– *Sigma* No. 3. 2002. *The London Market in the Throes of Change*. Zurich: Swiss Reinsurance Company

Taylor, C. 1992. 'To Follow a Rule.' In M. Hjort, ed., *Rules and Conventions: Literature, Philosophy and Social Theory*, 167–85. Baltimore: Johns Hopkins University Press

Teasell, R., and H. Merskey. 1999. 'A Call for Caution.' *Recovery* 10 (2): 9–10

Thompson, W. 2002. *One Year Later: The Fiscal Impact of 9/11 on New York City*. New York: Comptroller of the City of New York

Tillman, R. 1998. *Broken Promises: Fraud by Small Business Health Insurers*. Boston: Northeastern University Press

– 2002. *Global Pirates: Fraud in the Offshore Insurance Industry*. Boston: Northeastern University Press

Treaster, J. 2002a. 'Airlines Approve Plan for an Industry Insurance Company.' *New York Times*, 3 March

– 2002b. 'The Race to Predict Terror's Costs.' *New York Times*, 1 September

Trimble, M. 1981. *Post-Traumatic Neurosis: From Railway Spine to Whiplash*. Chicester: John Wiley and Sons

Tyndel, M., and M. Egit. 1988. 'Concept of Nomogenic Disorders.' *Medical Law* 7: 167–76.

Tyrer, S. 1994. 'Repetitive Strain Injury.' *Journal of Psychosomatic Research* 38: 493–8

Van den Hoonaard, W., ed. 2002. *Walking the Tightrope: Ethical Issues for Qualitative Researchers*. Toronto: University of Toronto Press

Von Storch, H., and N. Stehr. 2000. 'Climate Change in Perspective.' *Nature* 405 (6787): 615 (8 June)

Waddell, G. 1998. *The Back Pain Revolution*. Edinburgh: Churchill Livingstone

Walker, C., and M. McGuiness. 1997. 'Political Violence and Commercial

Victims: High Treason Against the Political Economy.' Unpublished paper, Faculty of Law, University of Leeds

Wallace, L. 1997. 'Recovery.' In S. Brun et al., *Coping with Natural Hazards in Canada: Scientific, Government and Insurance Industry Perspectives*. Toronto: Institute for Environmental Studies, University of Toronto

Wallace, L., and R. White. 1997. 'The Impact of Natural Hazards in Canada: Scientific, Government and Industry Perspectives,' 5–14. Toronto: Institute for Environmental Studies, University of Toronto

Weintraub, M. 1995. 'Chronic Pain in Litigation.' *Neurological Clinician* 13: 341–9

Wilkinson, R. 1996. *Unhealthy Societies*. London: Routledge

Workers' Compensation Board of British Columbia. 1996a. *Annual Report – Statistics '96*. Victoria: Workers' Compensation Board of British Columbia

– 1996b. *Work Safe Focus Report: Protecting Young Workers*. Victoria: Workers' Compensation Board of British Columbia

Zelizer, E. 1979. *Morals and Markets: The Development of Life Insurance in the United States*. New York: Columbia University Press.

– 1997. *The Social Meaning of Money: Pin Money, Paychecks, Poor Relief, and Other Currencies*. Princeton: Princeton University Press

Zimring, F., and G. Hawkins. 1993. 'Crime, Justice and the Savings and Loan Crisis,' in M. Tonry and N. Morris, eds., *Beyond the Law: Crime in Complex Organizations*, 247–92. Chicago: University of Chicago Press

Index

Abbate, G., 170
Abbott, A., 114
ABC-TV, 281
absorbing risk, 34, 36, 180–211 *passim*, 287
academic literature on risk, 19
accident prevention, 30, 130, 287, 291
accidents: bodily injury, 108, 118, 174; with catastrophic consequences, 214; and compensation for pain and suffering, 106; and disability insurance claims, 29, 163; fatal, 90–1; and medical policing, 146; and neutral wording, 31; nuclear energy and chemical plant, 284; personal injury, 41, 129, 152, 173, 286; and property damage claims, 105; railway, 99, 147; and restrictions on eligibility, 145; of science and technology, 20; and solidarity, 129; and vocational rehabilitation, 143; work and vehicle, 94, 96, 98, 101–4, 122, 124–5, 131, 133, 177, 290; and work-hardening regimes, 141–2. *See also* whiplash
actuarial science: and analysis of group life insurance, 216; data on mortality and morbidity, 47–8; history of, 48–9; and life insurance, 59, 69, 93; and market segmentation, 70; and medical investigation, 82; quantitative precision of, 263; tables of, 18, 285; and terrorism, 234–5; and underwriting vehicle insurance, 127

Adams, J., 6–7, 9, 13, 156
Addenbrooke's Hospital (Cambridge), 145
administrative expenses: for governmental audits, 267; and lapse calculus, 51; and life insurance underwriting, 48, 52–3, 59–60, 78, 93; and life tables, 23–4; and losses on underwriting, 240; management of, 19; withdrawn by insurer, 55
adverse selection, 15, 28, 50, 69, 80, 126, 257–8, 287, 293
aesthetic reflexivity, 10
agent as medical interrogator, 81–3
aggregation risk. *See* concentration/ aggregation risk
airline industry, 225, 243, 255, 259–62, 295